Pursuing Justice

Second Edition

Pursuing Justice

Traditional and Contemporary Issues in Our Communities and the World

Second Edition

Ralph A. Weisheit

Frank Morn

LONDON AND NEW YORK

First published 2015 by Anderson Publishing

Published 2015 by Routledge
2 Park Square, Milton Park, Abingdon, Oxon OX14 4RN

and by Routledge
711 Third Avenue, New York, NY 10017

Routledge is an imprint of the Taylor & Francis Group, an informa business

Library of Congress Cataloging-in-Publication Data
Application submitted

British Library Cataloguing in Publication Data
A catalogue record for this book is available from the British Library

ISBN-13: 978-0-323-29459-1 (pbk)

We dedicate this book to
Ryan "The Jazzman" and Carol – RW
Carlos and Maura – FM
And to those who pursue justice in search of a better world

Contents

Acknowledgments

We would like to thank Michael Braswell for his encouragement along the way. We also appreciate the hard work and encouragement of Ellen Boyne and the staff at Anderson Publishing who agreed to take on the project and have been tremendously supportive throughout the process.

Online Resources

Interactive resources can be accessed for free by registering at www.routledge.com/cw/weisheit

Preface

This book was designed to introduce the reader to the many dimensions of the concept of justice, to provide several examples of the range of issues relating to justice, and to highlight some of the strategies that have been used to achieve justice. It is designed to fill a gap in the literature on justice by combining a discussion of the concept of justice with efforts to pursue it. Some academic fields, such as philosophy, deal extensively with the concept of justice but stop short of applying the concept to real-world efforts to pursue justice. Reading about philosophical views of justice provides little insight into the concrete steps that individuals, organizations, communities, or nations might take to achieve it. In contrast, more applied academic programs, such as criminal justice, political science, and peace studies, often examine strategies for pursuing justice without defining justice or providing a sense of the variety of ways the term might be used.

That a gap in the literature exists may seem surprising given that for each of the chapters in this book there are dozens, sometimes hundreds, of books and thousands of articles. That so much has been written about issues of justice has complicated the task of writing an introductory overview. For us, the chapters represent broad overviews of each topic rather than comprehensive coverage. Space restrictions also made it necessary to limit the number of topics included in the book. This has meant leaving out such important issues as poverty, domestic violence, police brutality, and privacy. The topics selected for inclusion were chosen to encourage the reader to think about the issue of justice more broadly. It is hoped that the information in these chapters will serve as a springboard for further study, and the reader who wants to pursue the topics in this book further is encouraged to begin with the many references provided with each chapter.

Not a day goes by without news of some injustice in the world. Whether it is rape and torture committed by paramilitary groups in a developing country or more local concerns about the sentence given a drunk driver, we are continuously faced with issues of justice. Our awareness of these issues is heightened by improved communications systems that show us real-time images of injustices around the globe—including hunger, child prostitution, and the civilian casualties of war. Deciding what constitutes injustice and what is the best way to right a wrong is not always easy. One purpose of this book is to stimulate the reader to think about the meaning of justice and strategies for achieving it.

Part One considers key sources of thought about the concept of justice. Talking about justice is, at the same time, simple and maddeningly complex. On the one hand, justice is an idea that we hear about every day. We use the terms justice and injustice on a regular basis and routinely apply them to everyday situations, often without thinking through what we mean by the terms. While most people know what they mean when they use the term justice, few of us are able to give a concise definition that fully captures its meaning. Justice is something that is difficult to precisely define but "We know it when we see it."

While justice may be a short simple word, the concept it describes is quite complex. Religion, philosophy, and political science each provide a perspective on the concept of justice, and the chapters in Part One illustrate how the concept of justice has evolved in each of these areas. These chapters are important in helping the reader to recognize the many dimensions of justice and to appreciate that justice is a constantly evolving concept, one that both shapes and is shaped by world events.

Simply talking about justice does not always convey a sense of how the concept might apply to real-world situations. Two sections of the book specifically address this issue. In Part Two, formal systems for achieving justice are described. It is often the case that people living under a particular justice system are unaware of alternative ways of structuring formal justice systems. Someone who understands alternative systems of justice will find it is easier to recognize the strengths and weaknesses of their own system. These chapters also reinforce the idea that justice is not a fixed concept, but is shaped by the culture and time in which it operates.

Part Three provides concrete examples of issues related to justice. These issues were selected to represent both domestic and global concerns, with the focus on issues that have far-reaching implications. Domestic terrorism, slavery, genocide, and the environment each illustrate issues pertaining to justice. These selected issues also make clear that questions of justice pervade our everyday lives, whether we are aware of it or not. When we buy clothes made by slave labor we are supporting injustice. Becoming aware of how justice issues are woven through our everyday decisions is an important first step in righting wrongs.

Finally, Part Four addresses the issue of responding to injustice. The discussion ranges from what individuals can do, to the role of organizations, to global approaches to justice. Most people are aware that individuals can make a difference and that organizations have a role to play in pursuing justice. While individuals and organizations will continue to be important agents in the pursuit of justice, global approaches are increasingly necessary as the world moves toward a global economy. Global approaches are relatively new, and have yet to be fully developed, but as the globe continues to shrink these approaches will become crucial.

Ultimately, there will always be injustice, but ignoring injustice only breeds further injustice. Governments, agencies, and people who are perceived as unjust quickly lose their legitimacy and ultimately their authority. Injustice is also an underlying cause of war. "No justice no peace" is more than a slogan, it is a reflection of reality. The battle for justice may be never ending, but it is a battle that must be fought. Recognizing injustice and taking steps to correct it is one of the things that distinguishes us from animals.

PART

I

What Is Justice?

What is justice? What constitutes a just society? What are the responsibilities of citizens to their neighbors, their government, other humans? Should everyone be treated equally? Or should people be treated based on some special status? Is there any just war? Why do we punish people? What is our responsibility to the environment? These have been questions raised by every civilized society. Answers to such questions are embedded in ancient traditions, mythology, philosophy, theology, history, law, and political theory.

In the final analysis, the notion of justice is a human construct used to describe the actions of humans. We do not describe earthquakes as "unjust" although we might use that term to describe inequities in the way assistance is provided to the victims of an earthquake. As Aristotle has observed, if we lived in a perfect society, we would not need to define and dispute this notion of justice.

Generally speaking, justice may be divided into two main spheres. One is concerned with the justice of the individual in relation to other human beings and to the organized community itself, the state. The other is concerned with the justice of the state—its form of government and its laws, its political institutions, its military postures, and economic arrangements—in relation to the human beings that make up its population.

In the language of justice five words act as justice markers. They are **equality**—everyone being given the same treatment and access to goods; **merit**—getting what one deserves; **need**—some sort of "safety net" for those who cannot function in society; **rank**—many institutions such as military, universities, churches, think in terms of rank structures as a means to think about justice, and, finally, there is **fairness**—justice is treating people fairly if not equitably. Law is often the last interpreter on what is just, even if a law is considered unjust.

Although justice is a short, simple word, it is a complicated idea with many dimensions. Presenting a broad overview of these dimensions is the task of the next three chapters. In these chapters, the discussion will focus on religious and philosophical perspectives, justice and the state, and social justice.

CHAPTER

Religion and Justice

1

From the beginning of human existence, people have wanted to understand the mysteries surrounding them. Primitive humans lived in a fearful world. Forces of nature needed to be understood. Bad things—such as drought, flood, disease, and death—happened all around people in an arbitrary way. Good people suffered, and bad people prospered. Religion sought to give meaning to the world, to help people understand mysterious things. It also tried to account for injustice and to outline proper responses to injustice. Perhaps the first formal efforts to delineate the meaning and implications of justice can be found in religion. Though questions of justice were present from the beginning, answers evolved over time.

Because natural forces were everywhere, they were readily worshiped. The weather, the seas, the mountains, and, above all, the sun were made gods. The mystery and complexity of life was such that worship of multiple gods, polytheism, developed early. There was little room for one god in a world that demanded so many players.

The Incas of the Andean regions of South America created monumental sacred spots like Machu Picchu and Saksaywaman. The Mayas and Aztecs did similar things in Central America. Babylonians in the Euphrates Valley created stories assimilated by a variety of tribal peoples that would become sacred texts that lasted for thousands of years. Egyptians posited an afterlife based on decisions after a judgment day. Greeks, Romans, and Norsemen had supreme councils comprised of many gods who were deeply involved with human history and divine justice.

Initially, justice in these religions was harsh and vengeful. In the ancient Babylonian culture, which arose on the banks of the Tigris and Euphrates Rivers (an area known today as Iraq), issues of justice were being addressed as early as 1750 BCE. *The Hammurabi Code*, an ancient text of laws, reflected a rigid static society in which obligations and responsibilities were well known and fixed. Consequently, justice was rigid, uncompromising, and absolute. For example, if a building collapsed because of faulty design, the architect could be put to death. If a person under medical care died, the physician likely would face death. However, there was some proportionality. For example, if the daughter of a gentleman was struck and suffered a miscarriage, the fine was 10 shekels. If the same thing happened to the daughter of an ordinary man, the fine was 5 shekels. In a similar fashion, if an ordinary citizen's daughter died, the perpetrator was liable for a heavy fine; if it was a gentleman's daughter, the wrongdoer could face execution. This code established the concept of an eye for an eye and a tooth for a tooth, an idea that found its way into the law outlined by Moses in the Bible. It was harsh, but it shows that ancient peoples struggled to find justice.[1]

JUDAISM

The earliest stages of Old Testament justice were theocratic and tribal, with God's reactions swift and uncompromising. Written around 1000 BCE, the Pentateuch, or Torah, contained stories with themes that have continued in Western culture for centuries. Jews, Christians, and Muslims, all considered The People of the Book, believe these stories to be sacred.

When Adam and Eve were tricked into sin by Satan disguised as a serpent, the creature and its progeny were condemned to crawl the earth forever. The couple was then exiled from the Garden of Eden because they wanted knowledge and the ability to reason. Eve, and all women thereafter, was to suffer in childbirth, and man was to toil by the sweat of his brow. When Cain murdered his brother Abel, God did not condemn the killer to death but to a life as a fugitive and vagabond. A mark was placed on him so that no one would take revenge on him. Legend has it that he became a builder of cities, a negative thing for these tribal people. The story of Cain and Abel has been used by generations of reformers to defend alleged murderers against the death penalty. Later the wickedness of the world compelled God to destroy all the inhabitants of the earth, with the exception of a small party of elect gathered into an ark. Young and old alike were drowned in the deluge. In a classic example of rural fundamentalism versus urban secularism Sodom and Gomorrah met a similar fate. Even Lot's wife, whose only sin was to look back on her home with longing, was condemned and turned into a pillar of salt. Moses brought plague and death to thousands of Egyptians, even innocent children, because of the actions of the Pharaoh.[2]

When Moses was crafting a new set of tribal laws, to be found in the first five books of the Bible (Genesis, Exodus, Leviticus, Numbers, and Deuteronomy), he set forth a justice system that affected much of Western culture for thousands of years. After his people had lived for generations in Egypt, Moses needed to slough off the alien ways they had adopted. None but their one tribal god should be worshiped. Family ties needed to be strengthened. Due to the social chaos of slavery, proper relations between people had to be established. They were guided by a new set of laws, the Ten Commandments.

As the roaming Israelites settled and began to build a distinct culture in a new homeland, issues of justice emerged. In an attempt to bring some softness, proportionality, and reason to justice, they borrowed *lex talionis*, or an eye for an eye, from the Babylonians. For example, Leviticus 24:17-22 states,

> *If anyone takes the life of a human being, he must be put to death. Anyone who takes the life of someone's animal must make retribution—life for a life. If anyone injures his neighbor, whatever he has done must be done to him: fracture for fracture, eye for eye, tooth for tooth. As he has injured the other, so he is to be injured. Whoever kills an animal must make restitution, but whoever kills a man must be put to death. You are to have the same law for the alien and the native born. I am the Lord your God.*

While today we may think of "an eye for an eye" as a call for harshness, at the time it called for *no more than* an eye for an eye, thus limiting harshness.

Numerous offenses warranted capital punishment. For example, profaning the Sabbath could result in death (Exodus 35:2; Exodus 31:14-15; Numbers 15:32-36). Blasphemy and sacrifice to other gods resulted in death (Leviticus 24:11-14; Exodus 22:20). The 20th chapter of Leviticus commanded death for a variety of familial and sexual violations, including adultery, incest, homosexuality, and bestiality (Leviticus 20:9-16).

The history of the Jews is one of captivity, occupation, and dispersion by foreign empires. In 598 BCE, the Babylonian empire destroyed the Jewish state and then carried off the population for enslavement for over 60 years. In 63 BCE the Roman Republic made Israel a protectorate. Jews were allowed their religious practices but politically they belonged to Rome. For the next century a variety of rebellious leaders, called messiahs, arose to preach against Roman occupation.[3] They were rounded up and executed. Rebellion became so prevalent that by 73 CE the Roman Empire stepped in and destroyed Jerusalem. The Jewish state came to an end as Jews were dispersed (the diaspora) throughout Africa, Asia, and Europe.

Three ethnic traditions developed as the Jews scattered throughout the world. By the seventh century CE many moved to the Iberian peninsula and became the *Sephardim*, flourishing in Spain until expelled in 1492 along with the Moor or Muslim population by King Ferdinand and Queen Isabella. The *Mizrahim* Jews moved eastward to what became known as Iraq and Iran and other parts of Asia. Following the waterways, by the eighth and ninth century CE the *Ashkenazim* were settled in Germany, Northern France, Poland, Lithuania, Latvia, and Ukraine. They formed a new dialect called Yiddish.

Though tolerated in some places, widespread persecution occurred for over a thousand years.[4] Besides various pogroms in Russia and Poland, anti-Semitism was widespread. Christians commonly blamed the Jews for the crucifixion of their god. In addition, there was the belief that Jews were part of an international conspiracy to take financial, and eventually political, control of the world. Such luminaries as Henry Ford were avowed Jew-haters. Of course, so was Adolf Hitler as the Holocaust of the 1940s attests. After World War II, because of the shock of the Holocaust and feelings of guilt, the Jews were given a Jewish state in Palestine. The rest of their history will be connected to the Palestinian people they displaced and the Arab neighbors who resent their presence.

Today Judaism may be viewed as three groups, each with a different emphasis on justice. The Orthodox Jews are the most traditional with bearded men wearing furry shtreimel hats and side locks (peyot). Women wear long skirts with high necklines and full-length sleeves. They maintain and abide by the traditional rituals and obligations of the ancient law. Though strong in modern-day Israel, they are a minority elsewhere. The Reform Jews adhere to the ethical laws but believe the rituals should be adapted to the modern world. A product of nineteenth century Germany, and flourishing in the United States, their dress and manners are not distinguishable from any secular citizen. The reform branch is very humanistic and very different than the orthodox. The Conservative Jews are midway between the Orthodox and Reform Jewish persuasion. They study the ancient texts and laws but believe they need to adapt to modern conditions.

Though few in number worldwide the Jewish people have made contributions to politics, the arts, scholarship, and issues of justice.

CHRISTIANITY

In the midst of the turmoil caused by the Roman occupation of Israel, many peasant prophets arose. To name a few, there was Athronges the Shepard, John the Baptist, Hezekiah, Simon of Peraea, and Judas the Galilean.[5] One who stood out was Jesus of Nazareth. These were Jewish nationalists, zealots challenging the Roman Empire. Like others Jesus was duly arrested, tortured, tried, and executed. Many stories were written about him in the 100 years after his death but only four were voted as sacred by the Nicaea gathering in 325 CE.[6] These were the books of Matthew, Mark, Luke, and John. Mark, the earliest, was written around 70 CE, Matthew and Luke between 90 and 100 CE, and John was written between 100 and 120 CE. All of them were largely based upon oral traditions, and all of them were written after the fall and destruction of Jerusalem.

Raised in a small village, Nazareth, in the province of Galilee Jesus came from a family of woodworkers. Like his neighbors Jesus was poor. As a young man he came under the influence of a local zealot named John the Baptist. When his mentor was arrested and executed Jesus took to the country with a message of justice. He was a spokesman for the poor against two insidious influences in society—the Jewish religious elites and the Roman occupation forces.

At the time, there were two main priestly classes: the Pharisees and Sadducees. The Pharisees believed in strict adherence to the Law of Moses with themselves being its main interpreters. They believed in an afterlife of heaven and hell where one went depending on the extent to which one had followed the law. They also believed in a messiah but he was to be a political and military savior. The Sadducees were the elitist, priestly class. To them rituals were the most important part of Jewish life, and they profited from the fees charged in the temple. Also they seemed less pure, willing to allow Greek ideas to come into the faith. Tradition has it that from an early age Jesus challenged the scribes and priests in local synagogues. These were the enemies of Jesus.

Traveling through the countryside Jesus challenged the keepers of the local synagogues and temples in Jerusalem and the fees that were demanded of the poor. As a Jewish nationalist aware of his Jewish traditions, he picked 12 followers to represent the 12 tribes of Israel. Numerous healers and miracle workers roamed about performing magic for a fee, but Jesus endeared himself to the poor by doing likewise for free. Village people and hill farmers, astonished and pleased, gathered to hear his attacks on the religious establishment. He taught a different law than that of the scribes, Pharisees, and Sadducees. Jesus preached in Matthew 5:

> *You have heard that it was said, "Eye for an eye, and tooth for tooth." But I Tell You, Do not resist an evil person. If someone strikes you on the right cheek, turn him the other also. And if someone wants to sue you and take your tunic, let him have your cloak as well. If someone forces you to go one mile, go with him two miles. Give to the one who asks you, and do not turn away from the one who wants to borrow from you.*

Boldly he moved closer and closer to Jerusalem, the seat of religious and political power. After riding into town like a triumphant conqueror, he shocked the temple elite when he disrupted the tax collectors, money changers, and shop owners at the entrance to the temple. He was directly attacking a sizable portion of the revenue for the priests.

The Romans tolerated most zealots until they crossed the line. Jesus was a nationalist. Israel was to be a new Kingdom, one governed by Jews. To love one's neighbor was not taken literally; Jews were to love fellow Jews. Foreigners such as the Romans were despised. As he entered Jerusalem preaching the Kingdom of God, the Roman leadership joined the religious elite in viewing him as a rabble-rouser, a revolutionary. And he sounded like one. Radical change was imminent, he claimed. "I tell you, there are those here who will not taste death until they have seen the Kingdom of God come with power" (Mark 9:1). One of the first questions asked of him during interrogation was "Are you King of the Jews?" Though his answer was guarded, the Romans boldly posted their beliefs on the cross upon which they hung him. Ordinarily, for defying religious law, he would have been stoned for blasphemy; crucifixion was for political criminals.

Executed for sedition and treason Jesus' sect might have disappeared into history like others if not for followers like Paul and Peter. For the next two centuries, missionaries and martyrs brought this tribal religion to the sophisticated world of the Greeks and Romans. Its message and organization changed as it went from a nationalistic Palestinian religion to a universal (catholic) one. Eventually named Rome's official religion some 300 years after the death of Christ, Christianity grew in power and influence as the empire declined.

In the next 1500 years, the Catholic Church began to dominate the religious and political world of Europe. One faction broke away early to form the Eastern Orthodox Church based in Byzantium, or Constantinople. In Rome, the Catholic Church took on many attributes of the Roman Empire and it flourished. The Papacy, with Pope and Cardinals, and rituals and holy days, looked much like the Rome of olden days. Its history is replete with authoritarianism and dogma. Pronouncements of clergy became the source of justice. Because they held the "keys to heaven," many Popes were stronger than any Christian monarch. Not only could the Church excommunicate people, thus locking them out of heaven, but they could, as done in Spain's Inquisition take the lives of freethinkers. Corruption was so great that dissent arose. Heretics, like the zealots earlier, were quickly executed.[7]

The religious revolt against the entrenched elitism of the medieval Catholic Church in the sixteenth century was caused by a desire for reformation. Key figures—such as Martin Luther, John Calvin, and Huldrych Zwingli—led the breakaway called the Reformation. During the age of discovery in the sixteenth and seventeenth centuries, Catholic clergy accompanied the conquistadors spreading Catholicism to indigenous populations in Central and South America. On one level, the Roman Church adapted to the new peoples joining the faith. On the other hand, the Church remained very conservative and uncompromising.[8] Some Catholic theologians, particularly in the Third World, felt their Church did not address issues of justice strongly enough. This point of view has been called Liberation theology. Jose Porfirio Miranda (*Marx and the Bible*) and Gustavo Gutierrez (*The Power of the Poor in History* and *A Theology of Liberation*) are two significant writers who thought about justice from the liberationist point of view. Although not limited to Latin America, the liberationist view has found greater expression in these Spanish-speaking countries. The basis of the Liberation theology is a rereading of the Bible. Miranda and other liberationists believe the Bible should be read from a Marxist perspective with the goal of liberating the oppressed. Capitalism is evil, they think, and it tramples on the poor for a few rich people. Multinational corporations in the developing world have made the poor into nonpersons and robbed them of their dignity. Private ownership of property has come about by injustice. To them Jesus chose to be born poor and to live with and teach the poor; God loves the poor. Justice is recognizing the realities of poverty and oppression and the importance of struggling to liberate the oppressed.[9]

Protestantism had similar developments. These churches could be just as repressive as the Catholic Church, witness the Puritans in Colonial America and their treatment of dissidents. The Protestant Ethic promised that hard work, obedience to authority, and frugality would lead to success. But it did not always work that way and during the industrial revolutions in England and America thousands slipped into poverty. Capitalism and the constant quest for profits crushed the workers under foot. Some Protestant thinkers did address the issues of injustice stemming from the industrial revolution. The Social Gospel Movement in the United States (1870-1920) focused on the poor workers. Charles Monroe Sheldon wrote *In His Steps, "What Would Jesus Do?"* (1897) and Walter Rauschenbush's *Christianity and the Social Crisis* (1907) addressed the injustice of a rampant capitalist system.

Perhaps the greatest twentieth century theologian to address issues of justice was Reinhold Niebuhr, who saw justice as the balance of power between classes. Niebuhr (1892-1971) spent most of his academic career at the Yale Divinity School and influenced generations of theologians. Absolute justice was likely unattainable, he thought, but the ideal would be harmony in which the weak were protected from the strong. Two principles must be addressed before there can be justice. These principles are freedom and equality. Even though freedom is a cherished notion, if left alone it would harm the poor. Therefore, freedom cannot stand alone unregulated. Equality is Niebuhr's highest standard of justice, and Niebuhr believed that equal justice is the greatest goal for society. He says in *Moral Man and Immoral Society* (1932), "the oppressed have a higher moral right to challenge their oppressors than these have to maintain their rule by force." His most popular statement is called the *Serenity Prayer*: "Father, give us courage to change what must be altered, serenity to accept what cannot be helped, and insight to know the one from the other."[10]

ISLAM

Islam, like Judaism and Christianity, was born in the deserts of the Middle East.[11] These religious traditions were connected by legend and lore. The Torah tells that the Patriarch Abraham and his wife Sarah were barren. A servant, Hagar, was given to Abraham and a child, Ishmael, resulted. When Sarah finally conceived Hagar and Ishmael were forced to leave the tribe. They went off to be the progenitors of the Arabs. Such stories bind the Jews and the Arabs together but strain their relationship as well.

By the sixth century CE, the Arab peninsula was filled with diaspora Jews, Christians, and a variety of nomadic tribes. The center of trade and religious activities was the Ka'ba, (the cube) a sacred stone in a square-like edifice in the center of Mecca housing numerous images of gods and holy persons. Even images of Abraham, Jesus, and Mary were part of the mix in this highly polytheist culture. A powerful tribe, the Quraysh, dominated the care of the Ka'ba and the trade of the city. Into this environment in the seventh century CE was born a man who changed history.

Orphaned shortly after his birth in 570 CE, Muhammad fell under the care of an uncle who was a merchant and caravan trader in Mecca, a major trading city in the Arab peninsula. At an early age he was leading camel caravans throughout the area establishing business connections with diaspora Jews, Christians, and Arab tribesmen. A strikingly handsome man at 25 years—broad-chested with a full beard, hooked nose, and penetrating black eyes—he could have been sought after as a son-in-law by many tribal leaders. Instead he attracted the attention of a wealthy widow, Khadija, a woman 35 years his senior, and they married. He settled down to be a wealthy respected businessman in Mecca.

Muhammad was a unique character in pre-Islam Mecca. While others had multiple wives he had but one, Khadija, whom he cherished. He was increasingly wealthy but remained modest in habits and life-style. Although religious he preferred to go out into the desert to meditate. On one such occasion, he was overcome and fell into a semiconscious state in which he heard a voice commanding him to "recite." There was no book or script to recite from but there was a flood of words. Muhammad became the "messenger of God." These oral utterances would not be written down during his lifetime. Instead, they were memorized by a group of followers called Qurra. When finally compiled and written down in Arabic, they were called the *Qur'an*, literally "the Recitation." The book was not only religion, it was poetry, and was always to be read in Arabic. Calligraphy became a signature art form with verses from the *Qur'an* in beautiful script on all religious places. Even better it was meant to be listened to and repeated.

The first to convert to Muhammad's new religion were his family. As his "companions" increased, tensions broke out with other tribes, especially the Quraysh, and pressures to leave Mecca mounted. In 622 CE, he and his small group of believers stole away to an oasis village named Yathrib (later to be called Medina). The time marking this *Hijra* (flight or departure) established year 1 AH (After Hijra) in the Muslim calendar. He then set up a new kingdom in Medina and after several battles with various tribes was soon able to return victorious to Mecca.

His earliest messages, later written into verses in the *Qur'an,* were twofold. First, he was a social reformer attacking the tribal system that exploited the poor. Like Jesus before him, Muhammad became a spokesman for the poor, attacking economic and social practices that enslaved people. He decried the mistreatment of the weak and the unprotected. "Do not oppress the orphan and do not drive away the beggar," it is proclaimed in the *Qur'an* (93:9-10). The taxes and fees enforced by the Quraysh tribe were unjust, he felt. Unlike Jesus, who was a poor outsider, Muhammad was a wealthy insider attacking his own kind.

Economic and social inequalities were to be avoided. Those who did receive riches were not to be condemned, however, if they used this wealth to help others. The decay of any society is caused by neglect and self-absorption of the prosperous. The *Qur'an*'s main purpose is to prevent people from corrupting the earth by falling into decadent ways. When a civilization becomes decadent and decrepit, it needs to be swept away and a new one started. Therefore, vengeance and retribution are central, but they are to be tempered by mercy. In Islam, the poorest and most incapacitated person still has a claim on equal rights; all are the servants of God in this world and the next. Therefore, alms giving is not a charity, a sign of one's goodness, but rather it is a duty. The goal of the *Qur'an* is to establish an ethical and egalitarian society.

Second, Muhammad preached forgiveness. "The retribution for an injury is an equal injury, but those who forgive the injury and make reconciliation will be rewarded by God," (*Qur'an* 42:40). Central to Islam is submission to and fear of Allah (the Arabic word for God), who is both "terrible in his retribution," and "all-forgiving and compassionate."

> *O ye who believe! Be ye staunch in justice, witness for Allah, even though it be against yourselves or parents or kindred. (*Qur'an *4:135)*

And again:

> *Let not hatred of any people reduce you that ye deal not justly. Deal justly, that is nearer to your duty. (*Qur'an *5:8)*

Considerable justice and mercy is extended to fellow believers with warnings against being an aggressor:

> *And fight in the way of God with those who fight with you, but aggress not; God loves not the aggressors. And slay them, and expel them from where they expelled you; persecution is more grievous than slaying. (*Qur'an *2:185-190)*

And again later:

> *O believers, be you securers of justice, witness for God. Let not detestation for a people move you not to be equitable; be equitable—that is nearer to godfearing. (*Qur'an *5:11)*

Islam can be quite forgiving of the killer of a nonbeliever:

> *Whom God leads astray, thou wilt not find for him a way. They wish that you should disbelieve as they disbelieve, and then you would be equal: therefore take not to yourselves friends of them, until they emigrate in the way of God; then, if they turn their backs, take them, and slay them wherever you find them. (*Qur'an *4:91-94)*

Unlike the Jewish/Christian tradition, killing a believer of Islam called forth a much different consideration.

> *It belongs not to a believer to slay a believer, except it be by error. If any slays a believer by error, let him set free a believing slave, and bloodwit is to be paid to his family unless they forgo it as a freewill offering. If he belong to a people at enmity with you and is a believer, let the slayer set free a believing slave. If he belong to a people joined with you by a compact, then bloodwit is to be paid to his family and the slayer shall set free a believing slave. But if he finds not the means, let him fast two successive months-God's turning; God is all-knowing, All-wise. And whoso slays a believer willfully, his recompense is Gehenma [hell], therein dwelling forever, and God will be wroth with him and will curse him, and prepare for him a mighty chastisement.* (Qur'an *4:94-95)*

After Muhammad's death in 632 CE (10 AH) the faith was ruled by a series of Caliphs (meaning successors) beginning with Abu Bakr. Over the next 800 years, under various Caliphates, Islam spread throughout North Africa, the Indian subcontinent, and parts of Europe. The Moorish Kingdom of Spain with its magnificent palace in Granada tolerated Jew and Christian alike until both Jew and Muslim were kicked out in 1492. Meanwhile the power center of Islam shifted from Arabia to Damascus.

By the ninth century a sacred law, the Shariah, was formulated. It set the rules for living the just, the virtuous life. Five categories of behavior were outlined. They include the following:

1. Actions that are obligatory, in that their performance is rewarded and their omission punished
2. Actions that are meritorious in that their performance may be rewarded, but their neglect is not punished
3. Actions that are neutral and indifferent
4. Actions that are considered reprehensible, though not necessarily punished
5. Actions that are forbidden and punished

By the eleventh century The Five Pillars of Faith became required of the faithful.[12] They are:

1. Salat or ritual prayer. Five times a day (sunrise, noon, afternoon, sunset, evening) the faithful are to face Mecca and be led in prayer.
2. Zakat or the giving of alms. It was not a voluntary tithe but a religious obligation.
3. Sawm or month-long fasting during the month of Ramadan
4. Haji or pilgrimage to Mecca
5. Shahadah most importantly the profession of faith: "There is no god but God, and Muhammad is God's messenger."

While growing at a rapid pace the succession to Muhammad's rule became an issue. Two contending schools arose. One is the Shiite (representing 10-15% of the Muslim population today). Muhammad's successor was his son-in-law Ali, they believed. Shiites believe that the ruling of the nation is not a public matter; it is a theocratic one. Religious leaders called Imams have tremendous power, more so than the political leaders. A small number of Imams called Ayatollahs emerged to guide the faithful as they awaited a messianic restorer of the purest Islamist state called the Maldi. These religious rulers are infallible and never make mistakes. Shiites believe the Imams and Ayatollahs reflect the will of Allah. The people have no right to select or challenge them.[13]

The Sunnis represent 85-90% of the Muslim world today. According to Sunni beliefs, the successors to Muhammad were the caliphs or religious leaders that assumed power after his death. Government is a secular matter without any religious authority. Rulers come and go from power based on the will of the people.

Over time, many Muslim countries modernized and deviated from the pure teachings of the *Qur'an*, they were becoming too secular. A fundamentalist backlash resulted. Most notable is that of Muhammad ibn Abd al Wahhab. He sided with a desert prince, Muhammad bin Saud, founder of the dynasty that eventually took over Arabia giving us Saudi Arabia. Today Wahhabism represents an austere conservative brand of Islam. Followers of Wahhabism believe the *Qur'an* is the ultimate blueprint for life. All questions can be answered by a careful reading and application of that holy book. Some countries—Saudi Arabia, Iran, and Afghanistan, for example—construct their entire political and social structure around this sect. The Muslim Brotherhood in Egypt had similar feelings. Punishments come right out of the *Qur'an*. Theft results in the right hand being amputated. Adulterers are stoned to death. Murder and sexual deviation warrant beheading. Women should be covered and largely secluded. In more modern interpretations of the *Qur'an*, many fundamentalists would not allow females to drive an automobile or attend school. There are no theaters in Saudi Arabia because the Saudis detest the mixing of the sexes and the corrupting influences of Western culture. These Muslims see deviation from the *Qur'an*, or their interpretation of it, as sacrilege. Any government that goes contrary to The Book is the Great Satan.

HINDUISM

Hinduism, a Persian word for Indian, is an ancient religion in India, Malaysia, and Sri Lanka. It is the world's third largest religion. It's most sacred text is the *Bhagavad Gita*, a poetic conversation between a warrior and his charioteer, Krishna.

Hindus believe in the divine unity of the universe and all life in it. This unity (Brahman) is visualized as a triad. Brahma is the creative force and creates new realities continually. Vishnu, the Preserver, preserves the creations. Whenever dharma (eternal order, righteousness, religion, law, and duty) is threatened Vishnu travels from heaven to earth in 1 of 10 incarnations to save the world. Shiva, the Destroyer, rounds out the threesome. It recognizes that the opposite of creation is destruction. In addition there are hundreds of Gods and Goddesses worshiped as various aspects of the unity of the Divine.

Hinduism has been very stratified. Five classes, though officially abolished in India in 1949, still exist and shape social relations and issues of justice. They are:

1. Brahmin (priests and academics)
2. Kshatriyas (military)
3. Vaishyas (farmers and merchants)
4. Sudras (peasants and servants)
5. Untouchables

Humans are trapped in a cycle of birth and rebirth. Karma, the accumulated sum of good and bad deeds, determines how one comes into the next life. Good deeds mean a rebirth into higher levels of wealth and status until there is an escape from rebirth altogether. Bad deeds cause a lower rebirth. Therefore, justice issues such as unequal distribution of wealth, prestige, and suffering are the natural consequences of previous acts in previous lives. But one needs to have guidance in this life to attain a favorable rebirth. This is done by the Six Pillars of Justice. These six doctrines are Dharma, Karma, Ahimsa, Sahanshakti, Justice, and Meditation.

Dharma. The purpose of life is to help every human discover their Divine potential. Everyone has talents and when they use them to serve mankind wealth and happiness will follow.

Karma. The eternal law of justice is strict accountability for our actions, it is cause and effect. Behaving badly will bring unhappiness in this life and a lower rebirth later. Behaving well brings happiness now and a greater rebirth.

Ahimsa. Nonviolence in thought, word, and deed should guide our lives. Love of self, of others, and of all forms of life is key. Mother Earth is sacred and the environment should be protected. Environmental justice is an essential part of Hindu belief.

Sahanshakti. This doctrine is tolerance. Justice without tolerance is not justice. Essential to human life and development is the acceptance and celebration of diversity. There may be one truth but many paths to it.

Justice. The doctrine of justice addresses the contradiction of liberty and equality. Increasing one diminishes the other, Hindus believe. Too much liberty can create inequality. Too much equality stifles individual liberty and incentive. Neither are the ultimate good, they need to be regulated to serve others. A major challenge to justice is ethical relativism. Hindus believe that injustice follows the belief that "greed is good," and that winning is the ultimate good.

Meditation. Some believe reason is the ultimate explanation for the advance of humans. Hindus think the heart is superior to the brain. The inner voice of the heart, most pronounced through meditation, is the important voice that needs to be listened to.[14]

BUDDHISM

Buddhism stands in contrast to both Christianity and Islam. It is, however, very close to Hinduism. Gautama Siddhartha was born a royal prince in 624 BCE in Lumbeni, originally in northern India but now in Nepal. He lived a lavish and protected life in a palace until his 29th year. On an outing he was stunned at the suffering of the world. He left the palace and went into the forest to meditate for 6 years when he attained enlightenment under the Bodhi tree in Bodh Gaya, India. Thereafter, he was the Buddha.

His teachings were recorded in the Tripitaka or Three Baskets. One basket contained the discourses of Buddha (Sutra), the second held guidelines for his monks (Vinaya), and in the third were the teachings of his disciples (Abhidharma).

Buddhists are guided by the Four Noble Truths. First, human suffering is natural. There is the universal pain of birth, growing old, and death. Much of our individual situation is caused by our own actions in this life and previous ones. In this sense, justice is a cosmic phenomenon and society has little to do with it. In this justice system, what a person is now is the result of accumulation of what they had been before. Second, much of suffering is the attachment to things that do not last: wealth, status, privilege. Third, we can eliminate much suffering by letting go of these impermanent things. However deterministic this seems, there is a desire to live a just life now to ensure a better life later. For the individual, the good or just life is the middle path. One needs to avoid extremes. Do not pursue worldly things nor be an ascetic. The Fourth Noble Truth is to live a good life by following the Eightfold Path.[15] Individuals, rulers, and the human community should have the correct:

1. Views
2. Thoughts
3. Speech
4. Conduct
5. Livelihood
6. Effort
7. Mindfulness
8. Concentration

CONCLUSION

For much of human existence religion has offered solace for our future fears and guidance for our current complexities of life. Across the world, though different doctrines and rituals arose, there has been a common theme. The good life and the just society must be a caring one. The poor, whether doomed because of previous lives or victims of circumstance, must be cared for. Many of the religious stories are fantastic, based upon myth and miracle; they require suspension of reason, they are based on faith. Some people came forth exploring the same questions but placed their beliefs on reason. They were the philosophers, a topic to which we now turn.

DISCUSSION QUESTIONS

1. Can you think of examples in which religion and religious values shape problems between countries?
2. Using the example of the main religious leaders discussed in this chapter can you think why there might be different or similar views on capital punishment?
3. How do the religions of the Middle East (Judaism, Christianity, and Islam) differ from those of Asia?

Endnotes

1. C.R. Driver and John C. Miles (eds.), *The Babylonian Laws,* Vol. 2 (Oxford, England: Clarendon, 1956-1960), pp. 58-108, 406, 494, 501.
2. See Alan Dershowitz, *The Genesis of Justice: Ten Stories of Biblical Injustice That Led to the Ten Commandments and Modern Law* (New York: Warner Books, 2000), pp. 48-59, 94-102.
3. Reza Aslan, *Zealot: The Life and Times of Jesus of Nazareth* (New York: Random House, 2013), pp. 23-24, 106-107.
4. See Eric S. Gruen, *Diaspora: Jews Amidst Greeks and Romans* (Cambridge, MA: Harvard University Press, 2002), and Irving M. Zeitlin, *Jews: The Making of a Diaspora People* (Cambridge, UK: Polity Press, 2012).
5. Aslan, *Zealot*, p. xxiv.
6. See Elaine Pagels, *The Gnostic Gospels* (New York: Vintage Books, 1989), and Bart D. Ehrman, *The Lost Gospel of Judas Iscariot* (New York: Oxford University Press, 2006).

7. Justo L. Gonzalez, *The Story of Christianity, Vol. 1: The Early Church to the Dawn of the Reformation* (New York: HarperCollins, 2012).
8. Philip Jenkins, "The Next Christianity," *Atlantic Monthly* (October, 2002), pp. 53-68.
9. Jose Miranda Porfirio, *Marx and the Bible: A Critique of the Philosophy of Oppression*, John Eagleson [trans.] (Maryknoll, NY: Orbis, 1974), and Gustavo Gutierrez, *A Theology of Liberation: History, Politics, and Salvation*, Caridad Inda and John Eagleson [trans.] (Maryknoll, NY: Orbis, 1973).
10. Karen Labacqz, *Six Theories of Justice* (Minneapolis: Augsburg, 1986), pp. 83-90.
11. For a superb account see Reza Aslan, *No god but God: The Origins, Evolution, and Future of Islam* (New York: Random House, 2011).
12. Fazlur Rahman, *Major Themes of the Qur'an* (Chicago: Bibliotheca Islamica, 1980), pp. 37-64.
13. Aslan, *No god but God*, pp. 184-192.
14. See Bansi Pandit, *The Hindu Mind: Fundamentals of Hindu Religion and Philosophy* (India: New Age Books, 2007).
15. Trevor Ling (ed.), *The Buddha's Philosophy of Man* (Rutland, Vt.: Everyman's Library, 1981), pp. 119-121.

CHAPTER 2

Philosophy and Justice

Similar to religion, philosophy sought to understand universal mysteries. Instead of relying on faith, philosophy used reason. That is not to say philosophers were not religious, but their approach was plodding reason, not leaps of faith. The term philosophy has its origins in the ancient Greek for "love of wisdom." There are many approaches in philosophy. **Epistemology** is concerned with the nature of knowledge. Can we truly know something without experiencing it? Is some knowledge innate or are we the sum total of our experiences? **Metaphysics** ponders the features of reality, such as existence and time. What is the true nature of being? What is the universe? **Ethics** deals with morals. What is the proper way of dealing with others? **Political philosophy**, a topic we will explore more fully in Chapter 3, looks at government and its relation to individuals. **Logic** studies the principles of correct reasoning.

These philosophical orientations might seem dense, incomprehensible, and irrelevant to the average person. The language of philosophy can be hard to understand and arguments sometimes seem convoluted, yet philosophers have established positions and arguments relevant to the questions we face every day. This chapter focuses on issues of justice. How can we live the good life? How can we make the right decisions? What is ultimately the fair way to deal with others? These philosophical questions, some of them hundreds of years old, remain important today.[1]

The Maxims of Ptahhotep, from twenty-fifth century BCE Egypt, are some of the earliest philosophical thoughts from the ancient world. Presented as advice from a father to a son *The Maxims* extoll truthfulness, self-control, and universal kindness. These ancient Egyptians believed that the pursuit of justice marked the good life. Other examples of early philosophical thinking can be found in Confucianism and Taoism in China. Confucianism is at least 2000 years old. At one time, more than 200 years before Christ, it was so popular that it was the official state ideology in China. Among its principles is the belief that people should engage in acts that are right and just. Taoism, originating some 500 years before Christ, was at some point in history so popular in China that it was named the official state religion. Taoism emphasizes living in harmony with the universe.[2] In Hindu philosophy, justice is based on dharma, or duties that must be performed to achieve freedom from rebirth. Prominent in Hindu belief is the philosophy that all people should be treated as equals.[3]

While these early thoughts were influential at the time, it was in ancient Greece where philosophy flourished and set the foundations for modern-day philosophical thinking.[4] One of the earliest philosophical discussions of justice was in Plato's *Republic, or Concerning Justice*, written around 380 BCE. Plato's mentor, Socrates, chose to die by execution rather than give up his principles. He wanted the freedom to teach even if it went against current orthodoxy. Perhaps Plato used his teacher's example when he equated justice with personal and civic virtue. Arguing against those who thought a person or society does good only under threat of being caught, Plato suggested that people and states were just because it is the right thing to do. Consistent with the Socratic belief that no one sins on purpose, Plato believed that justice should be "corrective," not just punitive. Justice becomes a quest for harmony in the soul and in the state. However, that can lead to some confusion. One Greek word for justice was *isotes*, which means equality. When Plato spoke of justice, he used *dikaiosune*, or righteousness. Justice is performing the functions for which one's nature is best fitted. The just ruler is unselfish; his one aim is the welfare of the citizens. A just citizen is wiser, stronger, and happier than an unjust one. Plato believed that as humans we are incapable of seeing the world as it truly is, and we only see a rough approximation of the world. He illustrates this idea with a parable about people kept chained in a cave, facing a wall and unable to turn their heads. Behind and above them is a fire that causes shadows of beings outside the cave to be reflected on the wall. According to Plato, our understanding of the world is comparable to these prisoners' understanding based on their ability to only see shadows. As his parable of the cave shadows suggests, we live in a prison of existence and see only dim images of ideals that are perfect. The good life is trying to discover, to teach, and to live according to those ideals.[5]

Socrates' death leads us to think of loyalty, particularly loyalty to ideal principles. Humans have several relationships demanding loyalty. We have obligations to family, friends, the state, and ourselves. Two children, one yours and the other a stranger, are in jeopardy; who do you save first? Two aging people, one your parent and the other a stranger, need care; who do you care for first? Your nation is at war but you think it is an unjust one; how do you serve your country without being a traitor?

One classic example of the agonies of loyalty is that of General Robert E. Lee, a military genius living in mid-nineteenth century America. President Abraham Lincoln asked Lee to head up the army when the South declared its independence from the United States. Lee had served his country for years, disliked secession, and was skeptical about slavery, yet his loyalty to Virginia was greater than to the United States and he chose instead to lead the Confederate troops. Another example has to do with average college students. Today there is a cheating culture in most colleges and universities. One student blatantly cheats on homework assignments, but when other students were asked if an honest roommate should turn in the cheater they overwhelmingly said he should not. Universal principles of honesty were trumped by loyalty to roommates and fellow students.[6]

Aristotle, a student of Plato, felt that people need a moral compass, something for guidance in doing the right thing. In his *Nicomachean Ethics* (ca. 322 BCE), Aristotle divided justice into two categories: distributive and rectificatory.[7]

Distributive Justice

Distributive justice is giving people what they deserve. Aristotle would have us live in a meritocracy in which people achieve based on their hard work and ability, not because of the class into which they were born or other characteristics they did not achieve on their own. Making unequal things equal is the worst form of inequality, he thought. There is and should be differences among people according to merit. Justice is a matter of fit, making certain that honors and privileges go to those who deserve them through their own work and ability. Most debate today tries to divorce fairness from arguments of honor and moral desert; strict neutrality is sought. Aristotle disagrees. Justice requires discrimination based on ability. For him it is important to find the *telos*, the purpose or essential nature of the social practice. Aristotle uses an example of flutes. When flutes are distributed, who gets the best ones? he asks. The best flute players should get the best flutes, he determines. Yes, we all would benefit in hearing great instruments played by great musicians, but that is not the reason for the distribution. The better players, due to their nature, deserve the best flutes, whose *telos* is to be played by masters.

One can encounter this in some modern debates. Affirmative action is a social policy attempting to redress past harms visited upon minority groups in American society. In the name of justice, minorities need to be given a preference, say the advocates of this policy. Suppose a white student worked hard, got good grades, and did well on entrance exams but was passed over to allow a minority student with fewer accomplishments admission to the university. The argument might be made that the university has a responsibility to give minorities an opportunity to advance, serve as role models for their minority population, and that contact with minorities is an educational opportunity for white students. Aristotle would disagree. Those most fit should go to the university; they merit it. More profoundly, the Aristotelian question is: What is the *telos* of the university? Is it a place of scholarship honoring research and intellectual achievement? Others believe the university needs to be socially active and promote civic ideals. In either case Aristotle's *telos* comes into play. It demands that we ask essential questions about the purpose of the university.[8]

Another recent debate takes us back to Aristotle. The Purple Heart, one of the oldest and most honored medals in the United States, is given to those wounded or killed in combat. Wars in Iraq and Afghanistan have increased the awarding of these medals. Many want to give the Purple Heart to those suffering from posttraumatic stress disorder, as well as to accident victims injured while deployed. The 2009 shootings of service members at a recruiting station in Little Rock, Arkansas, and at Fort Hood, Texas, have caused debates about the merit of those victims. Veterans groups—thinking like Aristotle—believe expanding medal-giving demeans the honorific goals (*telos*) of the Purple Heart. They argue that only those wounded in combat should get the medal. In New Hampshire, in 2013, an emotional debate arose over allowing family members to keep Purple Heart license plates after the recipient of the medal had died. Representative Frederick Rice, R-Hampton, said the Purple Heart is unique because it is only given to those who shed blood in combat. Those related to the soldier should not benefit. Aristotle would agree. Other representatives said that the spouse honors the veteran by keeping the plate. The state assembly allowed surviving spouses to keep the plates.[9]

Casey Martin, by all accounts a gifted golfer, made it to the highest ranks of the game. But he had a disability that would not let him walk the course. He petitioned authorities to allow him to use a golf cart. The Professional Golf Association (PGA) and most professional golfers felt an essential part of the game, its *telos*, was walking the course. Justice, for Aristotle, was a matter of fit, a fit between a person and his role and the honors to which he could lay claim. Was Martin unfit to claim the honors of professional golf? Even more deeply it raised questions as to whether golf was a game or a business. The honor of the game was at stake. The issue was profound and made it to the United States Supreme Court in *PGA Tour v. Martin (2001)*. Once again Aristotle was engaged in modern debates.[10]

Another example of modern-day issues in which Aristotle's thinking is appropriate has to do with same sex marriage. Successes of the Gay Rights Movement have raised issues about marriage. Should the government and the church sanction marriage between people of the same sex? This reflects the *telos* of marriage. If it is for the purpose of propagation of offspring then it should be disallowed, but if it has other equally important purposes such as fostering loving relationships then it should be allowed. Once again Aristotle's ideas are called into play.

Rectificatory Justice

Aristotle wanted harmony. Justice was maintaining and restoring equilibrium or balance. The purpose of justice was rectifying or correcting imbalance. The state became so essential in this that Aristotle devotes an entire book on *Politics*. Two things were important to Aristotle. First, the good life was participating in politics. Democracy was earned and learned by participation. He believed those who did not participate did not deserve the benefits of living in a democratic society. Of course, there was a dark side to Aristotle and citizenship. Ancient Athens was a slave-holding city-state and he defended the practice. Some people were meant (fit) to be slaves, he felt. Also, slaves were necessary to allow other citizens the time to be active in politics. Those who ruled were those who deserved to govern. One's citizenship was to be judged by participation in politics. Second, the state was to cultivate virtue. Citizens were to be guided to a virtuous life by the state. Ordinary citizens should not have the freedom to live life as they choose.

One can see this concept in modern policies striving to prohibit activities. One obvious example was the attempt to make alcohol illegal. Popular culture and politicians declared prohibition wrong and repealed it. It is not clear that prohibition did fail. It took up to the 1960s for per capita consumption of alcohol to reach preprohibition levels, suggesting that prohibition altered America's drinking habits.[11] Other crusades against vice are conducted by the state. Prostitution is illegal in most places, although a few rural counties in Nevada have set up legal brothels. The most dramatic prohibition crusade has been against drugs. Few would argue the war on drugs has been successful, but from Aristotle's perspective healthy debates about the government's role in prohibiting such activities are necessary in a just society.

Pondering the difference between high culture and low culture is another area reflecting Aristotelian thinking but allowing the introduction of others. The "good" life and "good" state are those filled with higher pleasures. Base culture demeans all society. Aristotle would certainly argue that real art represents inner significances and not outward appearances. Government, in the quest to bring virtue to the lives of citizens, should promote high culture, Aristotle might say. What is the difference between the two pleasures? When asked which is preferred, Mozart or Madonna, most would choose the twentieth century singer over the Austrian composer. Others prefer to watch an episode of *The Simpsons* on television than a Shakespearean play on stage. But all would admit that Mozart and Shakespeare are of higher value. How do these people, those who love to watch and those who do not, come to such conclusions? The higher pleasures need to be cultivated and that could be a job of society, of government.[12]

Utilitarianism

John Stuart Mill (*Utilitarianism*, 1863) and Jeremy Bentham (*On Liberty*, 1859) would disagree with Aristotle. To these thinkers, and the philosophy associated with them called utilitarianism, those who govern, and individuals in their own lives, should choose the action that will produce the greatest amount of happiness. The ends justify the means. Justice is the chief part of morality. An action is just if it increases happiness and wrong if it decreases it. So people and policy makers need to think of the consequences of choices in life and in governing. If the greatest number receives happiness from *The Simpsons* or Madonna then they are the better choices. Of course, though the majority's desire might prevail, there will be some who are not pleased. Those in the minority must accept the choice or policy if it pleases the greatest number.[13]

Some examples might show the problematic nature of utilitarianism. Slavery was widespread for centuries. The majority opinion, that of those in positions of power, favored this institution. It was bolstered by using racism as justification. To be sure, slaves did not favor such a practice, but they lacked the power to change the institution. Utilitarian thinkers, along with Aristotle on this issue, believed the owner's pleasure outweighed the pain of slavery and it was continued for hundreds of years.

Another historical example has to do with murder on the high seas in *The Case of Queen v. Dudley and Stephens*. In 1884, a British ship broke apart with all but four drowning. After 8 days it was clear that the survivors would die before any rescue could happen. Captain Thomas Dudley and First Mate Edward Stephens noticed that the cabin boy, Richard Stevens, was very ill from drinking sea water. Though in a weakened state, Stevens did not give consent and he was killed and consumed for 4 days. After 24 days, the remaining men were rescued. They were arrested and brought to trial and the defense argument was utilitarianism. Those who survived had committed murder out of necessity and it was morally permissible. It was better that one perished rather than all four. The prosecution argued that it was morally wrong and they were guilty of murder and cannibalism. Would it have mattered if Richard Stevens had given his consent?[14]

Society's response to suicide provides another illustration of the application of utilitarian principles to issues of justice. How should we view suicide and assisted suicide? Of course only heavenly judgment could deal with the individual who commits suicide. But the law and criminal justice system could deal with those who helped people commit suicide. In either case, if the mental and physical pain could only be alleviated by death, the utilitarians might argue that suicide was the better choice. Jack Kervorkian helped more than 100 terminally ill people end their lives in 1990. Their pain was so great that it was their wish to die. His argument was that "If we can aid people coming into the world why can't we aid them in exiting the world?" Crisscrossing the state of Michigan, he defied the law and court system until he was finally arrested and sent to prison for 8 years. To utilitarians he was a hero; to others he was Dr. Death. Laws allowing doctor-assisted suicides were passed in Oregon in 1997 and in the state of Washington in 2009. Other states refused to sanction assisted suicide. One's individual pain was not enough to sanction suicide. Although utilitarians thought in terms of consequences, these people believed it was categorically wrong. Their hero might be Immanuel Kant.

CATEGORICAL THINKING

Immanuel Kant (1724-1804) grew up in Konigsberg, East Prussia, on the southeastern shore of the Baltic Sea. Though economically secure, his family of harness makers was of modest means. He studied and eventually became a popular lecturer at the University of Konigsberg. Through his teachings and writings he became one of the greatest philosophers of the modern era.

In his *Critique of Pure Reason* Kant rejected utilitarianism. The individual was sacred and could not be reduced to majority and minority groupings. Freedom, not happiness, is the goal of morality. People could achieve freedom only if they examined their intent. Freedom is living by your own reason. You are not free if you are a slave to advertising and vast shopping malls. You are not free if addicted to alcohol or tobacco. People should do the right thing because it is the right thing and not for some other reason. Morality lies in the intent. And the foundation of intent is that all humans must be treated with respect. Therefore, he would be against suicide, no matter the suffering of the person, because it demeans humanity. The suicide victim is responding to pain and not rising above it. Indeed, he would be against capital punishment as well.

According to Kant, the countless religious people throughout history who did good just to go to heaven had it wrong. Doing good for no desire of reward was the moral and just thing. Goodness for goodness' sake should be the intent underlying all decisions. Kant uses the example of a shopkeeper who saw that a customer could be duped into paying a higher price. But he chose not to do so because he feared being caught. That was doing good, or at least not doing a bad thing, for the wrong reason, and there was no moral worth to his decision. Like most universities suffering from an epidemic of student dishonesty, the University of Maryland created an honor system. Students who signed the pledge to be honest were offered discounts at local stores. According to Kant such a policy had no moral worth. Students should not cheat because that was the appropriate choice.[15]

Kant believed in the moral worth of the individual. If he had been in the lifeboat with Dudley and Stevens he would not have allowed the killing of the cabin boy. But some moral dilemmas push Kant to the limit. Say you are driving down a hill when your brakes give out. Straight ahead there is a sharp curve and a cliff that will result in your death. A turn to the left would result in plowing through a group of senior citizens on an excursion. To your right a little girl is riding a tricycle. Someone has to die but who should it be? To many the turn toward the old people makes the best sense; they have already lived their lives. Killing the young tricycle rider would be wrong; she has so much life ahead of her. The noble thing would be driving over the cliff, Kant would suggest. It honors the life of others, and with the sacrifice it honors the driver's life as well.

Worldwide terrorist attacks have become a major concern. Particularly after the September 11, 2001, attacks in New York and Washington, DC, the United States and others have waged a war on Middle Eastern terrorist groups. Many have ended up in a variety of prisons like that found in Guantanamo, Cuba. Getting information about terrorist organizations and plans is essential. Questioning captives has been difficult and a variety of torturous techniques have been used to get important information. Utilitarians would applaud such activity. The ends justify the means, they would say. Kant would argue against it. Such practices are categorically wrong.

Most of us lie. A vast spectrum of lies has been created, from "white lies" to grand harmful ones. Kant believes all lies are bad because they demean the person being lied to; they are an affront to humanity. But there are some tricky problems here. Suppose a dear friend rushed into your house begging to be hidden from someone intending to commit murder. Shortly, the prospective murderer arrives, asking for your friend. What obligation do you have toward your friend or the killer? Unlike most of us, Kant says you should not lie. Perhaps misleading truths might be acceptable. Telling the killer that you told your friend "to run and hide" is true and vague enough to meet Kant's standards of honesty. President Bill Clinton had a sexual dalliance with a White House intern. Before millions of people on television, he claimed he "did not have sexual relations with that woman." Was that an outright lie or merely a misleading truth? What does it mean to have "sexual relations"? Is oral sex without vaginal penetration not sex? Though he faced humiliation, Clinton's actions, and his statements that they did not constitute sex, walked the line between truth and deception that represent the "misleading truths" that Kant never fully addresses.

NATURAL RIGHTS

Like Kant, John Locke believed there are fundamental rights possessed by all humans. These natural rights are: life, liberty, and property. In our prepolitical state everyone was equal; we were in a state of complete liberty. What happened to those rights as society and state were created? For example, how just was it for the various conquistadors in Central and South America and the settlers of the American West to take property from peoples who had possessed the land for centuries? Of course, the framers of America's founding documents left out property and put in the "pursuit of happiness."

How does the issue of capital punishment play out in Lockeian terms? What does it mean to force young people to serve in the military? How fair is it to tax the rich to support the poor? Such matters will be covered below and in Chapter 3. According to Locke, in forming a society we have joined a social contract in which some individual rights must be given up for the benefit of the whole group. A society without the police, law, and penal system could not be sustained, Locke would admit. These natural rights should not be taken away in an arbitrary manner. But to ensure liberty some liberty must be given up. Locke's thinking about "natural rights" would prove to be an important component of contemporary thinking about justice proposed by John Rawls.

FAIRNESS

Much of modern philosophical discussions about justice have revolved around the work of John Rawls (1921-2002). A professor of philosophy at Harvard and Oxford Universities, Rawls wrote *A Theory of Justice* (1971), the primary philosophical text in the last half of the twentieth century that revitalized Locke's social contract tradition. *Justice as Fairness* (2002) was written shortly before his death.[16]

According to Rawls, only principles that everyone can accept serve the purpose of giving us a fair distribution of goods and privileges, and this leads to justice. But from where did this societal agreement come? Rawls asks us to imagine we are at a meeting at the beginning of time when we bargain and hammer out principles that would shape the fundamental institutions of human society. An environment for such a bargaining session can only occur if those at the bargaining table are under a "veil of ignorance" in which future gender, race, religion, wealth, intelligence, or special gifts would not be known. Those qualities will exist in life but are unknown in this preexistence. Decisions are arrived at not knowing what lot in life the individual will be given. Rawls thinks that stripped of the knowledge of the advantages and disadvantages that will befall us, with everyone operating on a level, moral plane, these principles would emerge as a foundation of justice:

1. Each person has an equal right to a fully adequate scheme of equal, basic rights and liberties.
2. Social and economic inequalities will exist but they must be attached to offices and positions open to everyone under conditions of fair equality of opportunity.
3. All rewards enjoyed by the best advantaged must be shared with those least advantaged.

Our freedoms to think and speak, to choose careers and lifestyles, and to differ in political and religious beliefs need to be safeguarded. These liberties are so precious that we cannot afford to put them at risk, not even to increase overall happiness. Rawls recognizes that some inequalities will exist, but they are tolerable if sufficient surplus trickles down to the least advantaged. If it turns out you are a day laborer and your boss gets a thousand times more income, this seems unjust. Rawls insists that the rewards coming from these inequalities also help those worst off. The advantaged are privileged by birth, talents, and luck. Their particular skills just happen to be those to be prized by society at a historic moment. A few examples might clarify Rawls' position.

Professional athletes make large amounts of money. Society prizes these games and showers the athletically inclined with rewards of high salary and status. But Rawls would argue that these athletes do not own these talents; they are due to the luck of birth. Besides the enjoyment for fans of watching talented players some of the athlete's money should go to the less talented. Television stars make millions of dollars a year, but a schoolteacher makes $40,000. US Supreme Court Justices make $200,000 a year, but a popular TV judge makes $25 million. Such inequality can be moral as long as sizable portions go to help the less advantaged.

Justice as fairness is not just academic speculation. Rawls has a political agenda. For example, he rejects free market capitalism, welfare-state capitalism, and state socialism. Rawls demands an activist government to ensure justice. His approach endorses a system in which economic power is shared by companies and workers. This system uses taxation to keep the differences between rich and poor close. That all—those wanting gay rights, women's rights, racial rights—have access to the basic rights he sees as coming from that agreement arrived at under the "veil of ignorance." As Rawls shows, indeed as Aristotle shows, philosophers see the importance of government in achieving justice. This is a topic to which we now turn.

DISCUSSION QUESTIONS

1. Should those soldiers injured outside of combat receive the Purple Heart?
2. You are a student living with a roommate who cheats on homework and exams. Should you report the student?
3. Is it unfair for universities and colleges to consider race or ethnicity as a factor in admissions?
4. Should the government recognize same sex marriages?
5. Should doctors help terminally ill people die?
6. Should professional athletes be paid such high salaries?
7. Should athletic teams be allowed to use Native American images and names as team symbols and names?

Endnotes

1. This chapter is deeply indebted to Michael J. Sandel's *Justice: What's the Right Thing to Do?* (New York: Farrar, Straus and Giroux, 2009).
2. See Yu-lan Fung, *A Short History of Chinese Philosophy* (New York: Simon and Schuster, 1997) and Bryan W. Van Norden, *Introduction to Classical Chinese Philosophy* (Indianapolis: Hackett, 2011).
3. Ron Neufeldt, "Justice in Hinduism," in *The Spiritual Roots of Restorative Justice*, Michael Hadley (ed.) (Albany, NY: State University of New York Press, 2001), pp. 143-160.
4. For readings on these philosophers, the reader is directed to Solomon and Murphy, pp. 66, 74, 81, 95.
5. G. M. A. Grube, *Plato's Thought* (Boston, 1958), p. 288.
6. See David Callahan's *The Cheating Culture: Why More Americans Are Doing Wrong to Get Ahead* (Orlando, Florida: Harcourt, 2004) and Sandal, pp. 236-239.
7. Earnest Baker, *The Political Thought of Plato and Aristotle* (New York: Dover, 1959), pp. 81-119.
8. Sandel, pp. 167-183.
9. Sandel, pp. 10-12.
10. Sandel, pp. 203-204.
11. See Daniel Okren's *Last Call: The Rise and Fall of Prohibition* (New York: Scribner, 2011).
12. Sandel, pp. 54-56.
13. John Stuart Mill, *Utilitarianism*, Oscar Piest (ed.) (Indianapolis: Liberal Arts, 1957), p. 62; and *On Liberty* (Chicago: Henry Regnery, 1955), pp.109-137.
14. Sandel, pp. 31-33.
15. Sandel, pp. 104-118.
16. John Rawls, *A Theory of Justice* (Cambridge, Mass.: Belknap Press of Harvard University Press, 1999), pp. 3-22; *Justice as Fairness: A Restatement* (Cambridge, Mass.: Belknap Press of Harvard University Press, 2001), pp. 39-52; and *Political Liberalism* (New York: Columbia University Press, 1993), pp. 4, 47-48.

CHAPTER

Justice and the State

3

As the nation-states emerged in the late Middle Ages, more profound questions arose about justice. At first, remnants of the old world remained, in such concepts as the divine right of kings. The king was thought to act under the guidance of God, and as a representative of God the monarch had considerable leeway to draw the lines of justice. This approach also made it difficult to challenge the king's interpretation of justice, for to challenge the king was to challenge God.

Perhaps one of the earliest treatises on the concept of governance and of justice to drift away from the view that government was a divine creation was outlined in Machiavelli's book *The Prince* (1513). Niccolo Machiavelli was born and raised in politically chaotic Italy. After a frustrating career in the politics of Renaissance Florence, Machiavelli wrote *The Prince*. He longed for a ruler who would bring order, stability, and unity to Italy. Questions of a moral or immoral state were wrongheaded, he thought. The state is amoral. The prince must be honest and just but deal with the world as it is and not as it should be. People are devious, gullible, corrupt, and greedy, and must be treated accordingly. Being feared by the citizenry was better than being loved. Obtaining and retaining power was the first priority. Every ruler in Europe achieved power by force. The state and its ruler are more important than the people who make up the state. Therefore, the ruler may do unjust things in the name of preserving the state. Hence, politicians must break promises, conceal their deals, distort the facts, ignore the masses, and pose as righteous even if circumstances force them to be unrighteous. Until one gets power, he or she must be ruthless and, if necessary, evil; the prince must be both the "fox and lion." The ends justify the means. To those who would argue otherwise, he would counter: "If the ends do not justify the means then what does?"[1]

As part of divine right, Machiavelli assumed a just and right state, but, as sensibilities changed, questions arose over what justified the state taking away a person's property in the form of taxes. How could a politician compel a young man into military service? How could a government draw up laws and punishments? In short, what gave legitimacy to the government? Of course, the main justification had been that a just and virtuous state was presupposed, having been created under divine guidance. Both divine right and Machiavellian perspectives on justice and the state assumed that everyday citizens had no role in decisions made by the state, and that they *should* have no role. But as the Middle Ages were replaced by the Renaissance, more humanistic voices were heard.

THE SOCIAL CONTRACT

The basis of social contract theory is that states and governments are legitimate or illegitimate only to the degree that they are formed and supported by the mutual agreement of the citizens of that state. This presupposes that society exists before the state does. Following this line of thinking, America—its society and sense of community—existed before the United States came into existence. The Constitution created a structure of government but it did not form a society. England existed long before modern

Great Britain appeared on the scene. This is true of most modern states. Humans, seeing that they would have to compromise some of their individualistic self-interests, created the modern state-ism through an unwritten contract or agreement among members of the society.

The first expression of this social contract was Thomas Hobbes' seventeenth century book called *Leviathian* (1651). Before the formation of society and the state there was brutish anarchy, according to Hobbes. The natural condition of man was animalistic and counterproductive to civilization. All humans were vane and hostilities erupted over a person's desire for deference. To Hobbes, humans were guided by self-interest, and in the absence of political authority selfish motivation and natural inequality would degenerate into war and chaos. In this barbaric state there was no justice or injustice. Therefore, a social contract was needed to protect humans from themselves. To assure a modicum of liberty and tranquility, man had to give up total liberty. Justice then results when people in a society carry out the agreements implicitly made among its members.[2] Harkening back to the Greek notion of justice and righteousness, Hobbes declares that:

> *A just man is he that takes all the care he can that his actions may be all just; and an unjust man is he who neglects it. And such men are more often in our language styled by the names righteous and unrighteous than just and unjust, though the meaning be the same. Therefore a righteous man does not lose that title by one or a few unjust actions that proceed from sudden passion or mistake of things or persons; nor does an unrighteous man lose his character for such actions as he does or forbears to do for fear, because his will is not framed by the justice but by the apparent benefit of what he is to do.*[3]

John Locke came to the social contract too, but with a different perception of human nature. In his *Second Treatise of Government* (1690), prepolitical humans were seen as good and industrious, working to make society a better place. Mankind had natural rights to property but some wayward people tried to take those rights away. Locke's social contract, therefore, was to protect man's property and the fruits of his labor. Government was formed to do this. It is to acknowledge and enforce these natural rights that political authority is instituted by contract.[4]

A similar theme was expressed in Jean-Jacques Rousseau's *Discourse on the Origins of Inequality* (1754) and *On the Social Contract* (1762). Rousseau saw primitive men as happy and healthy individuals, too. But they were indifferent to each other. As they slowly acquired property they formed law and government to protect their possessions, but in so doing they lost their innocence. The invention of private property, and the inequalities that followed from it, resulted in the end of our primeval happiness and independence. It is from the institution of private property that all of our unhappiness arose—the artificiality and competitiveness of contemporary society, the exaggerated differences between the rich and the poor. But there was no going back to the paradisal state. Therefore, a social contract was necessary, not to protect us from ourselves or our property, but to elevate us from mere humanity to the morally more important condition of citizenship.[5]

NATURE OF LAW

A very important part of the legitimacy of the state has to do with just laws and just lawmakers.[6] Where does law come from? Many philosophers, going back to the ancient Stoics, began to think in terms of **natural law**, a system of rules and principles of human conduct that were independent of enacted law or of the systems particular to one people. These laws preexisted humans, were fixed and unchangeable, and could be discovered by the rational intelligence of humans. The Stoic doctrine grew out of the proposition of a life ordered according to nature. The Stoics believed in the existence, in ancient times, of a "state of nature," a condition of society in which people universally were governed solely by the rational and consistent obedience to the needs and impulses of true human nature before it was defaced by dishonesty, falsehood, and baser passions. In ethical terms, this consisted of universal rules of conduct that had been established by the author of human nature as essential to the Divine purposes of an orderly universe.[7]

Such a concept became essential in terms of justice. It became a way to determine just laws and just governments. Just societies, laws, and leaders are those who conform to natural law.

It was in the founding of America, with the proclamations made in the Declaration of Independence, where the natural laws were articulated as principles for guiding state authority. As justification for throwing off the yoke of an unjust government, Thomas Jefferson alerted his readers that humans had inalienable rights. This declaration of the individual rights of life, liberty, and the pursuit of happiness became the bedrock of a new nation and a statement of natural rights. Much like Locke, Jefferson declared that government was created by the people and if it failed to live up to the desires of the people it could be done away with and another would replace it.

The Constitution of 1787 created a tripartite government with executive, legislative, and judicial branches carefully balancing each other so that no concentration of power would predominate. Initially, the Constitution did not address individual rights, and, as an afterthought, ten amendments were added to assure the government did not overbear the individual. A reading of the Bill of Rights indicates the restrictions placed upon government, particularly its police power. These natural rights were to override any development of government. Such a concern was important because the justness of law and governmental authority had other defenders.

Besides natural law others advocated **positivism**. Those advocating this school of thought felt that law came from those in power. It was not transcendental. Of course, it was very important to have just people in power or heading the state or its subjects would be enslaved by human greed and lust for power. Laws do change, but they change as those in power change. This was less offensive in a democracy than in a despotic state. In a democracy, it was presumed that those who came to power did so with the agreement of the citizens. Even the losers, as part of the social contract, agreed to abide by the will of the majority. Those who chose not to abide by the government had to prove the laws and the state unjust or suffer the label of outlaw.

Another group, identified by the description **sociological jurisprudence**, believed that changing conditions altered the law no matter who was in power. The evolving conditions of human society demanded laws to change. The ending of slavery and granting women the right to vote are two examples. The creation of hate crimes is another such response (see Chapter 10). Public sensitivities have evolved, the argument might go, and the law has adjusted to them.

How law emerges has implications for how one views the state—the state as something that protects rights and promotes justice, or the state as something from which to be protected. Natural law, positivism, and sociological jurisprudence provide very different perspectives on the link between justice and the state.

LIBERTY, EQUALITY, AND JUSTICE

A free society suggests liberty. But how much liberty? Can society interfere with a person's exercise of his or her freedom? Does justice imply that everyone is equal or that everyone is treated equally? But everyone is not equal; some are more intelligent than others, some have more talents than others, some are more attractive than others, and some are healthier than others. Should people who are different be treated equally? Should two students be given the same grade when one studied hard and another cheated? Should two bank robbers be given the same sentence even though one did it to feed his hungry children while the other did it for fun? Should a person who has talent and the courage to make a fortune in the free market be punished for his or her success? Should a person who is a failure because of lack of intelligence and energy be rewarded with government sponsored giveaways? A society that bases its ideology on equality and the freedom to engage in the pursuit of property finds itself in a bind. Capitalism and the free market, unlike socialism, do not guarantee equality. To the contrary, capitalism is based on the idea that many will fail while a few will succeed.

A central question for those concerned with a just society has to do with these notions of liberty and equality. This has been particularly relevant in the past century in which so many countries have moved to democratic societies. Ideally, a society would hope to maximize both liberty and equality. But these two principles may work at cross purposes.

At polar extremes you have **libertarians**, those who place the highest values on liberty even at the expense of equality. They want unlimited liberty and freedom even if it results in inequality of conditions. The only equality they want is equality of opportunity because it encourages freedom of enterprise and a meritocracy based upon talents and hard work. Vast inequalities will result and are acceptable because otherwise there would be a loss of individual liberty, which, from this perspective, is of the highest value. An equality of conditions can be achieved only by the loss of individual freedom.[8]

In contrast to libertarians, **egalitarians** regard equality of conditions as the supreme value and are willing to achieve this by infringing upon the liberty of others. To egalitarians, if individual freedom is unrestrained, inequality of conditions—poverty, housing, privilege—will result, and this is to be avoided. They hope to maximize equality of conditions even if individual liberty has to be sacrificed. Egalitarians as social activists are often in the forefront of social justice movements. They consider capitalism as a major problem unless it is socialized and the workers are given a stronger voice and share of the economic and political benefits of society.[9]

So how does one determine the proper balance between freedom and liberty? There are at least two sources of freedom and liberty. First, there are the freedoms implicit to all humans based on the fact that they are human. These may be called natural rights. They are life and the pursuit of happiness. These encompass other entitlements. For example, a human, in a just society, is entitled to enough economic goods to sustain life. Health and education are additional requirements to give humans access to humanity and humane treatment. Second, there are circumstantial rights and freedoms. These have to do with the freedom to exercise one's talents to the fullest and enjoy the benefits of such gifts. This requires an environment, one regulated by justice, which allows the greatest pursuit of happiness without infringing upon the happiness of others.[10]

Of course, all people are equal in their humanity. But after that there is a wide divergence in talents and skills. There is the question of equality of conditions—not all people have the same basic skills or intelligence. Then there is equality of opportunity. Mortimer Adler, in his book *Six Great Ideas*, illustrates the difference using the foot race as an example. The race starts with everyone having an equal opportunity to win. There are no hidden barriers or obstacles for some and not others. When the race is over, these same individuals end up unequal; some come in first, second, third, and last based upon their athleticism, training, and determination. This is equality of conditions. It is up to a just society to insure the equality of opportunity. It is up to the individual to succeed or not based upon his or her conditions.

Equality under the law is another example. Society cannot guarantee that some will or will not break the law. But in the law all should be treated the same, or with equality of conditions.[11]

Furthermore, when one abides by the laws, even if the laws curtail some freedoms, one does not lose his or her freedoms. As Adler says in reference to America:

> *The Constitution to which the citizen has given consent by exercising his suffrage provides for a decision by the vote of the majority. He has accepted the principle of majority rule and, having done so, the citizen has also accepted, in advance, the results of majority rule, whether or not the voting places him in the majority or in the adversely affected minority.*[12]

Although liberty and equality are important values that may appear to be in conflict, these conflicts need not lead to paralysis of thinking. A just society is one that balances these two competing values. Freedom and liberty cannot be exerted contrary to the best interests of the community.

WAR

Some of the most difficult issues of justice to be faced by nation-states concern the conduct of war. War has been a part of every nation's history.[13] It has been a means to acquire territory, resources, wealth, women, and pride. Early wars were localized to competing armies or navies; ordinary citizens were largely left alone. Soldiers were a professional class who were often not even emotionally attached to the nation for whom they were waging war. Sometimes war took on religious overtones. The crusades are an example of how Christian Europe attacked and fought to free the Holy Land from Moslem conquerors.

Modern war took on new attributes. First, many nations did away with mercenaries and professional soldiers, and ordinary citizens who had a more emotional interest entered the scuffle. Second, total war in which the land and lives of noncombatants were swept up in the destruction became common. Third, war became more mechanized and lethal with tanks, artillery, and bombs. By nature war is cruel, but this is particularly true in modern times. People are killed and property is destroyed. It is something that should not be entered into lightly.

To describe some wars as just and others as unjust, one must assume that there are some higher moral and legal standards that can be used to make this distinction. In an earlier time, such standards were provided by religious leaders and institutions. St. Augustine, in his *The City of God*, was perhaps the first to articulate the concept of a "just war." Thereafter, the Catholic Church assumed the role of defining and guiding the use of force along Christian ethics.[14] In modern times these standards are drawn up by an international community of nations[15] (see Chapter 16). These standards can be applied to the cause of the conflict, the carrying out of war policy by the state, the manner of individual behavior in war, and the treatment of the vanquished after the conflict.[16]

On the surface the cause of war seems to be a simple assumption. A nation that aggressively attacks another has done an unjust thing. Consequently, the state that has been attacked must go to war in the name of self-defense. Such countries may posture themselves as morally superior—they did not start this war; they are victims fighting for survival. For nations whose international policies reflect this attitude, including America in the twentieth century, war is a necessary evil. Preventive war, going to war early so as to prevent a future aggressor, is wrong according to this perspective. The just nation would generally have a non-warlike posture. Diplomacy and treaties to negotiate disputes and deter aggression would be the first and most just approaches. But a nation might create conditions that force another to be aggressive. For example, the Japanese attack on Pearl Harbor launched a just war for the United States. But America had numerous policies in the 1930s that threatened Japan's desires for oil supplies. Those policies maneuvered Japan into an attack, making the issue of justness cloudy.[17]

Once an aggressor has started a war, the victim nation, in the name of military necessity, can be very aggressive and violent. The act of instigating a war changes things; however, there are some restraining considerations. One is based upon the "evil few" concept. Even in the aggressor nation, only a few evil people are truly responsible for the act of war. The "many good" are simply brought along through patriotism and propaganda. Ordinarily, a just war policy tries to avoid citizen casualties. Of course, in the name of military necessity, total war, that in which many of the innocent majority are caught up in the violence of war, may occur and be justified. For example, the nuclear bombing of two Japanese cities in 1945 was argued to be necessary because of the many more Japanese and Americans who would have been killed and injured if an invasion of the country were forced. However, international rules dictate how combatants are to be treated (see Chapter 16). Proper prisoner of war camps and appropriate humane care need to be established. The Japanese role here, particularly in the death marches in Bataan, reaffirmed that the allies were fighting a just war. Nazi treatment of the Jews posed them in villainous roles so that certain leaders could be tried as "war criminals" at the Nuremberg trials after the war (see Chapter 16). Several German and Japanese war leaders were executed for their unjust waging of war.[18]

Even fighting a just war does not free individual soldiers to do inhumane things. Fighting for one's life can bring the individual soldier down. To see death and destruction all around is demoralizing. Being trained and forced to kill, which some argue is contrary to human nature, may blunt one's humanity. Such problems can emerge in any war. But in a particularly frustrating war they may be greater. For Americans, such a war was waged in Vietnam. Clearly defined goals and morally repressible enemies were not present. Moral support from home was tenuous. Issues of the enemy being the aggressor were elusive. Massive bombing and killing of people and destruction of the landscape were debatable. But two incidents point to the unjust behavior of individual soldiers. During the Vietnam war, first, there was the patrol duty of Lt. Calley at My Lai in which numerous, apparently innocent, villagers were slaughtered. Calley was later convicted of a war crime. Second, there was the career of a navy seal who invaded and slaughtered a village of apparently innocent people. He won numerous medals and a U.S. Senatorial seat before exposure years later. These are just two of countless incidents in Vietnam. The nature of war suggests that countless other examples may be found in all wars.[19]

Finally, there is the treatment of the defeated after the conflict. This is a matter of no small consequence. Hitler used the treatment of Germany after World War I as a means to achieve power and bring on the second World War. Forgiveness is not an easy thing to obtain, especially if the war was a particularly costly one. This dilemma has been beautifully captured by Simon Wiesenthal in *The Sunflower*. In the book, a young Jewish prisoner, having undergone horrendous treatment in a Nazi death camp, is summoned before a dying German soldier. The soldier, stricken with enormous pangs of guilt for what he and his comrades had done, pleads for forgiveness. Bewildered, the prisoner leaves, only to be summoned again and given mementoes the soldier wants delivered to his mother. The prisoner takes the items but still finds it impossible to forgive the soldier. He leaves, never to see the dying man again. After the war the prisoner goes to the soldier's mother and is told what a sweet, honest, peaceful young man the soldier had been. Now the old prisoner faces another dilemma, whether to tell the mother what a demon her son had really been. After *The Sunflower* was published, scholars, theologians, and philosophers debated the moral and ethical dimensions of the book. Clearly, issues of a just war have to do with events before, during, and after the conflict itself.[20]

In the last half of the twentieth century a new type of war, terrorism, has emerged. Here, a war is not officially declared, citizens become a main target, suicide warriors have no respect or regard for life, and gangster psychology is part of the aggressor's mind-set. For many in the Western world, such aggression falls into the unjust war category. But terrorists assume this strategy because they are too weak to fight legitimate wars. They are the dispossessed and, having little to lose, they resort to outlandish tactics.

CRIMINAL JUSTICE

Very early justice was connected to the processing and punishment of criminals, and it remains so today. In every human society, no matter what political and economic form it takes, there are people who violate the rules of society. Society's response is delivered through a system of criminal justice.

What constitutes a just processing of criminals? Processing of criminals might be defined as steps in the criminal justice system, including arrest, interrogation, charging, representation by an attorney, courtroom ceremonies, sentencing, and punishment (see Chapter 8). In this regard justice is a process. On one level, this process needs to be fair. On another level, the system is guided by its own set of desires and agendas that shape the nature of this fairness. Two mind-sets exist about the appropriate processing of criminals. Herbert Packer (1968) has described these approaches as the **crime control** and **due process** perspectives.

Those who subscribe to the **crime control** mentality believe that a major problem of modern society is crime. The criminal justice system—the police, the court personnel, and those in corrections—needs all the power it can get to process criminals. Victims of crime are of the most concern. In their minds, efficiency overtakes fairness. An appropriate metaphor for the system is the assembly line. Justice is a smoothly operating, efficient system run by professionals who should have the resources to do their job with little oversight by outsiders. Although not uttered, the presumption is that the accused person is guilty.[21]

Others approach criminal justice from a **due process** perspective. They feel that, along with criminals, the criminal justice system itself is a potential threat to justice. While efficiency is a good thing, too much efficiency might define a police state in which citizens have no rights. Therefore, the just system is one in which the police and others in the system have controls on their behavior. While respect towards victims is necessary, people accused of crimes also need protections. The presumption here is of innocence. An appropriate metaphor for the system is the obstacle course. High standards of procedures, accountability of actions, and close scrutiny by outsiders are characteristic of this perspective.[22]

These are not abstract concerns; they are bureaucratic ones. Criminal justice systems need to process large numbers of cases and do so as efficiently as possible. The just society is one that strives to find a balance between these two perspectives.

A fundamental question remains: why do we deprive people of life or liberty? John Stuart Mill and Jeremy Bentham believed in punishment and defended it in terms of rational ideas. To them, societal good came from punishing its wrongdoers. Jeremy Bentham, in his *Introduction to the Principles of Morals and Legislation* (1789), even expressed his belief that society should have a guiding principle to help make decisions for society. That master rule was the principle of utility—does the good outweigh the bad? All actions, rules, and institutions are justified only to the extent that they bring about the greater overall good, or the maximum of pleasure and the minimum of pain. Punishment is the intentional infliction of something unpleasant or the intentional deprivation of something pleasant by the state. From this **utilitarian** perspective, society should determine the amount of punishment based upon a cost/benefit analysis of suffering inflicted versus social gains achieved.[23]

The classic alternative to utilitarianism was **retributivism**. Those guilty of crimes need to be punished because they deserve to be punished. Utilitarians would determine punishment based upon the amount of good it would do society. Retributivists would rely upon the idea that the punishment inflicted should be in proportion to the severity of the offense. Immauel Kant, in his *The Philosophy of Law* (1797), stated it most clearly. The reason for punishing someone was the commitment of a crime. The crime should be punished according to the principle of equality; the severity of the punishment should equal the severity of the crime.[24]

Others have presented ideas outside the utilitarian and retributivist debate. For example, Hegel, in his *The Philosophy of Right* (1821), claimed that punishment was self-chosen, that the wrongdoer actually invites his or her own punishment. He distinguishes between injury to the state and injury to an individual. It is injury to the state that requires the punishment. For example, even if the victim forgives the offender, the state still needs to punish. That is why, Hegel explains, punishment often does not fit the crime, for the seriousness of the injury to the person may have little relationship to the threat to society. It is the sanctity of the particular society that is the main concern, not the interests of the various citizens or even the public good.[25]

Michael Moore, in *The Moral Worth of Retribution* (1987), defends retribution simply because wrongdoing deserves punishment. He gives several atrocious cases taken from newspapers and asks what should be done. In every case a natural abhorrence arises demanding some kind of pain. Reform and rehabilitation are not considered; issues of utility fall to the wayside. A natural impulse demands retribution, or "just deserts." He asks us to imagine a situation:

> *A murderer has truly found Christ ... so that he or she does not need to be reformed; he or she is not dangerous for the same reason; and the crime can go undetected so that general deterrence does not demand punishment (alternatively, we can pretend to punish and pay the person the money the punishment would have cost us to keep his or her mouth shut, which will also serve the ends of general deterrence). In such a situation, should the criminal still be punished?*

Moore believes that most of us still would favor some punishment.[26]

Robert Nozick, in his *Philosophical Explanations* (1981), distinguishes between retribution and revenge. Retribution is impersonal, he thinks, while revenge is personal. Retribution is for a wrong while revenge sometimes is merely for a slight. Retribution is limited in its severity by the offense; revenge is not. He defends retribution because it sends a message to the offender and likely to the wider society as well.[27] Robert C. Solomon, in his *A Passion for Justice* (1990), also addresses the issues of revenge and retribution. He argues that much of the supposed irrationality and excess of revenge has been overstated. In fact, seeking revenge lies at the very foundation of our sense of justice. The desire for vengeance seems to be an integral aspect of our recognition of evil. Uncontrolled vengeance might be bad, but to deny it as a legitimate motive would be as wrong. Therefore:

> *Justice is not forgiveness nor even forgetting but rather it is getting one's emotional priorities right, putting blame aside in the face of so much other human suffering and thereby giving up vengeance for the sake of larger and more noble emotions.*[28]

Many philosophers do not like retribution (which has a close kinship to vengeance, according to Solomon) because it is "backward looking," or undoing a past offense. These people argue for deterrence and reform as forward looking. But Solomon thinks this is wrongheaded. Why punish at all? Let us forget past misdeeds and move on to the future. In fact, carrying it further, why not punish innocent people as object lessons and warnings to future possible wrongdoers? Of course, that is ridiculous and even unjust. Vengeance can be dangerous (an old Chinese saying states "If you seek vengeance, dig two graves."); that is why it must be left to the state and not individuals. Solomon claims, therefore, that "vengeance deserves its central place in any theory of justice and, whatever else we are to say about punishment, the desire for revenge must enter into our deliberations along with such emotions as compassion, caring and love." Of course it also explains why some countries still have capital punishment.[29]

CAPITAL PUNISHMENT

Perhaps the most controversial of punishments society can inflict is death. Capital punishment, once so widely spread across the world, has been abandoned by much of Europe. Ironically, the country that has been such an exemplar to the world when it comes to politics and economics, the United States of America, still practices capital punishment.[30] Empirical evidence seems to suggest that capital punishment does not deter others from committing murder. However, in a Supreme Court case, *Gregg v. Georgia* (1976), the majority upheld the constitutionality of the death penalty in light of arguments of retribution and deterrence.

> *The instinct for retribution is part of the nature of men, and channeling that instinct in the administration of criminal justice serves an important purpose in promoting the stability of a society government by law. When people begin to believe that organized society is unwilling or unable to impose upon criminal offenders the punishment they "deserve," then there are sown the seeds of anarchy—of self-help, vigilante justice, and lynch law.*[31]

Justices representing the minority opinion in the case dismissed retribution as vengeance and deterrence as not supported by evidence.

Justice Thurgood Marshall, going back to arguments given by Socrates, believed that it was wrong to return evil for evil. There was no evidence, he felt, that capital punishment would have a greater deterrent effect than a life term in prison.[32]

Hugo Bedau, in his *Death Is Different*, argues that capital punishment is an ineffective deterrent and unnecessary for finding appropriate retribution. Although criminals need to be punished and the punishment should fit the crime, capital punishment does not do so. Bedau points out that death is not administered to all killers. Furthermore, it is unjustly applied. Wealthy white murderers do not receive that punishment. A very large number of those executed are poor and members of minority populations. Furthermore, who gets sentenced to death frequently has more to do with aggressive prosecutors and incompetent defense attorneys than anything else. Capital punishment cheapens and degrades human life rather than enhancing respect for it, claims Bedau.[33]

In contrast, Earnest van den Haag, a prominent conservative thinker, supports the death penalty because it is better to err in favor of potential victims than in favor of convicted killers. He thinks that despite the rhetoric, rehabilitation and deterrence are not really part of the American penal system. To be sure there is uncertainty in the impact of the death penalty. But by executing real killers we assure they will never kill again. Furthermore, there is a slim chance future victims might be saved by the example of killing a killer. Van den Haag thinks execution is worth it for the sake of these possible future victims.[34]

CONCLUSION

As abstract as the notion of justice might be, its presence or absence in a society is most evident in the workings of government. The political environment has the greatest immediate impact upon individuals and justice. Some totalitarian states only make insignificant gestures towards justice. Democratic ones are caught on the horns of a dilemma. They not only talk justice but must practice it.

The relationship between the people and their government raises all kinds of issues. Perhaps first is the issue of legitimacy. Is the government—its people and policies—a reflection of the people or is it imposed by force? Laws—those written or proclaimed statements by the government that bind the citizenry to order—directly affect the lives of citizens. Where do these laws come from and how are they to be interpreted? What if the activities of the government belie any philosophical or fundamental principles? When it comes to foreign policy and war, to what extent is the government just? No soldier wants to fight for an unjust cause. Internally, one of the most dramatic agencies of government is the criminal justice system. If it is true that a society will be judged by how it treats those it hates most, the treatment of criminals tests a people's sense of justice. For those countries that retain the death penalty, issues of justice are even more vivid. This chapter has tried to introduce the reader to those areas of justice. But there are a variety of other issues of justice that need to be discussed; they are categorized as social justice.

DISCUSSION QUESTIONS

1. Why is it essential for the state to be involved in issues of justice?
2. Does the "social contract" allow for dissent and disobedience?
3. Do you believe in natural law, positivism, or sociological jurisprudence?

Endnotes

1. J. W. Allen, *A History of Political Thought in the Sixteenth Century* (New York: Barnes & Noble's University Paperbacks, 1960), pp. 445-494.
2. Thomas Hobbes, *Leviathan: Or the Matter, Form and Power of a Commonwealth Ecclesiastical and Civil* (London: Collier Books, 1962), pp. 28-31. See also Johann P. Sommerville, *Thomas Hobbes: Political Ideas in Historical Context* (New York: St. Martin's Press, 1992), pp. 29-31, 57-63.
3. *Ibid.*, p. 116.
4. John Locke, *Second Treatise of Government*, Peter Laslett (ed.) (Cambridge, England: Cambridge University Press, 1967), pp. 336-348, 368-371. Also see Ian Harris, *The Mind of John Locke: A Study of Political Theory in Its Intellectual Setting* (Cambridge, England: Cambridge University Press, 1994), pp. 36-39, 189.
5. Jean-Jacques Rousseau, *On the Social Contract and Discourse*, G. D. H. Cole (trans.) (New York: E. P. Dutton and Co., 1959), pp. 176-282. Also see Lester G. Crocker, *Rousseau's Social Contract: An Interpretive Essay* (Cleveland: Case Western University Press, 1968), pp. 43-101.
6. For an introduction, see Thomas W. Simon, *Law and Philosophy: An Introduction with Readings* (Boston: McGraw Hill, 2001).
7. Paul Hazard, *The European Mind, 1680-1715* (Cleveland and New York: Meridan Books, 1968), pp. 266-283.
8. Mortimer J. Adler, *Six Great Ideas* (New York: Macmillan Publishing Co., 1981), p. 137.
9. *Ibid.*

10. *Ibid.*, pp. 164-173.
11. *Ibid.*, p. 157.
12. *Ibid.*, p. 148.
13. David Welch, *Justice and the Genesis of War* (Cambridge, England: Cambridge University Press, 1993), pp. 7-23.
14. Williston Walker, *A History of the Christian Church* (New York: Charles Scribner's Sons, 1959), pp. 160-172.
15. John Hagan and Scott Greer, "Making War Criminal," in *Criminology*, Vol. 40, No. 2, 2002, pp. 231-264.
16. James E. Childress, "Just Wars Theories," *Theological Studies*, 1978, pp. 427-445.
17. Robert W. Tucker, *The Just War: A Study in Contemporary Doctrine* (Baltimore: The Johns Hopkins Press, 1960), pp. 18-30.
18. *Ibid.*, pp. 27-30.
19. Kenneth W. Kemp, "Just War Theory: A Reconceptualization," *Public Affairs Quarterly*, Vol. 2, No. 2, 1988, pp. 57-74.
20. Simon Wiesenthal, *The Sunflower: On the Possibilities and Limits of Forgiveness* (New York: Schoken Books, 1997), pp. 3-98.
21. Herbert Packer, *The Limits of the Criminal Sanction* (Stanford, Calif.: Stanford University Press, 1968), pp. 154-163.
22. *Ibid.*, pp. 163-173.
23. J. H. Burns and H. L. A. Hart, *An Introduction to the Principles of Morals and Legislation* (London: Athlone, 1970), pp. 11-15.
24. Edward Caird, *The Critical Philosophy of Immanuel Kant*, 2 vols. (New York: Kraus Reprint Co., 1968), pp. 315-378.
25. Georg Wilhelm Friedrich Hegel, *The Philosophy of Right* (Chicago: Encyclopedia Britannica, 1952), pp. 64-78.
26. Robert C. Solomon and Mark C. Murphy (eds.), *What Is Justice? Classic and Contemporary Readings* (New York: Oxford University Press, 2000), pp. 236-245.
27. Robert Nozick, *Philosophical Explanations* (Cambridge, Mass.: Harvard University Press, 1981), pp. 363, 366-368.
28. Robert C. Solomon, *A Passion for Justice: Emotions and the Origins of the Social Contract* (Reading, Mass.: Addison-Wesley, 1990), p. 286.
29. *Ibid.*, p. 285.
30. For a perceptive discussion of the problem of capital punishment in America, see Franklin E. Zimring, *The Contradictions of American Capital Punishment* (New York: Oxford University Press, 2003).
31. *Gregg v. Georgia*, 428 US. 153 (1976).
32. *Ibid.*
33. Hugo Bedau, *Death Is Different: Studies in the Morality, Law, and Politics of Capital Punishment* (Boston: Northeastern University Press, 1987), pp. 32-34, 238-247.
34. Ernest van den Haag and John Conrad, *The Death Penalty: A Debate* (New York: Plenum Press, 1983), pp. 28-35, 55-56, 67-70.

CHAPTER

4 Social Justice

For most people discussions of justice become too abstract and academic. Social justice makes it more practical. Because of religious, political, or economic differences, many people find themselves at a disadvantage. Social justice focuses on the redistribution of resources to ensure fairness in meeting the basic needs of people. Social justice has to do with distributing society's benefits and burdens. These thinkers and activists are concerned with the gaps in society. A just society tries to diminish significant disparities. A classic social justice statement was made by Karl Marx: "From each according to his abilities, to each according to his needs."[1]

John Stuart Mill's argument for social justice and utility forms a significant part of his *Utilitarianism* (1861).[2] It is just to respect and unjust to violate the legal rights of any person. Justice means adherence to law. However, sometimes there are bad laws. Humans have moral rights that transcend such laws. In addition, people should get what they deserve.

> *Speaking in a general way, a person is understood to deserve good if he does right, evil if he does wrong; and in a more particular sense, to deserve good from those to whom he does or has done good, and evil from those to whom he does or has done evil.*[3]

For Mill, impartiality becomes a keystone in the definition of justice. And then in ringing terms Mill sees a critical aspect in the name of social justice.

> *The entire history of social improvement has been a series of transitions by which one custom or institution after another, from being a supposed primary necessity of social existence, has passed into the rank of a universally stigmatized injustice and tyranny. So it has been with the distinctions of slaves and freedman, nobles and serfs, patricians and plebeians; and so it will be, and in part already is, with the aristocracies of color, race, and sex.*[4]

Thus, social justice focuses on fairness and equality of opportunity for **classes** of people, rather than focusing on the justice due to individuals.

HUMAN RIGHTS

Many issues of justice are closely connected to human rights, basic rights that everyone should enjoy simply because they belong to the human family.[5] In general, human rights come from two perspectives: negative and positive rights. Those who advocate "negative rights" seek to protect individuals from others interfering with their efforts to build a future of their choice. They guarantee individuals freedom from coercion. Much of the early discussion of political theory was concerned with **negative rights**. The Bill of Rights of the U.S. Constitution is one example of negative rights. In the Bill of Rights, citizens are protected from the power of the government.

The **positive rights** perspective posits that people also have rights to food, clothing, medical care, education, and housing. These rights are not protections but statements of entitlement. The assumption here is that human rights are a minimal requirement for full, dignified, participation in the community.[6]

In 1948, the General Assembly of the United Nations adopted the *Universal Declaration of Human Rights* (see Appendix and Chapter 16). This was a result of the violations of human rights by the Nazis during World War II. The *Declaration* announced that the dignity and equality of all members of the human family were the foundation of freedom, justice, and peace in the world. Everyone had the right to life, liberty, and security. Slavery and the slave trade were condemned. Punishment that was inhuman and degrading was prohibited. No one was to be subject to arbitrary arrest or exile. Strikingly similar to the United States' notions of due process, the signatory nations agreed on the basic humanity of all people. Problems of human rights remained and the United Nation's authority was not enough to ensure compliance. Almost 20 years after the original *Declaration,* the United Nations' position was emphasized, clarified, and expanded upon. In 1966, the United Nations issued the *Covenant on Civil and Political Rights* and the *Covenant on Economic, Social, and Political Rights.*[7]

JUSTICE AND ECONOMICS

Jesus Christ said that the poor would always be in the world. Slaves, serfs, and peasants dot the historical landscape to suggest the wisdom of Christ's declaration. However, poverty puts people at risk for many problems, including poorer health, shorter life spans, greater exposure to crime, and unfruitful life styles. In a country such as America—with all of its wealth and opportunity—the existence of poverty is perplexing. In fact, 17% of children in the United States live in poverty, a rate two to three times higher than that of most Western industrialized nations.[8]

Some philosophers have addressed this troublesome issue of economic disparity. John Locke in his *Second Treatise on Government* (1690) believed that private property was a natural right. The earth belongs to all humans as a gift of God. People are entitled to the fruits of their labor. However, as a brake on future "robber barons" this acquisition did not go so far as to take and harm other humans or nature. "Nothing was made by God for man to spoil and destroy," declared Locke.[9]

Adam Smith, in his *A Theory of Moral Sentiment* (1759), acknowledged the importance of self-interests (greed) but insisted that it was balanced by something called moral sentiments. This meant that humans had feelings and sympathies for the suffering of others that held in check any desire to exploit or harm. Foremost of these feelings that prohibit us from harming is a sense of justice.[10] Unlike his friend, Hume, Smith felt this was a natural feeling. Therefore, justice is the desire not to harm others, a desire for approval from others, and above all a useful way to make society stable. Smith went on in *The Wealth of Nations* (1776) to argue the virtues of the free market system. Such a capitalist system, he believed, would ensure the greatest prosperity for all citizens. However, this free market, with its quest for private property, necessarily led to many inequalities between the few rich and many poor. He believed the natural enmity between the classes made civil government necessary.[11]

Immanuel Kant, in his *The Philosophy of Law* (1797), also argues for some natural right to property. Property is so important, Kant believes, that the violation of a person's property is an attack on their freedom. G.W.F. Hegel's *The Philosophy of Right* (1821) sets forth that property is not just a right but rather an expression of the self. One can give away or sell the products of one's labor, and it is because of this that the institution of contracts came into existence. However, if one gives, or is forced to give, so much away, they lose a sense of self and this becomes an unjust situation. People like Karl Marx would use such an idea to attack the entire capitalist wage system that he believed reduced humans to slaves.[12]

Perhaps no other thinker has had such a profound impact as Karl Marx. His influence on the political and economic landscape of the world cannot be denied. Marx felt that human society could be only understood through the ways its individuals obtained subsistence, in short their labor. His most fully developed ideas appeared in *Das Capital*, the classic denouncement of capitalism. History was the struggle between economic classes. The minority—the ruling class—was pitted against the vast working class who controlled very little. The working classes—first as slaves and serfs, then after the industrial revolution as workers—were exploited by the capitalist. The proletariat produced much but received few rewards. Capitalists produced very little but received great rewards. Capitalism and all class-oriented societies were unjust. They not only violated human rights, but because they were based upon flawed notions of economic production, they made it necessary to consider the issue of justice. As one author noted: "The demands of justice cannot be satisfied in the circumstances which made concepts of justice necessary; thus efforts to achieve justice inevitably fail."[13] For Marx economic justice could only be achieved when the means of production were turned over to the workers. History proved that dramatic changes could occur such as the transformation from feudalism to capitalism. He called for a new revolution, one from capitalism to communism.

Not everyone subscribed to the notion of economic justice. The social Darwinists of the nineteenth century were leery of perpetuating the weaker sorts and poverty was seen as a sign that the person was not well equipped to compete in society.[14] In the 1970s and 1980s, these ideas found expression in a new form of conservatism. Friedrich von Hayek, in his *The Mirage of Social Justice* (1978), was a major exponent of this belief. Hayek believed that any effort to predetermine distribution of wealth required placing power in the hands of government and taking it away from individuals. For example, it would require taking wealth from a few and depriving them of their liberty. What is often overlooked, according to Hayek, is that the free market system does not always reward merit and talent. Strong elements of luck are involved. No one—not the untalented who are deprived nor the talented who are overlooked— likes to go unrewarded. "Level playing fields" and equal opportunity are impossible to attain and any attempt to do so only strengthens the government and encourages dangerous meddling, making the free market less free, thought Hayek.[15]

GENDER JUSTICE

On a number of fronts women have a unique standing that forces the addressing of justice. The issue of sex—in terms of rape, prostitution, and harassment—is very large. Furthermore, issues of childbearing, domestic violence, lesbian identity, economic equality, and standards of beauty, to name a few, address the issue of gender justice.

Traditionally, there have been two gendered roles. First, is that of man as macho, or masculine, with certain male entitlements in terms of economics, politics, and sex. Second, women have been classified as seductresses. As seductresses, women are responsible for the "Eve Problem," ever ready to exploit the sexual weakness of males. Some societies are so concerned with this that they desexualize the female in public with strict dress codes or seclusion. Others require surgical processes, such as clitoridectomy to desensitize the woman's sexual organs. Centuries of foot binding in China, wife scalding, and Sati (widow burning) in India are other examples of injustices directed at women.[16]

It is clear that in most societies women have not shared justice equally with men. Historically, women were the property of men; the property first of their fathers then their husbands. Although several exceptional women obtained commanding positions in dynastic politics, very few women had political rights in such patriarchal arrangements. Take rape as an example. Throughout history, the perpetrator of a rape was often the significant male in women's lives—fathers, husbands, king. In fact, women had to demonstrate that they truly resisted. In addition, as the tale of Potiphar's wife in the Bible suggests, the female might instigate or claim a false rape. In that story, Joseph worked for a high official in the Egyptian government named Potiphar. Joseph became the target of a seduction by his boss' wife. When he refused, Potiphar's wife claimed a rape attempt and had him cast into prison. For centuries women had to demonstrate resistence and prove they were not "loose women."[17]

Prostitution, frequently called the "oldest profession" is a world-wide phenomenon. Often males are part of the industry as pimps and procurers. Of course, they predominate as the customer base. Prostitution takes many forms: call girls, strip club dancers, in many massage parlors, escort service providers, and street walkers. Elaborate rings of criminals abduct women and enslave them into prostitution. The Russian Mafia has taken over much of this activity in eastern and southern Europe. Some countries legitimize prostitution and in some cities such as Bangkok and Amsterdam, the "red light districts" are widely advertised tourist attractions. Regular "sex tours" are quite common in Asia. In the United States where prostitution is illegal, except in a few counties of Nevada, enforcement is slack. However, when crusades—frequently called "operation angels"—are implemented they are gender biased. They go after the prostitute and not her customer. In recent years, the problem of prostitution has been compounded by the increasing use of children as prostitutes, including females as young as nine.[18]

Sexual harassment has been a persistent problem in the work place. Women have been subject to sexual demands in order to secure a job or be promoted in it. Leering men making suggestive comments contribute to a hostile work environment. Title VII of the Civil Rights Act of 1964 addressed and forbade this problem of harassment in the work place. However, women are the ones who have to determine harassment, confront the perpetrator, and face judgmental coworkers. A particular problem has been found on university campuses where lecherous professors prey upon vulnerable female students; it goes on extensively in overt and covert ways. These problems seldom confront men at work.[19]

When it came to work in the agricultural economy women had an important and equal position with men. But, as industrialization occurred, women were forced out of most labor markets and relegated to domestic roles in the home. Many assumed that women, once given the opportunity to have a family, would not fully commit to any other profession or job. Of course, women have been hard at work throughout history. This "reproductive work," having to do with raising a family, has never been defined as real work. When allowed into the marketplace, most women were segregated into predominately female occupations, serving mostly as secretaries, elementary education teachers, and flight attendants. Furthermore, women were paid far less than men for doing the same work and "glass ceilings" prohibited advancement. For example, one study found that women and men had the following median annual earnings.[20]

	High School	College	Professional Degree
Women	$18,252	$27,840	$33,604
Men	$26,790	$40,624	$46,978

Childbearing suggests several issues of justice. For example, for a long time a woman had no paid leave to give birth and assume motherhood in those crucial first months. Child care places a tremendous physical and economic burden on a woman. Finding appropriate child care facilities becomes very important. Negotiating flexible work arrangements adds new burdens. Of course, the entire debate over abortion has been framed along women's control, or lack of such, over their bodies.[21]

Women make up the majority of the population in most societies. India might be an exception because of the practice of aborting an unwanted female fetus. But to have over 50% of a society being discriminated against raises many issues of justice.

RACIAL JUSTICE

All people make judgments about others. Xenophobia, or the fear of the foreign and the strange, has been a part of most societies. The history of the United States shows many ethnic tensions. As each wave of immigration arrived American reaction was swift and discriminatory. From the Irish, disparagingly called Paddies, to Eastern and Southern European immigrants, to Jews, to African Americans, to Latinos there has been a history of suspicion and segregation of the newcomer. Internment camps for Japanese Americans during World War II are thought by many to have been unjust. Treatment of Arab Americans after the terrorist attacks of 2001 provide another example of such prejudice.

Frequently, the marker of color is used. Whites or lighter colored indigenous people achieved higher status than darker colored peoples. Slavery was one way to keep a people in its place and achieve some economic benefits as well. Slavery has been part of human history for thousands of years. Much of America's economy before the Civil War was built upon the slavery of Africans. Even after a bloody war to free the African Americans a system of Jim Crow segregation kept them in their place for over 50 years. Lynching and the rise of the KKK helped to do this[22] (see also Chapter 10).

One racially charged part of American history was reflected by the plight of those indigenous peoples already living on the continent. Native Americans posed an alien culture and an obstacle to western migration. Their views on history, ownership of property, religion, integrity, and other attributes of culture were the opposite of the Anglo-Saxon's. Considered to be a "nation" these disparate tribes were given promises and treaties that were quickly broken. Numerous wars on the eastern sections of the country ended with either tribal annihilation or forced movement as in "The Trail of Tears" as tribes were forced to move from Georgia and the Carolinas to an "Indian Territory" that would be called one day Oklahoma and Kansas. As precious minerals were discovered and land-hungry settlers pushed westward, conflicts arose. Instead of protecting the indigenous populations from such intrusions the government used the military to wage war on Native Americans. Two theaters of battle were established, one on the northern plains and the other on the southern desert lands, both ending in massacres and decimation of cultures. To this day, most Native Americans reside on reservations, segregated from the dominant culture. Though there have been attempts at a civil rights movement for the Native Americans (called the American Indian Movement or AIM), those attempts have been weak and unsuccessful. Frequently, the larger issues of varied cultures, poverty, alcoholism, and crime have been overshadowed by debates about sports mascots.

In the 1960s and 1970s, following a Civil Rights movement, a national social policy aimed to end discrimination in voting was implemented. Soon other "equal opportunity" legislation was passed to end discrimination in hiring practices. According to some of these early social adjustments, various quotas were used to ensure ample representation of minorities. However, in the name of justice some claimed that injustices resulted. For example, some felt that reverse discrimination occurred when numerous white males were passed over in the name of having a racially diverse work environment. Enough pressure was exerted to scale back many affirmative action practices. Questions of racial justice continue to divide the United States to this day.

ENVIRONMENTAL JUSTICE

Justice as it is applied to the environment takes the earth and its resources and purity into consideration (see Chapter 13). Ancient peoples even made the earth a god, Gaia, and any damage to her was sacrilegious. In his thoughtful book, *Ishmael* (1995), Daniel Quinn has his hero, an ape, advertise for those who want to save the world. Ishmael instructs his pupil about two types of inhabitants of the world: the leavers and the takers. The former lived in harmony with the world. They took only what they needed and were not wasteful. They held the earth and nature in high regard. The takers were those who wasted natural resources. Like a man who jumps from a cliff and flaps his arms frantically, there is an illusion of flight until the ultimate crash to the canyon floor. If humans continue to consume, and waste, and spoil the earth, there may be an illusion of progress but it will end in a crash of destruction, declared Quinn's ape.[23]

For much of world history, industry and population were small enough not to jeopardize the earth. Even in countries with large populations, such as India and China, people tended to utilize resources in a way that left little waste. But during the industrial revolution in western society, concerns arose over the natural resources and the purity of the environment. Although this is a worldwide concern, particularly in developing countries, much of this discussion will be directed at the United States.

In the 1890s, two separate discoveries were made: the U.S. Census Bureau announced that the frontier, that line separating civilization from wilderness, had ceased to exist; and a group of investigative journalists, called "muckrakers," were exposing the industrial and corporate world's exploitation of the nation's natural and human resources.

The demise of the frontier had profound social impact. Before, with open western lands available as a safety zone, individual success was thought to be insured by just picking up and moving westward. Land, timber, water, minerals, and opportunity were thought to be the right of every American citizen. With the end of that frontier, though in reality there was still ample land available, the symbol was gone; now people had to stay put and succeed. There was a growing sense of limitation.

At the same time, people and government became aware that industry was consuming resources in a wasteful way. In the era of the "Robber Barons," those industrialists who were revolutionizing the economic structure of America, capitalism in its basest form was seen. Minerals and timbers were extracted with little regard for nature. Smoke-filled skies were seen as a sign of progress and not pollution. Ida Tarbell's *History of the Standard Oil Company* revealed in detail the practices that made that business the giant in the refining industry. Authors like Theodore Dreiser wrote about *The Titan* and *The Financier*, characters who had reckless disregard for human and natural resources.

Two distinctive strands can be seen in the rise of environmental justice in reaction to the closing of the frontier and the exposure of the industrialists. One is the **conservation movement**. Although there were some small concerns earlier, the major thrust of this movement came in the Progressive era, 1890-1920. These conservationists wanted to protect natural resources—timber, minerals, land—to ensure the quality of future generations. Conservationists are human-oriented, they are concerned over the needs of future generations and their right to these resources. George Perkins March, in his *Man and Nature: or Physical Geography as Modified by Human Action* (1864), argued that the decline and death of all past civilizations occurred because they destroyed their environment. Frederick Law Olmsted, creator of New York City's Central Park, thought nature was necessary in urban settings. He believed in land management and the creation of city and national parks. John Wesley Powell explored and mapped the western wilderness and in his *Report on the Lands of the Arid Region of the United States* (1878) to Congress he advocated a system of dams and canals to reclaim the land. The Reclamation Act of 1902 resulted.[24]

Under President Theodore Roosevelt political leaders took up the conservationist cause. A variety of agencies were set up to safeguard the environment. Numerous acres of federal land were set aside as national parks. Actually the first, Yellowstone National Park, had been created earlier, in 1872. But now, under Roosevelt and presidents who followed him, 365 parks were created to comprise a national park system. In 1916, the National Park Service was established. After the depression and the election of Franklin D. Roosevelt the economic and climactic devastations across much of the country were attributed to poor management of the lands and rivers.[25]

Another movement was that of the **preservationists**, those who wanted to protect the environment for its own value. They were nature-oriented and were less concerned with human need and consumption. Some of the earliest preservationists linked nature to God. George Catlin, Henry David Thoreau, and John Muir (the first president of the Sierra Club) all believed that nature was necessary as an inspirational and spiritual place. Humans needed nature as a spiritual compass for their daily lives. Wilderness was needed to preserve human civilization. Today much of their thinking has influenced the ecology movement and radical environmentalism. For example, Aldo Leopold, in his book *A Sand County Almanac* (1949), believed "the opportunity to see geese is more important than television, and the chance to find a pasqueflower is a right as inalienable as free speech."[26]

As the industrial, urban, and suburban expansions after World War II occurred, new issues having to do with the environment arose. The need for resources such as oil compelled many to side with business over the conservationists and preservationists. Politically, the conservatives were less environment-friendly than the liberals.

Perhaps the single most important book that kindled the modern environmental movement was Rachel Carson's *Silent Spring*, released in 1962 (see Chapter 14). Born in a small town in western Pennsylvania she developed passionate interests in nature writing and scientific research. She took a job in the Bureau of U.S. Fisheries in the late 1930s and began a career writing about undersea life. *Under the Sea-wind* and *The Sea Around Us* showed her concerns for the harm being done to the sea. *Silent Spring* became immediately successful and controversial. Her theme was that pesticides were ruining the environment. She argued that public health and the environment were inseparable. The petrochemical industry reacted vigorously with its scientific experts. Carson advocated that this issue was too important to be left to the experts, it had to be a democratically-grounded public issue. As one author noted "The mission of *Silent Spring* became nothing less than an attempt to create a new environmental consciousness."[27]

A variety of environmental issues arose in the 1970s. Global warming and the problem of greenhouse gases became evident as ozone holes in the atmosphere were discovered. The disposal of nuclear waste became urgent. Traffic congestion and automobile pollution in large cities threatened the public health. Endangering the foods and soils with pesticides called many to action. Saving endangered species and the tropical rainforest became a rallying theme.

An environmental justice movement was the product of the early work of the conservationists, preservationists, and several "environmental presidents."[28] Some environmentalists were concerned that issues of class and race were part of the problem (see Chapter 13). Wealthier communities could prevent locally unwanted land uses whereas poorer communities lacked the political and economic resources to do so. As a result, low income, minority communities received unwanted facilities.[29] Numerous organizations—such as Greenpeace and Earth First!—arose to fight for environmental justice.[30] Others were afraid that in the quest for the "bottom line" businesses would even break the law. Environmental crime became an important issue. Finally, the federal government created the Environmental Protection Agency in 1970.[31] But all societies of the world are caught in the balance between satisfying the demands of an ever-increasing population and guarding the ever-diminishing supply of natural resources.

CONCLUSION

Rather than talking of justice as it applies to individuals, social justice looks to larger segments of society and nature. Four themes emerge in discussing social justice. First, **egalitarianism** suggests that everyone, as part of the human family, deserves to be treated equally. Second, **membership** demands a concern for the exclusion and inclusion of people who might not enjoy the benefits of society. Third, there are issues of **time**. Time not only looks at the responsibility society has to those in the future, but to those who suffered in the past. Fourth, social justice advocates have expanded the **scope** of justice to include animals and nature.

Increasingly, issues of social justice are making their way into policy discussions and into the public consciousness. The issues raised in this chapter are complex and cannot be covered thoroughly in this brief discussion. The purpose of this chapter has been to introduce the concept of social justice and to illustrate some of the many dimensions of the concept.

DISCUSSION QUESTIONS

1. To what extent is it the government's responsibility to address issues of social justice—such as poverty, racism, and sexism?
2. In a society in which "majority rules" what rights should minorities have?
3. From the perspective of gender justice, what are the arguments for and the arguments against legalizing prostitution?

Endnotes

1. William Hefferman and John Kleining, *From Social Justice to Criminal Justice: Poverty and the Administration of Justice* (New York: Oxford University Press, 2000), pp. 1-21.
2. See F.L. van Holthoon, *The Road to Utopia: A Study of John Stuart Mill's Social Thought* (Assen, Netherlands: Van Gorcum & Co., 1971), pp. 68-85.
3. John Stuart Mill, *Utilitarianism, Liberty, and Representative Government* (New York: E.P. Dutton & Co., 1910), quote on p. 41 but see also pp. 38-60.
4. *Ibid.*, p. 59.

5. For an overview of some of these issues see Thomas W. Simon, *Democracy and Social Injustice: Law, Politics and Philosophy* (Lanham, Md.: Rowman & Littlefield, 1995).
6. Carol S. Robb, *Equal Value: An Ethical Approach to Economics and Sex* (Boston: Beacon Press, 1995), pp. 19-21.
7. David M. Smith, *Geography and Social Justice* (Oxford, England: Blackwell, 1994), pp. 41, 47.
8. *Child Poverty Fact Sheet, 2001.*
9. John Locke, *Two Treatises of Government,* Peter Lassett (ed.) (Cambridge, England: Cambridge University Press, 1967), pp. 288-290.
10. Robert L. Heilbroner (ed.) *The Essential Adam Smith* (New York: W. W. Norton & Co., 1986), pp. 65-66, 91-97.
11. *Ibid.*, pp. 248-257.
12. See Solomon and Murphy, pp. 151-154, 155-166.
13. Allen E. Buchanan, *Marx and Justice: The Radical Critique of Liberalism* (New Jersey: Rowan and Littlefield, 1982), p. 51.
14. Richard Hofstader, *Social Darwinism in American Thought* (Boston: Beacon Press, 1963), pp. 13-50.
15. Norman P. Barry, *Hayek's Social and Economic Philosophy* (London: Macmillan Press, 1979), pp. 124-150. For a classic statement of his views see Friedrich A. Hayek, *The Road to Serfdom* (Chicago: University of Chicago Press, 1965), pp. 88, 181. Also see Alan Ebenstein, *Friedrich Hayek: A Biography* (New York: Palgrave, 2001), pp. 217-226.
16. Sakuntala Narasimhan, *Sati: Widow Burning in India* (New York: Doubleday, 1990), pp. 61-78.
17. Susan Brownmiller, *Against Our Will* (New York: Simon and Schuster, 1975), pp. 16-30.
18. Kevin Bales, *Disposable People: New Slavery in the Global Economy* (Berkeley: University of California Press, 1999), pp. 43, 74.
19. Robb, pp. 51-71.
20. *Ibid.*, p. 30.
21. *Ibid.*, pp. 31-50.
22. Walter White, *Rope and Faggot: A Biography of Judge Lynch* (New York: Arno Press, 1969), pp. 19-39.
23. Daniel Quinn, *Ishmael: An Adventure of the Mind and Spirit* (New York: A Bantam/Turner Book, 1995), pp. 151-184.
24. Sally M. Edwards, "A History of the U.S. Environmental Movement," in *Environmental Crime: Enforcement, Policy, and Social Responsibility*, Mary Clifford (ed.) (Gathersburg, Maryland: An Aspen Publication, 1998), pp. 36-37.
25. *Ibid.*, pp. 37-41.
26. *Ibid.*, pp. 34-36.
27. Robert Gottlieb, *Forcing the Spring: The Transformation of the American Environmental Movement* (Washington, D.C.: Island Press, 1993), p. 84.
28. Jonathan P. West and Glen Sussman, "Implementation of Environmental Policy: The Chief Executive" in *The Environmental Presidency*, Dennis L. Soden (ed.) (Albany, New York: State University of New York Press, 1999), pp. 77-111.
29. Patrick Novotny, *Where We Live, Work and Play: The Environmental Justice Movement and the Struggle for a New Environmentalism* (Westport, Connecticut: Praeger, 2000), pp. 11-27.
30. Sally Edwards, pp. 44-50.
31. Bill Hyatt, "The Federal Environmental Regulatory Structure," in *Environmental Crime: Enforcement, Policy, and Social Responsibility*, Mary Clifford (ed.) (Gathersburg, Maryland: An Aspen Publication, 1998), pp. 115-141.

PART

Formal Systems of Justice

It is tempting to think of justice in terms of individual cases. Did the rapist or child molester get what was coming to him? Were employees treated unfairly because of their race or gender? Justice at that level is important to the individual victim and to others in similar situations. Justice at the individual level is also important for society because long-term failures to address these forms of injustice can bring into question the legitimacy of society as a dispenser of justice. Ultimately, the legitimacy of society itself is brought into question.

Focusing on justice at the individual level while pursuing larger societal goals is one of the main reasons for creating and maintaining governments. Numerous government agencies attempt to deliver justice. Some bureaucracies deal with poverty, race relations, work place safety, and environmental protections. Those agencies are worthy of discussion. However, here, discussion is limited to general systems of justice, with specific reference to those agencies dealing with law and order.

There are two great justice systems throughout the world: Common law and civil law. Common law systems are more familiar to Americans. They come from medieval England. Civil law systems are the oldest, most wide spread, and most influential, as found in France and in many parts of South America. They come out of the ancient organizations of the Roman Empire and the Catholic Church. In addition to these two distinct systems, what might be called Colonial systems are hybrids, drawing from both the civil and common law traditions. Countries that had been colonies of civil or common law countries often take those traditions and add a particular ideology or heritage that puts a unique stamp on their notions of justice. For example, some Communist countries have civil law structures but a Marxist/Maoist ideology that make their systems distinctive. Many Islamic nations, such as Egypt, have legal systems based on a civil law tradition, but they are also influenced by the teachings of Islam and its scriptures in the *Qur'an*.

In addition, to common law and civil law systems, a small number of countries have opted to have their legal system guided by Islamic law. Although such legal systems are not common, the rapid spread of fundamentalist Islam may give rise to more such systems. Islamic law systems have a number of features that distinguish them from common law, civil law, or colonial systems. Finally, this section concludes with a brief overview of the American justice system, a system that has put its own twist on the common law tradition.

CHAPTER

5 Common Law Systems

Common law is a body of principles and rules deriving its authority from usage and customs of "immemorial antiquity" or from the judgments and decrees of the courts recognizing, affirming, and enforcing such usages and customs. It is a body of law that comes from judicial decisions as opposed to legislative actions.[1] It is a specific justice system that emanated from England after the Norman Conquest of 1066 CE.[2] The common law system is distinctly different from the other great justice system called the *civil law system*, which will be discussed in Chapter 6.

The influence of the common law tradition is far flung because many of the most powerful countries today use it as a model for their systems of justice. Its distribution has occurred in one of three ways. Those countries "seeded," such as Hong Kong and India, were well developed before the arrival of the English, and the system was imposed upon them. "Settled" colonies, such as the United States and Canada and Australia, were not well developed when the English came. The English founders of those nations simply copied the system of the mother country. Finally, there were "conquered" colonies, such as South Africa, who were under the influence of another power before control was taken forcefully by England.[3] Most of the references made in this chapter are to England. However, on numerous occasions the United States is used to illustrate a point. The common law tradition in England developed from three historical sources: feudal practices, custom, and equity.[4]

After several centuries of Roman occupation, England was free of imperial control by the fifth century CE. Though the Romans influenced the building of roads and language, unlike those countries on the Continent, the law was largely absent. The next 500 years were marked by invasions of various tribes, most notably the Angles, Danes, Jutes, and Saxons. Some Christian missionaries brought elements of canon law (church law), too, but otherwise tribal law predominated. There were monarchs, but the law of the land was localized, with no set of laws common to the entire country.[5] Before the invasion by the Normans, disputes were settled by assemblies of freemen sitting in shire and hundred courts. These might be interpreted today as county and village courts.[6]

FEUDALISM

The invasion by the Normans and the rule of William (often called William the Conqueror) are taken as the beginning of feudalism. This medieval concept required strict obedience and obligations based on a society arranged along superior/inferior class structures. Upper classes gave protection to the lower classes, and in return they expected loyalty and public order.

Actually, two legal systems emerged: a very strong local one in the various counties and villages and a national one based at Westminster. These were called the "people's peace" and "King's peace," respectively. Many of the Anglo/Saxon traditions and institutions were kept at the local level, with courts making decisions based on local custom. The lord of the manor, the main landholder of the locality, frequently was looked to for the settlement of differences. Royal courts, which sat at Westminster, were concerned with disputes between large landowners.

The king's power was limited to controlling the roads, protecting forest preserves from poachers, securing the sanctity of religious sites, and assuring peace on certain holy days. Crimes among ordinary people were to be settled at the local level. Crimes against Norman royalty and lands called the kings' courts into action. On occasion, when ordinary crimes threatened the peace of the land with a feud, the king would step in to restore order. For example, for centuries rape was a crime against the father of the attacked girl, and family revenge often led to disorder. The king simply redefined the identity of the victim, transferring it from the father of the girl to the father of the land, the king.[7]

No separation of powers within government existed in feudal times. William and his successors ruled as executive, legislature, and judiciary. Royal courts (*Curia Regis*), often called the Courts of Westminster, became a centralized court system. This court evolved and reformed into three entities: the Court of the Exchequer focused on financial issues, the Court of the Common Pleas dealt with the common people though the king's direct participation was limited, and the King's Bench heard cases that had a direct royal interest. Slowly, these courts replaced the local courts, which were heavily influenced by canon or church law.

Ecclesiastical or religious courts persisted as rivals to the royal courts. These church courts continued to be a challenge to the monarch. A showdown occurred in 1170 when a leading proponent of the church court system, Thomas à Becket, was murdered in Canterbury Cathedral by henchmen of the king. Thereafter, the power and influence of the ecclesiastical courts diminished.

The monarch held considerable power and began to centralize much of the system, taking away power from the local jurisdictions. For example, King Richard I appointed "Keepers of the Peace," knights commissioned to keep the peace in their local areas. Later they were called Justices of the Peace. Though representatives of the king, they were regarded as local persons and were readily accepted by the people. They were a means for the local people to gain access to the royal courts. In fact, being heard by the royal courts was not easy. A system of writs developed early whereby a person had to make formal request, provide proof of the necessary action, and pay a fee before the court would hear the case. Over time, the royal courts continued to expand and by the end of the Middle Ages they were the only courts of justice.

CUSTOM

The Crusades of the twelfth century brought home returning soldiers who had seen the world. Dissatisfaction with conditions in England rose, and disorder became an issue. Already a king's representative, the Shire Reeve, or Sheriff, existed as the king's man in the counties. But such outsiders were resented. Remember the story of Robin Hood, a criminal who was a hero, and the Sheriff of Nottingham, who was portrayed as a villain. In order to stabilize society and the legal system Henry II (1154-1189), frequently known as the Father of common law, set up the Constitutions of Clarendon in 1164, which listed 16 customs practiced for the past 100 years that should be a basis for contemporary law.[8] Of course, much of Anglo/Saxon law for years had been based on custom. But various tribes and villages had different customs. Without some unifying thread, customs could lead to legal anarchy. Henry II attempted to define the process of a law based on these "immemorial customs." Several characteristics emerged. They were:

1. Ancient. No one should be able to remember its beginnings.
2. Continuous. It has never been abandoned or interrupted.

3. Peaceable. There was common consent of those using it.
4. Reasonable. There was a legal logic behind it.
5. Compulsory. Everyone was obliged to recognize and respect it.
6. Consistent. One custom could not contradict another.[9]

Although it would take years of development, this notion of custom set the stage for precedent or *stare decisis*.[10]

EQUITY

Unlike civil law, which is discussed in the next chapter, common law made no distinction between private law and public law. Because the legal system was so closely tied to the development of the monarchy by the end of the Middle Ages, all law became the king's law. Local barons and clergy resented the weakening of the local courts where they had considerable influence and banded together in 1215 to force the king to sign a charter, which was called the Magna Carta. This was an attempt to halt the erosion of their power in the local courts. But the charter also contained certain guaranteed rights for ordinary citizens, and later it took the force of a fundamental document in legal history.

However, common law was often deficient and frequently did not satisfy individuals. An appeal system grew up by the fifteenth century as a remedy. This was called Equity, which was meant to mean fairness or "just." A set of practices, known as *equity procedures*, were developed to help people bring their grievance before a court without using the complex common law system.[11] And an entire set of rules and lawyers grew up that were distinct from common law. Some of these equity principles still exist. For example, much of the modern-day writ system is based upon equity. Such writs are documents ordering some element of government to do something. For example, a *writ of mandamus* requires public servants to do their jobs. An *injunction* is an order to prevent harm that would occur if the case went through the system. A writ of *habeas corpus* requires the government to present someone before the courts. Of course, the monarch could not hear all such claims and a chancery court was set up to do so. The chancery courts did not make law that was binding on other courts. Common laws were honored, hence the saying "Equity follows the law," and equitable intervention was applicable in the name of morality. Chancery courts decided conflicts between law and morals based upon morality. Decisions were based on the equity of the case without reference to procedural technicalities. Even the language of the courts shows the distinctions. The procedure before the chancery court was a suit not an action. The Chancellor granted a decree and not a judgment and awarded compensations rather than damages. Procedures were more inquisitorial, were written, and were inspired by canon law. Never would there be a jury present to participate. Today common law is comprised of criminal law and the law of contracts and torts. On the other hand, equity includes the law of real property, trusts, partnerships, bankruptcy, the interpretation of wills, and the settlement of estates.

CHARACTERISTICS OF COMMON LAW

Definition of Crime

Definitions of crime have gradually become the function of the legislatures; that is called "substantive law." In a democracy like the United States, judges are elite. Having the legislatures, who are made up of elected people, pass laws seemed more democratic. This statutory law became important early in the new nation's existence (1791-1835) with the rise of the "Republican Code movement." Severe blows were aimed at common law tradition as the new states began to create statutory law. Obviously, murder, rape, and robbery were concepts coming from common law. But different jurisdictions had slightly different definitions and punishments for these crimes. Furthermore, in places like the United States, supreme courts made judgments about the constitutionality and appropriateness of the law [judicial review] and the procedures of the justice system. In addition, criminal procedure in the United States developed case law over the appropriate practices of search and seizure, interrogation, legal defense for the accused, prison facilities and features, and the place of capital punishment in the justice system. This was called "procedural law." During the "due process" revolution of the Warren court (the U.S. Supreme Court under Chief Justice Earl Warren) in the 1960s, many of the restrictions placed on the federal criminal justice system by the Constitution were applied to state and local justice systems. All of these are examples of judge-made law and are part of common law. Therefore, even though most common law countries have moved to create statutes, the ultimate arbiter of the appropriateness of those laws and the actions of the government in implementing those laws is common law.

Statute

England has no written constitution. Instead, there is a series of rules, sometimes in the form of statutes but most often judicial in origin, that guarantees fundamental rights and liberties. In a democracy, the laws coming from a legislature—duly elected by the people—are given some respect. But in a strictly common law country, a legislature is not seen as the normal avenue for making law. Since World War II, the laws of Parliament in England have increased in number and in acceptance. But English law still is basically judge-made for two reasons. First, judicial decisions set the framework for the development of most statutes. Second, legislators still think in terms of judge-made law and make their statutes in the language of judges. Historically, in English law only after a statute had been tested by a court decision did it achieve any legitimacy. Today, statutory law has become increasingly important, but it still must be tested by the courts before it is fully accepted.

Process as Justice

Procedure has primary importance in common law. "Forms of action" characterize the common law system, and it is the successful completion of these procedures that were necessary for a judgment to be rendered. Such a focus on procedure was necessary because it had a single function: The procedures followed shaped the facts to be put before a jury. According to David and Brierley, "The Common law was not so much a system attempting to bring justice as it was a conglomeration of procedures designed, in more and more cases, to achieve solutions to disputes."[12] This was particularly evident in criminal law. The definition of crime was determined by the legislature, the Parliament in England and the Congress in the United States. But common law dominated the procedural aspects of criminal justice. "Most of the criminal procedure rules that are set forth in the Fourth, Fifth, Sixth, and Eighth Amendments to the U.S. Constitution, as well as the rules about bringing the accused before a judge to question his incarceration (*habeas corpus*), were adapted from the common law rules and from Parliamentary decrees based on the common law."[13]

Because it is the starting point for so much common law development in the United States, a review of some of these basic principles in the Bill of Rights might be useful. Note how many times the Congress is warned away from creating statutory law and how often the issue of procedure is raised.

1. Congress shall make no law respecting an establishment of religion, or prohibiting the free exercise thereof; or abridging the freedom of speech, or of the press; or the right of people peaceably to assemble; and to petition the Government for redress of grievances [1791].
2. A well regulated Militia, being necessary to the security of a free state, the right of the people to keep and bear Arms shall not be infringed [1791].
3. No soldier shall, in time of peace, be quartered in any house, without the consent of the Owner, nor in time of war, but in a manner prescribed by law [1791].
4. The right of the people to be secure in their persons, houses, papers, and effects, against unreasonable searches and seizures, shall not be violated, and no Warrants will be issued, but upon probable cause, supported by Oath or affirmation, and particularly describing the place to be searched, and the persons and things to be seized [1791].
5. No person shall be held to answer for a capital or otherwise infamous crime, unless on a presentment or indictment of a Grand Jury, except in cases arising in the land or naval forces, or in the Militia, when in actual service in time of War or public danger; nor shall any person be subject for the same offence to be twice put in jeopardy of life or limb; nor shall be compelled in any criminal case to be a witness against himself, nor be deprived of life, liberty, or property, without due process of law; nor shall private property be taken for private use, without just compensation [1791].
6. In all criminal prosecutions, the accused shall enjoy the right to a speedy and public trial, by an impartial jury of the State and district wherein the crime shall have been committed, which district shall have been previously ascertained by law, and to be informed of the nature and cause of the accusation; to be confronted with hostile witnesses against him; to have compulsory process for obtaining witnesses in his favor, and to have Assistance of Council for his defense [1791].
7. In suits at common law, where the value in controversy shall exceed 20 dollars, the right of trial by jury shall be preserved, and no fact tried by a jury, shall be otherwise reexamined in any Court of the United States, than according to the rules of the common law [1791].
8. Excessive bail shall not be required, nor excessive fines imposed, nor cruel and unusual punishment inflicted [1791].
9. The enumeration in the Constitution, of certain rights, shall not be construed to deny or disparage others retained by the people [1791].
10. The powers not delegated to the United States by the Constitution, nor prohibited by it to the States, are reserved to the States, respectively, or to the people [1791].

The concern of the founders of the United States derives from common law. Shortly after the creation of the United States another event occurred that validated the role of the courts in common law. The Judiciary Act of 1801 created numerous courts and judicial positions. President John Adams, as he was leaving office, quickly filled these offices. A new president, Thomas Jefferson, resented such action and tried to withhold the appointments. The Supreme Court, not yet tested and looking for direction, had a strong Chief Justice in John Marshall. In the case of *Marbury v. Madison* Marshall addressed these appointments and established that the court could invalidate federal statutes that it deemed contrary to the Constitution. Such judicial review was a common law principle.

Procedure

Throughout the history of English law procedure was most important. This brings up the interesting dichotomy between "factual guilt" and "legal guilt." An individual may indeed be factually guilty of a crime; evidence has been gathered, witnesses assembled, and cogent arguments made. However, if the justice system has acted inappropriately, "legal guilt" might not be established, and the defendant could be released.

Procedure was carefully developed to solicit the real points of disagreement between litigating parties. Unlike civil law systems (see Chapter 6), where the dossier (or case file) is most important, these distinctions must emerge in oral testimony with the answering of questions by "yes" or "no." This must be done in open court. Historically, this information was to be provided to a jury—a group of laypersons (many of whom were poorly educated)—in the simplest of ways. Rules of evidence were developed to exclude evidence not obtained through proper procedures. To the continental (civil law system) lawyer, it would seem that real justice was being thwarted by technicalities. The concept of justice for the common law practitioner was in the process rather than the outcome. English courts accept that the accused must have a fair trial. Strictly adhered-to procedure called *due process* must occur for justice to be met. It is presumed that observing a regulated procedure, fair in all respects, will lead to a just solution.

The English tradition also pays considerable attention to the enforcement of judicial decisions. Unlike the continental systems where there is considerable disregard for judicial decisions, in common law countries the disregard of a court's decision becomes a crime itself. In a common law system, courts can issue orders to other parts of the government. Therefore, the administration of justice becomes a critical activity of common law courts. For example, courts can require certain administrative steps be taken with a *writ of mandamus*. The police can be ordered to release a person through a *habeas corpus* writ. Refusal to follow the orders of the court can result in contempt charges and sanctions.

Lawyers: Education and Practice

Of course, such an emphasis on procedure had an impact on the practice of law. In common law systems, knowledge of the law was not as important as courtroom performance. For example, in America during the early history of the profession of law, the reading of the law as an apprentice to a practicing lawyer was quite enough. Law schools were slow to develop, with most founded in the late nineteenth century. When they were created, they had a distinct common law orientation. For example, Christopher Columbus Langdell—Dean of Harvard Law School from 1870 to 1895—introduced the Case Method. This pedagogy required the student to read decisions made by judges to discover the points of law and understand the process of legal reasoning. In 1871, Langdell published the first casebook on contracts. It was largely made up of English decisions because he felt law and legal thought should be most like that of England. Before then, instructors of law were practicing lawyers who shared their experiences. Langdell wanted to give students a grounding in legal logic and principles and leave the practical stuff to be learned on the job. Langdell's model would become the standard for the elite law schools of America.[14]

However, there was a countermodel in the "sundown schools." At the beginning of the twentieth century, many immigrants, in the name of economic upward mobility, wanted to go to law school. Because of finances or ethnic prejudices, most of these people could not go to a standard law school.

In response, numerous "proprietary" law schools arose. These schools were not connected to a university, their entrance requirements were minimal, and classes were conducted in the evening so that students could hold down a job during the day. These "sundown schools" did two things. First, with little focus on legal reasoning, they taught the student to pass the local bar. Second, they emphasized courtroom techniques and tactics. In short, both the university law school and the proprietary law school in their own way demonstrated an ongoing connection to common law.[15]

Furthermore, in America the common law emphasis placed a premium on courtroom style, with oratory and persuasion of greater importance than legal thinking. The list of great courtroom lawyers in the history of the United States is made up of skilled orators. John Adams, Daniel Webster, Henry Clay, Abraham Lincoln, Clarence Darrow, and William Jennings Bryan, to name a few, were known for their oratory and theatrical skills more than their knowledge of the law. All one has to do is remember the ability of Johnny Cochran in the O.J. Simpson trial. Simpson had been asked to try on a bloody glove that was a key piece of prosecutorial evidence. Prosecutors argued that Simpson had been wearing the glove when he committed the murder. However, Simpson struggled to put it on and failed. In his brilliant summation, Cochran reminded the jury that "[i]f it does not fit you must acquit." The jury found Simpson not guilty.

Also, it is no small wonder that in most common law countries, but most notably in the United States, the law became a means for establishing a career in politics. At no time in their education or practice of law do lawyers learn to make laws. However, the skills of oratory and public performance are those most easily translated into a career in politics.

Decisions of the Courts

In most common law countries, the court structure today is largely divided between superior and inferior courts. The inferior courts hear most of the cases, but it is in the superior courts that judge-made decisions have the greatest strength because of the principle of precedent or *stare decisis*. Precedent means that decisions in court are influenced by past court decisions.

In the continental (civil law) systems, legal principles have always been derived from a body of rules, a legal code. Court decisions do not contain rules of law. Common law countries are quite different. The purpose of judicial decisions is not to just apply but to define legal rules. This simply means that a decision of one court is binding on all courts of equal and lesser power in the court hierarchy. Early English judges did not have to give reasons for their decisions. However, judges soon did begin to explain why the decision was made to instruct future lawyers, students who received most of their education by attending court. Soon these decisions were published for large numbers of students to ponder, such as in the case of *Landauer v. Asser* [1905] 2 K.B. 184. Landauer was the plaintiff (the person bringing the charges), and Asser the defendant. This case can be found in the law reports of the King's Bench series in the second volume published in 1905 on page 184.

Legal Literature

If law was unwritten, not put in statutory form, it was important to record the decisions of the judges. Making judicial decisions widely available to other courts became more common in the nineteenth century. These records became more formalized in England by 1865, with judicial reports being published as the Law Reports. This case law became a basis to study and understand the law. Several scholars began to write about the law, too. These authors became important for the aspiring student of law. Perhaps, the most famous and influential of these authors was William Blackstone (1723-1780). Written when common law was at its zenith his *Commentaries on Laws of England* describes the law in the late eighteenth century and became a major source of information and instruction for American lawyers and nation builders.[16]

Public and Private Law

Unlike the civil law systems, common law jurists rejected any distinction between public and private law. English law as it developed made the trial a public and not a private matter. Thus the royal courts enlarged their jurisdictions by developing the idea that all intervention was justified in the interest of the crown and kingdom. Technically, criminal violations were not against people but against the state. The courts emerged as independent branches of the *curia regis* (or king's courts) and were political rather than judicial organs because they were intended to resolve problems involving the interests of the king and the kingdom—the general interest—and not principally the private interests of individuals. Unlike the systems on the continent, the English legal system's development was tied to the rise and strength of the centralized government.

Jury

England had two competing trends. One was the growth of the central government and its monopolization of the court system. The other was the historic suspicion of the monarchy as seen in the Magna Carta. Because so much of the law was going to be judge-made and there was no clear distinction between public and private law, it was necessary to have representatives in the court who were not part of the court. Judges remained the keepers of the law, but juries became assessors of the facts. Of course, in such a stratified society, these juries were not meant to be gatherings of lowly types. Qualifications and checks were needed to ensure that neither the monarchy nor the peasantry gathered too much strength. Ideally, these juries were to be made up of one's peers. Those present at the signing of the Magna Carta would be like those who found their way onto juries.[17] In a real way, juries reflect the basic nature of common law. Law was not as absolute as in the civil law systems; it was being "discovered" by judges as they went along. So the juries, with their ability to upset the law by nullification, also made law. Nullification is when a jury, in spite of overwhelming evidence of guilt, refuses to convict. A jury may nullify the law for one of two reasons: Either they believe the law is a bad law that should not be enforced, or they believe the law is a good law but should not have been applied in this particular case.

An important question may be: To what extent do juries and judges agree or disagree in trial decisions? Some researchers have examined over 3500 criminal trials in which a jury played a part. Evidence indicates that juries and judges agree about 75% of the time. One study suggests that juries do tend to be more lenient; the conviction rate of juries was 64% while that of judges was 83%.[18]

Another attribute of common law that arose because of the presence of the jury was guarding these laypeople from hearing things from crafty lawyers that might unduly sway their opinions; these were called "rules of evidence." A classic example was hearsay, or secondhand information. Only dying declarations and excited utterances were exceptions to prohibitions based on hearsay. Another rule of evidence has to do with the common law notion of privilege. Wives could not be forced to testify against husbands, priests against confessors, doctors against patients, or writers against sources of information. Therefore, both judges and juries were reflectors of the common law system.

MODERN-DAY STRUCTURE OF THE LEGAL SYSTEM

Perhaps the best single example of a modern-day common law country is England. Of course, historical forces are such that there is no pure common law country. But, because England started it and continues in the tradition today, it is a good contemporary example.

Atop the political structure of England sits the monarchy. At first, this institution was very powerful, but today it is more symbolic; it represents the unity of the country. More important is the Parliament, which is made up of the House of Lords and the House of Commons.

The House of Lords, the most ancient division of Parliament with roots as deep as the monarchy, has diminished in power, too. It consists of about 1200 members today who fall into one of three groups. First, there are the religious lords consisting of the archbishops of York and Canterbury and the several bishops of the Church of England. In addition, this group includes the law lords, to be discussed later. Second, there are the hereditary lords, about 800 of them, who hold seats because an ancestor was knighted as a duke, marquess, earl, viscount, or baron by some monarch in the past. Third, there are the life peers, those people knighted for public service or some other achievement and whose peerage lasts only during their lifetime.

The House of Commons is the more important branch of the Parliament. Created in the thirteenth century but not prominent until the sixteenth, it is today the major legislative body in England. There are 658 elected members, and it is the most representative body in Parliament. Two political parties predominate: the Conservative Party and the Labour Party. The leader of the country, the Prime Minister, and the cabinet sit in the House of Commons on the front bench. They are the leaders of the party that wins the most seats in the House. Across from them, the opposition sits with a shadow cabinet, the officials who would assume office if the existing administration should receive a vote of no confidence.

Even the police are part of this common law tradition. The organization of the police is centralized. A cabinet member, the Home Secretary, administers the police. Under the Home Office, there is an Office of Inspectors of Constabulary to assure the efficiency and effectiveness of the police. Under them are 41 Provincial Police Forces, the City of London Police, and the Metropolitan Police of London. These 43 entities are committees consisting of 17 members, nine of whom are politicians from the local area covered by the police. The common law heritage of the police was reaffirmed in 1929 by *A Report of the Royal Commission of Police Powers.*

> *The police of this country have never been recognized, either in law or by tradition, as a force distinct from the general body of citizens. Despite the imposition of many extraneous duties on the police by legislation or administrative action, the principle remains that a policeman, in the view of the common law, is only "a citizen paid to perform, as a matter of duty, acts which if he were so minded he might have done voluntarily."*[19]

It is the court structure that most reflects the common law traditions in England. The courts in England can best be understood by highlighting three officials. First, there is the Lord Chancellor, who is appointed by the monarch on the recommendation of the Prime Minister. Although this is a political appointment and the Lord Chancellor comes from the Prime Minister's political party, it is customary to select someone who is distinguished as a lawyer or jurist. He is given peerage and a seat in the highest court of the land, the House of Lords. The Lord Chancellor heads the entire judiciary and is responsible for five duties.

1. Participates in judicial appeals that reach the House of Lords.
2. Recommends all appointments to the courts.

3. Performs day-to-day administration of the courts.
4. Oversees the legal aid system.
5. Takes an active role in law reform.[20]

The second key figure is the Attorney General. This cabinet member and his subordinate, the Solicitor General, are the legal officers of the Crown and Parliament. These law officers are responsible for the criminal process in the courts. The Attorney General also answers all questions pertaining to law reform that come before the House of Commons.

The third figure is the Director of Public Prosecutions. This person administers a large staff of lawyers who specialize in criminal law. In addition, since 1985, this office has taken the power to prosecute from the police and instigates all prosecutions. They also watch over the police to see that investigations are carried out appropriately. The organization of the English courts is thus:

House of Lords. The oldest common law courts are Parliament. The House of Lords handles this function. Within the House of Lords there are a small number of distinguished law lords (their number varies from nine to eleven) who act as the supreme court of the land. Their work is limited to hearing appeals on civil and criminal matters from the Court of Appeal.

The Court of Appeal is an intermediate appellate court broken into two divisions: civil and criminal. The presiding judge of the civil division is called the Master of the Rolls. The presiding judge of the criminal division is the Lord Chief Judge. Twenty judges make up the Court of Appeal.

The High Court is a single court with both original and appellate powers. It is divided into three divisions: Chancery, Queen's Bench, and Family. The Chancery is largely concerned with property, trusts, wills, and estates. The Queen's Bench, the largest division, is concerned with civil and criminal matters. It has both original and appellate powers. The Family Division is concerned with matters of matrimony, guardianship, and adoption. All together the High Court has 80 judges, who are selected by the Lord Chancellor.

The Crown Courts deal with major crimes. They also handle appeals coming from the magistrates' courts. Three kinds of judges preside in these courts. Some justices from the Queen's Bench handle the more serious cases, approximately 400 circuit judges preside over the less serious cases, and 500 recorders (part-time judges) help the circuit judges with their case loads.

The *magistrates' courts* constitute the workhorse of the court system. There are more than 500 of these courts, and they handle 96% of the criminal cases in England. Two types of judges make up this court. There are stipendiary or professional magistrates, who are trained in the law and are paid for their services. In addition, there are nearly 27,500 magistrates, called justices of the peace, who are laypersons providing services without compensation.

Legal Profession

Since medieval times, the legal profession in England has been divided into two branches, solicitors and barristers. There are about 50,000 solicitors in England. Most are office lawyers who rarely appear in court. Instead, they are the legal advisors to the public. They help write wills and contracts, set up land and commercial sales, and deal with divorce issues. People become solicitors in one of two ways. They complete a university law degree, which is a 3-year undergraduate education, followed by a 2.5-year apprenticeship with an established solicitor. The other approach is to attend a college of law for 1 year and then serve a 4-year apprenticeship. After their training, they can apply to be a member of The Law Society, the professional society for solicitors.

Barristers are a second category of lawyers. Barristers present cases before the court. Oral advocacy is the greatest quality of the barrister. Solicitors may actually prepare the case, but the barrister argues it before the judge and jury. There are about 8500 barristers in England. They operate under a very strict code of conduct. For example, they cannot advertise their services. Cases must be brought to them from a solicitor. The bar is organized into 270 chambers or offices out of which the barrister operates. In each chamber, barristers are divided into two groups: Queen's Counsel (QC) and juniors. Junior barristers are those who have been practicing law for less than 15 years. Once the junior barrister has accumulated 15-20 years of experience, they can apply to the Lord Chancellor for appointment as QC. This is called "taking the silk" because they can then wear a silk rather than a cotton robe in court. In addition, they can have the initials QC after their name. Every barrister is a member of one of the four ancient organizations called the Inns of Court. These are Gray's Inn, Lincoln's Inn, the Inner Temple, and the Middle Temple. Any person who wants to be a barrister must join one of these Inns, take occasional meals there, receive instruction on the more practical aspects of court procedure, and develop a fraternal spirit with their fellow members.[21]

Judges are not a separate entity in the legal system. They are appointed by the Lord Chancellor from the ranks of the barristers. There is no popular election nor confirmation hearings before lawmakers as in the United States. There is no legislative input. It is purely ministerial with the Lord Chancellor in complete control of appointments.[22]

Juries are the critical indicator of a common law system. However, today, the jury system is used sparingly in England. The Grand Jury was abolished in 1948. Juries are no longer used in civil cases. They exist in criminal cases, but only 1 in 20 defendants selects a jury trial. To serve on a jury one must be between 18 and 70 years old, be a registered voter, and have resided in the United Kingdom for 5 years. A person can be disqualified from jury duty if they have been convicted of a crime. Anyone who has been sentenced to more than a 5-year prison term is disqualified for life. Those who work in the justice system are disqualified. So are members of Parliament, health care officials, and military personnel.[23]

The role of the university in shaping the law and legal structure is quite different in England than on the continent. As will be discussed later, the civil or continental systems were developed largely through the universities and academic thinkers. All training was received in the university, and emphasis was placed on history, reason, and logic. However, in England, law was not even taught at Oxford until 1758. Cambridge did not do so until 1800. Because the most important aspect of the legal profession was procedure, university training was less important in England. One could learn the job "practicing" under an experienced lawyer. English law was not a product of the universities, or a law of principles. It was the law of practitioners interested in procedure more than principles.

It has never been the tradition for English lawyers to be educated in universities; even today a university law degree is not mandatory in order to become a barrister, a solicitor, or a judge. Traditionally, these persons were educated in legal practice in which no mention was ever made of Roman law and in which attention was constantly focused on matters of procedure and evidence on which the success and indeed the receivability of the action depended.[24]

CONCLUSIONS

Common law systems are not widespread throughout the world, but their influence has been great, mainly because several of the common law countries—such as England and the United States—have assumed important roles on the world stage in the past two centuries. Of course, today there is no pure common law country. Instead, these countries have adjusted to historical forces and made compromises. The United States is a classical example; it has maintained common law principles in many areas but also made room for the decidedly democratic institution of statute. Nonetheless, even in America procedural law and judicial review maintain the power and influence of common law. Civil law countries far outnumber any other, and it is to them we turn. As we will see, civil law systems take a very different approach to justice.

DISCUSSION QUESTIONS

1. How does the Bill of Rights reflect the common law origins of the United States?
2. Why is procedure or process so important in a common law country?
3. There is a saying, "If you are guilty of a crime it is better to be in a common law country, but if you are innocent it is better to be in a civil law country." How can that be?

Endnotes

1. Henry Campbell Black, *Black's Law Dictionary*, 6th edition (St. Paul, Minn.: West Publishing, 1990), p. 276.
2. The use of the designation CE, which stands for "Common Era," instead of AD, Latin for "year of our Lord," is itself an issue of justice. It tries to take into consideration the multitude of readers who are not Christian.
3. Mary Ann Glendon, Michael Wallace Gordon, Christopher Osakwe, *Comparative Legal Traditions: Text, Materials, and Cases on the Civil Law, Common Law and Socialist Law Traditions with Special Reference to French, West German, English and Soviet Law* (St. Paul, Minn.: West Pub. Co., 1985), p. 279.
4. Philip Reichel, *Comparative Criminal Justice Systems: A Topical Approach* (Englewood Cliffs, NJ.: Prentice Hall Career & Technology, 1994), pp. 95-98.
5. Rene David and John E.C. Brierley, *Major Legal Systems in the World Today: An Introduction to the Comparative Study of Law* (London: The Free Press, Collier-Macmillan, 1968), p. 288.
6. Reichel, p. 95.
7. Susan Brownmiller, *Against Our Will: Men, Women and Rape* (New York: Simon and Schuster, 1975), pp. 24-30.
8. Theodore Plucknett, *A Concise History of the Common Law* (Boston: Little, Brown and Company, 1956), pp. 17-18.
9. Reichel, pp. 96-97.
10. Melvin Aron Eisenberg, *The Nature of the Common Law* (Cambridge, Ma.: Harvard University Press, 1988), pp. 50-61.
11. Erika Fairchild and Harry R. Dammer, *Comparative Criminal Justice Systems* (Belmont, Ca.: Wadsworth Thomson Learning Series, 2001), p. 52.
12. David and Brierley, p. 295.
13. Fairchild and Dammer, p. 53.
14. Kermit L. Hall, *The Magic Mirror: Law in American History* (New York: Oxford University Press, 1989), p. 220.
15. Jerold S. Auerbach, *Unequal Justice: Lawyers and Social Change in Modern America* (New York: Oxford University Press, 1976), pp. 74-99.
16. Roscoe Pound, *The Spirit of the Common Law* (Francestown, NH.: Marshall Jones Co., 1921), pp. 193-216.
17. Plucknett, pp. 106-138.
18. H. Kalven and H. Zeisel, *The American Jury* (Boston: Little, Brown and Company, 1966), pp. 55-65.
19. Richard Terrill, *World Criminal Justice Systems: A Survey* (Cincinnati: Anderson Publishing Co., 1999), p. 21.
20. *Ibid.*, p. 33.
21. *Ibid.*, p. 40.
22. *Ibid.*, p. 41.
23. *Ibid.*, pp. 41-42.
24. David and Brierley, p. 313.

CHAPTER

Civil Law Systems

6

Among the modern systems of justice, the civil law tradition is the oldest and most widespread. Western Europe, all of Central and South America, many parts of Asia, and a few places in North America (Louisiana, Puerto Rico, and Quebec) have civil law systems.

For many readers, there might be some semantic confusion. The phrase *civil law* has a particular meaning, especially for students in the United States. In the USA, it connotes a branch of the law, distinct from criminal law, which deals with conflicts between individuals. In the USA, this branch of law includes such things as divorce, contracts, house closings, alimony payments, and estate planning, to mention a few (see Chapter 14). That is not what is referred to in this chapter. This chapter concerns a family of justice systems practiced in other countries. Other phrases that might be used when studying civil law systems are the *Continental* or *Napoleonic systems of justice*. In this chapter, the three terms will be used interchangeably when discussing civil law traditions. Like common law systems, this civil law system is a product of historical development.

HISTORY

Rome

The civil law system comes from ancient Roman law. Early in the Roman Republic, two legislative bodies, the *comitia centuriata* and the *comitia tributa*, enacted statutes called *lex* or collections of laws. The earliest form of this law occurred in 450 BCE when a council of 10 men created the Twelve Tables that set forth the rights of a Roman citizen. During the Empire period, magistrates called *praetors* issued edicts that had the force of law. But the most important development was the codification of the law by Emperor Justinian in Constantinople. His *Corpus Juris Civilis* placed the law in written and codified form and became the sole authority on the law for hundreds of years. In the 11th century, the first European university was opened at Bologna, and civil law was its main curriculum.[1]

Canon Law

When the Roman Catholic Church assumed ascendency in Rome and later in Europe, its canon or church law was based on Roman models. Reichel believes that "[a]s the Roman civil law comprises the universal law of the worldly empire, canon law was the universal law of the spiritual realm."[2] Papal pronouncements, called *decretal* letters, had the force of law among Christians. Soon conflict arose between emperors and popes over who was the main source of the law. By the time of Pope Gregory I (590-604 CE) canon law had a secure place in the law of the Roman empire. However, it placed religion and religious institutions in the forefront of the system. In fact, many refer to the medieval church system as *inquisitorial*. As the Roman empire died, it was canon law that continued to have an influence throughout the Middle Ages. However, as nation states emerged and the Reformation of the Protestant churches began, the idea of a national law free from the history of Rome and the edicts of the Catholic Church became important. The French Revolution would address that idea.[3]

The French Revolution

The French Revolution was one of the greatest revolutions—equaled perhaps only by the Bolshevik Revolution of Russia—in world history. It not only disrupted the ruling structure of France but made way for profound changes in the law with the creation of the Napoleonic code. This codification movement was fundamental to the civil law tradition. First, it removed many of the religious laws that had been carried over from the dominant Catholic Church. Second, besides being anticlerical, the Revolution was antifeudal. Dislike of the aristocracy became intense. Judges and the judicial process, remnants of past elitism, were attacked as feudal and isolated. Third, there was a strict separation of powers in France, which led to a system of specialized courts and restrictions on judicial review. Power was taken from the courts and the lawyers and placed in the hands of the people in legislatures. Fourth, codification or written laws became important. One student of the civil law system declared that "[c]odification gives civil law a revolutionary character and written format that adds to its separate identity among legal families."[4] Written law was legitimate and binding for all because it was enacted by a recognized authority, generally a legislature, that followed formal procedures.

The United States

Conventional wisdom, and the preceding chapter, accepts that the United States is a common law country. However, there are strong historical antecedents of the civil law tradition in America. For example, though the thin strip of colonial America was attached to England and its common law, much of the continent was settled by France and Spain. The French were eventually eliminated, and their influence narrowed to parts of Canada. However, the Spanish had a much greater impact. The first permanent white settlement in America was established by the Spanish in St. Augustine, Florida, in 1565. Santa Fe, New Mexico, was settled in 1610 by Spaniards, and it became the first continuing capital city in America. Therefore, the Spanish—as representatives of Spain and later Mexico—were in America early and had a profound impact on California, Texas, and New Mexico. Early legal development in these areas brought both common law and civil law into proximity and shaped any debates on the direction of the law in the United States. The French also settled many parts of the American continent, bringing their civil law tradition with them. Today, Louisiana state law is primarily a civil law system.[5]

CHARACTERISTICS OF THE CIVIL LAW TRADITION

Definitions of the Law

The idea of a "Divine source" of law, essential to canon law, gave way during the French Revolution. Law came from the people or the state, particularly from the legislatures. Law did not come from external sources or local ones. Nationalism dictated that laws come from the central government.

Only statutes enacted by legislative power could be the law. Neither judicial decisions nor discussions by legal scholars had the force of law. The law was in the code.[6]

A legal code is the compilation of all the statues of a country. Common law countries have codes. But civil law countries have a distinct ideology when it comes to their codes. The purpose of the code is to weaken the role of the lawyer and the judge. The code needs to have no gaps or loopholes. There should be no conflicting provisions allowing judicial discretion. There should be no ambiguity that would allow for individual interpretation. If gaps and ambiguities are found, a special court, frequently called a *constitutional court*, assesses the problem and sends the law back to the legislature for clarification if necessary. Such an approach to law shapes the role of the judge, the legal training of lawyers, and the role of the prosecutor.[7]

Statute

Substantive law, a written statement defining what is a crime, in the civil law system becomes most important. As Reichel says, "Even though common law jurisdictions have moved toward statutory crimes and procedures, the civil law holds more closely to the principle that every crime and every penalty must be embodied in a statute enacted by the legislature. The civil lawyer sees common law courts violating this principle every time people are convicted of common law crimes and whenever judges prohibit relevant evidence and make rules regarding criminal procedure."[8]

A very important distinction in statute in a civil law country is between private and public law. First, public law deals with relations of people to public officials and agencies. It allows citizens to complain and hold accountable government agencies. Strictly speaking, it is more interested in administrative issues than legal ones. A series of Administrative Courts was put in place to deal with these issues. Early in the history of the civil law tradition a problem arose. Crime was originally a private matter; victims or families of victims were expected to bring people to court. However, as time went by, society began to recognize that crime affected more than the primary victims; it impacted all of society. So civil law countries had to decide whether to move crime into the public law arena. Most of these countries decided to leave such matters in the private law category.[9]

In private law, the government enforces an individual's private rights. The government is a referee in such matters. In public law, the government is much more active. Crimes fall under the category of private law. The two primary documents in criminal law are the Code of Criminal Procedure and the Penal Code. The former deals with the justice system's procedure; it is not left to the courts to decide such weighty matters as in the common law countries. The Penal Code is the substantive law.

Typically the Penal Code of a civil law country will have four sections or books. Book one will define the available punishments. Book two will explain criminal liability and responsibility. Book three will define the various offenses. Book four will do the same for lesser offenses, called violations. Criminal offenses will be divided into three categories: *crime* (serious offenses that we might call felonies), *delit* (less serious felonies and misdemeanors), and *contraventions* or violations. Such distinctions address the seriousness of the act and also indicate the kind of court to which they will go. For example, in France, crimes are punishable with imprisonment of more than 5 years to life and are heard at the highest level of courts called Courts of Assize. *Delits* are punishable by a fine or a prison term of 2 months to 5 years and are heard in a Correctional Court. *Contraventions* may result in a fine or a jail term of up to 2 months and are heard before a Police Court.[10]

LEGAL PERSONNEL

The Judge

In civil law systems, the judge is a civil servant, a functionary of the government. Decisions of the judge are different from the common law system. Clearly, the decisions of the court are procedural. Though they have an impact on the individual case, their decisions are not binding on other cases. There is no concept of precedent in a civil law country. The solution to a case is found in the written law; the judge has to show that any decision is based on provisions already written in the code.[11]

Becoming a judge is a quite different process from that of common law systems. After graduation from university, a student must decide on one of several career paths. If they decide to become a judge, they must take a state test. If they pass this rigorous test, they will then attend a special school for prospective judges. After completing their academic training, the individual will be appointed a junior judge, without ever having practiced law in court. Civil law countries do not have juries. Instead, a judge will have two or more subordinate judges to form a panel made up of these junior judges.[12]

The judge is to use only the written law, there is no *stare decisis* or precedent. Any unclear, incomplete, conflicting, or confusing legal issues will be sent back to the legislature for authoritative interpretation. The legislature might even create a "special court" to handle constitutional issues. These constitutional courts (in France they are called Cassation Courts, *cassation* meaning *to quash*) are established by the legislature because ordinary judges are not given the power to interpret the law. Thus the supremacy of the legislature is protected from judicial usurpation.[13]

The concept of certainty is important to all legal systems. Common law countries achieve this inductively. That is, general principles of law are established through the accumulation of a lot of cases. When it is not clear how a law is to be applied to a particular case, common law courts rely on what has been decided before to determine what to do in the current case—the principle of precedent. Thus, the general principle arises from individual cases. For example, a U.S. Supreme Court decision about an individual case will help establish a more general legal principle. Civil law countries achieve this deductively. Legislatively created statutes establish the legal principle to which individual cases are applied. There is a legal syllogism in civil law traditions. The major premise is the statute. The minor premise is made up of the legal facts of the case. The conclusion follows logically. In other words, individual case decisions emerge from general principles rather than general principles emerging from individual cases.

Equity is a principle to make the law fit the incident and person justly. In common law countries, the judge, using principles of mitigation or aggravation, may change the nature of the substantive law. This could not happen in a civil law system. The judge would not have such power.

Legal Scholars

Legal education in civil law countries is different than that in common law countries. Because case law is unimportant, the entire curriculum and pedagogy is different. Generally, in civil law countries, legal education is an undergraduate activity that is very general and interdisciplinary. Universities have law departments and students can specialize in law as an undergraduate. Furthermore, emphasis is given to studying the code, its history, and its philosophical foundations. Unlike legal training in a common law system, argumentation and moot court practice are not essential.[14]

Civil law systems use and have greater respect for legal scholars and scholarship than other systems. The teacher-scholar is the real power in the civil law tradition. This is very old, going back to the Roman "jurisconsult," an academic expert on the law who advised the legislature and the judge. In civil law jurisdictions, scholars look at the law in high levels of abstraction, relegating the facts to a minor place. Principles are taken out of their factual and historical context. As one scholar has said, "The legal scientist is more interested in developing and elaborating a theoretical scientific structure than he is in solving concrete problems."[15] Theories from the social sciences are notably absent in what is called "conceptual jurisprudence." These academic lawyers are very powerful because they mold and direct legal thinking. A cluster of disciples gather around their professor and "schools of thought" develop that influence legislators.

Lawyers

Other members of the legal profession have unique characteristics. For example, there are distinct legal careers. People in one area think of themselves as different and unconnected to other branches. There is a high degree of compartmentalization and immobility.

Public prosecutors, often called *procurators* in civil law countries, prepare and present the case to court. In addition, they have a greater role in the investigative process. The recently graduated law student may move directly into the field of prosecution. They may take a special government examination and then begin at the bottom of the ladder and build a career based on seniority. Actually, there are three types of prosecutorial roles, each of which may be chosen by the recent law graduate. There is the judicial police, the procurator, and the examining judge. The judicial police operate to investigate cases and to see that this is done legally. Procurators determine appropriate charges against the accused, prosecute minor crimes, and direct the judicial police. Examining magistrates, chosen from the court judges, direct all investigations.[16]

Advocates are defense lawyers. They meet with clients to give advice and representation in court. In most civil law systems the defense has a much more subdued role than in the common law systems.

Civil law notaries draft all important legal instruments such as wills and contracts. Notaries act as a public records office, keeping all original documents and providing *bona fide* copies to the public on request. The typical civil law country is divided into a number of notary districts, and the total number of notaries is limited. Therefore, it is a very competitive and cherished civil law position.

CIVIL PROCEDURE

The civil law procedure owes its origins to ancient Rome and canon law. There are three separate stages in the procedure. Generally, common law countries have an adversarial system. On the other hand, civil law countries may be called inquisitorial. The single most distinctive attribute of this inquisitorial system is the importance of the judge. In all stages of the process in civil law systems, the judge plays a prominent role while the lawyers play passive ones. Unlike the common law's adversarial competition between opposing sides, a trial in a civil law country is an ongoing investigation. While the common law system places an emphasis on the trial, civil law countries emphasize the preliminary screening process.

First, there is the very brief *preliminary stage*. Pleadings are submitted, and a hearing judge, usually called an *instructing judge*, is appointed.

Second, there is the *evidence taking stage*. At this point the instructing judge takes all the evidence and prepares a summary written report.

Third is the *decision-making stage*. New judges consider the report from the instructing judge. They then hear arguments and render a decision.

Trials and hearings in a civil law system may be thought of as "trials by files." Wordy trials with elaborate speeches and summations are rare. Typically, adjudication is a series of isolated meetings and written communications between lawyers and the judges. The appearances of witness and lawyers are brief and constitute a small part of the total case. Cross-examination is particularly foreign to a civil law system. Lawyers who want to question witnesses must first prepare a written statement of "articles of proof," which describes the matters about which they wish to question the witness. This document goes to the judge and opposing council in advance. Therefore, witnesses know in advance the types of questions that will be asked. This procedure is long and arduous, frequently taking up to 2 months. First, the lawyer asks in writing for a witness to be called; a copy of this request goes to the other lawyers. The instructing judge sets a date for the lawyers to present their reasons for calling the witness. Finally, a judge will decide and issue his ruling. Only then can the witness be called into the trial. Then the witness testifies, and the judge takes notes. There is no verbatim record kept during the trial.[17] In the adversarial setting of common law courts, opposing lawyers decide which witnesses will be called, what they will be asked, and what evidence will be introduced. In civil law systems, judges take on these responsibilities.

CRIMINAL PROCEDURE

Substantive criminal law—defining particular crimes in statutes and fixing the appropriate punishments—is not very different in common law and civil law countries. But criminal procedure, the process by which cases are handled, is very different.

There are three basic parts to the civil law criminal procedure. First, the **investigative phase** is under the direction of the public prosecutor. In some countries, the detectives operate directly under the prosecutor. Of course, because the investigation ultimately is under the judiciary, there is little worry about the legal appropriateness of the investigation. Large files or dossiers of evidence are compiled by the prosecutor at this stage. Inquisitorial systems assume that all persons are seeking the truth. Therefore, there is an expectation that the defendant will cooperate. This means providing information before the trial and at the trial, and it means that defendants are not fully protected from self-incrimination. In the adversarial setup of a common law country, there is no such expectation, which puts an added burden upon the prosecutor.[18]

Second, the **examination phase** is under the direction of an examining judge. Though the prosecutor is still active, the weight of the proceedings is shifted to the judge. This phase can be described as "trial by file" and is not very public. The main purpose is to see if there is sufficient cause and evidence to move to the next phase. There is no system of plea bargaining. Even if a person were to plead guilty and offer a confession, a trial—which is a fact-finding rather than an adjudicating ceremony—would go on. The confession and plea would simply be treated as evidence.

Third, the **official trial** finalizes an already developed system. That is why it is commonly felt that rather than a "presumption of innocence" as found in common law countries a "presumption of guilt" is attributed to civil law justice systems. The evidence has been collected. Judges—seeking a fuller understanding of the file of evidence—ask questions of the defendant and witnesses. At this stage with a presumption of guilt, the burden of proof shifts to the defendant. There is no right to remain silent. Any refusals to testify are taken as elements of culpability and held against the accused. Prosecutors and especially defense attorneys play minor roles. For example, there is no system of cross-examination of witnesses as might be found in a common law country. Though juries sometimes exist, they are rare. Particularly in those countries with wide economic or ethnic divisions, there is a distrust of popular participation in the justice system. These systems exist in highly bureaucratized countries where there is a belief in the efficiency and thoroughness of the system. Any resemblance to a jury is found in the existence of the lay judges.

Most trials do not have a single judge. Instead, there is a panel of at least three, a main judge and two assistant or lay judges. Together these three listen to the proceedings, then leave to deliberate and render a verdict. Theoretically, the lay judges can outvote the main judge, but they rarely do.[19]

Scholars point out a real difference between the civil and common law systems. If a person were guilty of a crime, they would have a better chance in a common law country where the process would be filled with rhetoric, argumentation, and emotion. With its emphasis on procedure, common law systems are more likely to allow the guilty to "get off on a technicality." If a person were innocent, however, they would be at an advantage in a civil law proceeding. In short, judgment in a civil law system—with its logic and strict adherence to unemotional bureaucratic proceedings—is more likely to distinguish factual rather than technical guilt or innocence.

MODERN-DAY STRUCTURE OF A CIVIL LAW SYSTEM: FRANCE

Political Structure and Background

Perhaps the best example of a modern-day civil law country is France. For centuries the French government was headed by a monarch. That came to an end with the French Revolution of 1789. Since that time the French have been guided by two ostensibly different goals. They have a profound desire for personal freedom and independence. At the same time, they have enormous respect and faith in authority, especially if it is wielded by a hero who unifies the country.[20] Throughout the nineteenth century, France was guided by a series of emperors. In the twentieth, this leadership role shifted to presidents. The one characteristic of these executives was their use of power and authority.

Today the French government is organized according to the Constitution of the Fifth Republic under Charles de Gaulle in 1958. There is a President of the Republic, who is elected to be head of state for a term of 7 years. But there are no limits to the terms the President may serve. The President appoints the Premier or prime minister, who is the head of the government. The Premier is the link between the national legislative body and the President. It is up to the Premier to explain and defend the President's policies. The Premier selects a cabinet called a *Council of Ministers*, whose members are career civil servants, university professors, or technical experts. Very few are politicians.[21]

The Parliament is made up of two houses: a Senate, which is the upper chamber, and a National Assembly, or lower chamber. The National Assembly is the more powerful. Its delegates are elected directly by the people for 5-year terms.[22] They represent one of the numerous political parties. For example, there is the National Front, representing the extreme right of the political spectrum. The Movement for France is also a very conservative party. The Rally for the Republic is a conservative party that owes its origins to the Charles de Gaulle era; it favors a market economy and regulation by the central government. The Union for French Democracy is a center-right party that attracts the moderate voters. The Socialist Party was not strong until François Mitterand revived it and won the presidential election in 1981. Throughout the 1980s, this party dominated French politics. The Communist Party has declined as the Socialist Party ascended. Most of the trade unions abandoned the Communist Party for the Socialist Party. There are three parties that specialize in ecological issues: the Greens, the Ecological Generation, and the New Environmentalists. The French believe in "proportional representation," which means in the Parliament all these parties will be present in number in proportion to the vote they got in the election. Such a proliferation of political ideologies—all subscribing to some measure of ideological purity—makes coalition building very difficult. But, in the name of political justice, it does ensure that large numbers of people with drastically different political views have representation in the government.[23]

ADMINISTRATION OF JUSTICE

Unlike England and the United States, with their desires for local input into government administration, the French have a history of highly centralized and bureaucratized government. Even in the 95 "departments," local levels of administration comparable to counties in America, there remain strong ties to the central government.

Police

Throughout the history of France, the police had been highly centralized in the national government. There is a pronounced connection between the French police and the military. Unlike England and the United States, where the police were kept distant from the military, the French police grew out of the military. This meant they were quickly uniformed, and those costumes were very similar to the ones worn in the military. Unlike in England and the United States, the French police were quickly armed. Another characteristic of the French police is the extent to which they can interfere in the lives of ordinary citizens. This is quite common in civil law countries and is caused by the notion that the collective needs of society are more important than individual rights. Historically, the French police—and this is also true of other civil law systems—have a close relationship with the judiciary. In fact, many of the earliest leaders of the French police—called *Lieutenant Generals*—were magistrates.[24]

There are two police systems in France. The **National Police** is the largest, employing over 133,500 people. It is responsible for policing the cities and towns with populations of more than 10,000 people. It is under the Ministry of Interior, one of the most important members of the Council of Ministers. The Director of the National Police is a civilian career bureaucrat who is concerned with the central administration of the National Police. The head of each local "department," the administrative subdivisions of France, is a Prefect. The Prefect is linked to the Director General but is the liaison to the local department.

To accomplish its mission, the National Police has several subunits. First, there is the Office of Inspector General of Police whose job it is to make sure the police are not too brutal or corrupt. Second, the Judicial Police, divided into 18 regions throughout the country, conduct all criminal investigations. Third, a General Intelligence Directorate, referred to sometimes as the "political police," collects all kinds of intelligence to safeguard the security of the nation. Fourth, there is the Public Security

Directorate, which consists of the uniformed branch of policing. This would be the urban uniformed patrol. Fifth, the Territorial Surveillance Directorate is a specialized unit concerned with protecting those at risk from terrorist attacks. Vital industrial, scientific, and technical industries fall under its protection. Sixth, the Directorate for the Control of Immigration and Illegal Employment, created in 1994, has an Air and Border Patrol to handle security at the airports and along the borders. Finally, there is the Republican Security Company or riot police. This directorate is highly militaristic, and its members are encamped throughout the country to quell public unrest such as student demonstrations and union strikes. They also protect the President of France and visiting dignitaries.[25]

The **National Gendarmerie** is the other principal police system of France. Administratively, it falls under the Ministry of Defense and does three tasks. First, it acts as the military police for the French army, navy, and air force. Second, it provides law enforcement services for the French overseas territories. Third, the Gendarmerie provides policing in France for all those communities with populations of fewer than 10,000 people.[26] Overall, the police of France are highly centralized and have powers and authorities much expanded over the typical common law police. In this regard, the French police are quite typical of all civil law justice systems.

Judiciary

There are two kinds of courts in the French legal system. Administrative Courts supervise the government. They try to regulate and balance any conflict between the general interests of the state and individual rights. The other branch is the Ordinary Courts, which handle all civil and criminal cases. The Ordinary Courts are of the most interest to us.

The Ministry of Justice, a cabinet position in the Council of Ministers, is the government overseer of the Ordinary Courts. This minister is concerned with the administration of the correctional system, the selection and appointment of magistrates (judges and prosecutors), and the general administration of the law.

The court structure of France is typical of civil law countries. In the United States, there is a Supreme Court that can rule on the constitutionality of the laws and practices of government agencies. Such a judicial review does not exist in France's court system. Instead, a special council, the Constitutional Council, is established to do this. This Council is composed of nine members who serve terms of 9 years. One third of the Council is appointed every 3 years. The President of France and the presidents of the Senate and National Assembly share in this appointment power. All former Presidents of the Republic serve as *ex officio* members. The Council has two responsibilities. One is to address complaints about elections. The second is to determine the constitutionality of legislation passed by the Parliament. This second activity occurs before a piece of legislation is signed into law. Such scrutiny occurs only when a special request is made by the President of the Republic, the Premier, or the presidents of the Senate or National Assembly.[27]

As shown in Figure 6.1, there are five layers of courts in France. The Court of Cassation is the actual highest court of civil and criminal appeals in France. The word *cassation* comes from the French verb *casser, to shatter*. This court listens to appeals on the interpretation of the law by the lower courts. The court has six chambers, three of which handle civil cases. The other chambers listen to issues concerning social, commercial, and criminal matters. Over 120 judges sit in this court. Eighty-five are senior permanent judges. About 40 are career judges, called "advisors," who are appointed for 10-year terms. Each case that is heard by the court will have a minimum of seven judges and two advisors.[28]

Court of Cassation
- highest court of civil and criminal appeals
- six chambers, three for civil cases, one each for social, commercial, and criminal matters
- hearings use panels of 7 judges and 2 advisors

Courts of Appeal
- 35 courts hear appeals from lower courts
- four chambers specializing in civil, social, correctional, and juvenile cases
- hearings use 3-judge panels

Courts of Assize
- 95 courts, one for each county in France
- two chambers, one for juveniles and one for adults
- hears appeals from lower courts and some criminal cases

Courts of Major Jurisdiction
- 181 courts
- hears civil cases, criminal cases, and juvenile cases
- hearings use 3-judge panels

Courts of Minor Jurisdiction
- 473 courts
- hears civil cases and minor crimes
- a single judge presides over hearings

FIGURE 6.1

Structure of the French Courts.

There are 35 Courts of Appeal that deal with civil and criminal appeals from the lower courts. These courts consist of four chambers each specializing in civil, social, correctional, and juvenile cases. Each case is heard by a three-judge panel. Two types of issues will bring an appeal to these courts: (1) cases that involve a point of law that needs clarification and (2) cases that may deal with some factual issue. In the latter case, this court's decision is the final decision.[29]

Ninety-five Courts of Assize, one for each of the departments (counties) of France, sit to hear appeals from lower courts and have original jurisdiction in criminal matters. These courts are divided into two chambers, one for juvenile and one for adult cases. Three judges sit as a panel to hear civil cases. For criminal cases, three judges and nine lay jurors will preside.[30]

Courts of Major Jurisdiction are the next layer of courts. There are 181 courts of major jurisdiction. Each court is divided into three chambers. When it hears civil cases, they are called *civil courts*.

When they hear criminal cases, they are called *correctional courts*. This court also sits as a juvenile court. Three-judge panels make up these courts.[31]

Courts of Minor Jurisdiction are the lowest courts in the hierarchy of courts. There are 473 of these courts. Each court is divided into two tribunals. They are civil tribunals when they hear civil cases. Minor crimes, called *contraventions*, are heard by a police tribunal. These courts are the only ones in the French system that have a single judge presiding.[32]

Legal Profession

At the pinnacle of the legal profession is the law professor. Legal education in France is an undergraduate interdisciplinary field of study. French universities are public institutions administered by the Ministry of National Education. Legal education takes 4 years, divided into two phases. In the first 2 years, the student studies history, economics, political science, sociology, and finance. There is a desire to have students obtain a general broad education during this initial phase. In the second 2-year phase, the student concentrates on law. At the end of the third year, a student is given a license in law, equivalent to a bachelor of law degree. At the end of the fourth year, the student is given a master of law degree. Instruction is highly theoretical and philosophical. Law professors operate in the realm of ideas and are little concerned with the practical aspects of the law or legal profession. As Terrill notes, "Their responsibility is to train people to think like jurists, not to produce legal practitioners."[33]

Judges are part of the judicial bureaucracy. Unlike the United States where judges are elected or appointed, French judges are civil servants. They tend to start and end their careers as magistrates. They are called *magistrates du siege* or sitting magistrates. Their training and career path is very different from that found in England and the United States. To become a judge, one needs to receive a license in law then attend the National School of the Judiciary in Bordeaux. It is at this school where a person learns to be a judge. This training is divided between very theoretical course work and an apprenticeship. It takes 3 years to complete this training. A graduate's first appointment will be as an assistant judge in a provincial city. From that point they slowly work their way up the career ladder. Judges are committed to theoretical purity and tidiness. Their decisions and writings are clear and brief, usually no longer than a page. Their thought processes are deductive. The general principle in the written law is the major premise. The facts of the case are the minor premise. The conclusion flows smoothly and logically. Any decision must show how it is in accordance with the law code.[34]

Procurators, called prosecutors in the United States, are another important part of the French judiciary. They are called *magistrates debout* or standing magistrates. Procurators also attend the National School of the Judiciary but opt for a different career path than judges. Unlike a prosecutor in the United States the procurator's job is not to secure a conviction. They seek to achieve justice and serve the interests of society. They are not the attorney for the state. For example, in a civil case where the state is one of the litigating parties the government must hire its own lawyer; they cannot use a procurator. There are two types of procurators. First, there is the public procurator, who represents the general public. Second, every lawyer who appears in court for a victim serves as a procurator.[35]

Before 1971 defense counsel was divided into two groups, *avocats* and *avoues*, similar to the British solicitor and barrister. They were merged, and now they are *avocats* only. They must obtain a license in law from their university, pass an examination, and register at a local bar association, of which there are 180 in the country. During a 3-year probationary period, the new *avocats* attend a specialized training school set up by the court of appeal in their region of residence. Historically, these lawyers practiced alone. However, legislation was passed by the Parliament that allows small partnerships to form. This has become the favorite form of legal organization in the last generation.[36]

Unlike many civil law countries, France does have a jury system. It is used only in the Courts of Assize. To serve on a jury a person must be a citizen, be at least 23 years old, be able to read and write, and be on the voting lists. Before a court session is opened, the names of 35 jurors and 10 alternates are placed on a list. On the day of a trial names are drawn from an urn. *Avocats* can challenge five potential jurors and procurators can reject four. Reasons for challenges and rejections need not be given. Nine jurors are finally selected and are seated on either side of the three judges. Jurors are to decide issues of guilt or innocence but are at a disadvantage. They are not provided any written record of the trial, nor are they provided any summation of the law before the trial begins. In other words, in the name of the revolutionary spirit of the Napoleonic era, juries were added, but they are powerless compared to the judges.

CONCLUSION

The civil law family is an important part of the justice systems of the world. Many argue that truly impartial justice can only be had by the rational, logical, and coldly bureaucratic civil law system. To these advocates, the common law system is too arbitrary and unscientific. Civil law systems tend to arise in highly centralized civil servant countries. The system of justice mirrors the political environment in which it finds itself. Most of Europe, Latin America, and South America have such systems. Even some former socialist countries, such as Russia, have law systems that resemble the civil law structure. Some civil law countries may have an ideological orientation that on the surface make them seem different. For example, China, with its Communist background, still appears to be a civil law system. This is true of those with a strong religious base such as Islam, a topic to which we now turn.

DISCUSSION QUESTIONS

1. How do civil law systems of justice differ from common law systems of justice?
2. How have some civil law traditions affected the United States?
3. Which is more efficient: a civil law or a common law justice system?

Endnotes

1. Reichel, p. 100.
2. Ibid., p. 101.
3. Fairchild and Dammer, p. 48.
4. Reichel, p. 102.
5. *Ibid.*, pp. 103-106.
6. John Henry Merryman, *The Civil Law Tradition: An Introduction to the Legal Systems of Western Europe and Latin America*, 2 ed. (Stanford, Calif.: Stanford University Press, 1985), pp. 19-25.
7. *Ibid.*, pp. 26-33.
8. Reichel, p. 141.

9. *Ibid.*, pp. 118-122.
10. *Ibid.*, p. 142.
11. Merryman, pp. 34-38.
12. Terrill, pp. 227-229.
13. *Ibid.*, p. 225.
14. *Ibid.*, pp. 232-234.
15. Merryman, p. 64.
16. Reichel, p. 225.
17. Merryman, pp. 111-123.
18. Reichel, pp. 149, 152-153.
19. Merryman, pp. 124-132.
20. Terrill, p. 193.
21. *Ibid.*, pp. 195-196.
22. *Ibid.*, p. 197.
23. *Ibid.*, pp. 197-200.
24. *Ibid.*, pp. 203-204.
25. *Ibid.*, pp. 206-208.
26. *Ibid.*, pp. 209-210.
27. *Ibid.*, p. 234.
28. *Ibid.*, p. 225.
29. *Ibid.*, pp. 225-226.
30. *Ibid.*, p. 226.
31. *Ibid.*
32. *Ibid.*
33. *Ibid.*, p. 233.
34. *Ibid.*, pp. 227-228.
35. *Ibid.*, pp. 229-230.
36. *Ibid.*, pp. 230-231.

CHAPTER 7

Islamic Law Systems

Common law and civil law systems form the basis for most Western images of how a formal justice system should be structured. For people living under such systems, they seem quite natural, and it may be difficult to imagine alternatives for dispensing justice. Islamic law provides a good illustration of a very different way of formally addressing the issue of justice. As the name suggests, Islamic law is based on the principles of Islam, a set of religious principles. Followers of Islam are called Muslims. While Western laws trace their roots to either court decisions (common law systems) or statutes enacted by lawmakers (civil law systems), the roots of Islamic law can be found in the Islamic holy book, the *Qur'an*. And, while Western legal systems tend to make a distinction between religion and government, that distinction is less clear under an Islamic system of justice.

Just as it is difficult to find examples of pure common law systems or pure civil law systems, it is difficult to find pure examples of countries governed by Islamic law. In a country that is a pure example of an Islamic law nation, the head of state would also be the head of the church, government proclamations would also be religious proclamations, and criticism of the government would be viewed as a criticism of Islam and ultimately of God. While there are no pure examples of Islamic law nations, there are nations in which Islamic law plays a dominant role in the systems of justice. Because in an Islamic law system there is such a close connection between religion and law, it is impossible to understand Islamic law without first understanding the religion Islam.

ISLAM

Among the world's religions, Islam is relatively young. Its origins can be traced to the city of Mecca, Arabia, where the word of God was revealed to the prophet Muhammad in 622 AD.[1] Those revelations were written in the book known as the *Koran*, or, as it is called in the Muslim world, the *Qur'an*. Islam shares many of the ideas found in the Old Testament of the Bible. For example, Muslims believe in a single God, who they refer to as Allah, and they believe in many of the Old Testament prophets, including Abraham and Moses. In fact, Muslims, Christians, and Jews all worship the same God, the God of Abraham.[2] Muslims also believe in Christ but view him as simply another prophet.

Although it began in the Middle East, Islam spread quickly throughout the world and is presently the second largest religion in the world.[3] Although Americans tend to associate Islam with the Middle East, the largest number of Muslims are in Asia, which has about three times the number of Muslims as the Middle East.[4] At present, Muslims make up the majority of the population in 49 countries. Islam is also among the fastest growing religions and is expected to grow at about twice the rate of other religions; by 2030, more than one quarter of the world's population is expected to be Muslim.[5]

Today the largest numbers of Muslims are in Asia and in parts of Africa, but there is also a large Muslim population in the United States. A study by the Council on American-Islamic Relations found that between 1994 and 2000 there was a 25% increase in the number of mosques in America and a 300% increase in the number of Muslims participating in religious activities in mosques.[6] It has been projected that the number of Muslims in the United States will more than double between 2010 and 2030 to 6.2 million, or about the same as the number of Jews or Episcopalians.[7]

ISLAM IS NOT THE SAME EVERYWHERE

Although Christians may follow the same Bible, there are large variations across denominations in their interpretations of the Bible and in the behaviors they expect of believers. Similarly, there are large variations in the practices of Muslims and in the applications of Islamic law. There are many countries with a large Muslim population that do not operate under Islamic law, there are some countries that have partially adopted Islamic law, and among countries that formally recognize Islamic law there are large variations in how that law is interpreted. For example, under the Taliban, Afghanistan was an Islamic law country in which there was a strict interpretation of the *Qur'an*. Police there arrested and punished citizens for behaviors that would have been ignored or viewed as minor indiscretions in other Islamic countries. When the Taliban was in power, the Islamic government in Afghanistan forbade both native and foreign women from working and from driving automobiles.[8] Other Islamic governments may forbid Muslim women from working but allow work by non-Muslim women. Still other Islamic governments may not place restrictions on women's work, or they may discourage it but not ban it.

There are also variations over time within individual Islamic countries. For example, officials in Pakistan and Egypt have become more restrictive over time in the behaviors they allow, while those in Sudan have become more tolerant.[9] Perhaps the most common situation is for a country to adopt a civil or common law system and integrate key elements of Islamic law into that system.[10] Under these blended systems, behaviors considered essential to following Islam are regulated under Islamic law, while other behaviors are regulated by secular law and processed through secular courts, similar to courts in much of Europe.[11] Often Islamic law is applied to what are considered moral issues while more secular law is applied to other areas of behavior.[12]

And, just as there are wide variations in how Christians interpret and follow the Bible, there are wide variations in the religious practices of Muslims living in non-Muslim countries. Muslims living in the United States, for example, generally recognize the criminal justice law of the United States but refer to Islamic law to guide moral behaviors, such as sex, gambling, and the use of alcohol and other drugs. This reminder of variation is to caution that the description that follows is what some social scientists have called an *ideal type*—a picture drawing on the essential elements of Islam, the exercise of which may vary from one country to another.

SOURCES OF ISLAMIC LAW

Collectively, the laws of Islam are known as the shari'a, which can be translated as "the path to follow God's law." There are four sources of Islamic law (Figure 7.1). The *Qur'an* is the primary source for Islamic law, with which all other sources must be in accord.[13] Muslims believe the *Qur'an* is a sacred document and as such is infallible. Thus, there are variations from one Islamic community to the next

Primary Sources
Qur'an: The Muslim holy book
Sunnah: Customs sanctioned by Muhammad

Secondary Sources
Consensus: Agreement among members of the Muslim community
Analogical Reasoning: Applying existing rules to a new situation that is similar to an existing situation

FIGURE 7.1

Sources of Islamic Law.[16]

in the interpretation of the *Qur'an*, but there is never a challenge to the *Qur'an* itself. This also means that compared with legal scholarship in the United States and Europe, scholars of Islamic law take a less critical approach to the subject. While American law journals are filled with articles criticizing particular laws or punishments, Islamic legal scholars never question laws or penalties spelled out in the *Qur'an*, only the interpretation of those laws.

Although the focus of this discussion is on the Islamic approach to criminal law, the *Qur'an* provides legal guidance on a variety of life issues, including religious obligations, commerce, family relations, and diet. In fact, of the 6237 verses in the *Qur'an*, only 190 deal with legal issues. Of those 190 verses, only about 30 deal with criminal law; the remaining verses cover such issues as family law and contracts.[14] This means there are many areas of criminal behavior not explicitly covered by the *Qur'an*. To deal with such problems, Muslims turn to three other sources of Islamic law. These are the *Sunnah*, the consensus of the Muslim community, and analogical reasoning.[15]

Second in importance to the *Qur'an* are the Sunnah, the words and actions of Muhammed, which have been written down and whose authenticity has been verified by religious scholars.[17] These ideas are thought to be from God through Muhammed as an extension and clarification of the *Qur'an*. If there are questions not addressed in the *Qur'an* or if some passages of the *Qur'an* require clarification, Islamic law judges turn to the Sunnah. In addition to clarifying the meaning of the *Qur'an*, the Sunnah also describes general judicial procedures and the use of evidence by the courts.[18] Violating the rules established in the *Qur'an* or in the Sunnah means not simply violating the rules of society but violating the rules of God.

When neither the *Qur'an* nor the Sunnah provide guidance about how to handle a case, judges may turn to consensus. This consensus requires the unanimous agreement among Muslim scholars who represent varied opinions.[19] In some cases, religious leaders may issue a religious edict or order that does not have the weight of law (this is known as a *fatwa*), but that order may solidify public opinion on an issue and lead to a new law. For example, a Muslim cleric in Lebanon issued an edict banning Muslims from smoking tobacco.[20] It was expected that most of the cleric's followers would obey the order although it did not have the weight of law. In a society guided by Islamic law, should there be general agreement among a cleric's followers and among other religious leaders that smoking should be banned, the edict might well become law.

Analogical reasoning is the fourth source of Islamic law. Through analogical reasoning the law can adapt to new situations while remaining true to the spirit of the *Qur'an* and the Sunnah. For example, the *Qur'an* specifically prohibits fornication but does not mention sodomy. Some scholars have argued that by analogy sodomy is comparable to fornication and should result in the same legal punishment.[21]

CRIME AND PUNISHMENT UNDER ISLAMIC LAW

There is an image of Islamic law as harsh and unyielding, but this is not entirely accurate. While the penalties for some offenses are much harsher than in many non-Islamic systems, strict enforcement of these laws is often difficult given the strict criteria that must be met under Islamic law. Further, there are offenses that are considered among the most serious in Western law that are, by comparison, treated less harshly under Islamic law. Islamic law also differs from Western law in that technically only God and the individual can be seen as victims—there are no crimes against the state. In addition, there is no provision in Islamic law for recognizing corporations as individuals or entities capable of being either an offender or a victim. Charges may be brought against individuals who control the corporation but not against the corporation itself.

While common law and civil law systems tend to categorize crimes by the relative harm that results, Islamic law categorizes crimes according to the nature of the punishment that follows a conviction. In general, there are three categories of crime under Islamic law: hudud offenses, quesas offenses, and ta'zir offenses (Figure 7.2).

Hudud offenses are those for which the offense and the penalty are explicitly defined in the *Qur'an*. Quesas offenses include crimes against the person, and punishments are designed to provide victims with a formal mechanism for retribution. Finally, ta'zir offenses are offenses not specifically listed in the *Qur'an* or Sunnah, for which the penalty is left to the discretion of the judge with a focus on correction or rehabilitation of the offender.[22]

Hudud Offenses: There are seven hudud offenses and their respective penalties listed in the *Qur'an*. The punishments for hudud offenses are presented in Figure 7.3, along with the standard of proof that must be met for there to be a conviction. These offenses are:

- *Apostasy*: This refers to followers of Islam who voluntarily renunciate Islam or its beliefs.
- *Armed rebellion*: This refers to attacks against the state with the intention of overthrowing it or giving aid to its enemies.
- *Theft*: Theft refers to taking the property of another in a secret manner. The object must have been in a secure place and the thief must have full possession of the property.
- *Highway robbery*: This includes both robbing highway travelers and, in some jurisdictions, murdering highway travelers.

Hudud Offenses:	These are offenses against God and the public good. Hudud offenses and their corresponding penalties are specified in the *Qur'an*.
Quesas Offenses:	These are offenses against individuals, either resulting in death or in serious physical harm. These offenses and their corresponding penalties are specified in the *Qur'an* and the Sunnah.
Ta'zir Offenses:	These are offenses that harm society or individuals but for which the punishments are not specified in the *Qur'an* or Sunnah. These offenses are decided by religious authorities and their corresponding punishments are up to a judge.

FIGURE 7.2

Categories of Islamic Law.

Offense	Standard of Proof	Punishment
Apostasy	2 witnesses or a confession	Death by beheading for males, imprisonment until they repent for females
Armed Rebellion	2 witnesses or a confession	Death if captured while fighting; a lesser punishment if they surrender
Theft	2 witnesses or a confession	1st offense: amputation of hand at wrist 2nd offense: amputation of second hand at wrist 3rd offense: amputation of foot at ankle or imprisonment until they repent
Highway Robbery	2 witnesses or a confession	Amputation of right hand and left foot, execution, crucifixion, or exile
Extramarital Sex	4 witnesses or a confession	Married offenders are stoned to death. Unmarried offenders receive 100 lashes
Slander/Defamation	Failure to prove adultery	80 lashes across the back of the offender
Drinking Alcohol	2 witnesses or a confession	80 lashes across the back of the offender

FIGURE 7.3

Hudud Offenses, Standards of Proof, and Proscribed Penalties.

- *Extramarital sex*: This includes both adultery and sexual relations between individuals who are not married to each other.
- *Slander/defamation*: This refers to accusing someone of extramarital sex without being able to meet the necessary standard of proof.
- *Drinking alcohol*: At the time the *Qur'an* was written the ban on alcohol appeared to refer to drinks made from grapes, but some Islamic scholars have interpreted the law to refer to any alcoholic beverage.

Strictly enforced, the required punishments for hudud offenses can be quite harsh. Although these offenses and their punishments are technically not subject to negotiation, in reality it is a common practice for Islamic officials to find ways to justify lesser penalties. For example, theft may be reduced from a hudud offense to a lesser offense if it can be shown that the thief was hungry or needy "for in this case the blame is attributed to the injustice of society or the ruler."[23] Similarly, having sex outside of marriage is made more difficult to prosecute by the requirement that there be four witnesses of the offense. However, the pregnancy of an unmarried woman may be such a visible and undeniable violation that religious leaders feel compelled to carry out the proscribed punishment.[24]

Although hudud offenses are not usually punished fully, such punishments are always possible. In 1989, the Iranian government offered a bounty for the death of author Salman Rushdie because his novel *The Satanic Verses* was ruled to be an affront to Islam and thus a form of apostasy. Before they were removed by American troops, Afghanistan's Taliban rulers announced that they would carry out the death penalty against any Muslim who converted from Islam to another religion.[25]

Quesas Offenses: These are commonly referred to as offenses against the person and include murder, voluntary killing, involuntary killing, intentional physical injury or maiming, and unintentional physical injury or maiming. The manner in which quesas offenses are handled and the punishments that accompany them make Islamic law quite distinct from either common law or civil law traditions.

While by Western standards the punishments for hudud offenses may seem harsh, the punishments for quesas offenses can be comparatively mild, depending on the wishes of the victim. Unlike common law and civil law, neither homicide nor battery are crimes against the state or against society. Instead they are seen as personal matters between individuals in which the state acts only as a neutral mediator.[26] Thus the victim has the option of seeking either retaliation or compensation. In the case of willful murder or manslaughter, the victim's family may choose among death to the offender, financial compensation, or a complete pardon. In the case of an accidental killing, the victim's family may seek compensation, or they may pardon the offender. For inflicting bodily harm, the victim may seek to have the same harm inflicted on the offender, compensation, or a complete pardon. In most modern Islamic states, the victim's family's wish to have a killer executed is carried out by the state, acting as a representative of the victim's family. Quesas offenses are crimes against individuals while hudud offenses are crimes against God. Consequently, hudud offenses are viewed as more serious. As a result, "[a] proven murderer thus has, at least in principle, a better chance of averting punishment than does the proven sexual offender."[27]

One provision of Islamic law that is unusual and controversial by Western standards is the practice of not punishing "a father or a teacher who kills a child in the course of correction."[28] This same provision allows for the killing of a female who has harmed the family name by having sex outside of marriage or by marrying a man unacceptable to the father or male guardian. According to a report by the United Nations, the number of these so-called honor killings is increasing worldwide, as is the number of countries in which they are practiced.[29] Within Islamic societies the practice of honor killing is controversial. Some argue it is required by the *Qur'an,* while others argue the *Qur'an* prohibits the practice. In reality, honor killing was practiced in the Middle East long before Islam came into being and is more accurately a reflection of tribal custom than of a religion. In fact, honor killing is mentioned in the Old Testament book of Deuteronomy, which calls for the death by stoning of any woman who is not a virgin at the time of her marriage. This book of the Bible is at least 1000 years older than Islam. While honor killing is common in some countries, it is against the law in every nation. Authorities may choose to look the other way, but they are violating the law in doing so.

Ta'zir Offenses: These offenses concern behaviors that are not specifically outlined in the *Qur'an* or the Sunnah and for which neither the *Qur'an* nor the Sunnah specifies penalties for violators. Religious scholars, guided by the principles outlined in the *Qur'an* and Sunnah, determine which acts will be defined as crimes. The judge, acting as a representative of the religious leader, decides the punishment, taking into consideration the specifics of the case, the offender's background, the likelihood that a particular punishment will bring about reform in the offender, the best interests of the society, and the range of punishments allowed by the *Qur'an* or the Sunnah. Ta'zir offenses include behaviors that do not rise to the level of a hudud offense, such as petty theft or unlawful cohabitation. This category of crime also includes behaviors that threaten the stability of society, such as bribery, or that violate important religious principles, such as the prohibition against eating pork.[30] For ta'zir offenses, more than for hudud or quesas offenses, there is an emphasis on using punishment to reform and rehabilitate the offender.

CRIMINAL PROCEDURE UNDER ISLAMIC LAW

The crimes and punishments emphasized by Islamic law are often very different from those in Western justice systems, but the procedures followed to carry out the law have much in common with those in both civil and common law systems. There is, for example, a strong sense of privacy underlying

Islamic law. Consequently, authorities must obtain a search warrant based on probable cause from the minister of complaints (not from a judge) or they must obtain the consent of the owner before they may search a home, a person, or letters.[31]

Islamic law also operates under the presumption that the accused is innocent until proven guilty beyond a reasonable doubt.[32] Consistent with this belief, in some Islamic societies people accused of crimes under Islamic law are not held in confinement while waiting for trial. In modern Islamic societies authorities are forbidden from using torture to force a confession from the accused. Further, the accused has the right to withdraw his confession at any time before the sentence is carried out. For hudud offenses the accused also has the right to remain silent, and his silence cannot be used against him in court.[33]

The presumption of innocence is accompanied by an emphasis on the fairness of the proceedings. Consequently, it has been observed that many procedural steps that Western societies would consider essential to fundamental fairness can also be found in Islamic systems:

> *The accused and his attorney are to be informed of the charges and the supporting evidence, and of any evidence in the possession of the prosecution that indicates the defendant's innocence. The accused has the prerogative of being present at all proceedings relating to the charges, is to be informed of what occurs at any proceeding that he or his attorney fails to attend, and is to be provided the opportunity to present rebuttal evidence to investigators.*[34]

At trial the accused has the right to a fair and impartial trial, to present a defense, to have an attorney to assist in his defense, and to appear before a competent judge.[35] In fact, it is a crime for a judge to intentionally issue an erroneous judgment, and the accused is entitled to damages in such a case.[36]

There is also a belief in equality before the law. The *Qur'an* requires that the law treat everyone equally, regardless of their income or whether they are Muslim or non-Muslim.[37] The concept of equality of the law is compromised in some jurisdictions in which non-Muslims may testify against other non-Muslims, but they may not testify against Muslims.[38] The concept of equality before the law does not always apply to equality between the sexes. In some Islamic systems, women are prohibited from being witnesses in criminal cases. An exception to this is that two women may testify in the place of one man where the charges involve extramarital sex.[39]

Affirmative Defenses: Those familiar with Western legal systems are also familiar with a number of defenses in which the accused admits to having committed the criminal act but denies legal responsibility. For example, the defendant who claims to have killed in self-defense admits to the killing but argues that the circumstances absolve him or her of criminal responsibility. Islamic law allows for many of the same affirmative defenses that are allowed under Western law, including insanity, intoxication, infancy, coercion, necessity, mistake, and self-defense.

1. *Insanity*: Islamic law recognizes the defense of insanity, and, as in Western law, insanity is generally based on the individual's ability to distinguish right from wrong. Some schools of thought will postpone a trial if the person is thought to be insane at the time of the trial, while for others the only issue is whether the person was insane at the time of the offense. Islamic law gives special consideration to the issue of mental retardation. In general, the mentally retarded offender is treated according to his or her mental age, not his or her physical age. That is, a mentally retarded adult with the mind of a 6-year-old child will be treated in the criminal law as if he were 6 years old.[40]

2. *Intoxication*: While consuming alcohol, and by analogy other drugs, is against Islamic law, there are different schools of thought about the criminal responsibility of someone who commits a crime while intoxicated. Some Islamic scholars believe the individual is fully responsible for any acts committed while intoxicated, others believe the individual is only responsible if the intoxication is voluntary, and a third group believes the intoxicated person cannot be held criminally responsible because he or she lacks the necessary criminal intent.[41]
3. *Infancy*: Like nearly all legal systems, Islamic law holds that someone under the age of seven cannot have criminal intent and cannot be held criminally responsible for his or her acts. Between the ages of seven and puberty the child has the same status as someone who is mentally retarded. Children at this age can be expected to make monetary compensation for damage they cause, but they will not receive the full legal punishment of an adult. In many cases, their families will be held accountable for their crimes. Finally, children who have reached puberty or older are treated as fully responsible for criminal acts.[42]
4. *Coercion*: Someone who is threatened or coerced into committing a crime will not be held legally responsible, providing the threat is real to them and the person making the threat is capable of carrying it out.[43]
5. *Necessity*: Islamic law, like Western law, does not hold someone legally responsible for violating the law if that violation was necessary to prevent some greater harm. Bahnassi cites the example of cutting off someone's leg to stop the spread of gangrene.[44]
6. *Mistake*: If someone injures or kills another by mistake, the person is generally not held criminally responsible for the injury or death. If that person mistakenly damages property, he or she may be required to compensate the victim for damages or to pay a fine.[45]
7. *Self-Defense*: The Islamic view of self-defense is very similar to that in most Western systems. Under Islamic law, self-defense is a natural right, but there are limits on its use. Self-defense can be used to prevent a crime when it is not possible that public authorities will be able to respond and when the person claiming self-defense uses only the force necessary to stop the crime.[46]

ISLAMIC LAW COURTS

Islamic law courts are presided over by judges known as *qadi*. These individuals are appointed by the ruler. They are almost always male and are expected to be intelligent, be knowledgeable about the shari'a, and have the highest personal integrity. *Qadi* not only administer criminal law but are expected to protect the weak, such as orphans and the mentally deficient.[47] The judge is assisted by several individuals, including a secretary who makes a record of the case and others who assist in such things as the division of property or in providing legal advice. Historically, the Islamic law court has been held in a mosque with the judge's back or front facing Mecca.

> *There is no direct appeal from the qadi's decision, but following the execution of the sentence, a defendant may appeal to the ruler. If the ruler determines that the defendant was wrongfully punished, the* qadi *will be removed from office and will be subjected to the same punishment that he imposed on the defendant.*[48]

In contrast to Western law traditions, Islamic law courts often limit the evidence admissible at trial. The greatest weight is given to eyewitness testimony, confessions, and religious oaths.[49]

CONCLUSION

In practice there are many variations on Islamic law. The *Qur'an* and Sunnah specify some offenses and penalties that to the outsider might appear to be both harsh and inflexible. However, the harshness of these penalties is generally tempered by the strict evidentiary requirements needed to obtain a conviction and in the day-to-day applications of these rules. Judges routinely find ways to reduce the penalties. For example, the hudud offense of extramarital sex requires four eyewitnesses, a difficult standard to meet. However, the judge may reduce the charge to cohabitation, a ta'zir offense with a substantially milder penalty.

Also, there are differences among Islamic societies in how strictly the laws will be interpreted. For example, some interpret the prohibition against alcohol to include only that made from grapes, while others include any form of alcohol.

This variation among Islamic societies and within the same society over time can make it difficult to provide a simple description that is both accurate and captures the essence of Islamic law. It is easy to get lost in the details that differentiate the laws of one Islamic nation from another. Even those who live under an Islamic law system may find themselves confused about what is allowed and what is forbidden. The situation is so complex that some Islamic nations have begun telephone hotlines on which people may call Islamic clerics with specific questions about what behaviors are allowed under Islamic law in their country.[50]

While there are many ways in which Islamic law can be interpreted and applied, there are basic ideas that guide Islamic law and that make it more understandable to the outsider:

- *All law ultimately flows from the Qur'an and the* Sunnah *and must be consistent with the teachings of Muhammad.* Thus, laws are a direct reflection of religious beliefs. Violating the law is not simply violating the will of the people, but it is violating the will of God.
- *While many passages in the Qur'an and* Sunnah *spell out offenses and punishments, these documents also emphasize compassion and forgiveness.* This compassion and forgiveness not only temper the apparent harshness of many Islamic laws but provide a religious justification for routinely making exceptions to administering the harshest of penalties.
- *Under Islamic criminal law, when judges are allowed discretion in sentencing, they must give the greatest weight to punishments that take into consideration the general public interest.* Punishments are not simply imposed for the purpose of demonstrating harshness but should ideally be used for the betterment of society. This may happen in a variety of ways, such as through compensation to victims or by serving as an example to others. For this reason imprisonment is a possible penalty under Islamic law but is not frequently used because it places a financial burden on society, keeps the individual from contributing to society, and exposes the individual to more hardened offenders.[51]
- *There is a considerable emphasis on the rights of individuals and on fundamental fairness in the process of justice.* Even at its harshest, Islamic law also strives to be fair and to provide those accused of crimes with a number of due process protections, including the right to be free from unreasonable searches, the right to an attorney, and the presumption of innocence.

Perhaps the most difficult aspect of Islamic law to accept without question is its treatment of women in general and in criminal law in particular. Even within the Islamic community this issue is a contentious one. Some view the treatment of women as oppressive, while others argue that the restrictions placed on women are for their own protection. In criminal law, Muslim women are forbidden from testifying in court for most crimes.[52] They are allowed to serve as witnesses in cases involving sex outside of marriage, but even here the testimony of two women is given the weight of the testimony of one man. In other matters of daily life the restrictions on women are much more severe. Under strict Islamic law women are not to work outside the home, are not to venture outside the home without their husband or a male relative, are to cover all parts of their bodies except for their palms and faces when in public to avoid arousing sexual desires in men, and are even to worship in a separate area of the mosque.[53] Further, women are only allowed to inherit half of the value of any estate that would have been left to a man. As Kristof and WuDunn note:

> *Of the countries where women are held back and subjected to systematic abuses such as honor killings and genital cutting, a very large proportion are predominantly Muslim. Most Muslims worldwide don't believe in such practices, and some Christians do—but the fact remains that the countries where girls are cut, killed for honor, or kept out of school or the workplace typically have large Muslim populations.*[54]

Kristof and WuDunn go on to note, however, that such attitudes often have more to do with culture than with religion. They also note that it is ironic that when Islam was created it was an important step forward for women, giving them rights and protections they had previously lacked. Some suspect that the influence of Western models of justice on the legal systems of Islamic nations will continue to grow, and as that happens Islamic criminal law will fall into disuse. Such a transformation would leave the *Qur'an* and Sunnah to serve as moral guides for behavior without the weight of formal law behind them.[55] However, there is nothing inevitable about this scenario. From the time of the Iranian revolution in 1979, which led to the creation of an Islamic republic, fundamentalist Islamic groups have grown in influence. In some countries they have come to dominate all levels of the justice system. Although these fundamentalists represent a minority of Muslims worldwide, there is nothing to suggest that movement will disappear in the near future or that other nations will not come to fully embrace Islamic legal principles. In Afghanistan, for example, the defeat of the fundamentalist Taliban by American forces led to an immediate loosening of restrictions on women, but over time many of those restrictions have returned because they reflect the deeply held beliefs of many citizens there.

For Americans, understanding Islam and Islamic law is important for several reasons. First, with the emergence of a world economy it becomes increasingly important that we be able to work with other nations and other cultures, and that requires the ability to work with other countries to pursue justice. That, in turn, requires being able to come to a common understanding about what is meant by justice and how it is to be pursued. As one example, U.S. efforts to reduce violence in the Middle East require being able to understand both Jewish and Muslim perspectives on the problem and their respective approaches to dispensing justice.

Second, as the number of Muslims in the United States grows, it will be increasingly important to understand Muslims' perspectives on justice. Non-Muslim Americans often have an incomplete and distorted view of the Islam religion and of the nature of Islamic justice. The absence of such an understanding sets the stage for prejudice, discrimination, and eventually acts of violence against Muslims.

DISCUSSION QUESTIONS

1. Islamic law views murder very differently from the way murder is viewed in either common law or civil law systems. In what ways might the Islamic perspective be a more just way of viewing murder, and in what ways might it be a less just way of viewing murder?

2. Islamic law lists seven hudud offenses. If you were to create a list of the seven most serious crimes that threaten the long-term existence of a society, how would the crimes on your list differ from those considered hudud offenses?
3. When you consider both crimes and procedures, which system would you consider more just—an Islamic law system or a common law system? Specifically, what makes one system more just than the other?

Endnotes

1. John L. Esposito, "Islam," in *The Oxford Encyclopedia of the Modern Islamic World*, John L. Esposito (ed.) (New York: Oxford University Press, 1995), pp. 243-254.
2. Charles Kimball, *When Religion Becomes Evil* (San Francisco, Calif.: HarperSanFrancisco, 2002), p. 50.
3. Pew Research Center, *The Future of the Global Muslim Population*. Report from the Pew Research Center's Forum on Religion & Public Life. Washington, D.C. (accessed online at www.pewforum.org, on 3 July 2013).
4. *Ibid.*
5. *Ibid.*
6. Ihsan Babgy, Paul M. Perl, and Bryan T. Forehle, *The Mosque in America: A National Portrait*, Report from the Mosque Study Project by the Council on American-Islamic Relations, Washington, D.C. available at www.cair-net.org/mosquereport; Internet; accessed on 26 June 2001.
7. Pew Research Center, 2011.
8. "Taliban Forbids Foreign Women to Drive, Defends Hindu Ids," *Chicago Tribune*, 1 June 2001, p. 3. After the September 11, 2001, attack on the World Trade Center in New York, American forces invaded Afghanistan and overthrew the Taliban. Despite this, many of the tenets of Islamic law persist in Afghanistan.
9. Philip Smucker, "Sudan Shows Signs of Erasing Its Enforcement of Sharia," *The Christian Science Monitor*, 14 May 2001, p. 7.
10. Farhat J. Ziadeh, "Criminal Law," in *The Oxford Encyclopedia of the Modern Islamic World*, John L. Esposito (ed.) (New York: Oxford University Press, 1995), pp. 329-333.
11. *Ibid.* For a general overview of Islamic criminal law, see Matthew Lippman, Sean McConville, and Mordechai Yerushalmi, *Islamic Criminal Law and Procedure* (New York: Praeger, 1988).
12. Bernard Weiss, *The Spirit of Islamic Law* (Athens, Ga: The University of Georgia Press, 1998).
13. Lippman, McConville, and Yerushalmi.
14. Abdullah Saas Alarefi, "Overview of Islamic Law," *International Criminal Law Review*, 9 (2009), pp. 707-731.
15. Lippman, McConville, and Yerushalmi.
16. Adapted from Table 2 of *Ibid.*, p. 29.
17. Norman Calder, "Law," in *The Oxford Encyclopedia of the Modern Islamic World*, John L. Esposito (ed.) (New York: Oxford University Press, 1995), pp. 450-456.
18. Alarefi.
19. *Ibid.*
20. Hussein Dakroub, "Muslim Cleric in Lebanon Bans Faithful from Smoking," *Chicago Tribune*, 7 June 2001, p. 3.
21. Taymour Kamel, "The Principle of Legality and Its Application in Islamic Criminal Justice," in *The Islamic Criminal Justice System*, M. Cherif Bassiouni (ed.) (New York: Oceana Publiations. Inc., 1982), pp. 149-169.
22. See Ziadeh.
23. Aly Aly Mansour, "Hudud Crimes," in *The Islamic Criminal Justice System*, M. Cherif Bassiouni (ed.) (New York: Oceana Publiations, Inc., 1982), pp. 196-201.
24. For example, see Agence France Presse, "Nigerian Girl to Be Lashed 180 Times," *The Christian Science Monitor*, 4 January 2001, p. 7.

25. "Taliban to Execute Converts from Islam," *The Christian Science Monitor*, 9 January 2001, p. 7.
26. See Weiss.
27. *Ibid.*, p. 156.
28. Lippman, McConville, and Yerushalmi, p. 50.
29. "UN Aide Says 'Honor Killing' of Women on the Rise Globally," *Chicago Tribune*, 8 April 2000, p. 8.
30. Ghaouti Benmelha "Ta'zir Crimes," in *The Islamic Criminal Justice System*, M. Cherif Bassiouni (ed.) (New York: Oceana Publiations, Inc., 1982), pp. 211-225.
31. Osman Abd-el-Malek al-Saleh, "The Right of the Individual to Personal Security in Islam," in *The Islamic Criminal Justice System*, M. Cherif Bassiouni (ed.) (New York: Oceana Publiations, Inc., 1982), pp. 55-89.
32. *Ibid.* Also see Ma'amoun M. Salama, "General Principles of Criminal Evidence in Islamic Jurisprudence," in *The Islamic Criminal Justice System*, M. Cherif Bassiouni (ed.) (New York: Oceana Publiations, Inc., 1982), pp. 109-123.
33. al-Saleh.
34. Lippman, McConville, and Yerushalmi, p. 65.
35. al-Saleh; Awad M. Awad, "The Rights of the Accused Under Islamic Criminal Procedure," in *The Islamic Criminal Justice System*, M. Cherif Bassiouni (ed.) (New York: Oceana Publiations, Inc., 1982), pp. 91-107.
36. al-Saleh.
37. Muhammad Salim al-Awwa, "The Basis of Islamic Penal Legislation," in *The Islamic Criminal Justice System*, M. Cherif Bassiouni (ed.) (New York: Oceana Publiations, Inc., 1982), pp. 127-147.
38. Lippman, McConville, and Yerushalmi.
39. *Ibid.*
40. Ahmad Fathi Bahnassi, "Criminal Responsibility in Islamic Law," in *The Islamic Criminal Justice System*, M. Cherif Bassiouni (ed.) (New York: Oceana Publiations, Inc., 1982), pp. 171-193.
41. *Ibid.* Also see Lippman, McConville, and Yerushalmi.
42. Bahnassi.
43. *Ibid.*
44. *Ibid.*
45. *Ibid.*
46. *Ibid.*
47. Lippman, McConville, and Yerushalmi.
48. *Ibid.*
49. *Ibid.*
50. Sarah Gauch, "Need to Know If *Koran* Allows Soccer? Call Islam Line," *Christian Science Monitor*, 6 April 2001, p. 7.
51. Benmelha.
52. Lippman, McConville, and Yerushalmi.
53. Weiss.
54. Nicholas D. Kristof and Sheryl WuDunn, *Half the Sky: Turning Oppression into Opportunity for Women Worldwide* (New York: Vintage Books, 2009), p. 149.
55. Weiss.

CHAPTER

8

Justice American Style

Any discussion of pursuing justice must take into account the criminal justice system. The previous three chapters presented very different approaches to structuring a criminal justice system: common law, civil law, and Islamic law. The systems outlined in these three chapters represent ideal types—models of justice that, in practice, are modified to fit the particular needs of a society. In any society the institutions, procedures, and personnel that make up the criminal justice system reflect the character of the country. A close look at a single system not only reflects the values that shape the country that uses it, but also highlights many contradictions the system must face.

This chapter focuses on the justice system in the United States, because America holds itself out as a beacon to the world when it comes to freedom, compassion, and justice. The discussion begins by providing a brief overview of the system and then turns to two examples of a contradiction built into the system. How those contradictions are resolved changes over time, reflecting changing concerns about justice.

As discussed in Chapter 5, the United States originally was culturally similar to England and had strong ties to the common law tradition. However, by its nature, common law is elitist. A small number of judges, none of whom were elected, made the law with their decisions. This was contrary to the democratic experiment fermenting in the late 18th and early 19th centuries. Shortly after the new nation was established, a "republican code movement" arose in the majority of states.[1] New constitutions placed greater emphasis on law making in popularly elected institutions called legislatures. This movement led the United States to drift away from a pure common law system and to draw in the elements of a civil justice system. Nonetheless, many common law traditions have remained to this day. For example, the American system relies heavily on precedent, using decisions in prior cases to make decisions where the written law might be vague, and appellate courts operate much as they did under common law. The American system, like other common law systems, is based on an adversarial system in which the prosecution and defense battle it out in court, while the judge sits as a referee making sure each side follows the rules.

Elements of the civil law tradition emerged as law came to be defined in statutes, a movement largely completed by the 1830s. Today, most laws are written down in statutes passed by the legislature, and courts are expected to follow these statutes. Judges may interpret the law, but if legislators don't like the interpretation, they may change the wording and compel judges to adhere to their wishes.

The contradiction inherent in the American system of justice reflects the basic definitions of justice: process versus outcome. America has historic antecedents in the common law tradition that emphasized procedure. The focus on procedure reflects a belief that orderly, predictable, fair processing will guarantee justice. This might be called "bureaucratic justice." Others care less for the process, but appeal to a higher law demanding a "transcendent justice," the righting of some wrong no matter how it is done. When President Reagan stood before a press corps, jokingly pointed his finger, and declared "Go ahead, make my day!" he was quoting a pop cultural character who in police movies believed that "the ends justify the means." As a rogue cop in San Francisco, "Dirty Harry" Callahan made his own justice outside the formal legal process. America's long tradition of vigilantism characterizes this mind set. When all else fails, citizens should take justice into their own hands, proclaim hundreds of historic examples. Hollywood latched onto this feeling when it produced a series of films, the first being *Death Wish*, in which an ordinary man obtains a gun and begins killing criminals after his wife and daughter were attacked. Such transcendent or abstract justice appeals to high emotions. The loved ones of homicide victims might not feel justice is done or emotions laid to rest until they have witnessed the execution of the murderer. Process becomes secondary to other feelings. In fact, a process that is too slow—for example, the passage of 20 years and countless appeals before the execution takes place—might get in the way of the families' perception of justice. Before we consider other examples of important contradictions, it is useful to first provide a framework and an overview of the system.

EFFICIENCY VERSUS INEFFICIENCY AND JUSTICE

The criminal justice system is part of a larger political system. Fair and efficient processing of offenders provides justice to the offender and to society. But the structure of the government does not always allow efficiency. First, a case can be made that the founding fathers did not want an efficient system. Many procedural obstacles were set up, largely in the Bill of Rights and subsequent case law, to keep the government from becoming too efficient. Furthermore, most founders of the U.S. justice system saw a diminished role for the national government. To them, government and justice systems functioned more effectively at the grass roots level.

Second, the nature of government in the USA shapes the justice system. America is a federal republic, which means there is a national government with its federal laws, police, courts, and prisons; fifty state governments with their state laws, police, courts, and prisons; hundreds of county governments with their ordinances, sheriff departments, courts, and jails; and thousands of town and city governments with their ordinances, police, courts, and lockups. Unlike a more unitary or a national system of justice, America seems to be fragmented into countless justice systems. Sometimes these different political divisions cooperate, but often they do not, and jurisdictional quarrels result.

Third, within various levels of government, there are many checks and balances. The cornerstone of the American political system is the system of checks and balances in which the executive, legislative, and judicial branches each have relative independence, while being expected to monitor the behavior of the other two. This system was designed to limit the power of the government, to make government actions tedious, and, in effect, to make the government inefficient. The executive branch might appoint high criminal justice officials, such as police administrators or prison wardens, but the legislative branch holds the purse strings and allocates or withholds money, while the judicial branch might determine the propriety of criminal justice actions.

Fourth, local criminal justice systems are constantly checked and held accountable by the larger system. Consider the following examples.

- Courts may limit the power of the criminal justice system by creating procedural law that regulates the process. The Miranda warning and various restrictions on search and seizure are examples.
- The police, who are part of the executive branch, must go to the courts for warrants, and the courts ultimately decide if the procedures followed by the police will be allowed in the prosecution of an offender.

- The legislature may curtail the power of judges to make decisions and to exercise discretion in sentencing by requiring mandatory minimum sentences.
- Governors and presidents can override decisions of the courts by granting pardons to people they believe wrongly convicted of crimes or whose punishments were thought to be too harsh.

Finally, citizens in the United States have a large voice in the way the criminal justice system works, though they might not always fully exercise their authority. Citizens elect mayors, governors, and presidents. They vote for legislators as well. More specifically, voters elect most prosecutors and judges in America. Citizen Review Boards, the watchdog groups that hold criminal justice agencies accountable, may threaten civil suits against the system. Membership on a grand jury or trial jury insures the layperson's check on the system. As the above discussion suggests, justice in America is a complicated thing. Attempts are made to ensure a fair process, one halted and obstructed by principles that guarantee some inefficiencies in the system. A look at the flow of the criminal justice system and several examples of tension between the quest for efficiency and the fear of it are illustrative.

OVERVIEW OF THE AMERICAN CRIMINAL JUSTICE PROCESS

The official criminal justice system adheres to a process. As long as that process is fair and impartial, as symbolized in the figure of a blindfolded goddess holding a book for reason and a sword for power, justice will be done. Such a methodical process not only insures justice, but also adheres to principles of efficiency. On the surface the procedure seems to be simple—a flow chart is always produced in standard introductory criminal justice textbooks—but there are a number of procedural checks to ensure accountability and to actually create inefficiency.[2] What follows is a simple outline of the justice process in America. Some basic contradictions related to the process are noted.

After a crime has been reported, an investigation occurs. Crime scene investigators and forensic scientists play an important part here. Rules of evidence dictate that the search and recovery of evidence must be done in appropriate ways. This notion of the "fruits of the poisoned tree," the idea that evidence obtained in wrongful ways taints that evidence, might lead to it being excluded at trial. Such a doctrine is a check on the police. Judicial permission, called a warrant, might be required prior to a search, adding to the labor of the police. Protection from unlawful search and seizure was so important to the framers of the Constitution that it was written into the Bill of Rights over 200 years ago. However, in the name of a more efficient process, numerous warrantless searches are allowed. Consent searches, searches incidental to an arrest, and most automobile searches are a few examples of warrantless searches. A considerable amount of law has evolved over the tension between bureaucratic and abstract justice related to search and seizure.

The disposition of the case follows. The disposition is a decision on how much resources are going to be put forth on a case. Some high profile crimes, such as murder, will get considerable attention, but others, such as robbery, might not. The police want a high degree of success, while still being economical with their resources. This means not all cases will be given the same work effort. Sometimes the differences in police effort have to do with resources. Other times they have to do with the amount of publicity surrounding a case. Some departments frequently "unfound" a case they do not want to work on. This means that they make a bureaucratic judgment that this crime did not actually occur. Such disposition decisions highlight the differences between process and outcome. Expending the most effort on cases with the highest probability of successful outcomes is contrary to the position that all crimes should be given equal treatment.

A follow-up investigation might lead to surveillance and arrest. Surveillance is spying and seems contrary to the American way of life. But it is an efficient way to collect evidence for search warrants or to acquire information for use in interrogations, arguments to force a plea bargain, and the prevention of further crime. While ordinary surveillance is intrusive, using electronic devices is even more so. Initially, there were restrictions upon such technology (in *Katz v. U.S.* in 1967, the Supreme Court proclaimed that the Constitution protects people, not places), but as crime became more prevalent, many restrictions were lifted. Another example has to do with arrests. Unless an officer sees a crime being committed or otherwise has strong probable cause to arrest someone, an arrest warrant is needed. A warrant is official judicial permission to make an arrest. Historically, when police conducted an arrest, it was important to make an "announcement." Officers had to proclaim who they were and the purpose of their presence. All citizens, even possible criminals, had the right to fair warning. Of course, the announcement took the element of surprise away from law enforcement officers and potentially put them in harm's way. Today, under dangerous circumstances, the original warrant might include a "no knock" privilege allowing officers to neglect making an announcement.

Another critical stage in building a case is the interrogation. Along with search and seizure, interrogation processes have generated considerable case law. In the name of efficiency, the police would like a confession. The entire system would operate more swiftly if only the suspect would confess and face his punishment. Historically, officers used physical force, the infamous third degree, to obtain admissions, until this was banned by the courts (*Brown v. Mississippi*, 1936). After physical abuse was prohibited, prolonged custody without access to friends or legal counsel was used until it was banned in the 1940s. In the 1960s, the U.S. Supreme Court defined interrogation as any questioning after an arrest, even if the questioning occurred on the crime scene or the back seat of a police squad car. Recently, considerable debate has arisen over the televised recording of interrogations, an innovation many police officers resist.

The case then goes to the prosecutor. Called the state's attorney or district attorney in some jurisdictions, the prosecutor decides to accept a case and proceed or to deny it (*nolle prosequi*). The prosecutor also acts as a check on police procedure, holding law enforcement officers accountable for their activities. At the same time, as a bureaucrat, the prosecutor seeks to pursue cases with the greatest odds of success. The decision to refuse a case because it might jeopardize a prosecutor's "conviction rate" might go against some people's notions of justice.

Initial appearance before a judge occurs next. Under the common law, the principle of habeas corpus requires people to be brought before a judge to determine the lawfulness of their detention. Issues of bail and right to council are addressed at this hearing. Justice requires that a person be protected from excessive bail. Of course, what is excessive for some might not be for others. Poor people are at a distinct disadvantage when it comes to bail. If a person cannot make bail and spends time in jail, there is a greater likelihood of being convicted later. Some people are considered so dangerous that they are denied bail. This is called preventative detention. In the name of process, propriety, and fairness, people who cannot afford a lawyer have counsel appointed to them by the court. This is achieved in several ways. There might be a public defender's office, while in other jurisdictions, a private attorney might be appointed. In an adversarial system, it is important that the defense attorney be at war with the prosecution. However, public defenders are actually part of the system, and the fees for a contracted lawyer come from the state.

A grand jury or preliminary hearing occurs in which the prosecutor seeks permission from a lay body (grand jury) or judge (preliminary hearing) to proceed. This step is another attempt to have laypeople or a judge check the system and hold it accountable. The prosecutor does not have to reveal all of the state's evidence during the grand jury or preliminary hearing, but enough evidence has to be presented to convince the deciding entity that the case should go forward.

Arraignment comes next, at which time the defendant stands before a judge, told of the charges, and asked to plead innocence or guilt. A majority of pleas at this time are guilty based upon a plea bargain, a bureaucratic way to get a conviction while avoiding a trial. Plea bargaining reveals the gap between procedure and outcome. The defendant, if truly guilty, might get a reduced punishment in the name of keeping the system running smoothly. In *Santobello v. New York* (1971), the Supreme Court declared the plea bargain to be constitutional and necessary. If every defendant had a full trial, the system would grind to a halt. If the accused pleads not guilty, a trial does result, however.

Before the trial begins, pretrial motions are given. Pretrial motions might seek to dismiss the charges, to suppress evidence because it was illegally obtained, to change the venue or location of the trial because of adverse pretrial publicity, or to obtain a delay of the trial called a continuance. Continuances, most often applied for by defense council, account for the largest number of delays in the adjudication process.

A bench or jury trial occurs. This is a highly ritualized ceremony during which the state makes its case and the defense rebuts it. Then the defense makes its case, and the prosecution rebuts it. Closing arguments by both sides summarize their cases. Historically, this process has lent itself to lawyers with oratory and theatrical talents more than to the importance of the evidence.

The judge offers instructions to the jury, and they retire to deliberate. In most felonies the jury's decision must be unanimous. On many occasions the jury might be unable to decide, and the case will be retried. On other occasions the jury might nullify. Jury nullification is when, in spite of overwhelming evidence to the contrary, the jury finds the defendant not guilty. They might do this out of collective ignorance or because they believe the person should not have been charged.

If there is a finding of guilt, a presentence investigation is conducted. The presentence report helps the judge determine the most appropriate sentence. Historically, judges have had considerable discretion in sentencing. Sometimes this led to sentence disparity, a process under which different judges looking at the same case gave different sentences. Attempts to regulate such sentence disparity have met with resistance from the judicial establishment. However, legislatures might require mandatory sentences as a way to limit such discretion and resultant disparity.

As punishment, most convicted offenders are required to pay a fine or to be released into the community on probation. Probation usually entails that the convicted individual follow certain rules, such as no alcohol consumption or payment of child support. Serious offenders or those with many previous convictions face incarceration in prison. Deprivation of liberty is painful to all those imprisoned. Here, too, there is a tension between bureaucratic and transcendent justice. Traditionally, incarceration was meant to reform the inmate. Old style penitentiaries and reformatories were set up to rehabilitate. Programs—be they religious, work, or educational—were created to treat and change inmate behavior. However, overcrowding made most of these programs and conditions ineffectual. Over time, "Truth in sentencing" laws demanded prisoners serve substantial parts of their sentence no matter the degree of reform. "Three strikes" laws sought to provide more severe penalties for habitual offenders, and "Civil death" measures permanently took away many of the prisoners' rights as citizens, such as voting or holding public office.

After sentencing, the convicted person might appeal to higher courts to examine the procedure of the system. Should the convicted person win the appeal, the original case will be re-tried.

This brief overview of the process shows the way in which the system is supposed to operate, as well as some of the obstacles that slow the process. Now we select two issues in American justice to further highlight the tension between bureaucratic efficiency and due process, described in Chapter 3 as a tension between due process and crime control.

ISSUES IN AMERICAN JUSTICE

The American justice system must accommodate strong contrasting forces that require speedy justice, while paying full attention to due process. While there are dozens of examples of this tension, the discussion in this chapter focuses on two: racial profiling by police and wrongful convictions.

THE POLICE AND PROFILING

The strongest and most powerful expression of government in civil society is law enforcement. The police have the power to inconvenience, take away liberty, and under certain circumstances, take life. Discretion, the necessity of making independent decisions on the street or tailoring justice to the situation, is an important part of policing. Ironically, the hallmark of any "profession" is the use of discretion. Lawyers decide which strategies to use in litigation, doctors decide which therapies to use in treatments, and professors decide what kind of tests to give in their classes. Police administrators try to eliminate or at least control independent officer discretion, but sometimes discretion is allowed by policy in the name of efficiency. This is best seen in the issue of profiling.

Informal profiling has been around for as long as the police have existed. Individual officers with years of experience developed "gut instinct" when crimes or suspicious behavior confronted them. But such profiling was unsystematic and inefficient. When a veteran officer retired, all of that occupational wisdom vanished, too. In the 1960s, more formal profiling emerged, and it played up its scientific credentials to establish legitimacy.

On the surface formal profiling seems to be scientifically based. It is built upon the **theory** that a group of behavioral, physical, or psychological characteristics, when brought together, can predict a person's actions or establish someone as the most likely perpetrator of a crime. It is based upon the assumption that criminal activities reflect the personalities of the offenders and that the offenders cannot or will not change their personalities. Criminal profiling uses attributes associated with a group of crimes, or **empirical** information, to develop a portrait of a likely culprit. Studying past offenses and behavioral patterns allows the profiler to **predict** the future. This makes the police process appear to be very efficient, as suspicion about a potential offender derives from science rather than hunch.

Formal profiling began in the 1960s with the problem of commercial airline piracy and hijackers taking planes to Cuba. In 1968, 18 American planes were hijacked, and the next year, 40 attempts were made, 33 of them successful. Specially trained U.S. Marshalls called "Sky marshals" were put on planes, but hijacking continued. A government task force came up with a profile of potential hijackers. Taking information on known hijackers, they developed a picture of a potential pirate. It was hoped that the criminal would be identified before boarding the plane. This approach did not work, and instead, all boarding passengers were required to undergo mandatory electronic screening before they boarded. By 1976, the number of hijackings of U.S. commercial airplanes decreased to four, a 90% decline from those of 1969.[3]

The more famous profiling has to do with serial killers. In the late 1970s and early 1980s, the FBI's behavioral sciences unit began to study violent people. The first attempt at profiling involved the case of Wayne Williams, the Atlanta-based killer of two young Black men. Williams fit the profile, although the profile itself did not lead to his arrest and conviction. The police believed he was responsible for 20 other killings, but he was never convicted of those crimes. In 1983, the Violent Criminal Apprehension Program was established. In 1987, the National Center for the Analysis of Violent Crime opened, and profiling was formalized. A serial killer profile was based upon interviewing those who had already been caught. In addition, officers who captured serial killers were interviewed. Using these interviews, the FBI created a profile to help apprehend serial killers as they became active.[4] Such a police technique captured the imagination of popular culture, but there is little evidence to prove its effectiveness. For example, serial killers such as John Wayne Gacy, Joel Rifkin, Jeffery Dahmer, and Theodore Bundy were captured without any notable input from profiling. In the Seattle area, the Green River Killer murdered 49 people from 1984 to 1988, but he was not captured for over a decade, after authorities received a tip from a relative.[5] In fact, one would be hard pressed to find a single serial killer who was caught because of a profile.

Also in the 1980s, profiling came into much wider use with the development of the "drug-courier" profile at airports. These profiles were much more similar to those aimed at hijackers than they were to the profiles of serial killers. Drug-courier profiles were less concerned with describing a perpetrator and more interested in predicting criminal activity. Given that so many of these profile characteristics could provide a basis for terrorist profiling today, it might be instructive to isolate them. According to the profile, a drug courier would most likely (1) pay for an airline ticket with a large amount of cash, (2) travel under a name different than the one under which their telephone was listed, (3) make a round-trip to a so-called drug-source city such as Miami, (4) stay in the destined city for a very short time, (5) appear nervous, and (6) not check any luggage.[6] Over time many drug profiles emerged, often based on completely contradictory criteria. A person could fit a profile if he was (1) the first to leave the plane, the last to leave the plane, or if he left in the middle group; (2) appeared too nervous or appeared too calm; (3) had too little luggage or had too much luggage; or (4) bought a one-way ticket or bought a round-trip ticket. A new government report in 2000 concluded that Black women were nine times more likely than White women to be X-rayed or forced to endure other intrusive searches. However, they were less than half as likely to be carrying drugs.[7] Of course, the possibility of an innocent person being inconvenienced and embarrassed is great. These profiling techniques were upheld by the U.S. Supreme Court in 1989 in *U.S. v. Sokolow,* but there are no reliable statistics to prove the technique's effectiveness.

Profiling on the highways has also become particularly widespread and controversial. This practice began in Florida in the 1980s to curtail the flow of drugs out of that state. Drugs were coming into Florida from South and Central American countries and were then being transported to other states by highway. Florida highway patrolmen made numerous successful stops and noticed "cumulative similarities" among the drug couriers. After stopping a driver on a traffic offense—all drivers commit some sort of driving violation every time they drive—Florida highway patrolmen used these cumulative similarities in the driver to justify a broader search. Some of these characteristics were the driver's demeanor, the vehicle not being registered in the driver's name, driving overcautiously, things that looked out of place such as a spare tire in the back seat, use of a large late model car, driving in the early morning hours, and drivers and occupants avoiding eye contact with officers. Unfortunately, this type of criminal profiling became racial profiling, as one significant attribute was the driver's race or ethnicity. Numerous state police systems began to use the Florida model. Even the Drug Enforcement Administration was impressed and began to fund and encourage the Florida model in something called Operation Pipeline.[8]

Just how successful is this highway profiling? Law enforcement officials think it is very efficient. But statistics indicate that "hit rates," the number of discoveries of contraband against the number of stops, are not significant. For example, in Florida, where it all started and was touted as most successful, the number of minorities stopped was astonishing. Research has shown that African Americans and Latinos made up only 5% of the drivers who used the I-95 in Florida. However, video tapes connected to troopers' cars indicate that minorities accounted for more than 70% of those stopped. When searches of the automobile occurred, 80% were directed toward to a minority.[9] In Maryland, African American drivers made up 17% of all drivers, but were 70% of those searched.[10] In both Maryland and New Jersey, Black motorists were five times as likely to be stopped on the highways as Whites.[11] A report by the American Civil Liberties Union in 1999 found that in Illinois 30% of the motorists stopped by state police were Hispanic, even though less than 8% of the state population was Hispanic. Studies of Philadelphia found that the police singled out minorities at least 71% of the time.[12] In Dallas, Texas, for every 50 White motorists stopped one was searched. With Blacks, the figure rose to one in 22. Hispanics underwent the most searches, one in 20. The "hit rate" for both Blacks and Whites was 10%. The hit rate for Hispanics was 6.5%.[13] Troopers found evidence on minorities they searched 28.4% of the time. They found evidence on White drivers 28.8% of the time.[14] Under a federal consent decree, the Los Angeles police department began recording and reporting their traffic stops in 2003. Blacks and Latinos were more likely to be stopped and searched. Of those stopped, 7% of the Whites were asked to step out of their car, compared with 22% of Latinos and 22% of African Americans.[15] The unstated argument was that minorities fit a profile of likely offenders. But "hit rate" information suggests otherwise. Minorities complained that they were stopped for the crime of "driving while Black" or "driving while brown." Justice—both bureaucratic and transcendent—did not seem to be served by highway profiling.[16]

Another form of profiling involves stopping people walking the streets. As early as the late 1960s, the Supreme Court allowed the police to stop and frisk, a pat down of the outer clothing of some suspected persons, for weapons in the name of officer and citizen safety. (*Terry v. Ohio*, 1968). However, when policy makers adopted more severe measures, such as those implemented by New York City in the 1990s, this stop and frisk technique became widespread and questionable as racial profiling. Using the social science concept called the "broken windows theory" the police went aggressively after low level crime and disorder in order to minimize bigger crime.[17] Extensive stops and frisks of ordinary citizens, mostly aimed at minority populations, in the name of efficient preventive police work occurred. In the strictest sense of the word, these were informal profiles based more on an officer's intuition than a checklist of characteristics.[18] Officials claimed that New York City became a safer city because of such practices. Many minorities did not think the city was so safe, especially after a young Black immigrant, Amadou Diallo, was shot and killed by New York City police. In 2003, the ACLU brought a civil suit against the Chicago police department for making racially biased stops.[19]

The gap in trust between the police and the minority population widened as Blacks were more likely to be stopped and frisked than Whites. Rational policing would expect a higher percentage of arrests of African Americans for carrying weapons since they are stopped more often. Researchers found that police made one arrest for every 15 Whites stopped on a suspicion of a weapons offense. Blacks had a ratio of one arrest for every 17.4 stopped. Latinos had a one for every 18 weapons stops ratio.[20] In other words, the "hunch" or racial profile was ineffective. Whites were less likely to be stopped, but were actually more likely to be carrying weapons. Courts have been reluctant to curtail police discretion and profiling. Still, five states have passed "DWB" (driving while Black) laws, and 24 others are considering such laws to limit the use of racial profiling by police.[21]

A similar situation existed in New York City, where crime dropped dramatically during much of the first decade of the 2000s. There were nearly four and a half million stops between 2004 and 2012, and the majority of those stops were of minorities. In 2013, a federal court ruled that the extensive use of stop and frisk by police in New York City was unlawful because people were stopped without any probable cause and because the stops disproportionately targeted minorities. The court also noted that, although Whites were more likely to be found with weapons or contraband, Blacks and Hispanics were more likely to be subjected to the use of force.[22]

September 11, 2001, saw the attack on the World Trade Center Buildings in New York City. Most of the hijackers were Arab. The following hysteria focused on a new victim of profiling, the Arab American. As might be expected, this ethnic profiling was widely accepted by the White population. In a new irony, however, the victims of previous racial profiling joined in to support the new racial profiling. Some African Americans remembered that Arab American taxi drivers often passed them by just because they were Black. One Black professional woman remembered how "Arab taxi drivers have passed me by too many times for me to feel much sympathy for them. Let them find out how it feels to be profiled."[23] A Gallup poll conducted in Boston found that 71% of the Black respondents favored special and more intense security checks for Arabs, including those who are U.S. citizens. Fifty-seven percent of Whites favored such a policy.[24] This issue is a key test of how many civil liberties Americans are willing to give up in the name of security. In 2013, some 12 years after the World Trade Center attacks, the issue of profiling Arab Americans continued when it was revealed that the New York City Police Department labeled Muslim mosques as terrorist organizations.[25]

The wisdom of profiling Arab Americans is further questioned by the observations in Chapter 10 that nearly three-fourths of terrorist acts that occur in the United States are committed by "home grown" terrorists, three quarters of whom are White. Focusing on Arabs or other people of color will lead police to miss some very dangerous people.

Profiling is a difficult issue, particularly in a country like the United States. When President George W. Bush was pressured to do something about the problem, his spokesperson, Ari Fleisher, commented, "It's not as if there's one federal police force, that the president can wave a magic wand and make a very difficult problem go away. It involves a lot of local jurisdictions that the United States government does not have direct control over. If it could be so easily done, I suggest that it would have been done a long time ago."[26] Profiling has some appeal because it appears to be a scientific way to spot offenders—a tool for improving efficiency. Although very popular, the success of profiling has been limited, and there are serious questions about whether the continued use of profiling can be justified. The efficiency it claims has not proven to be true, while it has shaken the belief of many citizens in the fairness of the system.

WRONGFUL CONVICTIONS

The American system of justice, with its emphasis on process and providing legal rights to the accused, can be incredibly slow. Trials can drag on for months, lawyers argue for hours over the smallest of details, and appeals may take years before the case is finally resolved—all in the name of making sure that justice is done. For the public the emphasis on process can be frustrating. Some people question why defendants who are obviously guilty should be provided a lawyer, why the convicted should be allowed an appeal, and why the entire process cannot move more quickly. They argue that "justice delayed is justice denied." In addition, the large number of cases faced by the criminal justice system each year puts pressure on police and prosecutors to quickly arrest and convict, and the pressure is particularly acute in high profile cases. Public defenders also face heavy caseloads and must resolve cases as quickly as possible. Thus, actors in the system struggle to resolve cases quickly, while at the same time following procedural safeguards.

Legal rights and procedural safeguards exist to make certain that innocent people are not convicted, and on the whole, it probably works quite well. There are exceptions, however, times when innocent people are sent to prison, or even executed. How often does this happen, how is it possible, and how does the system respond when these cases come to light?

How often does it happen? No one knows with any certainty. On the one hand, there are almost daily accounts of individuals who have been convicted and later exonerated, suggesting the actual number of cases may be quite large. On the other hand, the American criminal justice system handles millions of cases each year, and the percentage of cases in which someone is wrongfully convicted is probably quite small. One study conservatively estimated that wrongful convictions occur in only about one half of one percent of all criminal cases (0.5%), but given the large number of cases handled each year, this tiny percentage translates into about 10,000 wrongful convictions per year.[27] Whatever the actual numbers, the steady stream of revelations about wrongful convictions shakes public confidence in a system that relies on extensive due process and a strong presumption of innocence to prevent such errors.

The case of Illinois shows the impact that wrongful convictions can have on confidence in the criminal justice system. Republican Governor George Ryan, a man who personally supported the death penalty, first declared a moratorium on the death penalty and later commuted the sentences of all death row inmates in Illinois, after 13 individuals on death row were released because of new evidence of their innocence.[28] Death penalty cases undoubtedly represent only a tiny portion of wrongful convictions, but such cases stand out because of the brutality of the original crime and the harshness of the sentence. Such cases also represent the extreme in the conflict between due process and speedy justice. In death penalty cases, police and prosecutors are often under extreme pressure to solve the case, while it is in death penalty cases where we expect the full range of procedural safeguards to be in place. Between 1989 and 2012, there were 104 death row inmates exonerated for their crimes, and there were almost 500 people convicted of homicide who were later found to be factually innocent.[29]

How does it happen? There are a number of ways in which people who are innocent might be found guilty. A few of the more common reasons include: witnesses are mistaken, witnesses lie, police coerce suspects to falsely confess, laboratory technicians falsify reports, and prosecutors conceal evidence of innocence from the defense. Underlying all of these reasons is a failure of the system and an eagerness to bypass procedure to achieve justice as quickly and as easily as possible. As Huff, Rattner, and Sagarin have observed:

> *If we had to isolate a single, "system dynamic" that pervades large numbers of these cases [of wrongful conviction], we would probably describe it as police and prosecutorial overzealousness: the anxiety to solve a case; the ease with which one having such anxiety is willing to believe, on the slightest evidence of the most negligible nature, that the culprit is in hand; the willingness to use improper, unethical, and illegal means to obtain a conviction when one believes that the person at the bar is guilty.*[30]

The subsequent discussion follows the traditional pattern of considering several of the most common ways in which mistakes are made. As Westervelt and Humphrey persuasively argue, however, wrongful convictions are seldom the result of just one error. More commonly, mistakes at one stage ripple through the rest of the process:

> *For example, a poorly managed police lineup can lead to a mistaken eyewitness identification, which in turn can be used by police to pressure an innocent suspect into a confession. A prosecutor, relying heavily on the eyewitness and the confession, may choose to ignore or overlook evidence of the suspect's innocence and, believing that he or she has the correct person in custody, may choose to withhold that potentially exculpatory evidence from the defense. A jury, then, will hear only the flawed and incriminating evidence, not the potentially exculpatory evidence, and will most likely return a guilty verdict.*[31]

A compounding of errors is even more likely when the defendant is represented by inadequate counsel, as has happened in death penalty cases when lawyers sleep through significant parts of the trial, are obviously intoxicated in court, or never bother to interview witnesses or examine evidence.[32] Shockingly, the courts have generally held that such behaviors are not the basis for challenging a conviction.

One reason why an innocent person is convicted is *eyewitness error*, probably accounting for under half of all wrongful convictions.[33] While there is a tendency for the general public to believe there is no better evidence than the testimony of an eyewitness, in reality, eyewitnesses are notoriously unreliable. Witnesses can be rather easily persuaded to wrongfully identify a suspect and to genuinely believe this false identification. Anyone who has played one of many popular memory games knows how easily details can be forgotten. Witnesses often have only a brief look at the offender, and the trauma that accompanies a crime may further cloud a witness's memory. Consider the following example:

> *After serving more than 25 years in prison for the rape and murder of a 9-year-old girl, two Chicago men were released in January of 2003 after DNA evidence cleared them of the crime. They were convicted primarily based on the eyewitness testimony of a woman who swore she saw the girl being attacked just after 6:30pm. The girl's mother had said the girl left home at 8:00pm, but changed her testimony to say the girl left home at 6:30pm. She later said she changed her testimony to be consistent with the witness. The witness now says she never pointed detectives to the two men, who were teenagers at the time. Rather, she says police kept insisting the two teens were the offenders and she finally relented and agreed they must have been the boys she saw.*[34]

Experts often point to suggestive police interviews as a source of witness error.[35] In other cases, police act properly, but witnesses simply misremember. Whenever a false identification is made, the image of the falsely accused comes to be reinforced in the mind of the witness, so that as time passes, the witness becomes more and more confident in her (false) identification.

About half of the cases involve witnesses lying and providing false testimony.[36] One situation in which witnesses provide false information involves informants who provide information to the police in exchange for leniency or other personal gain. Jailhouse informants, for example, are individuals who share a cell or otherwise have contact with the defendant while in jail and then testify that the defendant admitted guilt in their presence. The use of informants has been harshly criticized because they are nearly always people of questionable moral character who have everything to gain and nothing to lose by providing false information.[37] "Of the thirteen Illinois death row inmates found to be wrongfully convicted and released from custody . . . five, or nearly 40%, were prosecuted using testimony of jailhouse informants."[38]

Official misconduct also plays a role in many cases of wrongful conviction.[39] Sometimes the misconduct is subtle. But, on other occasions, it is blatant, as when police or prosecutors hide evidence of an offender's innocence. For example:

- A police laboratory technician in Oklahoma City is accused of giving testimony falsely implicating defendants in a number of cases. In one case the defendant was executed before the misconduct was discovered and in another a man served 15 years on a 45-year sentence before being freed.[40]
- In March of 2003, the Justice Department revealed that as many as 3000 cases were being reviewed because the convictions may have been based on false testimony by technicians in an FBI laboratory.[41]
- Four county sheriff's deputies and three prosecutors in suburban Chicago were charged with conspiracy, perjury, and obstruction of justice in the wrongful capital convictions of two men, Rolando Cruz and Alejandro Hernandez.[42]

Finally, a surprising number of wrongful convictions (about 9%) occur because the individual *falsely confesses* to the crime.[43] Sometimes police pressure people to confess through long and grueling interrogations or even brutality.[44] Children, those with mental health problems, and those with low IQs are particularly susceptible to such pressure. On other occasions innocent people confess because they are facing a long prison sentence and don't want to risk going to court and losing. In Los Angeles, more than 70 cases were overturned after police admitted to planting evidence and lying in court. Of these more than 70 cases, the accused had entered guilty pleas in 55 cases.

There are even cases in which a suspect is coerced into confessing to a crime that never occurred. In Texas, for example, a man confessed to killing his ex-girlfriend, who later turned up alive in Arizona. In Arizona, a woman confessed to killing her three-month-old infant by letting another woman inject heroin and cocaine into the child. The child had died, but toxicology tests showed there were no drugs in the infant's system and that the cause of death was more likely pneumonia.[45] In Alabama, a mentally retarded woman was charged in the murder of her sister's baby, although no body was ever found, and no one ever reported having actually seen a child. She had her sentence reduced (but not overturned!!) when it was discovered that her sister had been sterilized several years earlier and could not have become pregnant.[46]

Furthermore, after a confession has been made, it is difficult for others to believe a recantation, or even to believe other evidence supporting innocence. In Illinois, a man confessed to a grizzly double murder. When he recanted and provided proof that he could not have committed the crime because he was in jail at the time of the offense, prosecutors proceeded with the case and persuaded a jury to convict.[47]

Just as disturbing as wrongful convictions is the official response when the error is discovered. While some prosecutors have worked hard to correct their errors, a disturbingly large number work hard to keep the wrongfully convicted in prison, or worse. In Missouri, for example, prosecutors argued before the state Supreme Court that new evidence proving the innocence of a convicted death row inmate should not stop the execution[48] because proper procedures had been followed leading to the conviction.

As the issue of wrongful convictions has come to public attention, there have been numerous efforts to identify such cases and bring legal challenges to their convictions. For example, The Innocence

Project at Yeshiva University lists 76 such projects in the United States alone and notes the list may not be complete. These groups often operate out of law schools, using law students to screen cases and gather relevant information. For the most part, the various innocence projects operate independently. One organization, however, seeks to shed light on the nature and extent of the problem by documenting wrongful conviction cases throughout the United States. The National Registry of Exonerations assembles detailed information about the wrongfully convicted.[49] To be included in the registry, the case must be one in which the individual has been shown to be factually innocent of the crime for which he or she was convicted. In other words, someone whose conviction was overturned because of procedural errors would not be included unless it also was clear he or she was completely innocent of the charges. The registry began in May of 2012, and by August of 2013, it had amassed detailed information about nearly 1200 cases. Periodic reports identify patterns in the data and document changes in those patterns since the first cases from 1989 were included. As might be expected, the most populous states—California, Texas, Illinois, and New York—contribute more cases than do other states. About one-third of the exonerations are based on DNA analysis, and the overwhelming majority of those exonerated are males. As might also be expected, the most common reasons for wrongful convictions are human factors, and sometimes more than one factor enters into a case. "For all exonerations, the most common causal factors that we have identified are: perjury or false accusation (52%); official misconduct (43%); and mistaken eyewitness identification (41%).[50]

Taken together the many examples of wrongful conviction rather dramatically demonstrate the dilemma of balancing expedient justice with a respect for due process. Too much attention to due process can bog down the system and make it almost impossible to convict the guilty. At the same time, too much emphasis on the quick and efficient resolution of cases can make it much too easy to convict the innocent.

Honest errors can occur in any system of justice, but the likelihood of error is also shaped by the structure of the justice system. Part of the problem of wrongful convictions is the adversarial process that characterizes the American system of justice.[51] In an adversarial system, the emphasis for both prosecutors and defense attorneys is on victory, not on truth-seeking. Prosecutors are rewarded for winning convictions, not for pursuing the truth.

CONCLUSION

The American system of justice draws heavily on the adversarial process characteristic of common law systems. One characteristic of such systems is a tension between expediently handling cases and affording the accused the full range of due process procedures. Because the tension between expediency and due process is built into the system, it is a tension that can never be resolved. Over time the American system of criminal justice moves back and forth between an emphasis on expediency and an emphasis on due process, never completely showing allegiance to either. For example, many Americans bristled at the sacrifice of due process that resulted from racial profiling, but those same Americans were quick to embrace racial profiling after the attack on the World Trade Center on September 11, 2001. Should fears of future terrorist attacks decline while abuses of profiling accumulate, public sentiment will likely again drift away from expediency in favor of due process restrictions on racial profiling.

Similarly, after a long period of restricting the rights of defendants and limiting appeals for those sentenced to death, the problem of wrongful convictions has led many to rethink the emphasis on expediency and move toward granting more due process rights. At some point, when examples of the abuse of due process have accumulated, the pendulum will undoubtedly swing again in the direction of expediency.

In the end justice comes neither from expediency nor due process alone, but from a careful balancing of the two. The numerous checks and balances on police, prosecutors, and judges are the mechanisms by which fine-tuning of the system is accomplished. The swing from one to the other over time represents an effort to reach that balance. Thus, the effort to create a just system of justice in America will never lead to a finished product, but will always be a work in progress.

DISCUSSION QUESTIONS

1. What are the advantages and disadvantages for justice of having citizens play a large role in regulating the justice system—such as by serving on juries, electing judges, and electing prosecutors?
2. What obstacles are thrown up to keep the American justice system from being too efficient?
3. Is using race to profile offenders always wrong? Are there any circumstances under which race-based profiling might be justified? Is there any way to stop police from using race as a factor when they decide which cars to stop on the highway?
4. What might be done to reduce the chances of a wrongful conviction, while still providing swift justice?

Endnotes

1. See, for example, William Nelson, *The Americanization of the Common Law: The Impact of Legal Change on Massachusetts Society, 1760-1830*, (Cambridge, Mass.: Harvard University Press, 1975) and Charles Cook, *The American Codification Movement: A Study of Ante-Bellum Legal Reform* (Westport, Conn.: Greenwood Press, 1981).
2. The number of introductory textbooks is considerable. I have listed just a few here. Jay S. Albanese, *Criminal Justice* (Boston: Allyn and Bacon, 2000); George F. Cole, *The American System of Criminal Justice* (Belmont, Calif.: Wadsworth Publishing, 1995); Larry K. Gaines, Michael Kaune, and Roger Leroy Miller, *Criminal Justice in Action* (Belmont, Calif.: Wadsworth Thompson Learning, 2000).
3. David A. Harris, *Profiles in Injustice: Why Racial Profiling Cannot Work* (New York: The New Press, 2002), pp. 17-18.
4. See as examples John Douglas and Mark Olshaker, *Mindhunter, Inside the FBI's Elite Serial Crime Unit* (New York: Scribner, 1995) and Robert Ressler, Ann W. Burgess, and John Douglas, *Sexual Homicide, Patterns and Motives* (Lexington, Mass.: Lexington Books, 1988).
5. Carlton Smith and Thomas Guillen, *The Search for the Green River Killer* (New York: Onyx, 1991).
6. Harris, pp. 19-21.
7. "Report: Customs Targeted Black Women Unevenly," *USA Today*, April 10, 2000.
8. Harris, pp. 21-23.
9. *Ibid.*, p. 63.
10. *Ibid.*, p. 79.
11. "Why Some Get Busted—and Some Go Free," *New York Times*, May 10, 2000.
12. "ACLU: Racial Profiling Threatens Justice System," *USA Today*, June 2, 1999.

13. "Police Sensitive About Being Profiled," *Chicago Tribune*, March 28, 2001.
14. Harris, p. 80.
15. "LAPD Offers 1st Data on Traffic Stops," *Los Angeles Times*, January 7, 2003.
16. Gary Webb, "DWB," *Esquire*, April 1999.
17. James Q. Wilson and George L. Kelling, "Broken Windows: The Police and Neighborhood Safety," *Atlantic Monthly*, March 1982.
18. "Why Some Get Busted—And Some Go Free," *New York Times*, May 10, 1999.
19. "ACLU to Bring Suit," *Chicago Tribune*, March 25, 2003.
20. Harris, p. 82.
21. "Courts Balk at Limiting Racial Profiling," *Christian Science Monitor*, July 6, 2001.
22. Joseph Goldstein, "Judge Rejects New York's Stop-and-Frisk Policy," *The New York Times*, August 12, 2013.
23. "My, Oh, My, Look Who's Profiling Now," *Chicago Tribune*, October 3, 2001.
24. *Ibid.*
25. Harry Bruinius, "NYPD Labeled Mosques as Terrorist Organizations, Report Says," *The Christian Science Monitor*, August 28, 2013.
26. "President: Profiling Will Be Under Review," *Ibid.*, February 10, 2001.
27. Ronald C. Huff, Arye Rattner, and Edward Sagarin, "Guilty Until Proved Innocent: Wrongful Conviction and Public Policy," *Crime and Delinquency*, vol. 32, 1996, pp. 518-544.
28. "Ryan: 'Until I Can Be Sure,'" *Chicago Tribune*, February 1, 2000.
29. The National Registry of Exonerations, *Update 2012: The National Registry of Exonerations* (accessed on line at: https://www.law.umich.edu/special/exoneration/Pages/about.aspx; on August 29, 2013).
30. Ronald C. Huff, Arye Rattner, and Edward Sagarin, *Convicted But Innocent: Wrongful Conviction and Public Policy* (Thousand Oaks, Calif.: Sage, 1996), p. 65.
31. Sandra D. Westervelt and John A. Humphrey (eds.), *Wrongly Convicted: Perspectives on Failed Justice* (New Brunswick, N.J.: Rutgers University Press, 2001), p. 10.
32. Adele Bernhard, "Effective Assistance Counsel" pp. 220-240 in *Ibid*. See Barry Scheck, Peter Neufeld, and Jim Dwyer, *Actual Innocence* (New York: Doubleday, 2000); Steve Mills, "Texas Case Highlights Defense Gap," *Chicago Tribune*, June 19, 2000; Henry Weinstein, "Judge Refuses to Intervene in Texas 'Sleeping Lawyer' Case," *Los Angeles Times*, October 29, 2002.
33. Ronald Huff, Arye Rattner, and Edward Sagarin, "Guilty Until Proven Innocent: Wrongful Conviction and Public Policy," *Crime and Delinquency*, 32, 1996, pp. 518-544; Rob Warden, "How Mistaken and Perjured Eyewitness Identification Testimony Put 46 Innocent Americans on Death Row," Center on Wrongful Convictions (accessed on line at www.law.northwestern.edu/depts/clinic/wrongful; on March 20, 2003); and Barry Schreck's *Actual Innocence*; The National Registry of Exonerations, *Update 2012*.
34. "When Jail Is No Alibi in Murders," *Chicago Tribune*, December 19, 2001.
35. George Castelle and Elizabeth F. Loftus, "Misinformation and Wrongful Convictions," pp. 17-35 in Saundra D. Westervelt and John A. Humphrey (eds.), *Wrongly Convicted: Perspectives on Failed Justice* (New Brunswick, N.J.: Rutgers University Press, 2001).
36. The National Registry of Exonerations, *Update 2012*.
37. Clifford S. Zimmerman, "Back from the Courthouse: Corrective Measures to Address the Role of Informants in Wrongful Convictions," pp. 199-219 in Saundra D. Westervelt and John A. Humphrey (eds.) *Wrongly Convicted: Perspectives on Failed Justice* (New Brunswick, N.J.: Rutgers University Press, 2001).
38. "Ryan: 'Until I Can Be Sure,'" *Chicago Tribune*, February 1, 2000.
39. The National Registry of Exonerations, *Update 2012*.
40. "Prosecutors See Limits to Doubt in Capital Cases," *New York Times,* February 24, 2003.
41. "3000 Verdicts Involving FBI Lab Reviewed," *Los Angeles Times*, March 17, 2003.
42. "Trouble for Officials in Cruz Case," *Chicago Tribune*, December 10, 1996.
43. The National Registry of Exonerations, *Update 2012*.

44. "Cops and Confessions: Coercive and Illegal Tactics Torpedo Scores of Cook County Murder Cases," *Chicago Tribune*, December 16, 2001; Richard A. Leo and Richard J. Ofshe, "The Consequences of False Confessions," *The Journal of Criminal Law and Criminology* 88 (2) 1998, pp. 429-496.
45. Leo and Ofshe, *Ibid.*
46. "Woman Freed Amid Doubt 'Victim' Existed," *New York Times*, July 18, 2002.
47. "When Jail Is No Alibi in Murders," *Chicago Tribune*, December 18, 2001.
48. "Prosecutors See Limits to Doubt in Capital Cases," *New York Times*, February 24, 2003.
49. The National Registry of Exonerations (accessed on line at: https://www.law.umich.edu/special/exoneration/Pages/about.aspx; on August 29, 2013).
50. *Ibid.*
51. Daniel Givelber, "The Adversary System and Historical Accuracy: Can We Do Better?" pp. 253-268 in Westervelt and Humphrey's *Wrongly Convicted.*

PART

Contemporary Issues

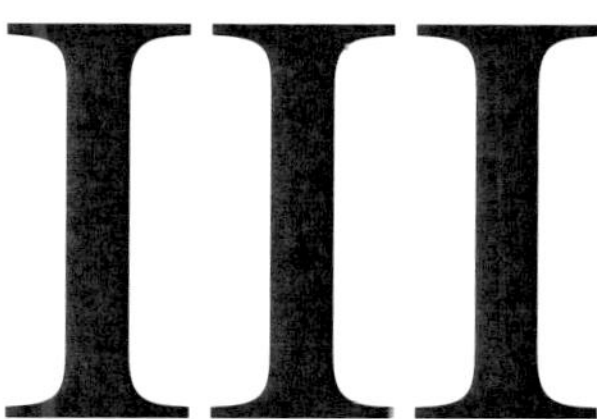

Injustice has been a constant throughout human history. In all places and at all times it is possible to find individuals or groups who have been wronged, and it is possible to find individuals who have committed themselves to correcting injustices. Thus far the book has considered some of the key perspectives on justice and some of the formal legal systems established to promote justice. This section of the book focuses on a few contemporary issues related to justice.

It is not possible in a single book, or even in a library of books, to comprehensively address all of the forms that contemporary issues of justice might take. The discussion that follows considers four issues that concern justice and that are of global concern. These issues were selected to represent a wide range of topics. This part of the book begins with a discussion of war and justice. Although there is some truth to the saying that all is fair in love and war, it is also true that over time rules have emerged about the proper conduct of war and about dealing with those who violate those rules of war.

The discussion of terrorism touches briefly on international terrorism but focuses primarily on hate groups and antigovernment groups in the United States. Although the discussion focuses on circumstances in the United States, the issue has far broader implications. Such groups are a problem in Europe, Canada, and nearly every developed nation. The violence undertaken by such groups is often engaged in under the belief that they are correcting injustices in society. Responding to these groups in a way that itself promotes justice is a major challenge.

What is known about contemporary slavery debunks the myth that slavery is a thing of the past. It is argued that slavery is more widespread today than at any time in history. Although the number of slaves in the world has increased dramatically, the form in which slavery appears is very different today. The problem is compounded by rapid population growth, abject poverty, and a global economy that demands ever-cheaper labor. In many ways contemporary slavery is more brutal and more insidious than slavery of the past—and more difficult to control.

Another contemporary problem is the issue of genocide. Like slavery, genocide appears more common than at any time in history. Advances in communications systems and in the technology of killing have made modern genocide substantially more efficient than genocides of the past. The promise of "Never Again," made by those who remember the Nazi Holocaust, rings hollow in many parts of the world. The discussion considers the factors that lead to genocide and ways that nations may intervene to stop the killing.

Finally, this section addresses the link between the environment and justice. The poor, many of whom are part of the minority, generate less than their share of toxic wastes. At the same time, they often live in the communities most polluted by industrial waste and in which toxic waste is stored. Although there are many dimensions of the environment that might be considered in a discussion of the environment and justice, much of the chapter focuses on the availability and use of water. Access to drinkable water is considered by some a basic human right, but as the world's population grows so does the number of people for whom clean water is not available.

The chapters in this section illustrate a wide range of issues concerning justice, and the complexity of responding to those issues to correct injustices. One purpose is to have readers begin to think of justice in broad terms and as an issue that touches on nearly every aspect of their lives.

CHAPTER

War and Justice

9

War—armed conflict between individuals, tribes, clans, nations, and empires—has been present for millennia. It takes many forms. Wars might be limited in nature or they might be "total." They might be internal, such as a civil war or insurgency. Or, they might be international, encompassing vast regions and taking place between nation-states. It is doubtful that there has been a period in history without war. Conflict seems to be part of the human condition. Some have argued that war is singularly human.[1] All animals fight for food, reproduction, and territory, but humans have organized and rationalized it. The rise of civilization is tied to war; similarly, nations often arise out of war.

There are those in the human family who thrive on war; either for personal reasons or out of national pride, these *warriors* seek out war. They become heroes in folklore, literature, movies, and video games. This warrior urge seems to totally overpower some. Quests for glory, geography, and wealth go back to the dawn of time. To these people war is necessary. Weapons become sacred symbols. Warrior inclination sees humans in negative ways. The enemy—its soldiers and nonfighting citizens—are seen as subhuman. Death and destruction in the name of victory are justified.[2]

On the other hand, there have always been those with a *pacifistic urge*, declaring war to be evil and avoidable and urging others to be active peacemakers. Historically, those who refused to fight for monarch or country were declared traitors, possible spies, and executed. Many religious persons—Jehovah's Witnesses, Quakers, and Seventh-Day Adventists, for example—refuse to wage war. The 14th Dalai Lama thought war should "be relegated to the dust bin of history." For many devout Buddhists and Hindus war is against their religious beliefs. Gandhi argued for peaceful disobedience. It was not until the late 20th century that these conscientious objectors were allowed to serve in nonmilitary capacities rather than being imprisoned or executed. Pacifists generally believe that war is evil and accomplishes nothing. They note that every war plants the seeds of future wars. For example, from 1816 to 1965 some pairs of nations seem to illustrate this tendency of one war leading to another: China and Japan, Great Britain and Germany, Russia and Turkey, Germany and Russia, and France and Germany.[3] These nations seemed to consistently square off against each other.

Teetering between these two polar extremes of pacifists and warriors are the *pragmatists*, those who detest war but recognize that it cannot be completely eliminated. They want to limit war and somehow regulate and legitimize it. It was this more practical pacifism that led to diplomacy between nation-states. This may be called the humanitarian urge. They are the proponents of a "just" war. With the possibility of nuclear devastation, these people feel the quest for a just war is even more compelling.[4] Much of this chapter deals with the efforts of this third group, those hoping to define a just and justifiable war. But it also shows how difficult that is to accomplish. To understand the move to create just and justifiable wars, it is helpful to first see the history of war and why it is so tantalizing for so many.

HISTORY AND THE IMPACT OF WAR

War was critical in ancient tribal cultures. Battle emphasized individual and clan pride. The Old Testament is as much a chronicle of war and nation building as it is religious development. Sumerian, Egyptian, Greek, Roman, and Asian civilizations were built upon war and warrior classes. Feudal Europe, with its knightly warriors, became nation-states due to conflict and conquest. Africa, the Americas, and Asia—though clearly having tribal conflicts sprinkled throughout their history—were subdued and dominated by European armies. With rare exception liberations of these colonies was by revolution and war. Most countries, as the USA's Revolutionary and Civil Wars attest, were radically altered by war. Though most wars are fairly localized, the 20th century's "world wars" suggest profound global dimensions. Devastating as past wars have been, history shows there has also been a commitment to conducting war as humanely as possible.

Although there is a tendency to emphasize the destructive nature of war, it is also true that war seems to have made profound contributions in many areas of human history. Politics and politicians have profited from war. The Bible's David created the state of Israèl through war. Julius Caesar, and those Roman leaders who followed him, created the Roman Republic and then the Roman Empire, sustaining it for generations through war. Russia's Ivan the Terrible and then Peter the Great created Russia with conquest. Napoleon Bonaparte did the same in France. George Washington, Andrew Jackson, Ulysses Grant, and Dwight Eisenhower became leaders in the USA due to their warrior reputations. Most U.S. presidents between 1865 and the twentieth century had been officers in the Civil War. Theodore Roosevelt used his reputation in the Spanish American War to political advantage. Although not warriors themselves, Abraham Lincoln in America and, later, Winston Churchill in England made their place in history because of wartime leadership. Some, like Mao Tse Tung and Ho Chi Min, restructured their countries through war. On the other hand, some leaders in history, like Lyndon Johnson who was diminished because of the conflict in Vietnam, have been undone by war. Obviously, people like Adolf Hitler brought ruin to themselves and their country by war.

War has an impact on a nation's economy, often benefitting the victors while devastating the defeated. Conflict is expensive, inspiring many factory owners to produce the tools of war. With men off to battlefields the home front industries stimulate full employment. Victors gain in new territories and resources, while losers have to suffer losses in land, reparations, and national pride. Those Americans, called loyalists, who supported the British during the Revolution, lost power and money and most fled the country.[5] The South, after the American Civil War, suffered economically for generations. Native Americans, after over 250 years of genocidal warfare, lost a way of life and cultural identity. Then they were relegated to rural confinement on reservations. The economic collapse of post-World War I Germany led to the rise of Adolf Hitler. America's economic depression of the 1930s ended with the Second World War. The postwar bump of America's economy in the 1940s and 1950s was due to the devastation of enemies and allies alike and the stimulation of the Cold War.

War inspires technology. Inventions of chariots in the ancient world and the crossbow in the Middle Ages shaped the outcomes of war. The butchery of battlefield hospitals gave rise to new medicines and medical techniques. In Vietnam, there was a 75% survival rate for the wounded. Thirty years later in Iraq, the survival rate was 90%. Poisonous gases, armored tanks, rapid-firing machine guns, and air bombardment were stimulated by World War I. Nuclear weaponry, which devastated two Japanese cities, arose because of World War II. The Cold War between the United States and the Soviet Union gave rise to an arms race and a space race. Now we have entered the era of "technowar" in which unmanned missiles and drone machines seek out and destroy the enemy.[6]

Popular culture is also affected by war. America's national anthem was penned at a battle site in Baltimore during the War of 1812. School children learned to pledge allegiance to the flag during the Cold War when the United States faced a "godless empire," the Soviet Union. Many pieces of great literature were inspired by war. Homer's *Iliad* and Thucydides' *Peloponnesian Wars* illustrate the point for ancient Greece. Julius Caesar's *The Conquest of Gaul* and Marcus Aurelius' *The Meditations* did so for Rome. Epic poems on Roland, Arthur, and Charlemagne romanticized medieval war and warriors. In the sixth century BCE, Sun Tzu wrote *The Art of War*, that became a classic for centuries. Over 1,000 years later, Carl Von Clausewitz's *On War* had a similar impact. *The Red Badge of Courage* by Stephen Crane captured the atmosphere of America's Civil War. Tolstoy's *War and Peace* became a classic about the Napoleonic war. Ernest Hemingway's *A Farewell to Arms* and *For Whom the Bell Tolls* talked of World War I and the Spanish Civil War. Finally, James Michener's *Tales of the South Pacific* and Joseph Heller's *Catch 22* used themes connected to World War II. One of the greatest oratories in history, "Pericles Funeral Oration" delivered in 431 BCE, praised the Athenian dead and extolled democracy. Lincoln must have been familiar with the ancient oration because his Gettysburg address, delivered at a battle site and praising the fallen, has remarkable similarities. Tchaikovsky's 1812 Overture commemorated Russia's victory over Napoleon. Numerous art works were influenced by war. Pablo Picasso's *Guernica* depicts the bombing of that Spanish town by Germans, leading up to World II. Hollywood has been fascinated by war. Nearly one-third of the 1700 movies made between 1941 and 1945 were war-related. From 1948 to 1968, over 1200 war movies were made. One of the greatest architectural wonders of the world, the Great Wall of China, was built because of the threat of war. Walled cities of Europe, modern tourist attractions, were a product of war and the fear of invasion.

War requires popular assent. As America's involvement in Vietnam showed, when the population disagrees with a war, the likelihood of success diminishes. This is particularly true if the goals of the war and the nature of the enemy are not clear. Propaganda plays an important role. If they are going to have to sacrifice health and wealth for war, the population needs to be convinced of the importance of the conflict. Propaganda's origins (from the root word propagation) were in religion. It was a means to spread the faith. Used effectively by abolitionists in the nineteenth century to garner support for ending the enslavement of Africans in America, propaganda became more powerful in the twentieth century. Largely due to the rise of corporate America and its need for advertisement, it became a permanent feature in modern life. The two world wars saw its use as a means to inspire popular support. It would take a separate book to catalogue propaganda techniques used in war. Wartime propaganda is relevant here because it reflects ethics and justice in warfare. Propaganda at best is exaggeration, at worst blatant lies. It appeals to latent racial and ethnic prejudice. Fear of the enemy or its ideology is created and emphasized. It places positions in black/white, either/or contexts. Any rational thinking is avoided. Managing information (disinformation) is critical.[7]

Just as it is important to manage information, it is also important to manage dissent. War is not tolerant of dissent. Every war leader not only wants to shape the public's views through propaganda but stifle those who raise objections. Those who question the war are thought to be treasonous. Even the most democratic societies stifle negative views and freedom of speech and the media are restrained. The French Revolution aroused anti-French feeling in the United States. This resulted in the Alien and Sedition Acts of 1789 prohibiting malicious writings and speaking against America.

During the Civil War, President Abraham Lincoln suspended *habeas corpus* (a legal request that the accused be brought before the court to challenge their arrest and detention) resulting in military justice replacing civil justice. The Sedition Act of 1918 restricted freedom of speech by making derogative language against the United States criminal. Even ministers who questioned the wisdom of the United States engaging in World War I risked imprisonment. Eugene V. Debs, Socialist Party presidential candidate, was sentenced to 10 years in prison for speaking out against military recruiting practices. In response to a series of anarchist bombings, a Justice Department roundup, called the Red Scare, resulted in hundreds being arrested and many deported because they were radicals. After the Japanese attack on Pearl Harbor, Hawaii, over 100,000 Japanese residents on the West Coast were put into 1 of 10 concentration camps in Arizona, Colorado, Idaho, Utah, and Wyoming.[8] As society developed, so did the arts and atrocities of war. Virtually every major philosopher weighed in on the perplexities of war. To name them all would be to write a history of philosophy. Because war seemed so tantalizing and unavoidable, there was a desire to legitimize it. This humanitarian urge became a body of principles on the proper conduct of war. Three broad categories might be used to discuss them. What were the reasons for going to war (*jus ad bellum*)? How was the conflict carried out (*jus in Bello*)? Finally, how were the vanquished treated (*jus post bellum*)? All of the thinkers, from ancient to modern, were reflecting the times and conditions in which they lived. Also, it should be noted, these ideas are values. They are Eurocentric. Unanimity could not be guaranteed if belligerents did not share the same values.[9]

JUST WAR DOCTRINE: GOING TO WAR

There are numerous reasons for a nation to start a war. They have alliances with other states that are threatened. Some want to extend their territories, feeling their racial or ethnic peoples should be united. Economics might lead a country to covet another's resources. Geographic closeness can lead to border disputes. Dictators, in order to solidify power and preoccupy their populations, will find war a good outlet. Historically, for dictators, starting a war was a good idea. However, the benefits of starting a war seem to have diminished over time. Before 1910, 80% of the wars were won by those who started them. Since 1910, however, only 40% of the instigators have been victorious.[10]

The ancient Greeks were some of the earliest to ponder the problem of war. Aristotle, the first to use the phrase "just war," talked about self-defense as the main reason to go to war. He did leave room to help an ally or to take vengeance upon those who have wronged the state. As the Roman Empire began to decline, Cicero argued that national honor joined with self-defense was a reason for war. Like Plato earlier, Cicero felt the ultimate goal of going to war was achieving a peaceful society.[11]

Early Christians, most notably Augustine in his *The City of God*, blended together Roman traditions and Christian principles. Like Cicero, he believed that the only purpose of going to war was to achieve peace but, staunchly Christian, he believed that fighting for Christianity was legitimate. Thomas Aquinas additionally thought national and individual sacrifice showed obedience to God. In the Middle Ages, starting in 1095, European invasions of Muslim-held territory in the Holy Lands occurred. The violent and widespread slaughter of Muslims (and Jews) by Christians came to be known as the Crusades. Aquinas felt such crusades, in the name of Christ, were justified. But because these crusades had been instigated by the Church, the question arose as to who had the authority to declare war. The *Decretum*, authored by Gratian of Bologna in 1149, was a religious attempt to regulate war.

Echoing Augustine's belief that war was fought in the name of peace, but reacting to the Crusades, *The Decretum* proposed that secular, and not religious authority, should instigate war. Of course, this was in keeping with the rise of nation-states. But it also gave rise to problems continuing into the modern day. What legitimacy does a host of "freedom fighters," rebels, and terrorists have in waging war? Clearly, declaring a "war on terrorism" gave legitimacy to those that philosophers concluded were not legitimate instigators of war.[12]

Most could agree that self-defense was a justifiable reason for going to war. But a range of other issues arose. First, had all peaceful means been exhausted? Such a principle gave rise to diplomacy as a feature of any national state. In more modern times, the rise of international organizations like the United Nations shows a desire to exhaust all peaceful ways to resolve disagreements between states. Second, had all reasonable concessions been made? In this calculus, short-term benefits run headlong into long-term ramifications. When Adolf Hitler made promises of peace to England and France for concessions in dismembering Czechoslovakia, short-term war was avoided. Devastating war followed shortly thereafter. Third, to what extent did the invaded country put itself into such a situation that war was inevitable? For example, though the United States was technically declared neutral, providing arms to England in World War II predisposed Germany to declare war on the United States. Japanese attacks on Pearl Harbor, Hawaii, starting U.S. engagement in the Pacific in World War II, seemed sneaky and unprovoked. However, did the American decision to cut off Japanese access to oil fields in Southeast Asia place Japan in a situation in which it thought it necessary to attack the United States? Fourth, what is the legitimacy of preemptive attacks? To what extent should a nation attack another to forestall greater threats later? The "Bush Doctrine" was used to defend a preemptive attack on Iraq in 2003. It was thought that the tyrant, Saddam Hussein, had and was about to use, weapons of mass destruction. He had used gas warfare on some of his population. Fifth, to what extent does humanitarian intervention justify going to war? In 1999, NATO sent troops to Kosovo to prevent a humanitarian catastrophe as a result of the genocide happening there (see Chapter 12). Lastly, there is the issue of proportionality. It is well established in the law that self-defense must be in proportion to the threat. So, too, should it be in war.[13]

JUST WAR DOCTRINE: CONDUCTING WAR

Once battles commence, war takes on a life of its own. The old saying goes that in war nothing goes as it is planned. But plans must be made and there are many levels at work. There are those high up who have ultimate authority for the conduct of the war. Kings, emperors, and presidents who lead the nation represent this level. Often these are military people who plan and execute the war operations. In some democracies, like the United States, civilian leaders are in ultimate charge. This can create tensions. President Abraham Lincoln had constant problems with his generals in the early stages of the American Civil War. President Harry Truman had so much trouble with General Douglas MacArthur that the civilian leader had to fire the military one. The next level would be the military leadership, those who advise the civilian leaders and carry out the war policy. The need for such military professionals gave rise to military schools. In the United States, special colleges and universities arose to train the officer class for the army, navy, and air force. These military experts operate from different viewpoints and in the name of "military necessity" want to twist and stretch any just war restraints. To them victory must be achieved at all costs. The last level would be the combat soldier. Survival and camaraderie are crucial and in the "fog of war" the boundaries of humane conduct may be crossed. A host of questions emerge about the conduct of war. Responses to them show the tension between the warrior urge and the humane one. This can be divided between treatment of combatants and noncombatants.

Combatants

One issue has to do with creating a corps of combatants. Some societies create a professional standing army. Others require all young males to spend 2 years in the military. America for a long time believed in the Cincinnatus Ideal, named after an ancient Roman general who returned home after his conquests, reshaped his sword into a plow, and took up farming. This is what is now known as the citizen army in which boys and men volunteer to fight for their country only to return home after the war is concluded. This model became firmly embedded in America's ideology and gave rise to selective service in which young men were forced into military service by a draft system. This was never very popular. In 1863, violent riots broke out in New York City as a reaction to the draft system. Massive marches showed displeasure over drafts during the Vietnam War. Since that war, the military has pursued a volunteer army policy.

Combatants are in harm's way; that is their job. Soldiers are meant to kill and be killed. But sometimes the means of killing becomes so grotesque that limits must be placed upon the tools of destruction. Because of the massive injury from lead bullets and hollow pointed bullets, the Hague Convention accepted metal jacketed missiles for military use in 1899. This not only made the bullets more accurate but made minor wounds less lethal. Poisonous gases had been used by the Chinese as early as 1000 BCE. Spartans used "noxious fumes" on Athens during the Peloponnesian War in the fifth century BCE, but it was the horrendous problems of poisonous gas during World War I that led to the Geneva Protocol in 1925. Sixteen nations promised to not use gas in warfare. The United States formally ratified it 50 years later.

Largely due to state propaganda and the passions of combat, enormous hatreds of the enemy are often aroused. Consequently, the taking and treatment of military prisoners is a critical issue. In ancient days, enemy soldiers were killed or enslaved. Most Roman gladiators were captured enemy soldiers. Throughout the Middle Ages, high ranking prisoners were ransomed and low ranking ones enslaved. During America's Civil War, over 50,000 soldiers died in prison camps. At Camp Douglas in Chicago, Illinois, 10% of its Confederate prisoners died in one winter month. In the South, at Andersonville prison in Georgia, 13,000 Union prisoners died. That was 28% of the total prisoners held there. Its commandant, Henry Wirtz, was convicted as a war criminal and executed in 1865. During World War II, 58% of the Soviet prisoners held by Germany died. Thirty-three percent of American soldiers imprisoned by the Japanese died. The Hague and Geneva conventions (1907), (1929), (1949), sought to protect captured military personnel from torture and inhumane treatment. Of course, most nations vary in adherence to these protections. Many criticize the United States for its treatment of imprisoned terrorists at Guantanamo Bay, a U.S. naval base, in Cuba.

Identifying the enemy can be a major issue. Wearing distinctive clothing, the uniform, was one way to ensure that one was fighting the appropriate enemy. Some soldiers might exchange uniforms of dead or captured enemy to dupe others on the battlefield. One problem in recent wars is the wide participation of citizens as warriors. Guerrillas and terrorists have always been problematic for conventional armies. During the Vietnam War, the Viet Cong was more troublesome to America's armies than North Vietnam's army. Terrorists in Iraq and Afghanistan were a major concern in those wars. Children have always been used as fighters. John Cook, a 15-year-old bugler during the Civil War, even won a Medal of Honor. Today many armies abduct young boys and girls and force them into combat. Myanmar, Sierra Leone, Colombia, and the Democratic Republic of the Congo have been active in sending children to war. The problem was so critical that the United Nations, in 2000, adopted the Optional Protocol on the Involvement of Children in Armed Conflict. Armed forces could accept volunteers less than 18 years of age but could not recruit them.[14]

Another area of concern has to do with soldiers being killed by their own. This "friendly fire" can be devastating and was so prevalent that the wearing of uniforms became common as a way to recognize fellow soldiers. Aerial and artillery bombardments during World Wars I and II frequently fell on friendly troops. Though the killing of officers by common soldiers in a collective mutiny or individual assassination goes back centuries, it peaked during the Vietnam War. All wars are demoralizing but the Vietnam conflict was particularly unsettling to soldiers. To claim an accident or lay blame on infiltrating enemy, the favorite device was dropping a fragmentation grenade near the intended victim, hence the word "fragging" used to describe the killing of a commanding officer. At least 230 officers were murdered by their own troops in Vietnam. Another 1400 deaths went unexplained.

Individual soldiers, caught up in the chaos of combat, needed to be held to high standards. Because most armies were largely male, sexual attacks on citizens were common. The Japanese during its "rape of Nanking" not only raped but supported prostitution for their soldiers.[15] American soldiers, after the invasion of Normandy, were accused of raping French women. In the invasion year (1944-1945), 151 death sentences for rape in France were given out.[16] Particularly in the twentieth and twenty-first centuries, females were allowed into the military. This resulted in revelations in the United States of female soldiers being raped by their comrades. In 2012, one governmental study concluded that 12,000 active duty women were victims of unwanted sexual contact. The following year the government announced that women could be in combat situations.

Finally, private armies, those outside the legitimate authority of the state, have long been criticized. Earliest philosophers wanted to keep private armies from going to war. In Medieval Europe, private armies roamed the countryside for hire. German mercenaries fighting for Great Britain during the American Revolution received severe criticism. Beginning in the late twentieth century, private businesses started offering services to military operations. Over eighty private military firms (PMFs) offer military services in Angola. Australia's military has outsourced recruitment to a U.S. firm called Manpower. Starting in the 1970s this industry has increased rapidly and today it operates in 50 conflict zones around the world. These private firms provide most support services for the U.S. Army. Halliburton, with one of its subsidiaries (Brown & Root Services), provides engineering, construction, food, laundry, mail delivery, and firefighting services, to name just a few. All of these were once provided by the military itself. Blackwater USA was formed in 1997 by Erick Prince in North Carolina. With the bombing of the *USS Cole* off Yemen in October 2000, Blackwater received a contract from the federal government. It trains Iraq's army and police force. In addition, it guards all officials in Iraq and Afghanistan and accompanies many convoys. Over 15,000 "corporate warriors" are in Iraq making PMFs the largest coalition partner of the United States. Many of these contract warriors get wounded or killed. Some carry out horrendous acts themselves.[17]

Noncombatants

Ordinary citizens have been exploited and brutalized throughout the history of war. Looting, rape, pillage, murder, and enslavement were common threads connected to all wars. Nonmilitary citizens were seen as supporting the enemy. Any hatred toward the enemy soldiers was easily transferred to the citizens. Old Testament Jews in the Kingdom of Judah, once defeated, were taken and placed in Babylonian captivity in the 590s and 580s BCE. A similar fate in the first century of the Common Era by the Romans led to the Diaspora, or their displacement and spread. The problem was so great during the Middle Ages that Pope Gregory IX came out with one of the most comprehensive statements on noncombatant safety in the thirteenth century. All priests, monks, friars, pilgrim's merchants, peasants cultivating land, women, children, and widows were to be protected from combating knights. But the tension between a just handling of citizens and the doctrine of "military necessity" remained. In one of the bloodiest wars in American history, the Civil War (or as it was called by the South the War of Rebellion), President Lincoln asked Joseph Lieber, a professor at Columbia University, to draw up a code of proper conduct for the Union troops. The Lieber Code became one of the earliest and most important documents addressing the suffering of noncombatants. Wanton violence toward civilian populations was criminal according to Lieber. However, forcing people to move from battlesites could be done. Destruction of property, in the name of military necessity, was not criminal.[18]

During war ordinary citizens suffer in several ways. No wonder that the Four Horsemen of the Apocalypse described in Revelation, the last chapter of the New Testament, are conquest, war, famine, and death. First, in war, more citizens are killed than soldiers. One scholar has estimated that 217 million citizens were killed throughout the world's wars of the twentieth century. Some were killed accidently or as "collateral damage." In World War II, when British and American precision bombings failed to hit their targets, they moved to carpet bombing in which entire cities and civilian populations were destroyed. Over 70,000 died during the firebombing of Dresden, Germany. A similar attack on Tokyo killed 100,000. In the name of military necessity, two cities in Japan, Hiroshima and Nagasaki, were annihilated by atomic bombs.[19]

Assuming all citizens are enemies, dangerous massacres frequently happen. Hundreds of men are lined up and shot. Genghis Khan swept across Europe and Asia massacring along the way. Protestant Huguenots were killed by the thousands in Paris by Catholics in the Middle Ages. The taking of Nanking, China, by the Japanese resulted in massacres. Native Americans were slaughtered by the U.S. military throughout the nineteenth century. Many more just disappeared, as in Latin and South America, in the twentieth century. Before they are killed many women are raped by invading troops. Massacres are not genocides. The former is killing to eliminate a potential combatant, the latter is to eliminate a culture. The Old Testament tells of the genocidal destruction of the Amalekites and Midianites in the second millennium BCE. Rome annihilated Carthage in a series of Punic Wars between 264 and 146 BCE. Though the Holocaust of the Jews by the Nazis has captured public outrage, numerous other mass killings have occurred. Pol Pot and the Khmer Rouge killed thousands in Cambodia. Rwanda in Africa was another example, suffering 800,000 deaths.

Second, noncombatants suffer from the results of war long after the battles. Forced out of ancestral lands thousands of civilians become refugees. Seeking asylum is an ancient fact of war. Cities of refuge are recorded in the Old Testament where refugees could flee. Ancient Jews experienced Egyptian and Babylonian captivities. In their diaspora, Jews were segregated into ghettos, the first set up in Venice in 1516. When Protestantism was outlawed in France in 1685 hundreds of thousands of Huguenots fled to England. In 2011, the major source of asylum-seekers is Afghanistan, the People's Republic of China, Iraq, and Pakistan. Concentrated in makeshift camps, these displaced peoples live in squalor. Disease, desperation, and death frequent the camps.

Third, if these refugees return home they find a land impoverished and dangerous. The tools and effects of battle remain behind. Land mines, explosive devises buried in battle zones, lie unexploded long after the war ends. Children and agricultural workers are particularly vulnerable. It is estimated that land mines kill or injure over 4000 people a year. Armies loot and pillage as they march across battle zones. Civilian victims of war lose their assets to destruction and theft. Bombs and battles destroy the countryside leaving people homeless and impoverished. Diseases attend all wars. Measles, influenza, tuberculosis, and sexually transmitted diseases traveled from Europe to the Americas with the Conquistadores. More American Indians died from European diseases than from musket balls.

Fourth, to lose loved ones and ancestral property to war and to live in constant fear and stress, takes enormous emotional toll. Citizens, just like soldiers, suffer from what used to be called "battle fatigue" but now is labeled post-traumatic stress disorder. Generations of survivors suffer the effects of war. How can humans condone and even participate in such violence and suffering?

"The Eighty Percent Rule"

Are there some people born evil and cruel? Indeed, there are a minority of people—usually, but not only, men—who are violent. But large majorities of citizens look the other way or even support violent behavior. Some scholars who study these things believe in the "80%" rule. According to this rule, given certain conditions, 80% of us would accept or participate in acts of violence. Ten percent would leave the scene or ask for other duties. Only 10% would actively resist such violence.[20] Dictators and violent ideologues intuitively know this and design plans accordingly. Ordinary people's emotions need to be inflamed to violence or cooled to passive acceptances. Such insight is important for two reasons. First, most of those people we see on TV newscasts who are yelling, burning, and destroying property are like us. Second, it urges us to understand the conditions that get people to slide into such violence. Some of these conditions are:

1. *Dehumanize the enemy*. People are portrayed as animals, less than human, or as some disease. By distancing oneself from the enemy they become easier to abuse.
2. *Conformity to authority*. Most people are conditioned to conform. Peer pressure is powerful. We are trained to respect authority. When strong authority commands and all around follow it is hard to resist. Ordinary men from Hamburg, Germany, were drafted to be Reserve Police Battalion 101 stationed in a Jewish village in Poland. These good men, prompted by higher authorities, massacred tens of thousands.[21] Later, in 1974, a social scientist, Stanley Milgram, carried out experiments where ordinary volunteers administered what they thought to be electric shocks to others based upon carrying out orders.[22]
3. *Bureaucratic and euphemistic distancing*. By erecting a division of labor, terrible tasks are divided so no one person takes part in all of the violence. Executors in America's penal system know this, and various aspects of the execution are assigned to different individuals. Using terms that cloud the act, massive killing becomes "cleansing"; citizen killing becomes "collateral damage"; massive firebombing becomes "strategic bombing"; and a holocaust deportation to death camps becomes "evacuations to the east."
4. *Altered states*. To do terrible things people cannot be themselves, they have to be changed in profound ways. This can be achieved in several ways. First, they need to take on a different look, such as face paint or camouflage, the cropped hair of U.S. Marines, tattooing, or scarring. Second, they have to have a different view of themselves. They must change from an individual to a member of a group instilled at a boot camp or some Al Qaeda. Frequently they take on new names, nicknames, *noms de guerre*. Wearing of masks or Middle Eastern keffiyeh or even dark

glasses frightens the enemy and creates a new persona. Third, using alcohol and other drugs alters the self-image and allows the warrior to do terrible things. A large problem, one that many returning American soldiers from Vietnam, Iraq, and Afgantanstan have had to address, is how difficult it is to undo this altered state. Lately, more U.S. soldiers have died of self-inflicted wounds than by enemy combat.

5. *Practice makes perfect.* The first act of violence is the hardest. Each subsequent act becomes easier and even pleasurable. Japanese soldiers in the 1930s and 1940s were forced to kill until it became second nature. They became desensitized. The purpose of taking captives was to have a ready group of victims for soldiers to bayonet or decapitate in front of fellow soldiers. By seeing peers doing it, new recruits would come along more quickly. Violence became a contagion.
6. *Hate and revenge.* One of the most powerful emotions is hatred. One can hate a leader, an ideology, an army, a race, and a religion. Such feelings can compel one into violent acts. "Displacement" of hatred is the shifting of rage to a weaker more vulnerable target when other targets are not attainable. Then there is self-hate, negative feelings toward yourself because of what you have become. Taking out on others the hatreds you feel for yourself is called "splitting." These feelings are inflamed if they are personal, if some violence has been done to you or your loved ones.
7. *Denial.* A powerful excuse for future violence is the denial of past and present brutality. Governments deny involvement in massacres and genocides. Such violence did not occur or they could not control it. Individual soldiers, those who raped and repeatedly killed citizens, deny their actions so often they begin to believe it themselves.[23]

When such factors are involved, these scholars of hate believe, 80% of all of us would resort to brutal violence. Often that hatred persists long after the battles end.

JUST WAR DOCTRINE: TREATING THE VANQUISHED

Post-war treatment of the defeated enemy can plant seeds for ongoing animosity and future conflicts. Often it shows the passions of the war persisting long after the battles. In addition, it shows the tension between the warrior and humanitarian urges. King David of the Old Testament had two-thirds of the entire Moabite citizenry executed after his victorious campaigns. At other times, the entire Jewish population was taken away to captivity. On the other hand, ancient Greek conquerors like Alexander simply incorporated the defeated into his empire and allowed them great autonomy. Rome treated its vanquished by forming the Roman Confederation and offering them Roman citizenship. Many wanted Napoleon executed after his defeat but others (particularly Britain) wanted him spared and exiled. Though Lincoln would have been more magnanimous, those who followed him treated the South badly. The old Confederacy was occupied for 15 years after the war and impoverished for generations beyond. Kaiser Wilhelm of Germany fled to Holland at the end of World War I. Ninety-one other German officials were tried at Leipzig but received minimal sentences. Germany did experience economic stress, as did many countries, but Hitler probably exaggerated the shame of the Versailles Treaty. After World War II the International Military Tribunal at Nuremberg tried 21 senior Nazis; 12 were eventually executed. In Tokyo the International Military Tribunal for the Far East tried hundreds. Eventually 920 were executed including Hideki Tojo, the architect of the Pearl Harbor attack. Emperor Hirohito was spared due to the work of General Douglas MacArthur. Post-war Germany was divided between the

United States and the Soviet Union and remained so for 45 years. Post-war Japan was occupied by American troops until 1951 under the control of General MacArthur, who allowed the country to be ruled by a Japanese government.

CONCLUSIONS

This chapter addressed the human problem of war. Conflict is part of human history. Such violence has impacted society in many ways. There is a warrior urge in all of us. For some it is an intractable part of their character. To others it is latent, needing to be inflamed by propaganda and societal pressure. It might be argued that the United States is a warrior nation. It is a nation that was conceived in war and whose national anthem was written about a wartime battle. The preservation of the nation was ensured by a Civil War coming some 84 years after its founding; the bloodiest war America has ever known.[24] Military mythologies developed to explain the conquering of the American frontier. No country's military spending comes close to that of the United States. America's spending accounts for just over one-third of military budgets worldwide. China and India are next in expenditures with China spending less than half as much as the United States and India spending only one-eighth as much. Further, since the start of World War II in 1941 the number of years in which the United States has been engaged in war has exceeded the number of years in which it has been at peace. To counter this tendency toward violence some peace seekers want an end to war. Even those who think in apocalyptical terms see eras of peace ushered in by war and chaos. More realistically, others want to control those passions that come with war. They want to seek a just war, a more humane war. It is those forces interacting that have characterized the human quest for war and peace.

DISCUSSION QUESTIONS

1. How has war shaped the political and economic fortunes of countries?
2. In the world of professional sports in the United States is there one that stands out as a metaphor for war?
3. Are humans naturally violent?
4. Why is paintball so popular in the United States?

Endnotes

1. See Dale Peterson and Richard Wrangham, *Demonic Males: Apes and the Origins of Human Violence* (New York: Houghton Mifflin, 1996), and David Livingstone Smith, *The Most Dangerous Animal: Human Nature and the Origins of War* (New York: St. Martin's Press, 2007).
2. Hugo Slim, *Killing Civilians: Method, Madness, and Morality in War* (New York: Columbia University Press, 2008), pp. 25-28.
3. Slim, pp. 31-33.
4. Jean Bethke Elshtain (ed.) *Just War Theory* (New York: New York University Press, 1992).
5. Maya Jasanoff, *Liberty's Exiles: American Loyalists in the Revolutionary World* (New York: Vintage Books, 2012), pp. 86-109.

6. See P.W. Singer, *Wired for War: The Robotics Revolution and Conflict in the 21st Century* (Yew York: The Penguin Press, 2009).
7. Philip M. Taylor, *Munitions of the Mind: A History of Propaganda from the Ancient World to the Present Day*, (Manchester, UK: Manchester University Press, 1990).
8. Geoffrey R. Stone, *Perilous Times: Free Speech in Wartime: From the Sedition Act of 1798 to the War on Terrorism* (New York: W.W. Norton, 2004).
9. Alex J. Bellamy, *Just Wars: From Cicero to Iraq* (Malden, Mass.: Polity Press, 2006).
10. Bellamy, pp. 121-126.
11. Bellamy, pp. 15-20.
12. Bellamy, 20-29; pp. 135-157.
13. Bellamy, pp. 158-179; 199-228.
14. P.W. Singer, *Children at War* (Berkely, Calif.: University of California Press, 2006), pp. 116-131.
15. Iris Chang, *The Rape of Nanking: The Forgotten Holocaust of World War II* (New York: Penguin Books, 1997).
16. Mary Louise Roberts, *What Soldiers Do* (Chicago: University of Chicago Press, 2013), p. 195, and J. Robert Lilly, *Taken by Force: Rape and American G.I.'s in Europe During WW II* (New York: Palgrave Macmillan, 2007).
17. P.W. Singer, *Corporate Warriors: The Rise of the Privatized Military Industry* (Ithaca, N.Y.: Cornell University Press, 2003), pp. 136-144.
18. Slim, pp. 12-13, 18.
19. Slim, pp. 37-70.
20. Slim, pp. 214-215.
21. *Christopher R. Browning, Ordinary Men: Reserve Police Battalion 101 and the Final Solution in Poland,* (London and New York: Penguin, 1992).
22. Stanley Milgram, "Behavioral Study of Obedience," in Nancy Scheper-Hughes and Philippe Bourgois (eds), *Violence in War and Peace: An Anthology* (Oxford, England: Blackwell, 2004), pp. 145-149.
23. Slim, 213-250.
24. See Richard Slotkin's *Regeneration Through Violence: The Mythology of the American Frontier, 1600-1860* (Middletown, Conn.: Wesleyan University Press, 1973). Also James William Gibson's *Warrior Dreams: Paramilitary Culture in Post-Vietnam America* (New York: Hill and Wang, 1994).

CHAPTER 10

Terrorism

The word "terrorism" brings to mind clear images of explosions and chaos. While these images may be clear in our mind, the term is far from clear and has been applied to a wide range of actions.[1] Bruce Hoffman has argued that it is important to distinguish terrorists from ordinary criminals.[2] In general, terrorism involves acts that are politically motivated. Terrorist acts are intended to make a political rather than personal statement and are not done for personal gain; these acts are seen by the terrorist as serving a higher purpose or greater good. Terrorist acts are also designed to generate fear beyond those who are the subjects of the immediate attack. As the name implies, terrorism is intended to breed terror, and, in the eyes of the terrorist, the more widespread the fear the better. Finally, terrorist acts are centered around the use or threat of violence. While violence is perhaps the most common and most effective tool of the terrorist, other nonviolent acts might be used. For example, hackers intending to bring down a country's financial system might easily be labeled terrorists if their actions had the potential to generate panic among investors.

For the sake of this discussion, there are three types of terrorism. First, *international terrorism* is that in which terrorist acts in one country are carried out by individuals from another country. The most noteworthy example is the September 11, 2001, attacks on the World Trade Center in New York and the Pentagon in Washington, D.C., in which nearly 3000 people were killed. The actions, in which 19 of the terrorists died, were planned and carried out by individuals from the Middle East and were said to be in response to U.S. policies in the Middle East. Some have argued that globalization has not only connected nations of the world economically and culturally but also has facilitated the rise of international terrorism.[3]

Second, **domestic terrorism** involves terrorist acts in which the actors and their ideology are from the country in which the terrorist acts occur. An example of this form of terrorism is in the April 19, 1995, bombing of the Alfred P. Murrah building in Oklahoma City, Oklahoma, in which 167 people were killed and hundreds were injured.[4] The act was carried out by Timothy McVeigh, a war veteran who sought revenge against the U.S. government for its actions against groups challenging the government.

Finally, **hybrid terrorism** is that in which citizens in the target country are swayed into action by a foreign ideology and often with the support of people in foreign nations. This form of terrorism is illustrated by the April 15, 2013, bombing near the finish line of the Boston Marathon. Three people died and 264 were injured. The act was carried out by two young American citizens who were said to have been influenced by radical Islamic beliefs and objections to the wars in Afghanistan and Iraq.[5]

International and hybrid terrorism are justifiably of great concern to both the public and government officials. It would be a mistake, however, to assume these two forms are the only ones worthy of concern. To the contrary, domestic terrorism happens many times more often than the other two combined. The National Counterterrorism Center estimates that globally domestic terrorist acts occur seven times more often than international acts.[6] For this reason, domestic terrorism is the primary focus of this chapter. This chapter also limits its coverage of domestic terrorism to that which occurs in the United States.

DOMESTIC TERRORISM

When Americans think of terrorism, they probably first think of foreigners entering the country to set off bombs or to engage in other acts of mass destruction. In reality, most terrorist acts that occur in the United States are committed by Americans, many of whom would define themselves as patriotic. According to the Federal Bureau of Investigation (FBI), between 1980 and 2000 there were 335 incidents of terrorism in the United States, and of these 247 (74%) were believed to have been committed by domestic terrorists, not by foreigners.[7] A study of federal terrorism prosecutions between 2001 and 2009 found that of the 804 prosecutions, U.S. citizens made up the largest group, with 273 offenders. Colombia was the next most frequent country of citizenship with 98 prosecutions, followed by Pakistan with 60 prosecutions.[8] As Jenkins has observed, "Americans have never needed instruction from abroad in launching the organized mayhem we call terrorism."[9] What is domestic terrorism? According to the FBI:

> *Domestic terrorism is the unlawful use, or threatened use, of force or violence by a group or individual based and operating entirely within the United States, Puerto Rico, or other U.S. territories without foreign direction committed against persons or property to intimidate or coerce a government, the civilian population, or any segment thereof in furtherance of political or social objectives.*[10]

Domestic terrorism presents a particularly interesting issue in the study of justice. Many who engage in domestic terrorism believe they are pursuing justice and are answering to a higher call. A democratic society is presented with the challenge of allowing free speech and free association while simultaneously identifying dangerous groups within its borders and preventing major acts of violence by them—and doing so in a manner that is itself just.

TYPES OF DOMESTIC TERRORISM

There are many ways to categorize domestic terrorism. This discussion focuses on three types: antigovernment, race-based, and religion-based domestic terrorism. As is true of any such categorization, there is a great deal of overlap among these categories. For example, some groups may have equal contempt for Jews, Blacks, and the federal government. The historical roots of the three categories are presented here separately to simplify the discussion. Examples of each in U.S. history will be presented, and then the focus will shift to their role in contemporary domestic terrorism, where more attention will be focused on how these categories overlap.

Antigovernment Terrorism

Antigovernment sentiments and antigovernment violence run through much of U.S. history. Before 1760, that is, before the Revolutionary War, there were between 75 and 100 riots in America, with as many as 40 of them efforts to overthrow regional governments.[11] The Revolutionary War itself was a fight against a strong centralized British government, and from the British perspective our founding fathers would have been seen as terrorists if that term were in popular use at the time. The nation that emerged was designed to have a weak federal government, keeping most power in the hands of state and local governments. Even this decentralized form of government was not enough for many early

Americans. Between 1750 and 1850, there were at least 20 uprisings by colonists who "emptied jails, burned public buildings, closed court systems, and organized their own government institutions."[12] In 1786, almost 9000 people took part in an uprising, known as Shay's Rebellion, against government-approved lending practices. This rebellion eventually became an effort to overthrow the government of Massachusetts.[13] Other rebellions occurred throughout the rest of the 1700s and through the 1800s, often arising in rural areas and spreading across the country.

Antigovernment violence continued through the early 1900s. In 1920, anarchists set off a series of bombs in eight U.S. cities, including one on the doorstep of U.S. Attorney General J. Mitchell Palmer. An additional 34 package bombs addressed to prominent Americans were discovered by an alert New York postal clerk.[14] Philip Jenkins vividly describes one antigovernment group, called the Christian Front, whose plot was uncovered in 1940:

> *The FBI smashes a dead-serious plot to overthrow the federal government and reveals that for more than a year the right-wing militias involved were undergoing army-style training, fired up by inflammatory talk radio. They planned to use their bombs, rifles, and machine guns to wage guerrilla warfare on American cities, and they claimed friends and allies in government and the military. They aimed, in one reporter's words, to "bomb selected buildings, seize public utilities, blast bridges, terrorize Jews, appropriate Federal Reserve gold, assassinate fourteen Congressmen, and set up a dictatorship." The goal: to remove all liberal and anti-Christian forces from government, not the least the liberal President and his activist wife.*[15]

In the late 1960s and early 1970s a left-wing radical group, the Weather Underground, advocated the violent overthrow of the government and was engaged in both militant protests and scattered incidents of bombing, including a bomb that exploded in the U.S. Capitol building.[16] In the 1980s, a right-wing group, known as The Order, underwent military-style training and engaged in armored truck robberies and counterfeiting in the hopes of raising money to stage a violent revolution.[17]

Perhaps the best example of how the thread of antigovernment sentiments has run through U.S. history is the case of Timothy McVeigh. On April 19, 1995, a fertilizer bomb exploded outside the Alfred P. Murrah Federal Building in Oklahoma City, destroying much of the building, killing 167 people, and wounding hundreds more. When he was arrested for his role in the bombing, McVeigh was wearing a T-shirt with a quote from Thomas Jefferson, who himself thought that to preserve democracy it might be necessary to have a violent revolution every 20 years. The quote, which was Jefferson's response to Shay's Rebellion, read: "The tree of liberty must be refreshed from time to time with the blood of patriots and tyrants."[18]

Religion-based Domestic Terrorism

From the time of the earliest settlers, America has had a history of religion-based hatred. The earliest hatreds targeted Catholics, later Mormons, still later Jews, and more recently Muslims. Coates made the following comment about the Catholic religion in early America:

> *Throughout colonial times Catholics were a tiny minority in the Americas . . . And their fellow colonists wanted to keep it that way. In 1704 the Maryland legislature enacted an "Act to Prevent the Growth of Popery," which imposed a heavy fine for attending Catholic religious services. In 1750 Harvard College offered lectures "for detecting and convicting and exposing of the idolatry of the*

Romish church, their tyranny, usurpations, damnable heresies, fatal errors, abominable superstitions and other crying wickedness in her high places." After the American Revolution, New Jersey incorporated in its state constitution a clause stipulating that Catholics might not hold state offices. Similar measures were included in the constitutions of North Carolina and Georgia in 1776. The 1777 Vermont constitution required all holders of state offices to swear they were Protestants.[19]

Public schools taught children about the evils of Catholicism and "Pope Night" festivals were held in which Catholics were depicted as in league with the devil. A popular game at these festivals was "Break the Pope's Kneck."[20]

In the early 1800s, anti-Catholic rallies were held, and rumors were spread that guns were hidden under the altars of Catholic churches to be used against Protestants. A series of popular novels described the secrets of life in a convent, which included the rape of young girls by priests, torture, starvation, and sexual sadism. The children born of these illicit affairs were said to have been killed and their bones bleached and collected in piles.[21] Nuns and priests were attacked, and in 1834 a mob burned to the ground the largest convent in Boston. For several decades, Catholic churches were vandalized, burned, and bombed. Some Protestant ministers saw the immigration of Catholics as a sign that Armageddon was near and gave sermons linking the Pope to the devil.[22] The inventor of the telegraph, Samuel F. Morse, published editorials in a New York newspaper warning about the Pope's conspiracy to take over the United States using immigrant Catholics as foot soldiers.[23] "When the Pope sent a block of Leonardo da Vinci's marble as a Vatican contribution to the Washington Monument, a nativist mob stole it from a shed and tossed it into the nearby Potomac River."[24]

A political party, the Know-Nothings, had a platform that was explicitly anti-immigrant, including a provision that no Catholic could hold any public office. At the height of their influence, "the Know-Nothings sent 75 members to Washington to serve in Congress and controlled several state legislatures,"[25] including the entire state government of Massachusetts. Through their political arm, the American Party, the Know-Nothings nominated former president Millard Fillmore as their presidential candidate in the 1856 election. Although he lost the election, coming in a distant third, he did receive 22% of the popular vote.[26]

By the early 1900s, large numbers of Jews were emigrating from Europe and were quickly added to the list of hated groups. During the 1920s, Henry Ford used the newspaper he owned in Detroit to print a series of essays titled "The Protocols of the Elders of Zion." The series itself was a modified version of a Russian manuscript though some believed Ford himself may have written it,[27] but it was more likely the work of the newspaper's editor, William J. Cameron.[28] These essays were then compiled in a book titled *The International Jew*, which claimed to describe a secret plan by Jewish leaders to take over America by manipulating the banking system and the media. Ford published additional copies of the document to be distributed at each Ford dealership.[29]

Race-based Domestic Terrorism

The third dimension of domestic terrorism that has run through the history of the United States is that based on race. The discussion here separates race-based domestic terrorism from the other two categories. That distinction is artificial but useful for organizing the discussion. Many of the groups that engaged in acts against religious groups also engaged in acts against racial minorities.

From the very beginning, colonial settlers made numerous attempts to wipe out Native Americans, killing them themselves, offering to pay one tribe to wipe out another—and then killing the first tribe rather than paying them—and even giving Indians blankets infested with smallpox. Native Americans also had their share of extremists committed to wiping out the foreigners who came to their land uninvited, and the violence of these extremists often matched that of the early settlers.[30] These attempts at mutual destruction continued until Native American tribes were either wiped out or segregated and brought under control on reservations. While both Native Americans and colonists were slaughtered, over the long term the advantage fell to the colonists whose casualties were quickly replaced by new waves of immigrants. In the end, violent colonists simply outnumbered violent Native Americans.

From the arrival of the first slaves, there were instances of behavior that clearly fit the definition of domestic terrorism. Domestic terrorist acts against Blacks became more organized with the formation of the Ku Klux Klan in 1865 by a group of Confederate soldiers in Pulaski, Tennessee. In 1867, Confederate General Nathan Bedford Forrest took charge of the Klan and gave it the organization it had lacked. The Klan arose to defend the Southern lifestyle opposed by the North—including clear ideas about the roles of Blacks in society. During its brief early history, it acted as a vigilante force, intimidating Blacks to keep them from voting, engaging in cross burnings, and conducting lynchings. Although Forrest attempted to control local units and coordinate their activities, his efforts failed, and the Ku Klux Klan became increasingly violent. The organization was officially disbanded by Forrest in 1869, but many of its activities did not end until 1871 when President Ulysses S. Grant ordered troops to help control Klan violence in South Carolina, resulting in the arrest of many Klan activists.[31] The sentiments that gave rise to the Klan did not disappear when the organization was disbanded. Some 30 years later, the Klan would reemerge.

The rebirth of the Klan in the early 1900s has been linked to two men. The first was Thomas Dixon, Jr., who had dabbled in Southern politics, having been elected to the North Carolina legislature when he was still too young to vote. He eventually left politics and became a Baptist minister and then a public speaker. In 1902, he wrote a book, *The Leopard's Spots*, about efforts to protect North Carolina from a movement to free Blacks and grant them equality. That was followed in 1905 by his most famous work, *The Clansman, an Historic Romance of the Ku Klux Klan*. The book, romanticizing the activities of the Ku Klux Klan and depicting Blacks as little better than savages, was a hit and was eventually turned into a stage production with Dixon himself playing a key character. More importantly, a young film director, D.W. Griffith, embellished on the basic story in the book to create the first full-length motion picture, an epic called *The Birth of a Nation*. The film was a lavish production, was scored by a 30-piece orchestra, and included panoramic battle scenes.[32]

It would be difficult to overstate the impact of *The Birth of a Nation*. As Coates observed:

> *In 1915, when a nickel bought dinner, a penny bought a daily newspaper and two cents covered a passable breakfast, The Birth of a Nation premiered in theaters that charged two dollars for a ticket. It grossed $18 million and was seen by an estimated 50 million people.*[33]

President Woodrow Wilson was said to have been touched by the film. The Chief Justice of the U.S. Supreme Court, Edward White, also gave the film his stamp of approval after making it known that he had at one time been a loyal Klansman himself.[34]

Two weeks before the film opened, William Simmons held a rally in Atlanta to celebrate the revival of the Klan, even burning a cross within sight of the theater. The film gave a great boost to Simmons' efforts, and Klan membership grew rapidly in both Georgia and Alabama. Then, in 1920, Simmons hired two publicists to take the organization national.[35] These publicists suggested that, to make the Klan appealing to a wider audience, the Klan should expand the list of groups it hated to include

Catholics and Jews. Both Catholics and Jews were immigrating to the United States in large numbers and including them would make the Klan appealing to Know-Nothings and other groups opposed to "aliens" of all sorts.

By the 1920s, the Klan had as many as four million members—electing governors in Oklahoma and Oregon and dominating Indiana politics.[36] The organization made an effort to reach out to fundamentalist ministers, with as many as 40,000 people joining the ranks of the Klan, many of them serving as local leaders.[37] Klan members in full regalia would recruit members during church services, after which they would make a contribution to the church.

The success of the Klan in the mid-1920s also gave them a visibility that led to news coverage of the violence supported by the Klan. Major groups began publicly denouncing the Klan. The position of the Klan further deteriorated when one of the most powerful Klan leaders in the nation, David Curtis Stephenson, was convicted for murdering a young White girl. By the end of the 1920s, membership had dropped to as low as 40,000.[38] In 1944, a substantially weakened Klan was dealt another blow when "its charter was revoked, the Internal Revenue Service placed a $685,000 tax lien on its assets, and the organization disbanded."[39]

From the late 1940s through the 1950s, the Klan was engaged in periodic acts of violence, but it seemed to gain a new energy in the 1960s, perhaps as a reaction to civil rights efforts. During the 1960s, Black churches were bombed and civil rights workers killed.[40] In 1966, a Congressional investigation led to the convictions of the leaders of seven major Klan organizations and the production of a report detailing the use of legitimate groups as fronts for Klan activity. Membership again declined, to as few as 5000 by 1973, perhaps as a result of an FBI program that targeted Klan organizations.[41]

From its low point in 1973, Klan membership gradually increased, and such leaders as David Duke began bringing young people into the Klan by recruiting on college campuses. Duke also welcomed women into the organization as equal members, and he welcomed Catholics.[42] By the 1980s, membership was again on the decline, and the organization faced lawsuits that threatened its existence.

The Ku Klux Klan remains one of the more visible examples of a group engaged in domestic violence with a focus on race. Although membership in the Klan has waxed and waned throughout the organization's history, it has shown a remarkable resilience and is likely to be a force to be reckoned with for some time. By the 2010s, the Klan had again bounced back to become a substantial force among American hate groups.

This discussion has included only a sampling of the more prominent cases, but the examples show that domestic terrorism has a long history in the United States. Indeed, it would be difficult to find any period in U.S. history when one or more of these three categories of domestic terrorism was not an issue. Our attention now turns to describing the contemporary face of domestic terrorism.

CHRISTIAN IDENTITY AS A UNIFYING THEME

Among domestic terrorist groups there has always been some overlap in the targets of their hatred. While there continue to be groups whose main focus is on the government, religion, or race, some believe that contemporary hate groups are more likely than those in the past to cooperate with other groups whose particular target for hate is unlike their own. The precise reasons for this are unclear, but one factor that may help unify these groups is an ideology known as Christian Identity. The Christian Identity movement has spawned Identity churches, but the power of the ideology is in its internal logic, which blends antigovernment sentiments with racism and religion-based hatred. Many of the ideas central to Christian Identity are familiar and comfortable to people who represent a wide variety of hate groups. Further, even if individuals do not buy into the entire package of Christian Identity ideas, elements of Christian Identity can be found in the beliefs of many of the most prominent domestic terrorists groups. And, as Coates observed:

> *Because it is a religion with all the traditional trappings, preached by Bible-quoting pastors from pulpits in churches very much like those most Americans grow up in, Identity allows its born-again men and women to practice with suddenly clear consciences the bigotry, hatred and even criminal violence that they had been taught from childhood were sinful.*[43]

The Christian Identity movement has been traced to a belief system known as British Israelism. British Israelism began in the 1600s and was characterized by the belief that the British were descendants of the 10 lost tribes of Israel. In its original form, British Israelism was neither anti-Semitic nor racist. When British Israelism moved to the United States in the 1930s, it began to take on its current form, which includes both extreme racism and extreme anti-Semitism.[44]

Christian Identity is fundamentalist in that followers believe the Bible is literally true and that their beliefs have a Biblical basis, but they are not to be confused with more traditional fundamentalist churches. However, because they use the Bible as the foundation for their hate, to challenge their beliefs is to challenge God, making it difficult to persuade members that they are wrong. They focus particular attention on the first and last books of the Bible, Genesis and Revelation. Genesis explains how things came to be as they are today, and Revelation shows what lies ahead. It is their interpretation of the Bible that sets Identity members apart from other fundamentalists.

According to Christian Identity our current "problems" began with creation. God created Adam and Eve in his image, and they had two sons, Cain and Abel. Abel was the fruit of a union between Adam and Eve and thus was created by God. All direct descendants of Abel are descendants of God's creation. Cain, on the other hand, was the product of a union between Eve and the devil, in the form of the serpent in the Garden of Eden. Consequently, Cain and his descendants are the products of the devil. Followers of Christian Identity believe that much of the world's history has been a battle between the "good" descendants of Abel and the "evil" descendants of Cain. The descendants of Abel eventually came to populate northern Europe while the descendants of Cain are the people we today know as Jews. When Identity members complain about the Jewish media, the Jewish control of banks, or the influence of Jews in politics they are expressing a deep concern about the devil taking control of major social institutions.

This interpretation of the Bible explains their hatred for Jews, but what about people of color? For followers of Christian Identity, people of color are not really people but are little more than animals. Some claim that people of color, who they refer to as "mud people," represent a first (and failed) attempt by God to create man. Because people of color are not really human, race mixing between "good" White descendants of Abel and people of color is akin to mixing species. Similarly, because Jews are the embodiment of evil, intermingling of Jews with "good" White Christians is also an abomination.

Identity followers also look to the Book of Revelation for a view of things to come. Their interpretation of Revelation leads them to believe the end will come through a great race war or through a war produced by economic collapse. The true children of God will survive and ascend into heaven if they are prepared to fight the forces of evil to the death—hence the appeal of Identity for some survivalists.

Drawing from the thinking of British Israelism, Identity followers believe that America's founding fathers were part of the true lost tribe of Israel, and they were guided to this country by God. Consequently, they believe the Declaration of Independence and the Bill of Rights are sacred documents, written under the direction of God. Amendments to the Constitution added after the first 10 are the product of a government that was infiltrated by agents of the devil. Their term for this corrupted government is Zionist Occupied Government (ZOG). As proof that the government has been corrupted they point to the number of Jews in policy-making positions in government, from the legislature to the President's Cabinet. They also point to such things as legalizing abortion. They believe that abortion is an attempt to breed the White race out of existence, arguing that it is most often practiced by Christian White women while people of color continue to proliferate. Identity's belief that Jews have taken over major institutions, including banks, is also palatable to conservatives living in the farm belt who believe that the lending practices of banks are designed to destroy the small farmer.[45]

Identity churches comprise only a small portion of the hate groups in America. A report by the Southern Poverty Law Center (SPLC) suggests that of the 1007 hate groups in the USA in 2012, only 54 were specifically identified as Christian Identity churches.[46] Beyond these relatively formal organizations, however, ideas from Christian Identity have made their way into the philosophies of many contemporary hate groups. What makes the ideology of Identity so powerful is that elements of it are appealing to members of many groups with widely differing orientations. It contains elements that are appealing to groups that emphasize antigovernment sentiments, to those emphasizing racism, and to those teaching anti-Semitism. These unifying themes may help explain why groups that at one time were at odds are increasingly working together. As Coates observed:

> *Under Identity, common ground is established for the first time between such normally antagonistic segments of the far right as the violently anarchist Posse Comitatus, which is out to end all governments, and the neo-Nazis, with their complex formulae for an extremely intrusive new government. Espousing Identity, Posse members and Nazis can join forces to oppose the ZOG establishment that each hates so thoroughly.*[47]

Thus, the influence of the Identity movement is likely many times greater than might be expected based only on the number of groups that define themselves primarily as Identity churches.

EMERGING TRENDS

Since 1981, the SPLC has routinely monitored trends and has issued reports concerning domestic terrorism. These reports suggest that domestic terrorist groups have been slowly changing over time. According to the SPLC, the number of antigovernment groups currently surpasses the number of religion- and race-based hate groups combined. The SPLC reports a dramatic increase in the number of these groups in response to the election of the nation's first Black president, efforts to enact strict gun control measures, and what they perceive as the government's efforts to suppress conservative government dissidents.[48]

Antigovernment groups have sharply increased in number. According to the SPLC, in just 4 years the number of antigovernment groups rose from 149 in 2008 to 1360 in 2012. These groups include antigovernment militias, antigovernment patriot groups, and various conspiracy groups that believe the government is planning to take away Americans' guns and is moving to create a one-world government in which the United Nations will "impose socialism on America and strip away private property rights."[49] Also included among these groups are those claiming to be sovereign citizens—those who believe it is "not necessary for most Americans to obey most criminal or tax laws."[50]

Among groups whose hatred is based on race or religion are the Ku Klux Klan, neo-Nazis, White Nationalists, Racist Skinheads, Christian Identity followers, neo-Confederates, and Black Separatists.[51] Since the terrorist attacks on September 11, 2001, there has also been a rise in the number of groups whose hatred is aimed at Muslims. The SPLC lists 36 such groups, including Aggressive Christianity, Bare Naked Islam, Christian Action Network, Jihad Watch, and the Sharia Awareness Action Network.[52]

The new century also saw the rise of neo-Confederate groups. As might be expected, neo-Confederate groups predominate in the South and rely heavily on symbols of the pre-Civil War Confederacy. Most neo-Confederate groups follow White supremacist ideologies and have a particular contempt for non-White immigration, affirmative action, school busing, and interracial marriage.[53] Neo-Confederates have actively sought leadership positions in Southern churches, espousing a theology that has much in common with Christian Identity.[54] Equally disturbing is the support these groups receive from elected officials. The Council of Conservative Citizens (CCC), for example, routinely publishes racist material and has members with links to such racist groups as the KKK and the National Alliance (a neo-Nazi group). The CCC also has a long list of national-level and state-level politicians who are either members or have spoken before the group, including 34 members of the Mississippi state legislature.[55]

Harkening back to the political party of the mid-1800s, the Know-Nothings, contemporary hate groups often include immigrants among the targets of their hatred, and they seem to have a particular animosity toward Latinos.[56] Contemporary hate groups have also targeted lesbians and gays. The Westboro Baptist Church became nationally known for celebrating the deaths of U.S. servicemen, which they saw as God's way of punishing the United States for its tolerance of homosexuality.[57]

There is also evidence of a growing sensitivity to environmental issues and globalization—issues traditionally associated with the political left. In his 1951 book, *The True Believer*, Eric Hoffer argued that the extreme left and the extreme right are closer to each other than either is to the political center—that it is easier to shift from one extreme to the other than to shift from an extreme to a moderate position. Trends identified by the SPLC seem to reinforce Hoffer's argument, suggesting that domestic terrorists are no longer drawing followers strictly from the political right.[58]

In recent years, hate groups have also made extensive use of technology to spread their ideology and recruit new members. The SPLC has identified more than 400 hate-based web sites. Hate groups have also used short-wave radio, broadcasting as many as 1100 hours of hate each month.[59] Finally, in an effort to attract youth to the movement, there is now a substantial business in hate-based music. There are at least 11 record companies that specifically produce and sell racist music.[60] Perhaps the best known is Resistance Records, a label specializing in youth-oriented hate-based music, which sells more than 50,000 music CDs each year.[61]

Domestic terrorist groups have traditionally been dominated by males, with women serving as support and occasionally forming auxiliary units. This, too, has been changing. Although men still hold most leadership roles, women are increasingly moving into these positions, and they are playing a more direct role in these organizations.[62] In addition, there appears to be an increase in the number of U.S. military, or former military, members who join hate groups.[63]

Over time particular organizations may come and go, and the particular targets of hate may shift from one period of history to another. Still, domestic terrorism has proven difficult to control and perhaps impossible to permanently eradicate.

JUSTICE AND DOMESTIC TERRORISM

How should society respond to domestic terrorism in a way that appropriately punishes offenders and deters acts of violence while also respecting freedom of speech and the right to peaceably assemble? There are no easy answers to this question, but several strategies have been tried. Beginning in 1964, the FBI undertook a program to

> *. . . disrupt and neutralize the KKK. This strategy involved infiltrating the Klan and included not only the use of informers and theft of Klan records, but also all manner of planted newspaper stories, rumors, and anonymous letters and postcards revealing Klan membership and accusing Klan leaders of everything from drunkenness, adultery, and misuse of funds to being informers for the FBI itself. By the 1970s, the Bureau claimed that one out of every six Klansmen worked for the FBI. This included at least one state leader, and there was talk of attempting to depose the United Klan's Imperial Wizard Robert Shelton and replacing him with an FBI informant.*[64]

While the FBI's program was effective in the short run, it eventually became known to the public and hurt the agency's credibility when it was revealed that it was also used against civil rights leaders. Further, the FBI's efforts may have set the stage for an organizational strategy that came to be known as "leaderless resistance," in which domestic terrorist groups work in small decentralized units of a dozen or fewer members. To protect themselves from police investigations, these units plan operations independently, keeping their plans secret from anyone not part of their small working unit. This strategy was advocated by William Pierce in his novel, *The Turner Diaries*, which some believe was a guide for Timothy McVeigh's bombing of the federal building in Oklahoma City.

One way to limit the spread of hate groups might be to penalize those who publish materials or make public statements advocating hate or questioning the legitimacy of the government. In many countries such speech is prohibited. In Germany, for example, it is a crime to display the swastika or other symbols of organizations that are banned by law.[65] Similarly, in Canada, it is a crime to make public statements that promote the hatred of any group.[66] While this approach may sound appealing, there are several problems with it. First, in the United States such restrictions are in conflict with the constitutional protection of free speech. There is probably no nation in the world with stronger protections for speech that most may find offensive.[67] Support for freedom of speech is deep and includes people from across the political spectrum, making it unlikely that banning hate speech will be considered constitutional in the near future. A second problem with banning hate speech is the lack of empirical evidence that it has much of an impact on the spread of hatred. Germany, for example, prohibits hate speech but continues to have an enormous problem with race-based hatred. We should not abandon our commitment to free speech without some evidence of what we will gain in return. Third, even if it is reasonable to ban speech that targets minorities or immigrant groups, it is another matter to ban speech critical of the government. As was seen in the Oklahoma City bombing, antigovernment sentiments are an important element of domestic terrorism. While repressive dictatorships often arrest or kill people who question the authority or integrity of the government, it is difficult to reconcile such a response with the principles of a democratic society. Finally, there is the issue of deciding what constitutes hate speech and what groups are to be included. For example, would it include Blacks who make derogatory remarks about Whites or Jews who make such remarks about Christians? Would making jokes about blonde women constitute hate speech?

Limiting hate speech may be appealing in that such limits make a moral statement about how society views such speech. However, the practical difficulties that arise from such an approach probably outweigh the benefits of making a clear moral statement.

Another response to domestic terrorism, particularly that aimed at minorities and protected groups, is the passage of hate-crime legislation. These laws provide for additional penalties if a crime was motivated, at least in part, by prejudice against a race, religion, or sexual orientation. In the United States, such laws did not exist prior to the mid-1980s, but since then they have proliferated.[68] In 1990, Congress passed the Hate Crimes Statistics Act, intended to keep a running count of the number of hate crimes each year. Unfortunately, neither hate crime laws nor efforts to keep track of hate crime numbers have proven very successful.

One of the biggest problems with prosecuting hate crime cases is that it is necessary to know not simply what someone did, but why they did it. Proving that an act was motivated by prejudice can be difficult, requiring the judge or jury to guess what was in the perpetrator's head at the time. Further, hate crime legislation seems to suggest that some victims are more valuable than others. For example, it suggests that killing someone during a robbery is less serious if the killer doesn't use racial epithets during the killing.

It is sometimes assumed that hate crime laws are designed to protect minorities, but this legislation has also been used against minorities. As many as 20% of hate crimes involve minority perpetrators and White victims.[69]

Deciding what offenses should be included is another complication of hate-crime legislation. Is the painting of racist or anti-Semitic graffiti a hate crime? In some jurisdictions, it is treated as a hate crime while in others it is not.[70] Although police agencies are encouraged to report hate crime statistics to the federal government, as many as one-third of the agencies do not report, and the consistency with which hate-based acts are reported appears to vary wildly from one police agency to the next.[71] The SPLC concludes that ". . . the system, already hobbled by the voluntary nature of reporting, is riddled with errors, failures to pass along information, misunderstanding of what constitutes a hate crime and even outright falsification of data."[72]

A final tool for responding to hate-based crime is to use the civil courts to sue organizations that promote race-based criminal acts (see also Chapter 14). The SPLC was formed in 1971 as a small civil rights firm. In May of 1979, it used a novel strategy for combating hate groups, taking the Ku Klux Klan to civil court and suing for monetary damages for the victims of KKK members' violence. This strategy has proven relatively effective against large organizations:

> *Center civil suits would eventually result in judgments against 46 individuals and nine major white supremacist organizations for their roles in hate crimes. Multimillion-dollar judgments against the United Klans of America and the neo-Nazi Aryan nations effectively put those organizations out of business. Other suits halted harassment of Vietnamese fishermen in Texas by the Knights of the KKK and paramilitary training by the White Patriot Party in North Carolina.*[73]

The strategy of taking hate groups to civil court holds promise and can be a useful tool for weakening their financial base. It is less useful, however, against small cells of domestic terrorists or against individuals acting on their own.

There is no magic formula for ending domestic terrorism. If efforts to stop domestic terrorism include infringing on basic legal rights, then the cure may be as offensive as the behavior it seeks to correct. Still, some of the strategies described here can play a role in chipping away at the base from which domestic terrorism arises.

CONCLUSION

Domestic terrorism is a part of the fabric of American culture. Hate-inspired acts against the government, racial groups, and religious groups can be traced back to before our country was formally founded. To say that it is ingrained in our culture is not to say it should be accepted and tolerated. It is easier, however, to label such acts injustice than to identify effective ways of responding that are consistent with democratic principles.

One of the ironies of domestic terrorism is that government efforts to control such groups may sometimes fuel the very behavior the government is trying to eliminate. While the government has a duty to respond to illegal activity, the nature of that response is crucial. Heavy-handed actions by the government may fuel further paranoia and extremism, and those who die in a conflict with the government may easily become martyrs.[74] For example, it has been argued that Timothy McVeigh set off the bomb at the federal building in Oklahoma City in response to the federal government's assault on the Branch Davidian compound in Waco, Texas—2 years to the day earlier.[75] Four agents for the Bureau of Alcohol, Tobacco, and Firearms (ATF) were killed and 20 more were wounded trying to execute a search warrant on David Koresh, leader of the Branch Davidians, for failing to register firearms. Six Davidians were killed and five were wounded, including David Koresh. A 51-day standoff followed. Then, on April 19, 1993, agents of the ATF and FBI stormed the wooden compound, arguing they could wait no longer because children were in danger within the compound and had to be rescued. A fire broke out, and when the smoke cleared, 76 Branch Davidians had been killed, including 25 children.[76] The government tactics used in the operation were questioned, and some thought government agents should be held directly accountable for the deaths. Such sentiments were particularly strong among those who, like Timothy McVeigh, already had a strong contempt for the government. For these individuals, the incident at Waco dramatically demonstrated a government out of control. Bombing the federal building in Oklahoma City would not only put the government on notice, but would serve as a wake-up call to all citizens. This scenario, of the government's response serving to fuel further acts of defiance, has been replayed on a number of occasions[77] and illustrates an irony. In responding to acts of injustice, the government may unwittingly sow the seeds for further violence. While the discussion in this chapter focuses on domestic terrorism, the implications for international terrorism are clear. The government's response to terrorism must be perceived as just. If it is not, the government's response will only fuel more terrorism.

DISCUSSION QUESTIONS

1. How do you respond to someone who looks back through history and concludes that hate groups are a natural part of American society?
2. How has technology facilitated the spread of hate groups?
3. What are some of the problems with trying to make hate speech a crime?

Endnotes

1. Sometimes the application of the term is taken to the absurd. For example, in Tennessee an official from the Tennessee Department of Environment and Conservation told a citizen that complaining about the quality of the water without scientific proof to back up the claim could be considered an act of terrorism. Brian Hass

"Official: Water Complaints Could Be 'Act of Terrorism.'" *The Tennessean* (electronic edition) (accessed online at www.tennessean.com on June 21, 2013).

2. Bruce Hoffman, *Inside Terrorism* (New York: Columbia University Press, 1998).
3. Audrey Kurth Cronin, "Behind the Curve: Globalization and International Terrorism," in *Terrorism and Counterterrorism*, 4th ed., Russell D. Howard and Bruce Hoffman (eds.). (New York: McGraw-Hill, 2012), pp. 57-78.
4. Kenneth S. Stern, *A Force Upon the Plain: The American Militia Movement and the Politics of Hate* (New York: Simon & Schuster, 1996).
5. Scott Wilson, Greg Miller, and Sari Horwitz, "Boston Bombing Suspect Cites U.S. Wars as Motivation, Officials Say," *The Washington Post* (electronic edition) (accessed online at www.washingtonpost.com on 20 June 2013).
6. National Counterterrorism Center, *2008 Report on Terrorism* (accessed online at www.nctc.gov on 20 June 2013).
7. Dale L. Watson, *The Terrorist Threat Confronting the United States*, Testimony before the Senate Select Committee on Intelligence, Washington, D.C., 6 February 2002 (available at www.fbi.gov/congress/congress02/watson020602.htm; accessed on 23 April 2002).
8. *The Terrorist Trial Report Card, 2001-2009*, The Center on Law and Security, New York University School of Law. January 2010, p. 20 (accessed on-line at: www.lawandsecurity.org/Portals/0/documents/02_TTRCFinalJan142.pdf on June 20, 2013).
9. Philip Jenkins, "Home-Grown Terror," *American Heritage*, September 1995, p. 40.
10. Federal Bureau of Investigation, *National Security Programs* (available at www.fbi.gov/contact/fo/sanfran/sanfran/sfnatsec.htm; Internet; accessed on 23 April 2002).
11. Catherine McNicol Stock, *Rural Radicals: Righteous Rage in the American Grain* (Ithaca, N.Y.: Cornell University Press, 1996).
12. *Ibid.*, p. 18.
13. *Ibid.* Also see Samuel Eliot Morison, *The Oxford History of the American People* (New York: Oxford University Press, 1965).
14. Samuel Walker, *In Defense of American Liberties: A History of the ACU* (New York: Oxford University Press, 1990).
15. Jenkins, pp. 38-39.
16. For an excellent history of this movement, see Ron Jacobs, *The Way the Wind Blew: A History of the Weather Underground* (New York: Verso, 1997).
17. A thorough account of this group is in Kevin Flynn and Gary Gerhardt, *The Silent Brotherhood: Inside America's Racist Underground* (New York: The Free Press, 1989).
18. Cited in Garry Wills, *A Necessary Evil: A History of American Distrust of Government* (New York: Simon & Schuster, 1999), p. 205.
19. James Coates, *Armed and Dangerous: The Rise of the Survivalist Right* (New York: The Noonday Press, 1987), p. 22.
20. A good overview of the evolution of hate in America is David Bennett, *The Party of Fear: The American Far Right from Nativism to the Militia Movement* (revised and updated edition) (New York: Vintage Books, 1995).
21. *Ibid.*
22. Coates
23. *Ibid.*
24. *Ibid.*, p. 24.
25. *Ibid.*, p. 28.
26. Bennett
27. Morison

28. An excellent review of this topic is in Michael Barkun, *Religion and the Racist Right: The Origins of the Christian Identity Movement* (Chapel Hill, N.C.: The University of North Carolina Press, 1994).
29. Coates
30. John George and Laird Wilcox, *American Extremists: Militias, Supremacists, Klansmen, Communists, & Others* (Amherst, N.Y.: Prometheus Books, 1996).
31. David M. Chalmers, *Hooded Americanism: The History of the Ku Klux Klan* (New York: New Viewpoints, 1981); James Ridgeway, *Blood in the Face: The Ku Klux Klan, Aryan Nations, Nazi Skinheads, and the Rise of a New White Culture* (New York: Thunder's Mouth Press, 1990).
32. Chalmers
33. Coates, p. 31.
34. Chalmers
35. Coates
36. Morison
37. Ridgeway
38. *Ibid.*
39. George and Wilcox
40. *Ibid.*
41. *Ibid.*
42. *Ibid.*
43. Coates, p. 81.
44. Barkun
45. For troublesome predictions about the future, see Joel Dyer, *Harvest of Rage: Why Oklahoma City Is Only the Beginning* (Boulder, Colo.: Westview Press, 1997).
46. "Active Hate Groups in the United States in 2012," *The Southern Poverty Law Center's Intelligence Report* no. 109 (Spring 2013), pp. 43-49.
47. Coates, p. 80.
48. Mark Potok, "The Year in Hate and Extremism," *Intelligence Report*, 149 (Spring 2013), pp. 39-42.
49. Potok, p. 42.
50. Ryan Lenz, "Sovereign Senator," *The Southern Poverty Law Center's Intelligence Report* no. 149 (Spring 2013), pp. 16-18.
51. Potok
52. "Active Hate Groups in the United States in 2012."
53. "Rebels With A Cause," *The Southern Poverty Law Center's Intelligence Report* no. 99 (Summer 2000), pp. 40-46.
54. "Confederates in the Pulpit," *The Southern Poverty Law Center's Intelligence Report* no. 101 (Spring 2001), pp. 51-55.
55. "Sharks in the Mainstream," *The Southern Poverty Law Center's Intelligence Report* no. 93 (Winter 1999), pp. 21-26.
56. "Raging Against the Other," *The Southern Poverty Law Center's Intelligence Report* no. 128 (Winter 2007), pp. 32-39.
57. "Westboro Baptist Church," *Wikipedia* (accessed online at http://en.wikipedia.org/wiki/Westboro_Baptist_Church on June 26, 2013).
58. "The Year in Hate," *The Southern Poverty Law Center's Intelligence Report* no. 97 (Spring 2000), pp. 6-7; "Neither Left Nor Right," *The Southern Poverty Law Center's Intelligence Report* no. 97 (Winter 2000), pp. 40-46.
59. "The Year in Hate," *The Southern Poverty Law Center's Intelligence Report* no. 105 (Spring 2002), pp. 6-7.
60. "Active Hate Groups in the United States in 2012."

61. "Money, Music and the Doctor," *The Southern Poverty Law Center's Intelligence Report* no. 96 (Fall 1999), pp. 33-36.
62. Mark Potok, "Secrets of the Sisterhood," *The Southern Poverty Law Center's Intelligence Report* no. 149 (Spring 2013), pp. 19-23.
63. Justine Sharrock, "Age of Treason," *Mother Jones* 35(2), March-April 2010, pp. 28-35, 95.
64. Chalmers, pp. 398-99.
65. Alexis A. Aronowitz, "Germany's Xenophobic Violence: Criminal Justice and Social Responses," in *Hate Crime: International Perspectives on Causes and Control*, Mark Hamm (ed.) (Cincinnati, Ohio: Anderson Publishing Co., 1994), pp. 37-69.
66. Jeffrey Ian Ross, "Hate Crimes in Canada: Growing Pains with New Legislation," in *Hate Crime: International Perspectives on Causes and Control*, Mark Hamm (ed.) (Cincinnati, Ohio: Anderson Publishing Co., 1994), pp. 151-172.
67. Samuel Walker, *Hate Speech: The History of an American Controversy* (Lincoln, Nebr.: University of Nebraska Press, 1994).
68. James B. Jacobs and Kimberly Potter, *Hate Crimes: Criminal Law & Identity Politics* (New York: Oxford University Press, 1998).
69. *Ibid.*
70. "Discounting Hate," *The Southern Poverty Law Center's Intelligence Report* no. 104 (Winter 2001), pp. 6-15.
71. *Ibid.*
72. *Ibid.*, p. 7.
73. The Southern Poverty Law Center, *Seeking Justice: A Brief History of the Southern Poverty Law Center* (available at www.splcenter.org/centerinfo/ci-index.html; Internet; accessed on 17 June 2002).
74. See Stuart A. Wright (ed.), *Armageddon in Waco: Critical Perspectives on the Branch Davidian Conflict* (Chicago: University of Chicago Press, 1995).
75. For a good discussion of this case, see Mark Hamm, *Apocalypse in Oklahoma: Waco and Ruby Ridge Revenged* (Boston, Mass.: Northeastern University Press, 1997), and Peter Kraska, *Militarizing the American Criminal Justice System* (Boston, Mass.: Northeastern University Press, 2001).
76. Hamm, pp. 103-145.
77. For other examples, see Daniel Levitas, *The Terrorist Next Door: The Militia Movement and the Radical Right* (New York: Thomas Dunne Books, 2002).

CHAPTER

Contemporary Slavery

11

INTRODUCTION

The end of the American Civil War in 1865 supposedly extinguished one relic of barbarism: slavery.[1] This "peculiar institution" had existed for centuries.[2] Some scholars believe that slavery began as civilization grew, first appearing in the ancient centers of Mesopotamia, Egypt, and India. These scholars believe that slavery started when ancient humans shifted from hunter-gatherer cultures to agriculture-based economies. Labor was needed to help farm crops, build pyramids, fight wars, and serve the ruling elites. Enslaved peoples were seen as the spoils of war, necessities in building an economy and supporting colonial systems throughout the world. Slavery validated racial hatreds and provided a means for upholding and supporting certain classes of individuals.[3] The scholars who promote such theories probably underestimate the beginnings of slavery, however. Most likely, slavery had existed for thousands of years before the dawn of civilization. Surely, the spoils of prehistoric wars must have included enslaving the vanquished. No matter the origins, the end of legal slavery in many parts of the world in the nineteenth century was considered a major step in the march toward civilization.

Nonetheless, today there are more enslaved people in the world than ever. It is estimated that 27 million people are currently enslaved.[4] In fact, there are more slaves now than all of the people stolen from Africa prior to the Civil War in America. The world's slave population might even be greater than the entire population of Canada and six times larger than the population of Israel.[5]

This new slavery touches most people of the world. For example, those who enjoy eating candy do not realize that slavery is used in a good deal of chocolate production. In 1998, the International Labor Organization (ILO), a UN agency, found the emergence of child slavery in the cocoa fields of the Ivory Coast, which is the source of 43% of the world's cocoa. Companies such Hershey's and M&M Mars were charged with complicity. These child slaves came from Mali, Burkina Faso, and Togo, nations even more destitute than the Ivory Coast. Parents in these countries sold their children in hopes that good jobs awaited them.

In Sudan, black Christians and animists have resisted those in the capital, Khartoum, who wished to impose an Arabic Moslem state and religion. Civil war resulted, with the Sudanese army being encouraged to turn captives and their families into slaves. In 1998, one automatic weapon could be traded for six or seven child slaves. In 1989, a woman or child from the Dinka tribe—a tall, proud people living along the Nile—could be bought for $90. The next year, as raids increased and flooded the market with captives, the market price slid to $15. Frequently, these slaves were forced to convert to Islam, and those who refused had their Achilles tendons cut, making it physically impossible for them to walk. Anyone caught trying to escape was castrated or branded like cattle.[6]

In March 2001, an explosion in a rural primary school in Jiangxi Province, China, killed 42 people, most of whom were 10- and 11-year-old children. Apparently, a money-strapped school system had set up an enterprise that made firecrackers, forcing children to work during and after school. Most of the money had gone into the pockets of corrupt school officials.[7]

The next month, a suspected child slave ship eluded authorities off of Africa. The ship, called *Etireno*, had made regular trips from Benin to Gabon for the past 5 years, and it was filled with human cargo, mostly young boys, to work in cotton and cocoa plantations, as well as girls destined to be domestics and prostitutes.[8]

SLAVERY IN MODERN AMERICA[9]

Even in contemporary America, there are examples of slavery. Most Americans think that slavery in their country was put to rest 150 years ago. Embarrassed by over 200 years of keeping African people in bondage, Americans think that the bloody civil war, the Emancipation Proclamation, and the Thirteenth Amendment finally put an end to slavery in their country. Yet, decades of sharecropping, lynching, and Jim Crow laws are overlooked as signs of slavery arising in different ways. While the look of slavery has changed over time, there has never been a time in U.S. history when slavery did not exist.

Christi Elangwe, from Cameroon, was a slave in Germantown, Maryland, for 5 years. Protection Project, a Johns Hopkins University program, estimates that there are one million undocumented immigrants trapped in slavery in America. Asian slaves are used in the sex industry. Latin American slaves work in the fields. Those from the Middle East and Africa become domestics. President Bill Clinton's Inter-Agency Council on Women declared slavery to be "the fast-growing criminal enterprise, behind guns and drugs, in this country."[10] At a conference on human rights in 2003, the U.S. Attorney General announced that "each year, tens of thousands of people—predominantly women and children—are trafficked into the United States." During the previous 2 years, the Justice Department successfully convicted 36 defendants in sex-trafficking cases, but this number hardly scratches the surface of the problem. The Justice Department estimates that as many as 50,000 victims of slavery end up in the United States each year.[11]

Slavery in America comes in several forms. One study conducted by the University of California at Berkeley estimates the breakdown of slavery in America as follows:

- Prostitution and other sex services (46% of all slaves in the United States).
- Domestic servitude (27%).
- Agriculture (10%).
- Sweat shops or factories (5%).
- Restaurant and hotel work (4%).
- Mail order brides, entertainment, and the sexual exploitation of children (8%).[12]

The most common type of American slavery is sex-trafficking. It is the third largest criminal enterprise in the world. Most of the victims are from South and Southeast Asia, the former Soviet Union, and Central and South America. The Russian mafia is responsible for many women in strip clubs. Asian traffickers supply massage parlor workers. One growing concern is the number of children being caught up in the sex slavery industry. Many victims are domestic, mainly young (starting as young as 12 years of age) runaways or abandoned girls living on the streets who are abducted and forced into sex slavery. Some girls are forced into slavery by their parents who have struck a deal with a trafficker.

The second largest group of slaves in America is domestics and nannies. Many of these women (and they are almost exclusively female) come to America expecting to be paid, have a car, go to school during leisure hours, and move on after a short time of work. Instead, they are placed in house seclusion. To maintain control and compliance, the supposed employers take passports and threaten beatings or reprisals against family in the home country. Overworked and sometimes physically and sexually abused, these slaves can be anywhere. A large number of them are held by diplomats and foreign government workers based in the United States.[13]

On the other hand, Florida has become "ground zero" for agriculture servitude, the third largest group of slaves in America. Immokalee and Cocoa, Florida, have been cited for slavery in the tomato fields. Hundreds of slaves work those fields. Some of them were found chained to poles, locked in trucks, beaten, and cheated out of pay. In 2010, the Department of Justice indicted Global Horizons, a labor-recruiting company, for sending 400 Thais into 13 states where they were enslaved as farm workers.[14]

Slave labor is not restricted to agriculture, however. It has been estimated that 75% of garment factories in Manhattan are sweat shops, with workers laboring in terrible conditions for little compensation. In 1995, in El Monte, California, 72 undocumented Thais were found locked up behind wired fences, working in sweat shop conditions. Some of them had been enslaved there for 17 years.

Finally, many high end hotels and restaurants have an army of cleaning and maintenance personnel who are undocumented and vulnerable to enslavement. As a cross over, some hotels also allow rooms to be used for sex-trafficking.

The United States has increasingly addressed human trafficking. Several nongovernment organizations have arisen to fight American slavery. Free the Slaves, the Coalition of Immokalee Workers, Goodweave International, and the Polaris Project are a few groups dedicated to end trafficking. The State Department's Office to Monitor and Combat Trafficking in Persons is the federal government's response. The FBI has also become increasingly involved in breaking enslavement rings. Still, as long as there are thousands of impoverished people needing work and criminal businessmen wanting cheap labor, the danger of slaves next door will remain.[15]

THE NEW SLAVERY

The "new slavery" has grown for several reasons. First, there has been a dramatic increase in population since the end of World War II. Second, this population growth has occurred at the same time as rapid social and economic changes. Third, the greed and chaos accompanying political and economic instability has allowed slavery to grow unnoticed. Fourth, slavery has become very profitable, not because slaveholders make expensive things, but because the modern slave is so cheap. As one student of this problem has called them, they are the "disposable people." Fifth, the international community, perhaps complacent over the victories of the abolition movement of the nineteenth century, has not noticed the presence of the new slavery.[16]

It is important to distinguish between the old and new slavery. Under the old slavery, legal ownership was asserted, but under the new slavery, such ownership is avoided. Slaves were expensive under the old slave system; today, the purchase price is very cheap. Profits from slavery in past times were low, but today high profits await the slaver. Historically, there was a shortage of slaves, but today they are abundant. Under the old slavery system, the relationship between slaver and slave was long-term and patriarchal; today, the relationship is short and more uncaring. Under the old system, slaves were maintained; under the new, they become disposable. Finally, under the old system, racial and ethnic differences were important in upholding and justifying the slave system. Today, such ethnic differences are not as important. The following table illustrates these differences.[17]

Old Slavery	New Slavery
Legal ownership asserted	Legal ownership avoided
High purchase cost	Very low purchase cost
Low profits	Very high profits
Shortage of potential slaves	Surplus of potential slaves
Long-term relationship	Short-term relationship
Slaves maintained	Slaves disposable
Ethnic differences important	Ethnic differences not important

New slavery also has taken different forms from its predecessor. Today, there are three types of slavery existing that, if not understood, might mask the presence of human bondage. First, there is *chattel slavery*. This is the oldest and closest to the old slave systems. Under this form a person becomes a slave through birth, sale, or capture during war. This form occurs most often in northern and western Africa and represents the smallest proportion of slavery. Mauritania is often used as an example of chattel slavery. Second, there is *debt bondage*, the most common form of modern-day slavery. Under this system a person pledges or sells himself into slavery as a surety against a loan, sometimes as small as $25. However, with high interest and hidden costs, the debt is never reduced, and the person becomes trapped in slavery. Even though ownership of the person is never asserted, complete control of the person is maintained. This form is most common in India and Pakistan. Third, there is *contract slavery*. Phony contracts for work are drawn up, and the workers are taken to a labor site far removed from their homes and isolated from their families. There, they are enslaved. This is most common in Southeast Asia, Brazil, and some Arab states. Brazil and Thailand offer examples of this type of modern slavery. Against those broad observations, let us turn to some specific examples.[18]

CHATTEL SLAVERY IN AFRICA: MAURITANIA

As a military dictatorship in Northwest Africa, Mauritania is a buffer between the Arab north and black Africa to the south, and it is characterized by its chattel slavery. Despite being the size of California and Texas combined, Mauritania has only 2.2 million people, making it the country with the lowest population density on earth. It is practically all desert, located at the western end of the Sahara. Over one-third of the country, the eastern region that borders Mali, is barren and is called the "empty zone." This zone, which is about the size of Great Britain, has no roads, no towns, and almost no people. In the more populous regions, generally around the capital of Nouakchott, there is ongoing tension between the people from the black south and those from the Arab north.[19]

This former French colony of slightly over two million people probably contains the world's largest concentration of chattel slaves. In 1993, the U.S. State Department determined that up to 90,000 Blacks lived as the property of North African Arabs (known as Beydanes or White Moors). Other sources add

300,000 part-time and ex-slaves, known as Haratins, many of whom continue to serve their owners out of fear or need. The slaves are chattel. Most often, they are used for house and farm labor, for sex, and for breeding. They may be exchanged for camels, trucks, guns, or money. Their children are property of the master and are born, live, and die as slaves.

Africans in Mauritania converted to Islam over a century ago. Though the *Qur'an* forbids the enslavement of fellow Muslims, racism outranks religious ideals. In fact, Black Muslim Mauritanians are forbidden the basic rights of other Muslims.[20] In 1990, Human Rights Watch/Africa reported routine tortures and punishments of Black Africans for the slightest fault. Beatings, denial of food, and prolonged exposure to the sun with hands and feet tied together were common. For serious reprimands, the notorious "insect treatment" was used. Tiny ants would be stuffed into the ears of the slave, which are then sealed with stones and bound with a scarf. Hands and feet were tied, and the errant slave was left in the hot sun for days. The presence of the insects in the ears could drive a person crazy. Such treatment guaranteed future compliance. In some respects, Mauritania is just a stone's throw away from the stone age.[21]

A comparison of old slavery, new slavery, and slavery in Mauritania is illustrative.[22]

Old Slavery	Mauritania	New Slavery
Legal ownership asserted	Ownership illegal but upheld by courts	Legal ownership avoided
High purchase cost	Relative high purchase cost	Very low purchase cost
Low profits	Relative high profits	Very high profits
Shortage of potential slaves	Shortage of potential slaves	Glut of potential slaves
Long-term relationship	Long-term relationship	Short-term relationship
Slaves maintained	Slaves maintained	Slaves disposable
Ethnic differences important	Ethnic differences accented	Ethnic differences not important

DEBT BONDAGE: PAKISTAN AND INDIA

Pakistan

In spite of some modern trappings of capitalism, Pakistan remains a feudal country.[23] Partitioned after India's independence movement in the late 1940s, it became a refuge for those Muslims living in the subcontinent who were displaced by the tumultuous end of British colonialism. This modern-day feudalism is characterized by a strict caste system. Relationships and interdependencies characterize the social structure. Power is the most important attribute of Pakistan's social structure. Those who have it can do just about anything because power trumps any rule of law. The peshgi system, or debt slavery, provides the underpinnings of life in Pakistan. It is estimated that one-third of all the land is owned by 0.5% of the population. Thus, there are about 15 million landless peasants available to work the kilns that produce bricks for building.[24]

Those highest in the caste system claim direct lineage from Mohammed. Strongmen or warlords come next in the power structure. At the bottom of the list are the Muslim Sheikhis, late converts to Islam who are derogatorily referred to as Musselis. Even below the Musselis are the Christians. These two groups will most often get caught up in debt bondage.[25]

Pakistan truly puts the feud in feudalism. Family fights going back generations continue unrelentingly. It is said in Pakistan that a person must have many sons because so many will die in feuds.[26] Armed gangs roam the countryside with modern weapons; murder, rape, and extortion are common occurrences. Even the government, the institution that should stabilize society, is involved in feuds. Political leaders are constantly being assassinated. Pakistan is an Islamic republic, and rival sects are involved in constant verbal and physical conflict. It is estimated that an average of 400 people are killed each year due to sectarian fighting. Of course, nonbelievers, such as Hindus and Christians, are often the first targeted and the most severely treated. Part of the problem has to do with the law. Pakistan has two sets of laws: state law (civil and criminal law) and Islamic law. Both are legal, but many times they are contradictory. In power struggles, Islamic law will frequently displace state law. For example, slavery is against state law. But it is not against Islamic law as long as the slave is a nonbeliever. Bowing to popular will and fundamentalist Islam, government officials break the law themselves. For example, the police, who are thoroughly corrupt, aid, perpetuate, and profit from the institution of debt slavery.[27]

Pakistan, particularly the Punjab region closest to India, is remarkably fertile. Advances in health care and greater agricultural productivity has made Pakistan's birth rate even greater than that of India's. One-half the country's population is under seventeen.[28] Brick-making has become a major industry. Brick structures are everywhere. Each family is allotted one eight-foot by eight-foot room in a brick complex of living spaces. There is a common toilet and shared water well. The water is not potable.

The soil of the region is particularly conducive to brick-making, and large kilns dot the landscape. There are at least 7000 kilns in the country, not counting the small backyard operations. The large operations can be the size of football fields, with 15-35 families doing piece-rate work. Once the furnaces are started, they burn continuously for 4-5 months. There are two seasonal closings, one in January and February when it is too wet, and another in July and August when it is too hot. The villages near the brick kilns are filled with families working off debts owed to the owner of the kiln. Children make up a large proportion of the workforce. Not only do they work along with their parents, but they may also be taken and used as hostages to prevent their families from leaving the kilns. Because a real opportunity to work off the debt is unlikely, these children often spend their lives working as slaves.[29] As one authority has observed, "The first generation of brick workers was drawn almost entirely from the ranks of the displaced farm workers. Today, their children and grandchildren inherit both the job and, often, the debt that holds them in it."[30]

The piece rate is so low that it is difficult to escape the debt. For example, on average, a family is paid the equivalent to $2.00 for every one thousand bricks made. If brick damage and rain is at a minimum, a family can earn about $14-$16 per week, about the amount a family needs for a subsistence diet. Even if some catastrophic event, such as illness or injury, does reduce their productivity, the family still cannot earn enough to pay its way out of debt.[31]

Then there are the munshi or kiln managers. Many of these managers are honest enough; they just let the dynamics of low income take care of the matter of perpetual debt. Unlike many countries that sustain slavery with high interest rates, Pakistan is Muslim, and the *Qur'an* clearly defines usury as sinful. Unable to rely on high accumulative interest, the managers resort to other means to enslave their workers. A significant number of these managers become corrupt. They miscount the weekly average brick production or overstate the amount of damaged bricks. They use intimidation to force the workers to stay at the kilns. They threaten to sell off a worker's promissory note, and thus the family and its debt, to other managers. If the head of the family dies or runs off, the manager can literally sell the family and its debts to other slave managers. Finally, they sexually exploit female members of the family.[32]

Unlike so much of the new slavery, the debt bondage system of Pakistan does not have a very high profit margin. Kiln owners, with all of their dishonest manipulations, barely make a profit of 10-15%.[33] Mechanization of the process could increase production, but the old peshgi system persists. Worldwide criticism has increased in the last decade. Some labor organizers have tried to reform the system by using the courts. Still the system continues. The large number of people begging for work sustains the slavery system. These are willing slaves. For some, slavery and bare subsistence seem better than the alternatives. As one authority puts it:

> *A brick kiln owner will be approached by a family that is looking for work. Perhaps they have lost the right to land where they were traditionally peasant farmers or were turned off the land when the landlord mechanized, replacing peasant cultivators with tractors. They might even be refugees, driven from their home by the fighting in Afghanistan or the Kashmir. Whatever the reason, the family will be desperate, willing to accept even the hard and hot work in a brick kiln.*[34]

Then there is the issue of honor. When a slave first signs up with a kiln owner, largely of his own free will, he incurs debt. This debt is in the form of money for food and fuel. Sometimes workers borrow additional money to fund the impending marriages of children, medical expenses, or funeral costs. Therefore, debt quickly accumulates. In this region of the world, honor is of prime importance. These slaves do have the opportunity to escape, however. During the off season, a worker, who is the male householder, can leave the kilns and travel the region. To do so, the worker must obtain a slip of paper from the kiln's owner stating the worker's name and amount of the debt. Workers can then go to other kiln owners and negotiate to have their debts purchased. The kiln owner who originally held the debt likely does not care. The workers are disposable people, there is a constant supply of labor, and if the worker does leave, the old owner still gets the money for the debt. The previous slave manager either keeps his slaves or receives hard cash that has been grossly and dishonestly inflated. The worker and his family simply move on, carrying with them past debt and future enslavement.[35] Slaves refuse to run away or seek other means of redress because they feel honor bound to pay off their debts, even though achieving this feat quickly seems impossible.[36]

Furthermore, in spite of window dressing protestations by political leaders, the system seems to have the support of the authorities. The peshgi system has too long of a history in this region of the world. The police in particular have been major supporters of the kiln owners and an obstacle to any meaningful reform. Across the country, the police are for hire. Although laws were passed in 1988 abolishing bonded labor, it continues unabated. Pakistan does not seem to have the will to end debt bondage.

India

Debt bondage has existed in India for thousands of years.[37] Not only is it ancient, but today it remains widespread. Reliable figures are hard to find, but it is estimated that the numbers are in the millions.[38] Slavery takes several forms. For example, in the practice of devadasi, a young woman is married off to a god. Poor families, in hopes of winning the favor of the gods, sell their daughter to a temple. She becomes a servant to that temple. In addition, she may be made a prostitute for that temple because many temples double as brothels.[39] Children are also commonly put into debt slavery. Parents are given money, and the children are required to pay it off. For example, in the state of Tamil Nadu, over 45,000 children between 4 and 15 years old are gathered up each day in school buses and taken to match and fireworks factories. There, they labor for 12 hours a day for 5 days (seven when an important holiday celebration is near).[40] A family working as bonded slaves in agriculture loses all freedoms and receives no wages. After taking on the debt and becoming slaves, the family gets two things: a daily bag of grain and access to a small plot of land where they can grow other food. The state of Uttar Pradesh is famous for its bondage. In this case, the debt bondage is supported by poor illiterate people's need to borrow money. These debts arise out of urgent crisis, such as illness, injury or famine, or the need to pay for death rites or marriage celebrations. In one cruel irony, there are some men who borrow heavily to get married only to eventually sell their wives into prostitution to pay off the original debt.[41]

The ancient caste system supports slavery. The upper classes own most of the land. The lower castes and untouchables are the impoverished ones who borrow money and get enslaved. Unlike Pakistan where Islam forbids usury, Indian landlords charge interest in excess of 60%. Working at subsistence levels, fighting an ever mounting debt due to interest, a family may be enslaved for generations. If a man runs away or dies, the debts of the father are assumed by the oldest son. One bonded servant declared that "I've always lived here, so did my father and grandfather. We've always been here and we've always worked for the same master. When my father died, I had to take over his debt; that was almost 30 years ago." When asked if he had ever been free of debt, he responded: "No, never; neither were my father or grandfather." There is some evidence of a family enslaved for nearly 300 years.[42]

There have been some attempts to rid India of debt bondage. Several factors stymie such reforms. First, there is history and the caste system. Although some reforms since independence have bettered the position of the untouchables, the caste system and the prejudice that sustains it remain fixed, serving as an obstacle to change. One landlord said the following in defense of keeping slaves: "After all, they are from the Kohl caste; that's what they do, work for Vasyas like me."[43] Second, government officials are corrupt and wink at the practice of debt bondage. There is an attitude that the system is actually good for the slave. Again, one landlord justified owning slaves this way: "They benefit from the system and so do I; even if agriculture is completely mechanized I'll still keep my bonded laborers. You see, the way we do it I am like a father to these workers. It is a father-son relationship: I protect them and guide them. Sometimes, I have to discipline them as well, just as a father would."[44] Third, there are profit issues. Landlords can expect profits of over 50% with bonded laborers. If they paid the daily local rate for workers, their profit would sink to 36%. If they paid the national minimum rate for workers, the profit would sink to 1%.[45]

Perhaps the most promising attempts to "rehabilitate" those in debt bondage have occurred in India. When an investigative reporter exposed the existence of bonded slavery in Tamil Nadu, officials swept in and released 321 bonded laborers, giving them 500 rupees to go home. A law had been passed setting up vigilance committees to spot bonded laborers, register them, cancel their debts, protect them from their former masters, and send them to their original homes with a small amount of money. Half the costs were carried by the central government, and the other half by the state government. As one student of the system noted, "It is the modern Indian equivalent of the forty acres and a mule that American slaves were praying for (but never received) at the end of the U.S. Civil War."[46] Some states even went further in this "rehabilitation" program. In Bihar, the grant money was doubled. Also, this state focused on children bonded in the carpet industry. In Karnataka, the freed slave was allowed to keep the land the master had originally bestowed for the slave's personal use. In Uttar Pradesh, vigilance committees tracked down brothels to release girls held as sex slaves. In Orissa, low level government jobs were set aside for freed laborers. Just in one state, Uttar Pradesh, 26,000 bonded laborers were rehabilitated between 1979 and 1989.[47]

However, much corruption has grown up around the rehabilitation programs. Officials keep unduly large parts of the money grants. Land allotted to the freed laborer was often unusable. Former masters took chunks of the land the government had set aside for the freed laborer. Fraudulent contractors supplied sick [or even, in one case, dead] cows to the freed slaves. There is no record of a former master or contractors being prosecuted for keeping or defrauding slaves. Little preparation for freedom was given. It has been noted that bonded slavery is like prolonged stays in a prison; one needs to be prepared for the "real world" to avoid failure. People were given equipment to start a small business—for example, a bicycle repair shop—but no training on how to repair bicycles. In spite of its failings, India remains the only example of a country trying to deal with the problem of modern slavery.[48]

CONTRACT SLAVERY: BRAZIL AND THAILAND

Brazil

Portuguese colonizers introduced slavery to Brazil early in its history.[49] From its beginnings in the sixteenth century to the nineteenth century, millions of slaves were shipped from Africa to Brazil.[50] In fact, their numbers were far greater than the number of Africans sent to the United States. The death rates for Africans transported to Brazil were so high, however, that their total number never became as great as in America. The African slave traffic ended in the nineteenth century, but slavery in the country continued. In 1888, Brazil emancipated its slaves, the old slavery, becoming the last country in the Americas to abolish legal slavery.[51] Then, in the 1960s and 1970s, Brazil underwent an economic boom. Infant mortality declined, city populations grew, industry expanded, and pockets of poverty grew. Enormous slums sprung up in the cities. Today, Brazil has some of the greatest economic disparities in the Western hemisphere. Fifty thousand Brazilians, out of 165 million, own nearly everything. Millions own little if anything, and the unemployment rate is staggering.[52]

The governments of Brazil have largely been corrupt, selling off huge lots of federal land at low prices to the elite classes. Some big companies, such as Nestle and Volkswagen, cut down the forests and use local contractors to make charcoal. Making charcoal is a skilled activity. As the forests in their home states are depleted, these charcoal workers congregate in small town ghettoes eager to find any means to feed their families. When recruiters, called gatos or cats, arrive, there are hundreds of workers from whom to choose. The gatos take these workers deep into the interior with promises of transportation home, money loans to provide for their families, and good food and lodging at the work site. The gato then takes the state identity papers and labor cards from each worker. Without these papers, the workers are trapped. When the workers get to the charcoal-making work place, however, they find a concentration camp with armed guards and threats to their freedom. While theoretically free to go, in reality, these workers now are enslaved. The gato and his thugs are in complete control and can use violence at any time. They are not enslaved for life; the period is from 2 months to 2 years. In fact, the gatos do not want to own them; they just want to exploit them until they are broken and then dispose of them.[53]

The work sites, called batterias, are isolated. Far from towns and villages, they are surrounded by desolation; tree-stripped and blackened terrain. In each camp, there are numerous furnaces to burn the wood. As many as 40 workers might be huddled in together in this wilderness. No matter how hard they work to pay off their debt, they constantly slip into more indebtedness. As one worker put it, "I haven't had anything, absolutely nothing. See, with this gato my debt is always running ahead of my earnings."[54] Not only are people enslaved, but the environment is ruined. Eucalyptus is burned using a minimum of oxygen so as not to consume the wood. The wood oils, intense heat, and lack of breathable air soon makes the workers ill. If they survive, most will suffer from black lung disease. Unfortunately, the charcoal burners in the backwoods are only one example of slavery in Brazil. Slaves are also used to cut down the Amazon rain forest. They harvest sugar cane, mine gold, and act as prostitutes. The rubber, cattle, and timber industries rely upon contract slave workers as well. Brazil has one of the highest number of slaves in the Western hemisphere.

Sex Slavery in Thailand

Thailand gives us one of the best examples of the new contract slavery. This slavery is connected to the sex industry. Modern-day Thailand has become notorious for its sex slaves. It has been estimated that there are one-half to one million prostitutes in Thailand, and one-fifth of them are enslaved. The Thai economy's annual profit from prostitution is estimated to be $1.85 billion. Thailand's reputation as a sexual playground has grown to such an extent that "sex tours" from other areas of Asia regularly come to Bangkok.[55]

There are several reasons for the pervasiveness of sex slavery in Thailand. First, there are geographical reasons. Southern Thailand is rich and fertile, and it has taken on industrialization rapidly. The north, however, has remained poor. Many of the mountain tribes are destitute.[56] So, the bustling metropolitan areas are a magnet to the impoverished rural people.

Second, the economic boom that hit Thailand in the 1990s was confined to the cities. Not only did the rich carry on a historic tradition of going to brothels, but during the economically prosperous times, many working class men could afford to do so as well. The rural areas, however, remained poor. But these areas were exposed to the goods enjoyed by the rich. Televisions, VCRs, and other consumer items were seen as desirable, even though they were outside the paltry budgets of rural families. Some families were willing to sell their girls in order to get these appliances.[57]

Third, there has been a tradition of men visiting prostitutes. Between 10% and 40% of married men visit prostitutes regularly, and 50% of single men do. For most Thai men, it is a legitimate form of entertainment done with friends after an evening of dining and drinking. In business circles, an interlude with a prostitute might be part of closing a business deal. In addition, there is a great desire for virgins. Asians think that sex with a youthful virgin will restore their youth and put off the aging process. Furthermore, as the HIV and AIDS epidemic hit Asia, many men felt that they were safer having sex with virgins. Many wives grudgingly support prostitution as better than their man having a mistress, which is a greater threat to the marriage.[58]

Fourth, there was the historic practice of Buddhism. Basic to Thai Buddhism is the belief that things in this life are due to the activities of past lives; in a cosmic way, the pain and frustrations of this life are just consequences for past sins. Furthermore, tradition has it that Buddha himself sanctioned prostitution. Sex was not a sin; it was merely one of many attachments humans had to this worldly existence, and therefore should be accepted. Impersonal sex—sex without romance and love—was accepted as normal. Popular Buddhism was also antifemale. Females were placed low on the ladder of existence. In addition, all children owed a large debt to their parents. From their earliest years, children were expected to contribute to their family's income.[59]

To recruit sex slaves, agents come to the poverty-stricken rural areas where the average income is $100 to $180 per month. These agents give the family between $88 and $2000 per girl based upon their physical beauty. They promise to bring back the girl once the "loan" has been paid. Most of the young women and girls are ignorant as to the nature of prostitution; many think it is merely sitting around in a restaurant. When they arrive in a major city such as Bangkok, they are put into a brothel. Brothels are usually nondescript places with signs saying "restaurant." The average number of girls per brothel is 20. The sex workers are rarely over 30; most are under 18. Expenses are constantly added on to the loan, and it becomes impossible for the girl to ever pay it off and return home. So, she becomes locked into the sex industry.[60]

These sex slaves face two major threats. First, violence is a constant problem. Customers might exert their will violently. Pimps use random and arbitrary violence to keep the prostitutes compliant. Police chase down and round up runaways and usually use them for sexual pleasure. One young prostitute was found murdered, and her pimp and the police were later found to have killed her. Then there is the psychological violence perpetrated against these young, imprisoned women. In time they come to feel that they are unfit for anything else but the brothel. They develop a dependence upon the pimp and madam.

The second major threat is disease. Thailand has one of the highest rates of HIV infection in the world. Culturally, it is difficult to get men to use condoms, and recently, a large number of women whose husbands visit prostitutes have become victims of sexually transmitted diseases. Forced contraception injected by pimps has also increased the spread of disease among the girls.[61]

Of course, everyone except the sex slave prospers from this industry. The parents of the girl receive some money or consumer goods. One girl who had to have an operation was pressured by her own mother to return to the brothel and fulfill her obligation to the madam and to the family. The procuring agent receives a profit for the girls brought to the brothel. The brothel receives an enormous profit. It has been estimated that the average monthly expenses for a single brothel are around $10,000. The average monthly income, however, is nearly $90,000. The girls are so cheap and plentiful that they become disposable. Very little money is spent on their care. The police receive bribes of money and sexual services for tolerating prostitution. Finally, the entire Thai economy is bolstered by the sex slave industry.[62]

Sex slavery is not limited to Thailand. In Laos and Cambodia, where the annual income is $300, a 12- to 16-year-old girl can be easily purchased. As a virgin in a Tokyo brothel, a girl could fetch $3000-$5000 for her first encounter. In other countries, such as Bangladesh, Pakistan, Nigeria, and some Caribbean or Central American countries, standards of living are low and unemployment high, and the lure to leave and take up prostitution is great. The Victims of Trafficking and Violence Protection Act of 2000 was passed after a U.S. Government report determined that 50,000 women were illegally trafficked into America for sexual exploitation. A government office was then set up to study and combat this problem. In December 2000, the United Nations adopted an international convention against organized crime as well as the Protocol to Prevent, Suppress, and Punish Trafficking in Persons, Especially Women and Children. Only 4 out of 40 nations needed to ratify the protocol have committed to doing so.[63]

CONCLUSION

New slavery is alive and thriving in the world today. The existence and pervasiveness of modern-day slavery comes as a surprise to most. In this modern world of globalization, it is virtually impossible for anyone to sample products that were not produced, at least in part, by modern-day slavery.

One important question is why, 150 years after the Emancipation Proclamation, does this institution still exist? There are several possible answers to that question that might even lead to reform.

First, there is the drag of history and tradition. So much of the new slavery discussed in this chapter exists in countries still experiencing feudalistic tendencies. Mauritania is a modern example of the existence of the old slavery in modern times. India and Pakistan have a mix of the old and new elements of slavery. Those countries are very feudalistic. Class lines are sharply drawn, and the expectations and advantages of the lower classes are marginalized. Furthermore, an intellectual rationalization has grown up that sounds strangely reminiscent of the pro-slave advocates in America before the War Between the States. This notion that the bonded person is childlike and is better off under the patriarchal rule of the owner is common throughout the places that host the new slavery.[64]

Second, perhaps the conceptualization of the new slavery itself contributes to its continued existence. The world community tends to think of slavery according to historical archetypes. Ownership has been a key part of any definition of slavery; this does not fit into any understanding of the new slavery. In reality, two other words are essential: control and violence. So, an important part of modern-day slavery is the violent control of a person. The image of an antebellum-America slave on a plantation crowds out the idea of sex slaves and debt bondage. On the face of it, people working off a debt do not seem to be real slaves. Only when you see the impossibility of getting out of debt, the force used to keep people in slavery, and the lack of regard for these "disposable people," does the magnitude and cruelty of the situation come to our attention.

Third, there has been a population explosion, particularly in poverty-stricken countries, that provides enormous numbers of "disposable people." When these people who already are living on the borders of starvation meet an additional economic crisis, they are likely to fall into slavery.[65]

Fourth, the globalization of business provided opportunity for slavery, while involving all consumers as conspirators. In the last generation, economic changes have pushed corporations into poor countries looking for the cheapest labor. With an eye to their own pockets and the well-being of their investors, businesses look for the best deal possible and do not worry about the politics of the host country. Multiple layers distance the corporate headquarters and Wall Street from the grime and crime of Third World new slavery. Haitian men, women, and children are enslaved in the cane fields of the Dominican Republic, producing sugar earmarked for export to the United States. Only on occasion do companies such as Nike and Gap have their complicity with modern slavery and sweat shops exposed. Then the dicey issues of corporate guilt and consumer responsibility mingle.[66]

Fifth, in spite of some protestations by international organizations such as the United Nations, the international community has been quiet and acquiescent over the problems of the new slavery. The League of Nations had drawn up a Slave Convention in 1926, the first attempt to address the issue in the twentieth century. The United Nations adopted the Slave Convention in 1953, and by 1990, 86 nations had ratified it, thereby setting out to prevent and suppress the slave trade and abolish slavery in all of its forms. A Working Group on Contemporary Forms of Slavery was then set up by the UN in 1975. Every year it evaluates the state of slavery in the world. It has been particularly interested in the problem of children as sex slaves. The International Labour Organisation (ILO) has adopted two conventions that require ratifying states to suppress any form of forced labor. The World Health Organization (WHO) has conducted hearings on sex exploitation, debt bondage, and the sale of children.[67]

Yet, other international organizations have been slow, unenthusiastic, or too poor to confront the problem of modern slavery. The main international group concerned with slavery is Anti-Slavery International (ASI). Founded in 1839, it has worked diligently against the old slavery. But today, it has only 6000 members, a very small number compared to those in Greenpeace and Amnesty International. Some other groups address slavery as part of their larger mission. For example, the Catholic Agency for Overseas Development (CAFOD), Oxfam, Human Rights Watch, and UNICEF have taken on the issue. But these groups work independently, and there is no uniform strategy. Even the United Nations has been particularly timid in labeling countries as slave nations.[68]

Sixth, the lack of democracy in host countries seems to be a problem. New slavery flourishes best in those societies that offer no voting opportunity for the slaves and do not have media institutions to publicize and outrage the public about the existence of slavery. Coupled with that lack of a voice for the people, there is the problem of governmental corruption. Slavery thrives in countries with dishonest officials. Even if there are laws against slavery, as there are in most of the countries cited in this chapter, implementing those laws is another matter. The police in Thailand, Pakistan, and Brazil are slave catchers. To hold and keep their slaves, the slaveholders must use violence, and the police must allow it to exist. Judicial and legislative officials in most of the countries with bonded labor are easily bribed. Very few slaveholders ever get punished. Without the rule of law, the rule of men prevails. And, frequently, men in these countries are greedy and corrupt.[69]

Seventh, local antislavery groups do not get the public support they need. All of the countries used as examples in this chapter do have groups trying to eliminate bonded labor. There is the Pastoral Land Commission in Brazil, SOS Slaves and El Hor in Mauritania, the Human Rights Commission in Pakistan, and the South Asian Coalition on Child Servitude in India. Members of these small but vocal organizations are in constant danger of bodily harm or arrest.[70] Some countries, such as India with its official Rugmark program that identifies carpets made by freed laborers, have moved ahead of others, but across the board, progress has been very slow. Lately, even the Rugmark program has been exposed as having corrupt carpet inspectors.[71]

Finally, there is a feeling among the nations of the world that this was a nineteenth-century issue laid to rest long ago. Perhaps a sense of moral superiority over our ancestors is in place. To acknowledge that we as apathetic consumers of the global economy live in a world of slavery, with as many slaves as in any other era, is too difficult and painful. Until nations show the moral strength and courage of the abolitionists of a previous generation, this relic of barbarism will remain.

DISCUSSION QUESTIONS

1. Why are most people ignorant about contemporary slavery?
2. If a person willingly enters into the new slavery, is it still slavery?
3. How does the slavery of "disposable people" relate to issues of economic justice?

Endnotes

1. See Eugene Genovese's *Roll, Jordan, Roll: the World the Slaves Made* (New York: Vintage, 1976), pp. 410-420.
2. Melton Meltzer, *Slavery: A World History* (New York: DaCapo Press, 1993), pp. 5-6. Also see Robin Blackburn, *The Making of New World Slavery: From the Baroque to the Modern, 1492-1800* (London: Verso, 1997), pp. 31-95.

3. For discussions of these principles, see David Brion Davis, *The Problem of Slavery in Western Culture* (Ithaca, N.Y.: Cornell University Press, 1966), pp. 62-125. Also helpful is Roger L. Ransom's *Conflict and Compromise: The Political Economy of Slavery, Emancipation, and the American Civil War* (Cambridge: Cambridge University Press, 1989).
4. Kevin Bales, *Disposable People: New Slavery in the Global Economy* (Berkeley: University of California Press, 1999), p. 8
5. *Ibid.*, p. 9.
6. *Chicago Tribune*, May 17, 1999.
7. *Los Angeles Times*, March 9, 2001.
8. *Chicago Tribune*, April 16, 2001.
9. Much of this section is based on Kevin Bales and Ron Soodalter's *The Slave Next Door: Human Trafficking and Slavery in America Today* (Berkeley: University of California Press, 2009).
10. *Newsweek*, December 18, 2000.
11. "A Crackdown on the Traffic in Humans," *New York Times*, February 26, 2003.
12. Free the Slaves and Human Rights Center, University of California at Berkeley, *Hidden Slaves: Forced Labor in the United States* (Washington, DC: Free the Slaves, 2004) (accessed online at www.freetheslaves.net on 11-2-2013).
13. Joy M. Zarembka, "America's Dirty Work: Migrant Maids and Modern-Day Slavery," in *Global Woman: Nannies, Maids, and Sex Workers in the New Economy,* Barbara Ehrenreich and Arlie Russell Hochschild (eds.) (New York: Metropolitan Books, 2002), pp. 143-53.
14. See John Bowe's *"Nobodies": American Slavery and the Dark Side of the Global Economy* (New York: Random House, 2007). Also Bales and Soodalter, *The Slaves Next Door*, pp. 43-77.
15. For a list of organizations fighting slavery, see Bales and Soodalter, *The Slave Next Door*, pp. 269-276.
16. Bales, pp. 12-13.
17. *Ibid.*, p. 15.
18. *Ibid.*, pp. 19-20.
19. Murray Gordon, *Slavery in the Arab World* (New York: New Amsterdam, 1989), pp. 18-47. See also U.S. Congress, Senate, Committee on Foreign Relations, *Slavery Throughout the World:* Hearing Before the Committee on Foreign Relations, United States Senate, One Hundred Sixth Congress, Second Session, September 28, 2002. Also helpful is U.S. Congress, Senate, Committee on Foreign Relations, *International Trafficking in Women and Children:* Hearing Before the Committee on Foreign Relations, United States Senate, One Hundred Sixth Congress, Second Session, February 22 and April 4, 2000.
20. Robert Segal, *Islam's Black Slaves: The Other Black Diaspora* (New York: Farrar, Straus, Giroux, 2001), pp. 183-187. Also see Humphrey J. Fisher, *Slavery in the History of Muslim Black Africa* (New York: New York University Press, 2001), pp. 63, 69, 93.
21. Bales., p. 118.
22. *Ibid.*
23. See a series by Cassandra Balchin in *The Nation* in September 1988 on the problem of slavery in Pakistan.
24. Bales, p. 154.
25. *Ibid.*, p. 173.
26. *Ibid.*, p. 175.
27. *Ibid.*, pp. 179-183.
28. *Ibid.*, p. 184.
29. *Ibid.*, pp. 150-151.
30. *Ibid.*, p. 155.
31. *Ibid.*, p. 156.
32. *Ibid.*, pp. 159, 167, 170.
33. *Ibid.*, p. 193.

34. *Ibid.*, p. 165.
35. *Ibid.*, p. 170.
36. *Ibid.*, p. 169.
37. Utsa Patnaik and Manjari Dingwanez (eds.), *Chains of Servitude: Bondage and Slavery in India* (Madras: Sangam Books, 1985), pp. 1-34.
38. Bales, p. 198.
39. *Ibid.*, p. 199.
40. See Human Rights Watch, *The Small Hands of Slavery: Bonded Child Labour in India* (New York: Human Rights Watch, 1996), pp. 14-16.
41. Bales, p. 203.
42. *Ibid.*, pp. 202, 210, 212.
43. *Ibid.*, pp. 218-219.
44. *Ibid.*, p. 219.
45. *Ibid.*, p. 220.
46. *Ibid.*, p. 224.
47. *Ibid.*, pp. 225, 228.
48. *Ibid.*, p. 229.
49. For an overview, see Alison Sutton, *Slavery in Brazil: A Link in the Chain of Modernisation* (London: Anti-Slavery International, 1994).
50. For an overview, see Robert Edgar Conrad, *Children of God's Fire: A Documentary History of Black Slavery in Brazil* (Princeton, N.J.: Princeton University Press, 1983).
51. Leslie Bethell, *The Abolition of the Brazilian Slave Trade: Britain, Brazil and the Slave Trade Question, 1807-1869* (Cambridge: Cambridge University Press, 1970), pp. 62-87. Also Robert Conrad, *The Destruction of Brazilian Slavery, 1850-1888* (Berkeley: University of California Press, 1972), pp. 3-19.
52. Bales, p. 229.
53. *Ibid.*, pp. 128-129.
54. *Ibid.*, p. 135.
55. *Ibid.*, p. 43.
56. *Ibid.*, p. 38.
57. *Ibid.*, p. 40.
58. *Ibid.*, pp. 46-48. See also Mark VanLandingham, Chanpen Saengtienchai, John Knobel, and Anthony Pramualratana, *Friends, Wives and Extramarital Sex in Thailand* (Bangkok: Institute of Population Studies, Chulalongkorn University, 1995), pp. 9-25.
59. I.B. Horner, *Women Under Primitive Buddhism* (London: Routledge, 1930), pp. 40-43.
60. Bales, pp. 41, 53-57.
61. *Ibid.*, pp. 58-60.
62. *Ibid.*, pp. 55, 57-59. See also Thanh-Dam Truong, *Sex, Morality and Money: Prostitution and Tourism in Southeast Asia* (London: Zed Books, 1990), pp. 175-179.
63. *Chicago Tribune* February, 14, 2002.
64. Bales, p. 233.
65. *Ibid.*, p. 234.
66. *Ibid.*, pp. 235-240.
67. United Nations High Commissioner for Human Rights, *Fact Sheet No. 14, Contemporary Forms of Slavery* (Geneva: United Nations, 1991), pp. 3-4, 6-7.
68. Bales., p. 260.
69. *Ibid.*, p. 245.
70. *Ibid.*, p. 247.
71. *Ibid.*, p. 257.

CHAPTER

Genocide

12

. . . [M]en must either be caressed or else annihilated; they will revenge themselves for small injuries, but cannot do so for great ones; the injury therefore that we do to a man must be such that we need not fear his vengeance.[1]

Machiavelli

There is nothing new about the mass killings we now call genocide. It has been suggested that modern man may have exterminated the Neanderthals, and the Old Testament books of Exodus and Deuteronomy specifically name ethnic groups that God ordered exterminated.[2] There is no period in history that was free of mass killings. It would be nice to think that as civilizations have advanced the practice has diminished, but all evidence points to the contrary. It seems that more people have been killed through genocide in the past 100 years than in any 100-year period in history.[3]

In the modern era, the commission of genocide has been greatly facilitated by advances in technology. The development of modern communications systems has made it easier to coordinate efforts to eradicate groups. Modern transportation has made it easier for killers to reach their victims, and advances in the machinery of death (e.g., automatic weapons, bombs, armored vehicles, armed aircraft, and chemical weapons) have made the process of killing more efficient.

Although the practice of genocide is ancient, the term is relatively new, having been created in 1944 by Raphael Lemkin. Lemkin was a Polish scholar who studied Nazi efforts to wipe out Jews and Gypsies in Europe during World War II, having lost his entire large family to the Holocaust.[4] The term *genocide* is the result of combining the Greek word *genos* (race, tribe) and the Latin *cide* (killing).[5] The term was created out of a need to describe the carnage of the Holocaust, and there is a tendency to equate the term *genocide* with the Holocaust. While the Holocaust fits anyone's definition of genocide, examples of genocide can be found far back in history, and there have been many examples since the Holocaust. As Melson has observed, "Since the Second World War many more people have been killed as victims of domestic massacres and partial or total genocides than by international war."[6] And, since Melson's 1992 statement, there have been hundreds of thousands, perhaps millions, of additional deaths from genocide. Genocide is a contemporary international issue of which the Holocaust is only one example.

DEFINING GENOCIDE

The term *genocide* has become part of our everyday vocabulary. Its popularity may be partly attributable to the powerful images it conveys. Describing killings as genocide makes them seem more sinister, calculated, and far reaching. Perhaps this is why it has been applied in a number of areas that some scholars of genocide would deem inappropriate, including family planning, race mixing, drug distribution, cocaine addiction, abortion, bisexuality, medical research, dieting, language regulation in the schools, and establishing Indian reservations.[7]

While most people seem to "know" what is meant by the term *genocide*, it has been surprisingly difficult to define in precise terms, and academics have argued about what should be included in the definition. In his original statement on the issue, Lemkin defined genocide as "a coordinated plan of different actions aiming at the destruction of essential foundations of the life of the national groups, with the aim of annihilating the groups themselves."[8] His definition referred to actions carried out by people working under the authority of the state and included such nonlethal actions against the group as efforts to destroy a group's "culture, language, national feelings, religion, and the economic existence . . . and the destruction of the personal security, liberty, health, [and] dignity."[9]

Lemkin worked hard to gain recognition of the term *genocide* and to encourage nations to work together to prevent future acts of genocide. In 1948, the United Nations adopted the Genocide Convention, including in its definition of genocide many of the elements found in Lemkin's definition (see Box 1).[10]

The United Nations thus created a law that, for the first time, recognized genocide as an international crime. While this action by the United Nations "has undoubted symbolic value, it has never had any practical effect."[11] In fact, although passed in 1948, the United Nations has been slow to charge member nations with genocide or to act against those engaged in genocide.

The definition of genocide offered in the UN's Genocide Convention has been frequently criticized. Ironically, though, many of those same critics then utilize the UN definition in their own work. This is because the UN definition is among the only internationally recognized definitions of genocide and because in the future the Genocide Convention is likely to serve as the basis for international actions against genocide. Discussing the criticisms of the UN definition is a useful exercise because it can clarify why the United Nations has sometimes been slow to act in situations where genocide has been alleged and because the discussion can highlight some of the difficulties in defining genocide.

One problem with the United Nations' definition is that it omits the mass killing of political and social groups, thus excluding a substantial number of contemporary genocides.[12] Thus, as Heidenrich observes, the UN definition excludes the case of Cambodia:

> *In Cambodia in 1975-1979, the Khmer Rouge, followers of Communist leader Pol Pot, murdered people for "political" reasons as inane as for simply wearing eyeglasses. The Khmer Rouge, being Communists, wanted to eliminate all bourgeois intellectuals—and they assumed that any Cambodian who wore eyeglasses must be one. In their effort to socially re-engineer Cambodian society using*

BOX 1 UNITED NATIONS' DEFINITION OF GENOCIDE

Article II

In the present Convention, genocide means any of the following acts committed with intent to destroy, in whole or in part, a national, ethnical, racial or religious group, as such:

(a) Killing members of the group;
(b) Causing serious bodily or mental harm to members of the group;
(c) Deliberately inflicting on the group conditions of life calculated to bring about its physical destruction in whole or in part;
(d) Imposing measures intended to prevent births within the group;
(e) Forcibly transferring children of the group to another group.

terror and killing, later dramatized in the motion picture The Killing Fields, the Khmer Rouge murdered an estimated 1.7 million Cambodians out of an original population of only 7 million. In per capita terms, the Cambodian nation suffered the worst mass murder ever inflicted upon a population by its own government. Yet according to the international legal definition of genocide, the great majority of those victims were not victims of "genocide" because they were killed according to a purely political, not a racial, criteria.[13]

A second problem with the United Nations' definition is that it is unclear how many people must die for a genocide to have taken place. It is obvious if the numbers are in the millions or even in the tens of thousands. What if 5000 people are killed? What about 500? What about five? Is it a proportion of the group's members, such as more than one-quarter or more than one-half? Similarly, what if there is an attempt to wipe out a group but the attempt fails, killing only 50 of the group's two million members? While only a small proportion of the group was killed, the intent may have been to wipe out everyone.

A third problem is that the UN definition requires that there be intent. It is essential to know what was in the minds of the killers. In some cases, such as the killing of Jews and Gypsies by the Germans, there is abundant documentation to show intent. A more common circumstance is for the killers to deny that destroying the group was the intent. Instead, they will argue the killings were the result of police actions to restore order, or that the victims were the casualties of war, not of genocide. Unless there is evidence to the contrary, one may avoid being charged with genocide under international law by simply denying intent.

A fourth problem is that the UN definition makes no distinction between acts of genocide and acts of war, but such a distinction is important. War involves killings that result from battles between two or more groups, each of which is in a position to fight. In contrast, genocide involves victims who are unable to defend themselves or to otherwise engage in battle. However, neither the United Nations' definition nor most other definitions of genocide facilitate making a relatively straightforward distinction between war and genocide. For example, on August 6, 1945, during World War II, the United States dropped the atomic bomb on Japanese civilians in Hiroshima and Nagasaki, killing at least 140,000 men, women, and children. Another 130,000 civilians were killed in the firebombing of Tokyo. The bombings took place in a time of war and were against a civilian population unable to defend itself. Some scholars argue that the bombing should be called an act of genocide.[14] Others disagree,[15] while still others confess they have difficulty resolving the issue.[16]

It should be obvious that there is no definition of genocide that is universally accepted and which can be easily applied across a range of specific situations. Leo Kuper, who wrote a great deal on the limitations of the UN definition, nevertheless resigned himself to working with that definition in his research.[17] Perhaps, it is best to think of current definitions of genocide as orienting frameworks for thinking about the general issue, rather than as tools for making precise distinctions in real-world situations.

CONDITIONS LEADING TO GENOCIDE

Genocide is a crime so horrible that it is hard to imagine why it might occur. A good explanation of genocide would allow us to better predict and perhaps prevent future acts of genocide. To date, none of the numerous explanations have been completely satisfactory.

An important first step toward explaining genocide is to develop a typology. Putting genocides into categories forces us to consider things that are common to all genocides. Developing a typology also encourages us to think more systematically about what we mean by genocide, thus having the added benefit of furthering the work of developing a good definition of the term.

Genocide and War

A number of typologies have emerged.[18] Some categorize genocides by the motivations of the perpetrators. Others make distinctions among genocides based on characteristics of the victims, types of perpetrators, and types of society. As an illustration, Chalk and Jonassohn's typology assumes that there are four types of genocide based on motive: (1) eliminate a real or potential threat; (2) spread terror among real or potential enemies; (3) acquire economic wealth; or (4) implement a belief, a theory, or an ideology.[19] Organizing past examples of genocide by using a typology helps us describe what genocide looks like, but is not enough to explain genocide. Chalk and Jonassohn's typology, for example, does not suggest why a potential threat is responded to with genocide in one society but not another, or why a group may be seen as a threat for decades before a genocide is undertaken. And, just as there has been no definition of genocide that has been universally accepted, there has been no typology of genocide to which most researchers would subscribe.

But if the reasons for genocide are difficult to fathom, it has been easier to describe conditions under which such acts are more likely to occur. Some have suggested that the stage is often set for genocide in conditions of war, colonization, or decolonization.

Most scholars make a distinction between acts of genocide and acts of war. While the two are not the same, periods of war may facilitate the surfacing of a society's genocidal tendencies. There are several reasons for this phenomenon: First, in times of war, normal restrictions on government behavior are lifted, and the state is granted the authority to take actions that might otherwise not be allowed. And, in times of war, citizens of the state are more likely to support this expanded authority. Second, the perceived threat to society posed by a group, such as the Jews in World War II Germany, may seem much greater in times of war when people are quite naturally sensitive to any threats to their national security. Third, the leaders of a country at war may find that the presence of a hated group is a useful tool for mobilizing the masses. Finally, the horrors of genocide may be less immediately apparent to other countries whose focus is on the war and who might well be initially fooled by claims that the killing is an act of war rather than of genocide. The result is a reluctance of other countries to intervene.

During World War II, the Japanese atrocities in Nanking, China, provide a good example of using war as an excuse for engaging in genocidal acts and using the climate of war as an excuse for other nations to do nothing. In 1937, after capturing several other key cities in China, the Japanese army attacked Nanking and killed as many as 300,000 in a period of only 7 weeks. The level of brutality is hard to imagine:

> *Chinese men were used for bayonet practice and in decapitation contests. An estimated 20,000-80,000 Chinese women were raped. Many soldiers went beyond rape to disembowel women, slice off their breasts, nail them alive to walls. Fathers were forced to rape their daughters and sons their mothers, as other family members watched. Not only did burials, castration, the carving of organs, and the roasting of people become routine, but more diabolical tortures were practiced, such as hanging people by their tongues on iron hooks or burying people to their waists and watching them get torn apart by German shepherds. So sickening was the spectacle that even the Nazis in the city were horrified . . .*[20]

Just as disturbing was the failure of the rest of the world to act, even though news of the holocaust quickly spread to other countries. For many years after the event, western countries remained silent, a silence that one author has described as the second Rape of Nanking. Even today, while nearly every American schoolchild has heard of the Nazi holocaust against the Jews, few are told about the Rape of Nanking.

Fourth, the "fog of war" may make it difficult for the outside world to understand what is happening. Only after the killing has ended will the true nature of the killing be understood. War is a messy, confusing business, and it is often true that atrocities committed during war are not dealt with until after the fighting has ended and a clearer picture of what has happened emerges.

Finally, when large nations are involved in war, they may not have the resources to intervene in a genocide occurring elsewhere. In the case of Sudan, for example, the United States publicly stated that a genocide was occurring, but did not intervene. The reasons for not intervening were many, but among them was the reality that, at the time, the United States was fighting wars in Afghanistan and Iraq and simply did not have the resources available to intervene in Sudan.

Genocide and Colonization

Colonization may be associated with genocide when the colonizers view their own actions as morally right, and the area being colonized as unclaimed—or more properly as not being claimed by any legitimate group.[21] In America, for example, much of the land found by Columbus was considered unclaimed, and the "savages" inhabiting it were often seen as less than human. Their skin was a different color, they were not Christians, their language was different, and they utilized substantially more primitive technology. All of this made it easier for "good Christians" to purposely infect Native Americans with smallpox and to send in armies to kill as many of them as possible (see Chapter 10). Similarly, Spanish and Portuguese are now the primary languages of South America because colonizing efforts successfully destroyed much of the existing culture throughout South America.

Genocide and Decolonization

The stage is often set for genocide when decolonization occurs. When a strong colonial power withdraws from a society, or when a strong unifying leader is replaced, existing ethnic tensions may rise to the surface, and the consequence may be genocide. There are numerous examples of this phenomenon throughout history, including the efforts at "ethnic cleansing" that occurred in the 1990s in Yugoslavia in what is now known as Bosnia Herzegovina. Until his death in 1980, Communist Yugoslavia was tightly controlled by its leader Tito who kept long-standing ethnic tensions under control. During the 1980s, Yugoslavia was led by a Serbian, Slobodan Milosevic, who encouraged tensions between Serbian Christians and Muslims. Then, in 1991, Slovenia and Croatia declared their independence from Yugoslavia, and a civil war broke out. While both the Muslims and the Croats were engaged in violence against the Serbs, the (Christian) Serbian response against Muslims was extreme, accounting for as much as 90% of the violence. Croatians accounted for only 6% of the violence, and Muslims accounted for only 4%.[22] Serbian atrocities included "killings, rapes, and other abuses against the Muslim civilian population . . . . It appears unquestionably to be the case that the victims of killings were selected because they were Muslims, that in the overwhelming proportion of cases they were defenseless, and that the killing was intentional."[23] Slobodan Milosevic and others were eventually arrested and put on trial for the crime of genocide.

In addition to these three general conditions that set the stage for genocide, several authors have suggested other relevant conditions. Porter provides a list that includes many of these key elements. He suggests that the likelihood of genocide increases in nation-states where the following conditions exist[24]:

(a) Historically and in the present, minority groups have been defined outside the universe of moral obligation by the dominant group. Such victims have been labeled "outsiders," "scum," or other epithets in order to stigmatize and dehumanize them.
(b) Pervasive racialistic ideologies and propaganda are found in the nation-state's society.
(c) There is a strong dependence on military security.
(d) Powerful, monolithic exclusionary political parties are present.
(e) The leadership has strong territorial ambitions.
(f) The power of the state has been reduced by defeat in war and/or internal strife.
(g) There is minimal risk of retaliation for genocidal acts by kin of the victims or of interference by neutral nations.

Thus, genocide is not a random occurrence but is likely to emerge when a variety of conditions are present simultaneously. The last item on Porter's list—the likelihood of interference from kin of the victims or from neutral nations—leads us to consider how genocide has been responded to in the past.

RESPONDING TO GENOCIDE

Complaints about the UN definition of genocide are not merely word games of academic interest. Whether particular actions fit the legal definition of genocide under international law will determine whether there is legal authority to bring charges against offenders. The UN Genocide Convention was purposely vague regarding how violators would be brought to justice and completely silent on appropriate punishments. Many countries were uncomfortable with developing an international court, because it might have meant giving up some of their own sovereignty. Such concerns may account for why the U.S. Congress did not ratify the UN Genocide Convention until 1986, nearly 40 years after it was initially passed by the UN.

As a compromise designed to gain the cooperation and signatures of as many countries as possible, the UN Genocide Convention called for signatory countries to pass their own laws against genocide and to determine their own penalties. Furthermore, Article VI of the Convention called for the trial of those charged with genocide to be held in the country in which the crime took place. Articl VI also instructed that trials should be conducted by a government tribunal, or by an international tribunal that *might* be formed by other UN signatory nations. Because genocide is most often carried out with the blessings of the government in power, it seems absurd to have that same government reach a judgment about whether genocide occurred, to conduct a trial, and to then determine the proper penalty for it.

The second option, an international tribunal, has rarely been used. In August 2001, a UN war crimes tribunal in the Netherlands found a Bosnian Serb general guilty of genocide for the killing of as many as 8000 Bosnian Muslims in 1995. This was the first genocide conviction since World War II. The general was sentenced to 46 years in prison.[25] In July 2001, the UN war crimes tribunal began actions against former Yugoslavian president Slobodan Milosevic. Unfortunately, he died before the trial's conclusion and so the outcome of the full trial will never be known. Whether these trials represent an emerging trend to bring charges of genocide before an international tribunal is as yet unclear. In the same year, the United States withheld its overdue payments to the United Nations because of objections to the UN's plan to establish a permanent International Court of Justice.[26]

For whatever reason, nations have been slow to respond to genocide and only rarely intervene to stop it. Furthermore, when the genocidal actions of a nation become known, it is unlikely that the nation will suffer consequences of any kind. Expressions of outrage by other nations are not unusual, but those expressions are seldom followed by meaningful action.

GENOCIDE IN THE PAST CENTURY

It would be nice to believe that humanity has progressed to the point that genocide is a thing of the past, a product of a simpler and less developed period in the development of the human race. However, there is little evidence to support such a belief. To the contrary, the twentieth century has witnessed more deaths through genocide than any other century.[27] Some have argued that genocide is fostered by pluralistic societies in which people of very different cultures and backgrounds are brought together. If that is true, then the increased interaction between cultures that results from modern transportation, modern communication, and the development of global businesses may set the stage for future acts of genocide. At the very least, these facts of modern life facilitate the movement of refugees threatened by genocide, who, in turn, may then attempt to retaliate.

It is not possible to describe all of the known acts of genocide, or even to describe all acts committed in the twentieth century. For example, Charny conservatively estimates that, between the years 1900 and 1987 alone, 170,000,000 innocent noncombatants were killed as a result of genocide.[28] Obviously, any estimates of the casualties of genocide are just that, estimates. By any account, however, the numbers are staggering.

Given the large number of genocides that have occurred in just the past century and the need to provide some background on each, this chapter elaborates on three instances to illustrate the concept of genocide with relatively concrete examples. All three are examples in which the nations of the world knew or should have known that genocide was happening, but did little or nothing to stop it, although there were expressions of outrage after the fact. The Armenian genocide is among the first of this past century, and the genocides in Rwanda and the Sudan are more contemporary examples.

The Armenian Genocide (1915-1918)

The Armenian people have lived in the area now known as Turkey for nearly 3000 years and were among the first groups to adopt Christianity. For at least a thousand years before their genocide, the Armenians occupied an area dominated by Muslim Turks. At the time of the genocide, the area was under the control of the Ottoman Empire, which was in serious decline, having lost many of the lands it had controlled in earlier centuries. The Armenians were a non-Muslim minority and were treated "as second class citizens subject to legal restrictions that denied them normal safeguards. Neither their lives nor their properties were guaranteed security."[29] They were not allowed to take part in government, were required to pay special taxes, and were not allowed to carry arms, and because they lived in a country guided by Islamic law, they could not testify in court against Muslim defendants.[30] Furthermore, most citizens had been segregated into their own religious communities known as millets, and this segregation made it easier to later target Armenians for extermination.

In 1913, the Young Turk Party seized power, gaining control of the army and putting sympathizers in key positions in every major town and city.[31] The Young Turks were ultranationalists who believed in the formation of an exclusively Turkish state, while also wanting to expand the boundaries of their country by attacking countries to the east, in an area controlled by the Russians. This area was also the historic homeland for the Armenians and is the location of present day Armenia.

For the Young Turks, having an exclusively Turkish state meant adopting policies that would "purify" the country by removing the Armenian people. A string of defeats in their efforts to expand the boundaries of their country was blamed on the Armenians. By claiming that the Armenians had collaborated with the enemy and had therefore caused the military defeat of the Turkish army, the Young Turks could more easily gain popular support for purification policies. Purification began on a large scale in 1915, just one year after World War I began. The war provided a convenient cover for the genocide, allowing the Young Turks to claim that the dead were casualties of war, not of genocide. The war also served to distract major world powers that might otherwise have intervened to stop the killing.[32]

The genocide itself began in 1915, although there were a series of lesser massacres before that. There were three strategies used to eliminate the Armenians: deportation, execution, and starvation. Armenian political, religious, educational, and intellectual leaders were separated from their communities and executed. To further reduce the likelihood of resistance, young able-bodied men were also executed, leaving women, children, and the elderly. By far, the largest number of victims occurred among women and children, many of whom were involved in the deportation process. In towns throughout the country, hundreds of thousands of Armenians were given as little as three days' notice to begin a journey on foot that covered hundreds of miles and lasted for weeks. The final destination was the Syrian desert to the south. However, most Armenians did not survive the journey, which was in actuality a death march. The government had made no provisions for food or water during the march, and when marchers passed near rivers, they were often killed if they tried to stop for a drink. In addition, women and children were often stripped naked and abused. Along the way, they were attacked and killed by bands of criminals. The criminals had been released from prison by the government and sent out with instructions to butcher as many of the Armenians as possible, and to do so in the most violent manner possible. The marchers were also attacked by citizens. "As columns of defenseless Armenians were marched through towns and villages they would be set upon again and again, sometimes by brigands but more often by Turkish or Kurdish villagers."[33] Young children who were not killed, or who did not die from exposure or starvation, were abducted and placed in Turkish and Muslim homes where they were required to adopt the language and religion of their captors.[34] For those Armenians who survived the long march:

> *The killing units completed their task at a place called Deir el-Zor. In this final carnage, children were smashed against rocks, women were torn apart with swords, men were mutilated, others thrown into flames alive. Every cruelty was inflicted on the remnants of the Armenian people.*[35]

When all of the killing was done, at least 1,500,000 Armenians had been slaughtered, and a people who had been living in the area for 3000 years had simply vanished from the face of the earth. Only a few Armenians managed to escape the carnage, but their culture and history did not. All art, literature, and other records of the history and culture of the Armenian people in Turkey were destroyed. Churches were destroyed, and even Armenian place names were changed.[36] Although symbols of Armenian culture were destroyed, throughout the 4 years of the genocide, there was relatively little destruction of Armenian property. Instead, as the Armenians were driven out, Turks simply took their homes, land,

and other property. In this way, everyday (non-Armenian) citizens of Turkey benefited directly from the genocide. The Armenian genocide is among the most tragic in this century because it is the genocide that most succeeded in completely destroying a people and all traces of their culture.

After the Armenian genocide, the Young Turks who coordinated the killings fled the country, and the world was finally ready to publicly acknowledge the extent of the killing. A Turkish military court tried and sentenced to death (in their absence) four organizers of the genocide. "No attempt was made to carry out the sentence, however, and thousands of other culprits were neither tried nor even removed from office. Within a few months the judicial proceedings were suspended, and even accused and imprisoned war criminals were freed and sent home."[37] Other nations agreed that Armenians should be returned to their homeland and compensated for their losses, but were unwilling to provide aid and did nothing to force the Turkish government to act. Instead, the Turkish government continued changing place names and destroying any cultural memory of the Armenians. The government tried to quiet any discussions of the Armenian genocide and even successfully pressured the U.S. State Department to stop the production of a Hollywood movie about the Armenians.[38] Turkish efforts were so successful that most people have never heard of the Armenian genocide, and most scholars describe it as the forgotten genocide.

Rwanda (1994)

Rwanda, located in west-central Africa, is slightly smaller than the state of Maryland, only about 125 miles at its widest point and only about 100 miles at its longest point.[39] At the time of the genocide, it was among the most densely populated countries on the African continent. Rwanda is also one of the poorest nations in the world, and in 1994, it was facing a drought in which "it was estimated that as many as 800,000 people would need food aid to survive."[40]

There are two major ethnic groups in Rwanda. The Hutu make up about 85% of the population, while most of the remaining people are Tutsi. These groups have lived in the region for over 2000 years, and over that time, they have developed a shared language and culture. Although far fewer in number, the Tutsi have historically held positions of power in Rwanda, while Hutu were more generally commoners. Rwanda came to be ruled by Belgium after World War I, and in the 1920s, the Belgians ordered that only Tutsi, who already held most positions of leadership, should be officials in the Rwandan government. This required differentiating between Hutu and Tutsi, and beginning in the 1930s, Rwandans were required to register with the government and declare their ethnicity.[41] By the 1950s, tensions between Hutu and Tutsi had grown, and the Belgium government sought to bring peace by placing some Hutu in positions of power. In 1961, Rwandans voted to establish a republic in which citizens elected their own representatives. Because of their overwhelming numbers, these elections placed many Hutu in positions of power. At this time, Hutu began to attack Tutsi who had previously held power, and they drove as many as 10,000 from the country. The Hutu depicted the refugees as enemies of Rwanda and eliminated any powerful opponents within Rwanda. The Catholic Church, which had supported the Tutsi and had many Tutsi among its priests, shifted allegiance and threw its support behind the new Hutu leadership. Other Christian churches remained officially neutral, but openly worked with Hutu officials.[42]

Tutsi refugees periodically launched attacks against Hutu-led Rwanda. They also orchestrated the slaughter of Hutu in neighboring Burundi in 1972, killing as many as 200,000. By the late 1980s, the number of Tutsi exiles had grown to nearly 600,000 people.[43]

By the late 1980s, Rwanda was at war with the Rwandan Patriotic Front (RPF), an organization led by refugees from Rwanda, many of whom were Tutsi. The RPF invaded Rwanda on October 1, 1990, and between that date and the victory of the RPF over the Hutu government in July 1994, "the killings wiped out one-tenth of Rwanda's population of seven million."[44] While Rwanda was in a state of war beginning in 1990, the killings on each side were limited until the spring of 1994.

On April 6, 1994, the Hutu president of Rwanda was killed when his plane was shot down. The genocide of Tutsi in Rwanda began in earnest with that event and lasted for 13 weeks, during which time as many as 800,000 people were killed. Although the primary target of the genocide was the Tutsi, Hutu who were sympathetic to the Tutsi or who refused to take part in the killing were also targeted. Throughout the genocide, the Hutu justified their actions as necessary for self-defense in their war against the RPF. Although the killing of Rwanda's president appeared to be the trigger for the genocide, it has been argued that planning for the genocide began months earlier. It has also been suggested that the president's plane may have been shot down by Hutu extremists hoping to use the event to mobilize citizens against the RPF and stir them to genocide.[45]

Rwandan military personnel often began the killing, later to be joined by Hutu citizens. At first they moved from house to house, but later they arranged to bring victims together in groups—in churches, schools, and other public sites—where they could be massacred on a larger scale.[46] The Hutu government also made extensive use of the media, including radio, television, newspapers, and magazines to stir up anti-Tutsi sentiments.[47] Before the genocide, at least 29% of Rwandan homes owned a radio. Immediately before and during the genocide, government officials handed out free radios to Hutu and used radio broadcasts to incite the public by reporting fabricated stories about massacres committed by the RPF. Radio broadcasts were also used to persuade Hutu citizens that killing Tutsi and Tutsi sympathizers was their patriotic duty.[48]

At the time of the genocide, poverty was extreme, and a drought left many in Rwanda starving. The government responded to the crisis by delivering food, drink, and clothing to those willing to kill. Killers operating in the countryside were often promised land, a scarce and valuable commodity. Hutu willing to take property and destroy the homes of Tutsi were sometimes threatened with punishment or even death if they did not also kill the inhabitants. The original slaughter, described to the outside world in the language of war, was focused on young males. Later the killing extended to women, children, and the elderly.[49]

The killing of Tutsi women was often accompanied by sexual and physical abuse. "Tutsi women were often raped, tortured, and mutilated before they were murdered,"[50] although some managed to escape with their lives by giving the killers sexual favors. Violence was particularly fierce against Tutsi women who had married Hutu men.[51] Such marriages were defined as race mixing, and it was believed that children produced from such a marriage would be part Tutsi and thus be racially impure.[52]

In preparation for their war with the RPF, the Hutu government had supplied both guns and machetes to civilian Hutu males, and had provided training for many. While guns were more efficient killing tools, machetes were often utilized because of the terror they caused. Many victims were simply hacked to death, or beaten to death with hammers or clubs. Victims sometimes had both Achilles' tendons cut before they were killed, so they were unable to run away.

It is now clear that other world powers were not only aware of the genocide as it was happening, but these powers knew about it in advance. In addition to a large number of early indicators that preparations were being made for genocide, the head of the United Nations Assistance Mission in Rwanda (UNAMIR) specifically warned the United Nations of a plan to annihilate all Tutsi.[53] This information was available to the United States, the French, and the Belgians, all of whom had peacekeeping troops in the country. The response was not to strengthen peacekeeping forces and protect Tutsi citizens, but to withdraw all forces, including diplomatic representatives.[54] The withdrawal included the UN soldiers who had been guarding refugee camps within Rwanda, camps that were subsequently raided, the inhabitants killed. The United Nations and other countries did not fail to act because they were unaware of the genocide. They failed to act because Rwanda was not of critical economic or political importance to them. As Lemarchand has observed, "That a carnage of this magnitude could have been going on day after day, week after week, without interference from the international community speaks volumes for the lack of resolve to deal with massive human rights violations."[55]

The genocide in Rwanda is striking because it was so thoroughly planned and executed, because the methods were extremely cruel and brutal, because it is among the first of the modern genocides in which a number of the killings were captured on videotape—making it easier for the outside world to directly see the horror of the killing, and because other nations failed to intervene when human decency dictated otherwise. Unlike the genocide of the Armenians, other countries could not claim the distracting influence of a world war. In fact, there were no credible excuses.

In Rwanda, the genocide officially ended in July 1994, but the killing has continued on a smaller scale. After the genocide, however, scattered fragments of the Tutsi-led RPF were doing the killing, and Hutu were fleeing the country for safety. In an ironic reversal of roles, some of the Hutu directly involved in the genocide of the Tutsi were refugees and became leaders organizing military forays into Rwanda in an effort to destabilize the government. The RPF, for its part, launched attacks against these refugee camps, driving hundreds of thousands of Hutu back into Rwanda and killing thousands in the process. Meanwhile, some of the Hutu who have returned to Rwanda have organized guerrilla groups to attack the government.[56] Although nothing with the scale and organization of the 1994 genocide has occurred, each side has engaged in smaller massacres, with little interference from other nations.

The international community has been slow to act, but has brought criminal charges against some of those involved in the genocide. In June 2001, a Belgian court convicted four people of war crimes for their actions in Rwanda. One was a factory owner, one a college professor, and two were Catholic nuns. The nuns "were charged with helping Hutu extremists kill more than 5000 people at their convent."[57] In February 2003, a doctor, a minister who headed the Seventh-Day Adventist Church in Rwanda, and his son were all convicted for aiding and abetting the genocide, and three Catholic priests were awaiting trial on the same charges.[58]

Sudan (2003–present)

The genocide in Sudan began in February 2003, in the western region of the country known as Darfur. Though some have labeled this conflict a civil war, as time has passed, evidence of genocide has increased, and the number of people and groups defining the conflict as genocide has grown. Nevertheless, the international community has been reluctant to commit the resources necessary to stop the fighting. As is often the case, hard numbers are difficult to come by, but most estimate that as many as 200,000 people have been killed and another 2-4 million people have become refugees in surrounding countries, including Ethiopia and Chad.

Sudan is about one-fourth the size of the United States, with a population of approximately 41 million people. The Darfur region is one of the least developed regions of Sudan, which itself is among the 25 poorest countries in the world.[59] The two largest ethnic groups are Black (52%) and Arab (39%).

Seventy percent of the population is Sunni Muslim. Muslim Arabs dominate national politics and have engaged in a series of civil wars with non-Muslim non-Arabs in southern Sudan since the country's independence in 1956.[60] This civil war was not only about Arab hostility toward Black Africans, but was also fueled by oil reserves in the region. The Chinese government had invested heavily in the oil industry in this region,[61] and it is perhaps no coincidence that the Chinese government has been among those reluctant to have the United Nations intervene with military force. Though the civil war in southern Sudan was supposed to have ended in 2005, a June 2006 report by Human Rights Watch indicated that the killing of innocent civilians by Sudanese military units has continued.[62]

In a separate action in 2003, citizens of Darfur came under attack by Sudanese military units and by the *Janjaweed*, nomadic Arab tribes that are technically beyond the control of the government, but who are believed to be armed and guided by them. The term "*Janjaweed*" roughly translates as "evil horsemen," and the group included bandits, common criminals released from jail, unemployed young men, and former military personnel.[63] Although the Sudanese government claims to be targeting rebel groups in Darfur, there is considerable evidence that the killings are motivated by a desire to "cleanse" the region of Black Africans.

As was true during the killings in Bosnia and Rwanda, the outside world initially debated whether the killings in Darfur constituted genocide. The situation in Sudan is different, however. In Bosnia and Rwanda, major nations were hesitant to label the killings genocide, because it might require them to respond and place their own soldiers at risk. In Sudan several world powers, including the United States, France, and Israel, have publicly called the killings in Darfur genocide, but have felt little compulsion to intervene. It appears that inaction by powerful nations is no longer cause for shame. For its part, the United Nations has been reluctant to label the killings genocide, citing a lack of evidence of intent on the part of the Sudanese government, despite mounting evidence to the contrary, including a report to the United Nations by the chief prosecutor of the International Criminal Court that "the entire Darfur region is a crime scene."[64] The chief prosecutor noted that the Sudanese government had been bombing schools, markets, and water installations, and that if the number of villages being burned was going down, it was only because there were fewer left. Sudanese and *Janjaweed* forces in Darfur have poisoned wells, raped, gang-raped, and murdered women, killed young men, most of whom were Black Africans, and have burned villages to the ground, while generally leaving adjacent Arab villages alone.

The Sudanese government learned much from the Rwandan genocide. Much of the world's reaction to the killing in Rwanda was prompted by the video footage of killings and by the reports of journalists on the scene. To blunt criticism and to promote their own view of events on the ground, the Sudanese government banned journalists from Darfur. In July 2008, the president of Sudan was charged in the International Criminal Court with war crimes, genocide, and crimes against humanity. This was the first time that a sitting head of state was charged with crimes before the International Criminal Court. On March 4, 2009, the International Criminal Court issued an arrest warrant for the president of Sudan without the genocide charges, though there was no mechanism for carrying out the warrant. The next day, the Sudanese government announced the expulsion of aid agencies from Darfur,[65] further endangering the health and lives of innocent civilians and further complicating efforts to unveil government actions there.

One of the distinguishing features of the genocide in Darfur is the extent to which science and technology have been used to document the situation on the ground. In 2007, the world could turn to Google Earth to view satellite images of burned-out villages—evidence of what was literally a "scorched earth policy."[66] In addition, it is only the second genocide to be documented through the use of modern survey research methods. The first was a survey of refugees from Kosovo.[67]

To better understand what was happening in Darfur, the U.S. State Department funded a 2004 survey of 1136 refugees from the region. The Atrocities Documentation Survey was based on multistage cluster-sampling in 20 refugee camps or clusters in eastern Chad, and respondents were asked a series of questions about what they had seen and experienced in Darfur.[68] A brief summary of the survey's findings provided the impetus for U.S. Secretary of State Colin Powell's 2004 testimony before the United Nations, during which he explicitly called the killings in Darfur genocide. This was the first time a victimization survey influenced U.S. foreign policy. John Hagan and his colleagues undertook a more elaborate analysis of the data, and their findings provide broad support for labeling actions in Darfur genocide.[69] In particular, they cited nine crucial elements supporting a claim of genocide in Darfur.

"The first element is the background of tension between Arab and Black groups in Darfur. The Sudanese state, especially in recent years, has implemented Arab-Islamic supremacist and demonizing policies that pit Arabs and Blacks against one another in an 'us' against 'them' kind of conflict."[70] The second element was the arming of *Janjaweed* militias by the Sudanese government. The third element was the bombing of Black villages by the Sudanese government, using Russian aircraft and helicopters. The fourth element was the ground attacks in which Sudanese soldiers raided villages, killing boys and young men, while raping—and sometimes killing—women and young girls. These were often joint ventures between Sudanese military forces and *Janjaweed*. The fifth element was the specific targeting of Black tribes. During these attacks, racial epithets made it clear that people were being targeted because of the color of their skin and not because of their participation in rebel actions. The sixth element was the widespread use of sexual violence against Black women, including gang rape and the mutilation of sex organs. The seventh element was "the confiscation of property—including animals, grains, seed, farm equipment, household items, and money. These possessions are required to sustain and reproduce a way of life for individuals and groups; indeed, they are necessary for physical survival."[71] The eighth element was displacing Black Africans from the land, preventing their return, and prohibiting them from making a livelihood. The ninth element was Arab resettlement of land abandoned by Black Africans, often with the help of the Sudanese government. Some dispute this last point, arguing that it is unlikely that nomadic herdsmen would suddenly become interested in agriculture.[72]

The sheer brutality of the attacks is illustrated in the following quotes from interviewed refugees:

> *First vehicles attacked the village. After one hour, planes came and bombed; after this military came on camels and horses and began shooting at random. They cut open the stomachs of pregnant women and split the throats of male fetuses. Bombs from airplanes killed a lot of animals and people. The military took women away. The village was burned and destroyed . . . Three boys were caught and slaughtered. Their throats were cut, a foot was cut open from big toe to the ankle, hands were cut off, brains removed, sexual organs cut off. Boys were 5, 6, and 7 . . . The 7-year-old's stomach was slit open and his clothes were torn off. A man who tried to return to the village was caught and killed. His skin was removed.*[73]

Although the global community has done little to directly intervene in Darfur, concern is growing as the killing extends beyond the borders of Sudan into the refugee camps in surrounding countries and as food and medical crises escalate in the camps. Hollywood celebrities, including Mia Farrow, George Clooney, Brad Pitt, and Don Cheadle (who starred in the film *Hotel Rwanda*) have traveled to the refugee camps in Chad in an effort to draw the world's attention to the plight of the refugees and the killing in Darfur, but with little effect to date.

The discussion of genocide in Rwanda concluded with an overview of events following the genocide, but for the ongoing genocide in Sudan, there is, as of this writing, no immediate end in sight. In 2009, the International Criminal Court issued an arrest warrant for the president of Sudan on five charges of crimes against humanity and two charges of war crimes, and in 2010, he was charged with three counts of genocide in Darfur. This was the first time the International Criminal Court issued genocide charges. However, there is little indication that any nation or group will step forward to enforce that warrant. In July 2011, a peace agreement was signed between Sudan and a Darfur rebel group, and there was hope that the bloodshed would end. That did not happen, however, and the violence against innocent civilians continues.[74]

PREVENTING GENOCIDE—WHAT CAN BE DONE?

Although a century has passed since the Armenian genocide, it appears that the world community learned little about preventing genocide or responding to it in a timely manner. Preventing genocide requires work at two very different levels. First, it requires identifying early warning signs of genocide. Second, it is necessary to find a way to motivate powerful nations to act when they become aware of genocide.

While it might seem that the conditions that foster genocide would be apparent to the outside world well before the genocide begins, history suggests that either other countries are unaware of these conditions or they are aware but choose to ignore them. The failure of nation-states to recognize when genocides are likely to occur cannot be attributed to a lack of information, but rather to the absence of any system for organizing hundreds or even thousands of scattered pieces of information from a variety of sources. In many cases the various pieces of the puzzle may be there, but not recognized until it is too late. One way to respond to the challenge of identifying and integrating existing information is to better educate a variety of people about genocide, including journalists, religious groups, foreign diplomats, politicians, and media news editors. An encouraging development in this regard is the rise of "Genocide Studies" programs at universities around the world. Another response, suggested by John G. Heidenrich,[75] is to develop early warning centers. Such centers could both identify likely outbreaks of genocide and bring these situations to the attention of political leaders and the public. In many ways such a center would be similar in principle to the Southern Poverty Law Center (aka Klanwatch), which monitors hate groups in America and issues alerts when serious problems are foreseen (see Chapter 10).

Ironically, in the past century, when communications were at their most advanced state in history and when methods for intelligence gathering had been finely honed, there were probably more deaths by genocide than at any time in the history of mankind. It seems clear that making powerful nations aware of an impending genocide is not enough, and awareness may not be the greatest challenge to preventing genocide.

The challenge is to engage those nations lacking the political will to intervene. An important element of this task is improving public awareness of genocides as they occur. Too often, the public is unaware of the nature and extent of a genocide until well after the fact. The same system of modern communication that can make world leaders more aware of impending genocides can also be used to educate the public about instances as they arise. An informed public is more likely to demand actions from its leaders. Thus, some of the same mechanisms for making nation-states aware of emerging genocides can also prompt them to act.

CONCLUSION

Genocide is a problem not only of the past, but also of the present and the future. It is likely that genocide will always be a possibility somewhere in the world. It is also possible, however, to stop genocides from actually being carried out. All that is required is knowledge that a genocide is occurring and the will to intervene.

DISCUSSION QUESTIONS

1. Other than the Holocaust, most Americans know very little about the many genocides that have occurred in the past 100 years. Why might that be so?
2. Why is it important to develop a specific legal definition of genocide that would apply to all countries? Why not let each country have its own definition and its own system for dealing with genocide within that country?
3. There have been more people killed in genocide in the past 100 years than at any time in history. Why might that be true and what might be done to change things?

Endnotes

1. Niccolo Machiavelli, *The Prince* (New York: The New American Library, 1952), p. 37.
2. Kiernan Ben, *Blood and Soil: A World History of Genocide and Extermination from Sparta to Darfur* (New Haven, Conn.: Yale University Press, 2007).
3. John G. Heidenrich, *How to Prevent Genocide: A Guide for Policymakers, Scholars, and the Concerned Citizen* (Westport, Conn.: Praeger, 2001).
4. Israel W. Charny, "The Dawning of A New Age of Opposition to Genocide," in *Encyclopedia of Genocide*, Volume I, Israel W. Charny (ed.) (Santa Barbara, Calif.: ABC-CLIO, 1999), pp. xi-xxiv.
5. Raphael Lemkin, "Genocide," *American Scholar* 15(2) 1946, pp. 227-230. See also Raphael Lemkin, *Axis Rule in Occupied Europe; Laws of Occupation, Analysis of Government, Proposals for Redress* (Washington, D.C.: Carnegie Endowment for International Peace, 1944).
6. Robert Melson, *Revolution and Genocide: On the Origins of the Armenian Genocide and Holocaust* (Chicago: The University of Chicago Press, 1992), p. 285.
7. For an example, see Frank Chalk and Kurt Jonassohn (eds.), *The History and Sociology of Genocide: Analysis and Case Studies* (New Haven, Conn.: Yale University Press, 1990); Helen Fein, "Genocide, Terror, Life Integrity, and War Crimes," in *Genocide: Conceptual and Historical Dimensions*, George J. Andreopoulos (ed.) (Philadelphia: University of Pennsylvania Press, 1994), pp. 95-107.
8. Raphael Lemkin, *Axis Rule in Occupied Europe*, p. 79.
9. *Ibid.*
10. United Nations, *Convention on the Prevention and Punishment of the Crime of Genocide. Resolution 260 A (III)* (available at www.unhchr.ch/html/menu3/b/p_genoci.htm; Internet; accessed on August 27, 2001).

11. Chalk and Jonassohn, p. 11.
12. Samuel Totten, in *Century of Genocide: Eyewitness Accounts and Critical Views*, William S. Parsons and Israel W. Charny (eds.) (New York: Garland Publishing, Inc., 1997); Chalk and Jonassohn; Leo Kuper, *Genocide: Its Political Use in the Twentieth Century* (New Haven, Conn.: Yale University Press, 1981).
13. Heidenrich, *How to Prevent Genocide.*
14. Kuper, *Genocide.*
15. Fein
16. To see the semantics of it all, see Israel W. Charney, "Toward a Generic Definition of Genocide," in *Genocide: Conceptual and Historical Dimensions*, George J. Andreopoulos (ed.) (Philadelphia: University of Pennsylvania Press, 1994).
17. Leo Kuper, *The Prevention of Genocide* (New Haven, Conn.: Yale University Press, 1985).
18. Peter duPreez, *Genocide: The Psychology of Mass Murder* (New York: Boyars/Bowerdean, 1994); Chalk and Jonassohn; Kuper, *Genocide: Its Political Use in the Twentieth Century*; Israel W. Charny, "The Dawning of a New Age of Opposition to Genocide," in *Encyclopedia of Genocide*, Volume I, Israel W. Charny (ed.) (Santa Barbara, Calif.: ABC-CLIO, 1999), pp. 3-7.
19. Chalk and Jonassohn, *History and Sociology of Genocide.*
20. Iris Chang, *The Rape of Nanking: The Forgotten Holocaust of World War II* (New York: Penguin Books, 1997). p. 6.
21. duPreez, *Genocide.*
22. Florence Hartman, "Bosnia," in *Crimes of War: What the Public Should Know*, Roy Gutman and David Rieff (eds.) (New York: W.W. Norton and Company, 1999), pp. 50-56.
23. Steven L. Burg, "Genocide in Bosnia-Herzegovina?" in *Century of Genocide: Eyewitness Accounts and Critical Views*, Samuel Totten, William S. Parsons, and Israel W. Charny (eds.) (New York: Garland Publishing, Inc., 1997), pp. 424-433.
24. Jack Porter, "Introduction," in *Genocide and Human Rights: A Global Anthology*, Jack Porter (ed.) (Washington, D.C.: University Press of America, 1982), pp. 9-10.
25. "Court Rules Genocide Was Committed at Srebrenica," *Los Angeles Times* (electronic edition) (available at www.latimes.com; August 2, 2001; accessed on August 2, 2001).
26. Naftali Bendavid, "Republican Spat Over World Criminal Court Holds Up UN Dues," *Chicago Tribune*, August 17, 2001, pp. 1-2.
27. Heidenrich, "How to Prevent Genocide."
28. Israel W. Charny, "Democide: A New Inclusive Concept Proposed," in *Encyclopedia of Genocide*, Volume I, Israel W. Charny (ed.) (Santa Barbara, Calif.: ABC-CLIO, 1999), pp. 15-18.
29. Rouben P. Adalian, "The Armenian Genocide," in *Century of Genocide: Eyewitness Accounts and Critical Views*, Samuel Totten, William S. Parsons, and Israel W. Charny (eds.) (New York: Garland Publishing, Inc., 1997), pp. 41-77.
30. Richard G. Hovannisian, "The Armenians in Turkey," in Frank Chalk and Kurt Jonassohn (eds.), *The History and Sociology of Genocide: Analysis and Case Studies* (New Haven, Conn.: Yale University Press, 1990), pp. 249-266; Richard G. Hovannisian, "Etiology and Sequelae of the Armenian Genocide," in *Genocide: Conceptual and Historical Dimensions*, George J. Andreopoulos (ed.) (Philadelphia: University of Pennsylvania Press, 1994), pp. 111-140.
31. Adalian, "The Armenian Genocide."
32. *Ibid.*
33. Melson, *Revolution and Genocide,* pp. 144-145.
34. Adalian
35. *Ibid.*, p. 45.
36. Melson.
37. Hovannisian, "Etiology and Sequelae of the Armenian Genocide," p. 126.

38. *Ibid.*
39. The Central Intelligence Agency, *The World Factbook: Rwanda* (available at www.cia.gov; Internet; accessed on September 26, 2001).
40. Alison Des Forges, *Leave None to Tell the Story: Genocide in Rwanda* (New York: Human Rights Watch, 1999), p. 1 (also available at www.hrw.org/reports/1999/rwanda).
41. *Ibid.*
42. *Ibid.*
43. *Ibid.*
44. Rene Lemarchand, "The Rwanda Genocide," in *Century of Genocide: Eyewitness Accounts and Critical Views*, Samuel Totten, William S. Parsons, and Israel W. Charny (eds.) (New York: Garland Publishing, Inc., 1997), p. 408.
45. Rene Lemarchand, "Rwanda and Burundi, Genocide," in *Encyclopedia of Genocide*, Volume II, Israel W. Charny (ed.) (Santa Barbara, Calif.: ABC-CLIO, 1999).
46. Des Forges.
47. Christopher Taylor, *Sacrifice as Terror: The Rwandan Genocide of 1994* (Oxford, England: Berg, 1999).
48. Des Forges.
49. *Ibid.*
50. *Ibid.*, p. 10.
51. Taylor, *Sacrifice as Terror.*
52. *Ibid.* See also Des Forges.
53. Des Forges.
54. Lemarchand, "Rwanda and Burundi, Genocide."
55. *Ibid.*, p. 511.
56. Taylor, *Sacrifice as Terror.*
57. "Two Nuns Guilty in Genocide," *L.A. Times* (electronic edition) (available at www.latimes.com; June 8, 2001; accessed on June 8, 2001).
58. Marlise Simons, "Rwanda Pastor and Son, a Doctor, Convicted of Genocide," *New York Times*, February 20, 2003 (available at www.nytimes.com; Internet; accessed on March 12, 2003).
59. Samuel Totten, "The Darfur Genocide," in *Century of Genocide: Critical Essays and Eyewitness Accounts* (3rd ed.), Samuel Totten and William S. Parsons (eds.) (New York: Routledge, Taylor & Francis Group, 2009).
60. Central Intelligence Agency (CIA), *The World Factbook: Sudan* (available at www.cia.gov; Internet; accessed on May 13, 2013).
61. John Hagan, Wenona Rymond-Richmond, and Patricia Parker, "The Criminology of Genocide: The Death and Rape of Darfur," *Criminology* 43(3) 2005, pp. 525-562.
62. Human Rights Watch, "No One to Intervene: Gaps in Civilian Protection in Southern Sudan" (available at www.hrw.org; Internet; accessed on June 21, 2009).
63. Gerard Prunier, *Darfur: A 21st Century Genocide* (Cambridge, Mass.: Harvard University Press, 2008).
64. Neil MacFarquhar, "Security Council Members Push to Condemn Sudan," *New York Times* (electronic edition) (available at www.nytimes.com; June 6, 2008; accessed on June 22, 2009).
65. Human Rights Watch, "Darfur and the ICC: Myths versus Reality" (available at www.hrw.org; Internet; accessed on June 22, 2009).
66. Elise Labott, "Google Earth Maps Out Darfur Atrocities," *CNN* (electronic edition) (available at www.cnn.com; Internet; accessed on June 23, 2009).
67. John Hagan and Wenona Rymond-Richmond, *Darfur and the Crime of Genocide* (Cambridge: Cambridge University Press, 2009).
68. Jonathan P. Howard, "Survey Methodology and the Darfur Genocide," in *Genocide in Darfur: Investigating the Atrocities in the Sudan*, Samuel Totten and Eric Markusen (eds.) (New York: Routledge, Taylor & Francis Group, 2006).

69. Hagan, Rymond-Richmond, and Parker, "The Criminology of Genocide"; John Hagan and Alberto Palloni "Death in Darfur," *Science* 313: pp. 1578-1579; John Hagan and Wenona Rymond-Richmond, "The Collective Dynamics of Racial Dehumanization and Genocidal Victimization in Darfur," *American Sociological Review* 73: pp. 875-902; Hagan and Rymond-Richmond, *Darfur and the Crime of Genocide*.
70. Hagan and Rymond-Richmond, *Darfur and the Crime of Genocide,* p. 5.
71. *Ibid.*, p. 11.
72. Prunier, *Darfur: A 21st Century Genocide*.
73. Hagan and Rymond-Richmond, *Darfur and the Crime of Genocide*, pp. 7-8.
74. Human Rights Watch, "World Report 2013: Sudan" (available at www.hrw.org; Internet; accessed on May 13, 2013).
75. Heidenrich, *How to Prevent Genocide.*

CHAPTER 13

The Environment

It may seem peculiar to talk about the environment as an issue related to justice, and such a discussion would probably not have taken place as few as 50 years ago. We depend on natural resources, such as air and water, to survive, but until relatively recently there has been little appreciation for injustices that might arise from mankind's relationship with the environment. We do not use or dispose of natural resources in a way that effects all people equally, and issues of justice surround the way in which the benefits and the costs are distributed throughout society and among nations.

Some use the term "environmental justice" to describe injustices in the way natural resources are used. Environmental justice concerns the way in which environmental damage is disproportionately suffered by the powerless—primarily the poor and minority. In America race and income are intertwined. Some view the problem as more rooted in race than economics. These individuals prefer the term "environmental racism." This discussion uses the more general term environmental justice to encompass inequalities related to both race and income.

In America concern with environmental justice is relatively new. In 1971, the Council on Environmental Quality issued a report that was among the first to mention the possible link between toxic risk and income. In 1978, public attention was drawn to the issue by front-page stories about the potential health consequences of buried toxic waste in the community of Love Canal, New York. Then, in 1982, a protest in Warren County, North Carolina, prompted the government to study the process by which sites were selected for storing hazardous waste.[1] The study found that three of the four hazardous waste facilities studied were in predominantly African American communities, and the fourth was in a low-income community. In 1987, the United Church of Christ issued a report concluding that race was a major deciding factor in the selection of sites for hazardous waste disposal. In the early 1990s, a series of studies found that across the nation non-Whites were substantially more likely than Whites to live in the most polluted areas.[2]

By the early 1990s, the environmental justice movement had enough visibility to influence national policy. In 1994, President Clinton signed Executive Order #12898 requiring the U.S. Environmental Protection Agency to consider environmental justice in the development of its policies and regulations.[3] The Department of Energy also began to require the consideration of environmental justice when determining compliance with Department of Energy guidelines.[4]

Ironically, environmental injustice might result from concerns about the environment and the subsequent efforts to clean contaminated land, water, and air. Once removed from the soil, air, or water, dangerous contaminants must be placed somewhere, and the disposal sites are too often in the poorest communities. As Faber has observed:

> *The waste, now commodified, becomes mobile, crossing local, state and even national borders in search of "efficient" (i.e., low-cost and politically feasible) areas for treatment, incineration, and/or disposal. More often than not, the waste sites and facilities are themselves hazardous and located in poor working class neighborhoods and communities of color. . . .*

For instance, in Sierra Blanca, Texas, the local economy has collapsed. Underemployment is so pervasive that 40 percent of the population lives below the poverty line. Since 1992, New York City and a "biosolids" company called Merco have shipped roughly 200 tons of processed sewage a day *to the small town. Due to concerns that the sludge is poisoned with heavy metals, petroleum, and pathogens, community residents see this practice as posing a significant health threat and therefore a form of environmental racism. There are more than 200 other such sewage sludge sites in Texas alone.*[5]

Europe also illustrates one of the ironies of introducing efforts to protect the environment, as environmental regulations have created large profits for those who illegally circumvent the law:

Exporting waste illegally to poor countries has become a vast and growing international business, as companies try to minimize the costs of new environmental laws, like those here [in Europe], that tax waste or require that it be recycled or otherwise disposed of in an environmentally responsible way . . . [In those poor destination countries] electronic waste and construction debris containing toxic chemicals are often dismantled by children at great cost to their health.[6]

The use and disposal of natural resources is a global problem. However, the United States is a key figure in the process. Although the United States has only about 6 percent of the world's population, it "consumes approximately 30 percent of all raw materials used by the human population in any given year."[7] However, almost every portion of the world is experiencing, or will soon experience, conflict and injustice related to the use of natural resources. While consumption practices in the United States contribute to the problem, it is not only caused by the United States. It is a problem of global proportions.

The discussion that follows takes a global perspective and includes more than the disposal of hazardous waste or environmental contaminants. Much of the discussion concentrates on issues of justice related to the ways in which resources are extracted and their benefits distributed.

Oil is the natural resource that comes to mind when we think about problems arising from shortages of natural resources and when we think about air pollution and other environmental contaminants. The Gulf War was fought over oil, and oil provides nations that produce it with the money to buy advanced weapons. Money from oil production probably funded the terrorists who brought down the World Trade Center in September of 2001. However, oil is only one of many valuable resources that play key roles in modern society and over which injustices arise. Such resources include natural gas, coal, uranium, gold, diamonds, timber, copper, iron, and water.

An interesting example of the complex relationship between natural resources and justice can be found in the Democratic Republic of the Congo in central Africa. The Congo sits on one of the most mineral and timber rich pieces of land in the world. Although only 2 percent of the land is suitable for farming, the country's wealth lies underground in the form of gold, silver, diamonds, oil, tin, uranium, iron, coal, timber, and more.[8] As a result of these riches, the country has been racked by war for decades, as armies from surrounding countries, as well as private armies, plunder the country. As many as 20 rebel groups fight for the resources of this country and in the process engage in violence so horrific it is hard to imagine: gang-raping women and then sewing them shut, murdering millions of people, forcing child soldiers to kill and rape, and even cannibalism.[9] While we tend to think of environmental justice as linked to a shortage of resources, the people of the Congo are raped, murdered, and brutalized *because* the country has so many resources.

There are many dimensions to problems related to the environment and justice. Klare has argued that several factors make it likely that conflicts and injustices over natural resources will be an increasingly serious problem.[10] These factors are the growing importance of some resources and a growing worldwide demand for those resources.

Some resources, such as oil, have become essential for maintaining our economy and way of life. Until the early 1900s, oil played a minor role in the U.S. economy. Its derivatives, including kerosene, were used for heating and for light, but it was not yet used to power vehicles or modern machinery. Even though the United States is a major producer of oil, the economy would collapse if the flow of oil into the United States were suddenly interrupted. Protecting oil resources was a primary consideration in the United States' decision to enter the Gulf War in 1990 and in its continued military presence in the Middle East.

A growing and nearly insatiable demand for resources, combined with limited supplies, contributes to injustices related to the environment. Advanced industrial countries consume far more resources than do developing countries. In the United States, for example, advances in technology and an improved standard of living have meant that energy consumption increases every year. The problem is compounded by population growth, which is most rapid in developing countries—countries with per capita energy consumptions that are relatively small but will increase dramatically as the countries develop. However, because supplies are limited, there will be increased competition, violence, and even war over resources. Furthermore, increasing demand in the face of limited supplies will mean that many basic resources will be available only to the wealthy.

It is not possible here to cover every resource and its possible connections to justice. To illustrate the many ways in which environmental concerns and justice are connected, this discussion focuses on the implications for justice of one natural resource—water. Most industrial societies require oil, coal, and natural gas to maintain their industries, generate electricity, and provide fuel for planes, trains, ships, and trucks. While these resources are essential for maintaining a modern lifestyle, they are not essential to life itself. There have been and still are societies that do not depend on fossil fuels. Water is quite another matter.

WATER

The first civilizations arose in river valleys, and most major cities were built along waterways.[11] Water permeates (quite literally) every aspect of modern life. The Earth is mostly covered in water, and the human body is made of more water than anything else, so that a 150-pound man contains 90 pounds of water.[12] Access to water is a matter of life and death, something important enough that people might kill to obtain or protect it. And, while there are substitutes for many resources (e.g., for some applications, oil from soybeans can replace oil extracted from the ground, and plastic can replace wood in building construction), to date there are no substitutes for water.

Although it would appear that water is everywhere, it is a finite resource. "Available fresh water amounts to less than one half of 1 percent of all the water on the Earth. The rest is sea water, or is frozen in the polar ice."[13] Furthermore, the amount of water on earth is exactly the same as the amount that was on earth a million years ago. The water you drink today was consumed (and excreted) by dinosaurs. Some have begun to refer to water as "Blue Gold,"[14] and in Texas water has become more valuable than oil and is now called "Liquid Gold" by some.[15]

Water is a finite resource that is not evenly distributed throughout the world. Some have an abundance of water, while others have little. For example, "the world's arid and semiarid regions—which together constitute approximately 40 percent of the earth's land mass and house perhaps one-fifth of its total population—receive only 2 percent of the global water runoff."[16] This division of the world in to the water haves and the water have-nots sets the stage for a range of justice-related problems from public health to war.

The water supply problem is even growing in the United States, which is among the countries with the largest supply of fresh water. In the Southeastern United States, Georgia, Alabama, and Florida are in a legal battle over access to water from the Chattahoochee River. Faced with growth outpacing the supply of water, the city council of Santa Fe, New Mexico, considered a ban on all commercial and residential construction.[17] Arizona has passed a law allowing counties to limit growth in areas where there may not be enough water to sustain a growing population.[18] In these rapidly growing states, the need for water is outstripping the supply, and the situation is reaching a critical level.[19] Along the border between Texas and Mexico, American farmers are going bankrupt because Mexico has drawn water from the Rio Grande at such a rate that none remains for irrigation by American farmers.[20]

While the world supply of water is fixed, demand continues to grow. As a result of population growth and industrialization, water usage is doubling about every 20 years.[21] As Klare has observed:

> *Of the amount [of water] that is readily available . . . half is already being appropriated for human use. As in the case of oil, population growth and higher standards of living are constantly boosting the global demand for water. If this pattern persists, total human usage will approach 100 percent of the available supply by the mid-twenty-first century, producing severe shortages in some areas and intensified competition for access to important sources of supply.*[22]

Much of the water that is consumed by people, either directly or through irrigation, comes from underground. On every continent the water table, or level of underground water, is falling. The situation aboveground is no better. Many rivers, including the Colorado River, which runs from Colorado to California, and the Rio Grande, which runs along the border between Mexico and the United States, are now drained of their water before they reach the sea.[23] In China, the famous Yellow River, which is 3400 miles long, failed to reach the ocean for the first time in history in 1972, and some now consider the river to be dying. There are similar concerns that China's Yangtze will also run dry.[24] Massive lakes in Russia and sub-Saharan Africa have nearly disappeared as water was diverted from the rivers that feed the lakes. As the lakes have disappeared, the climate around those lakes has also shifted. In Russia, for example, the summers are now hotter and the winters colder without the moderating effects of the Aral Sea, which at one time was the fourth-largest freshwater lake in the world.[25]

Mexico's Lake Chapala was 50 miles wide and was once called Mexico's inland sea. Today, fish and wildlife are disappearing from the lake that was once an average of 36 feet deep, but is now averages only 4.5 feet deep. The lake is the main source of drinking water for the city of Guadalajara, and the river that feeds the lake is a source of water for Mexico City, while also providing water to irrigate crops. In addition, beginning in the early 1900s, portions of Lake Chapala were drained for farmland.[26] What was once a beautiful oasis is rapidly becoming a desert.

DESALINATION

One response to a water shortage is to remove salt from sea water, a process known as desalination. Unfortunately, this process is not very efficient, requiring tremendous amounts of energy, which itself is often produced using water. Desalination is only affordable for the wealthiest nations, and there are no signs that less expensive and more efficient purification systems will be developed soon.[27] In San Diego County, California, a desalination plant is being built for one billion dollars. The plant will produce fresh water at double the current cost of water and will provide only 7 percent of the county's water needs.[28] In El Paso, Texas, where desalination is applied to a salty underground aquifer, the cost of desalinated water is double the cost of fresh groundwater and 70 percent higher than surface water. The El Paso plant does not run at full capacity because of the high cost of filtering the water and supplies only about 4 percent of the city's water.[29] Furthermore, the high cost of transporting water long distances means that desalination is unlikely to ever supply large amounts of water to people living inland.

WATER AND FOOD

Water is not just used for drinking. It is also essential for growing food. Most of the fresh water consumed in the world today is used for agriculture.[30] Worldwide, about 40 percent of all crops are grown through irrigation, and irrigation "accounts for two thirds of water use worldwide and as much as 90 percent in many developing countries."[31] Making the problem worse, most irrigation systems are inefficient, with as much as half of the water never reaching intended crops, because of leakage in transit to the farmland or because of evaporation. Even the choice of foods we eat has an impact on how much water is used. For example, producing meat requires much more water than producing vegetables, as the following table shows.[32]

Food	Water Required
One Pound of Beef	1857 Gallons
One Pound of Chicken	469 Gallons
One Pound of Corn	109 Gallons
One Pound of Potatoes	31 Gallons
One Cup of Coffee	37 Gallons

In addition, it can no longer be assumed that the oceans will provide an unlimited supply of food. By the year 2002, three-quarters of the world's fisheries had been overfished.[33] Not only is the supply of fish in the ocean diminishing, but the pollution of ocean waters has led to the contamination of fish. This is particularly true of larger fish that take more time to grow and, as a result, are exposed to toxic chemicals in the ocean for a longer period. A study of fish purchased from grocery stores in California found that "All fish samples tested contained measurable levels of mercury . . . [and] nearly one-third of the fish purchased at grocery stores contains levels of mercury the United States has deemed unsafe for consumption . . . ."[34] This is why pregnant women are sometimes urged to limit their intake of fish. Fish from freshwater sources are also threatened:

> *Eighty percent of China's rivers are so degraded they no longer support fish. China is facing the likelihood of severe grain shortages because of water depletion and the shift of water resources from agriculture to industry and cities. The resulting demand for grain in China soon could exceed the entire world's available exportable supply.*[35]

While much of this discussion focuses on water as a global problem, the United States is also facing water shortages related to food production. Oregon farmers, fearing the loss of their crops, have damaged federally owned canals to release water for irrigation—water that was being saved to rescue an endangered species of fish.[36] In reality there may not be enough water to save either the fish or the farms.

WATER AND HEALTH

The public health consequences of the uneven distribution of water around the world can be staggering:

> *. . . more than one billion people lack access to clean drinking water and two and a half billion do not have adequate sanitation services. Preventable water-related diseases kill an estimated 10,000 to 20,000 children every day, and the latest evidence suggests we are falling behind in efforts to solve these problems.*[37]

It has been estimated that 80% of the disease in the Third World is caused by contaminated water and that as many as 10 million people each year die as a result. The situation is worst in Asia and Africa.[38] "Half of the people in Africa, Asia, Latin America, and the Caribbean are estimated to suffer from diseases associated with inadequate freshwater and sanitation."[39] According to a report by the United Nations, contaminated water kills more people each year than violence and war combined.[40]

The conditions in impoverished nations contrast dramatically with those in more developed nations, where water-related illnesses are relatively rare. It has not always been the case, however. In 1842, New York became the first city in America with a municipal water system, following years of epidemics and fires that could not be put out because of a lack of piped water.[41] A little more than one hundred years ago, 20% of the deaths in central Illinois were from contaminated water, and that region had some of the best water in the nation.[42]

WATER AND MANUFACTURING

In addition to its role in food production, water is central to the manufacture and distribution of food products. "Alone, five giant global food and beverage corporations—Nestle, Danone, Unilever, Anheuser-Busch, and Coca-Cola—consume enough water to meet the daily domestic needs of every person on the planet."[43] Water is also an essential element in the manufacture of everyday products. For example, it takes 2900 gallons of water to make one pair of blue jeans, 2800 gallons to make one cotton bed sheet, and 766 gallons to make one cotton T-shirt.[44] While on a global level most fresh water is used for producing food, in the United States, food production is not the primary way in which fresh water is consumed. It may be surprising to many that in the United States the single biggest use for water is in the production of electricity in:

> *. . . coal, gas, and nuclear power plants for cooling and to make steam. U.S. electric utilities require seven times more water than all U.S. homes. They use 1.5 times the amount of water used by all farms in the country. In fact, 49 percent of all water use in the United States is for power plants.*[45]

And, these statistics do not account for electricity produced by hydroelectric dams.

As the world population continues to grow while the supply of water is relatively fixed, injustices related to the use of water will become more frequent. Our discussion now turns to some of the forms those injustices might take.

PRIVATIZATION OF WATER

Where clean water is scarce, it quickly becomes an expensive commodity, a product to be sold to the highest bidder. There are hundreds of companies that deal in water as a commodity. The two largest are French companies that together have water-related annual revenues of more than $10 billion. "The World Bank estimates the global market for water to be worth $800 billion. . . . In the U.S. alone, where the vast majority of water services remains in public hands, private water corporations generate revenues of more than $80 billion (U.S.) a year—four times the annual sales of Microsoft."[46]

Price is of little concern to the very wealthy, but for the poor, a lack of affordable water can have deadly consequences. A World Health Organization report "estimated that 25% of the population living in cities in developing countries bought water from vendors, typically spending 10-20% of household income."[47] In India some households pay as much as 25% of their household incomes for water.[48] Although the wealthy can afford to pay more, they often end up paying less, even receiving government subsidies for their water. "Poor residents of Lima, Peru, pay private vendors as much as $3 for a cubic meter for buckets of often-contaminated water while the more affluent pay 30 cents per cubic meter for treated municipal tap water."[49] "In Bamako, the capital of Mali, poor people pay as much as 45 times more per unit of water than do the rich, who get water piped into their homes, often at subsidized prices."[50]

The idea that water should be privatized has been promoted by the World Bank, which sometimes requires privatization as a condition for loans to developing countries. In January of 2000, thousands of citizens in the Bolivian city of Cochabamba took part in strikes that shut the city down for four days.[51] In February thousands of Bolivians attempted to march peacefully in the streets. Again in April, citizens shut down the city, leading the Bolivian government to declare martial law and to arrest peaceful demonstrators. People traveled as far as 70 miles on foot to join the demonstrations. Bolivians had taken to the streets to protest the skyrocketing water rates that went into effect after the Bechtel Corporation took private possession of Cochabamba's water supply. As part of the agreement, Bechtel assumed control of wells that private citizens had dug for themselves, and the corporation even demanded that people pay for water they collected from their own rooftops. Soon after Bechtel took over, families earning less than $100 per month were charged as much as $20 per month for water. On April 10, the government backed down, returning control of water distribution to the government. However, because the government itself did not have the resources to upgrade the water system, returning control of the water to the public sector did nothing to improve the broken down supply system or to improve the prospects for a long-term solution to the city's water shortage. In the end, there were no winners in this dispute.

Bolivia is not an isolated case. Around the world there is a move to privatize water. Privatization of water has been slowly emerging within the United States as well, and some of the arrangements are beginning to involve massive amounts of water. In Colorado a senator is accused of trying to privatize a federal reservoir for his own benefit.[52] In Southern California a private firm is scheduled to provide as much as 47 billion gallons of water per year.[53] In Texas an entrepreneur is offering to sell tens of billions of gallons of water to the highest bidder. He is expecting to make as much as $1 billion. Under Texas law he may pump as much water as he wishes from his land, even if that underground supply extends onto other property (which it does), and his business leaves the surrounding region without water.[54]

Most jurisdictions in the United States recognize what are known as "riparian rights." This refers to the right of landowners to use the water that flows through or near their property. Whether the water is considered private (and thus something that can be sold) or public depends on a variety of things. Is the water in a small stream or is it part of a navigable river? Is the water being taken at the source of the river or near its end? Bodies that govern riparian rights consider these factors in making judgments about who may take water from the river and how much they may take. Riparian rights also regulate such things as the amount of water that property owners may remove from a river or stream, so that other property owners downstream have fair access to the water. These rights also address what happens if the course of the river or stream changes. If the river no longer runs through the property, can the owner still use water from the river? Although riparian rights exist throughout the United States, they have been of particular concern in the American West, where water is most scarce. Unfortunately, riparian rights were designed to apply to water that flows above ground. In many jurisdictions there are no restrictions on landowners who tap underground water sources.

Privately supplied water is not automatically bad for consumers, but the potential for injustice is substantial. Corporations exist to make as much money as possible, and the temptation will be to sell to the highest bidder, even if that means the poor are left without water. This will be particularly likely if the market becomes concentrated in the hands of a few companies so there is little competition, and if the supply grows short—a situation that has been compared to that of the oil cartels in the Middle East.[55] In that case the poor will likely be priced out of the water market. A member of Newfoundland's legislature has been quoted as saying, "Water is the commodity of the next century and those who possess it and control it could be in a position to control the world's economy."[56]

WATER AND WAR

Because water is essential for life, it should not be surprising that wars have been fought over access to it. This was true in the past, and today there are many places in which wars have erupted, or are likely to erupt, over the issue of water. In 1995, the former chairman of the World Commission for Water in the 21st Century, who was also a senior official at the World Bank, made the following prediction: "Many of the wars of this century were about oil, but those of the next century will be over water."[57]

Several factors would seem to increase the likelihood of water-related conflicts. First, conflicts can be expected when different countries share common water sources. A single river might flow through several countries, or an underground aquifer might cross national boundaries. As it happens, the sharing of water systems is a relatively common occurrence. Researchers who have drawn maps of the world's water systems have found that major river basins are often shared by more than one country:

> *. . . 261 such basins extend over two or more international boundaries. These basins cover approximately 45 percent of the earth's land area, excluding Antarctica. No less than 145 nations depend on shared river systems for at least some portion of their freshwater supply, and a good number of these are almost wholly dependent on such systems. Many important underground aquifers, such as the vital "Mountain aquifer" lying beneath Israel and the West Bank, are also shared in this manner.*[58]

Some of the most volatile regions of the world include nations that must share water. For example:

The major shared [river] systems of the Middle East and Southwest Asia—the Nile, the Jordan, the Tigris-Euphrates, and the Indus—have been the sites of conflict throughout human history; indeed, many of the earliest recorded wars occurred along their banks.[59]

Problems arising from shared water systems are exacerbated when the countries involved also have differences in religion, political systems, or customs.

A second factor likely to facilitate water-related conflict is a shortage of water. As discussed above, many parts of the world have serious water shortages. Several factors can lead to extreme shortages. Population growth can lead to a dramatic increase in the demand for water. Unfortunately, some of the countries suffering the greatest water shortages are also those having the most rapid population growth. Industrialization and economic growth can also result in substantial increases in demand for water. Total annual water consumption in industrialized nations averages more than 1500 cubic meters of water per person, whereas countries with low levels of economic development may use less than 100 cubic meters of water per person each year.[60]

Water is not only a source of conflict between nations, it can also be a target for warring nations. For example, during the Persian Gulf War, "the Iraqis intentionally destroyed the water desalination plants of Kuwait and in turn suffered from the destruction of their water supply system by the allied forces assembled to liberate Kuwait."[61] Within the United States, right-wing extremist groups have long discussed the strategic importance of contaminating urban water systems as a tool for bringing social and economic chaos.

Although there are many examples of water-related international conflicts,[52] only the case of Israel and her neighbors, particularly Jordan, is summarized here to give the reader a sense for the nature of the problem.

Israel and Jordan: Israel and Jordan are located in a region with some of the most severe water scarcity problems in the world. Nine of the fourteen Middle Eastern countries face serious water shortages.[63] Since its formation in 1948, Israel has competed with Jordan for fresh water, and both countries face substantial shortages. While 1000 cubic meters of water per person is considered a healthy minimum, in 1990, Israel's renewable water supply was 467 cubic meters per person, and Jordan's was only 224 cubic meters.[64] Both countries rely on the same two major sources of water, the Jordan River and underground aquifers.

The Jordan River is relatively small, having only about 1% of the water that flows through the Congo River and only about 2% of the amount that flows through the Nile.[65] The Jordan originates to the north of Israel, fed by rivers in Lebanon, Syria, and Jordan. Over the years there have been several efforts by these countries to divert or capture water flowing through their lands and into Israel. In each case Israel has responded that such diversions would threaten Israel's security and would be tantamount to a declaration of war. In the Six Day War of 1967, Israel attacked sites where Syria was building dams to divert water from Israel. As a result of superior military forces, Israel was able to occupy parts of Syria and gain further control over the region feeding water into the Jordan. In recent years Israel has been in conflict with Palestinians living on the West Bank. Water is again a key element (though not the only one) in that conflict. Israel draws most of the West Bank's underground water supply for its own use and rations water to the Palestinians in a manner that is blatantly unequal, "with Jewish settlers receiving five to eight times more water per capita than the Palestinians."[66] This unequal distribution of water has added to Palestinian resentment of the Israelis and "helped fuel the Palestinian *intifada*, or uprising, that began in 1987 and lasted for several years."[67] Water has also been an issue of contention between Israel and citizens of the Gaza Strip, a small area to the southeast of Israel, from which Israel has been drawing underground water supplies at a per capita rate 10 times that of the Palestinians who live there.[68]

Not only is water from the Jordan River in short supply, but Israel and Jordan have also been taking water from underground aquifers at a faster rate than it can be replaced:

> *By the mid-1990s, Israel was overexploiting its water, drawing down its aquifers at beyond replenishment rates by about 15 percent a year . . . . Jordan was doing even worse: it was using 20 percent more water than it was receiving. The costal aquifers in the region . . . were seriously overpumped, and seawater intrusions were becoming a major problem—and a major political problem given that Jews were allowed to drill their wells deeper than Arabs or Palestinians. The already potent Palestinian grievances were being ratcheted up by the brutal politics of water.*[69]

Water isn't the only issue in dispute between Israel and its neighbors. Land, religion, and politics have often triggered violence in the region. However, the role of water in such disputes is likely to increase over time. Through the 1990s and into this century, there have been efforts to negotiate peace agreements in the region, with water often serving as a key negotiating point. In 1994, Israel and Jordan signed a peace treaty that included provisions for the distribution of water. How long the peace will last is unclear, but long-term peace in the region seems elusive. The supply of available water continues to decline while the population of the region continues to grow. It is estimated that between 1998 and 2025 the population of Israel will grow by one-third and the population of Jordan will double. It is difficult to imagine a scenario in which all sides will be able to receive enough water to meet their needs.

The Middle East is only one of many regions where water has played a role in conflict. In most cases water is not the sole reason for the conflict, but magnifies the problem, as when Malaysia, which supplies about half of Singapore's water, threatened to cut off that water in response to Singapore's criticism of government policy in Malaysia.[70] While such conflicts have occurred in the past, the frequency of these conflicts appears to be increasing, as can be seen in Table 13.1.

Table 13.1 Water-Related Conflicts by Decade[a]

Decade	Conflicts
1960s	12
1970s	14
1980s	15
1990s	37
2000s	59

[a]The Pacific Institute, *Water Conflict Chronology Timeline* (accessed online at http://www.worldwater.org/conflict/timeline/ on July 9, 2013).

It can be expected that the number of incidents will increase even more rapidly in the decades to come.

WATER AND OTHER NATURAL RESOURCES

Before we close our discussion of water and justice, it is worth noting that the rush to extract other natural resources often has an impact on the availability and quality of water for consumption or for growing crops. For example, on a Pacific island called Bougainville, a company established the world's largest open-pit copper mine, a "gaping chasm three-quarters of a mile deep, two and a half miles wide, and three and a half miles long."[71] The refuse from this mine was dumped into the local river system, where it killed the fish and contaminated the island's water supply. The nearby island of Papua New Guinea claimed to possess the island of Bougainville and received royalties from the mines, but the residents of Bougainville received almost nothing, and the government in Papua New Guinea showed no interest in helping them. Eventually, the residents rebelled against Papua New Guinea and asserted their independence. After several failed attempts by Papua New Guinea to retake the island, tensions between the two groups continues.[72]

While Bougainville is one good example of how the extraction or use of natural resources can lead to water-related conflict, there are additional examples throughout the world. In some places clear-cut logging results in such high levels of soil erosion that once safe streams and rivers are turned into mud. In other places subterranean water supplies are threatened by radioactive waste stored underground. And the list goes on. Water is a natural resource connected to many other resources, and it touches nearly every aspect of our lives. It is not surprising that some have called access to clean water a basic human right.[73]

EMERGING ISSUES

It is likely that the use and equitable distribution of water will increasingly become an issue leading to conflicts between and within nations. It is also likely that oil will play a larger role in international conflicts in the next few decades. Beyond the examples of water and oil, there are many resources that will raise issues of justice and will lead to conflicts in the very near future.

In recent decades endangered species, and in particular the trafficking in endangered species, have become an issue of international concern. Global recognition of the problem came in the form of the United Nations' 1973 Convention on International Trade in Endangered Species of Wild Fauna and Flora (CITES).[74] CITES has been ratified by 178 countries. Currently, the illicit trade in endangered species is highly lucrative. As it is an illegal activity, there are no precise records of the nature and extent of the trade in endangered species, but profits from the trade are estimated to be second only to those from illicit drug trafficking,[75] falling in the range of \$8-\$10 billion each year.[76] As an example, rhinoceros horns are ground into a powder and used in medicine in some Asian countries, where the powder sells for as much as \$1400 an ounce—about the price of gold.[77] There are hundreds of species at risk because of the illicit trade, but areas of particular concern include trafficking in rhinoceros (horns), elephants (tusks, skins, tail hair), tigers (skins, teeth, claws, bones), gorillas (meat, various parts as trophies), sharks (fins).[78]

There are concerns that high profits have attracted transnational organized crime groups to trafficking in endangered species.[79] Enforcing laws against trafficking in endangered species is complicated by the fact that many of the source countries are poor, limiting the resources available to fight the crime. Enforcement is also hindered by high levels of corruption among officials,[80] and the reality is that the odds of being caught are small and the punishments are likely to be relatively light.

Timber is another example of an environmental issue with implications for justice. Timber is technically a renewable resource, but it is not being regrown as quickly as it is being consumed. Consequently, timber has become extremely valuable. For example, large knot-like growths called burls create beautiful patterns in wood and are therefore particularly valuable. "A raw burl [from a single walnut tree] can sell for $5000 or more in California and as much as $30,000 in Italy on the rare woods market."[81] Similarly, a single cedar tree can bring as much as $20,000.[82] Much of the forest land in Indonesia has been stripped bare, and there are concerns that the forests will disappear altogether within the next decade. The market for timber is so lucrative in Indonesia that illegal loggers "are apparently evading arrest by getting their wives to strip naked and distract officials while they make a quick getaway with the valuable hardwood. . . . authorities were too embarrassed to take action when confronted by the women."[83] As time passes, timber will only become more valuable.

In Africa money from gold and diamonds has led to wars between nations, benefitting a few while leaving most Africans living in poverty. Also in Africa, as many as 15,000 children as young as 11 have been forced into slavery to harvest the cocoa required to make chocolate.[84] As discussed in Chapter 11, slavery continues to be a serious problem throughout the world, and the harvesting of natural resources is an important dimension of the contemporary slave trade.

As resources are becoming more scarce, they are also becoming more valuable and will fuel further injustices. It is now profitable for large corporations and nations to harvest natural resources from areas once considered remote. High profits also lead companies and nations to do things they might not do otherwise. Dictators use the wealth generated by the sale of natural resources to finance armies that crush political opposition. The Congo, for example, has some of the richest deposits of natural resources in the world, such as diamonds, gold, and timber. Although dictators and armies have become fabulously wealthy from the Congo's natural resources, its people are poor and are subject to random acts of violence.

One of the most disturbing trends is detailed by Klare.[85] The profits from natural resources are now so enormous that small nations and corporations can afford to hire private armies, mercenaries, to forcibly take those resources from anyone unwilling to hand them over. In many cases people who have lived on their land for many generations are driven away with no compensation, and in some cases, they are killed outright. These private armies, funded by the sale of natural resources, have also been tools for suppressing opposition to dictators who control the resources. These mercenaries generally don't concern themselves with doing what is right and just. They will kill, torture, and rape for anyone willing to pay their price. In the Congo, for example, tens of thousands of women have been raped by soldiers who have no fear they will ever be held accountable for their actions.

The distribution, use, and disposal of natural resources have often led to conflict and injustice. While it may not be possible to eliminate such conflicts, it is possible to minimize them. Klare suggests that, in a global economy, conflicts over resources can only be prevented through global cooperation.[86] Violence can only be avoided if the nations of the world work together to conserve scarce commodities and to arrange for their harvest and distribution in a just manner. Klare suggests that, for such cooperation to exist, it will be necessary to develop international institutions. These institutions would be expected to maintain "an accurate inventory of the world's supplies of critical commodities and to develop mechanisms for the global allocation of these materials in times of extreme scarcity or emergency."[87] These institutions would also serve to pool the world's scientific knowledge about the use of resources and about the development of substitutes for scarce natural resources. To be effective such institutions would need enforcement authority, and that would require some form of international court or tribunal.

While creating an international body to monitor and regulate the use of natural resources is an appealing idea, it is unclear whether such a body would work in practice. One major roadblock is the United States. As the United States is the largest consumer of natural resources in the world, its cooperation is essential to the success of any international body intended to regulate natural resources. However, the United States also has a long history of opposing anything that would undermine its sovereignty. The United States has traditionally been lukewarm to the United Nations, and it has generally not supported international treaties to protect the environment. And, the United States has long opposed the creation of an international court of justice that might enforce such treaties. Perhaps the best hope is that the world, including the United States, will come to appreciate that the nations of the Earth are increasingly interdependent on a finite supply of natural resources.

CONCLUSION

There are many connections between the environment and justice. First, natural resources are, in general, most available to those with the greatest economic resources. The gap in resource access between the rich and poor grows in direct proportion to the scarcity of natural resources. As resources become scarcer, the poor are eventually priced out of the market. For some resources, such as water, the consequences can be fatal. The justice of such a market-driven system is open to serious question, and injustices that arise from this system might easily lead to violent responses.

Second, murder, rape, and war all become tools for getting valuable resources. This is true today for such precious commodities as gold, diamonds, and oil. For example, the United States entered the Persian Gulf War to protect its supply of inexpensive oil, and soldiers in Africa use murder, torture, mutilation, and rape to maintain their access to gold and diamonds. Bales[88] has documented a variety of ways in which contemporary slavery is a tool for acquiring valuable resources (see Chapter 11). Money from the sale of resources can also be used to fund violence and oppression. Thus, environmental resources can provide both the incentives and the finances to engage in other forms of injustice.

Third, efforts to protect the environment can themselves be unjust and even deadly. The United States has seen relatively little extreme activism regarding its treatment of the environment. Even so, in 2002, Congress held hearings on "eco-terrorism" and were told that, in the previous 5 years, environmental activists had committed more than 600 criminal acts resulting in more than $43 million in damages.[89] Environmental activist groups such as the Earth Liberation Front have publicly announced they will no longer limit their work to nonviolence.[90] The incidence of eco-terrorism appears to be increasing over time, and one member of Congress has warned that "It's just a matter of time before a human life is taken."[91]

Finally, there is the issue of using the environment as a terrorist tool. For example, sabotaging just two dams on the Colorado River (Glen Canyon Dam and Flaming Gorge Dam) would "cause major damage to the water supply systems of more than 25 million people in the lower Colorado River Basin."[92] Similarly, America has 103 nuclear power plants, and a successful 9-11-style attack on any one has the potential to kill tens of thousands of people, perhaps hundreds of thousands.[93]

Except where severe shortages have already been felt, there is at present little appreciation for the full range of ways in which the environment and justice are related. As demand for resources grows and as shortages become more frequent, there will be a renewed appreciation for environmental justice. At this point the prospects are not bright for resolving large-scale injustices linked to the environment, and environment-related injustices can be expected to become more severe and more difficult to resolve. Of the justice issues discussed in this book, injustices related to the environment may be the most difficult to resolve.

DISCUSSION QUESTIONS

1. Why might some people use the terms "environmental justice" and "environmental racism" interchangeably?
2. What factors are related to a country's level of water consumption?
3. What are the advantages and disadvantages of privatizing water? Why are some people worried about privatization?

Endnotes

1. For this incident, see James P. Lester, David W. Allen, and Kelly M. Hill, *Environmental Justice in the United States: Myths and Realities* (Boulder, Colo.: Westview Press, 2001).
2. See Daniel Faber "The Struggle for Ecological Democracy and Environmental Justice," in *The Struggle for Ecological Democracy: Environmental Justice Movements in the United States*, Daniel Farber (ed.) (New York: The Guilford Press, 1998).
3. Environmental Protection Agency (EPA), *Index of Environmental Justice Publications* (available at www.epa.gov/swerosps/ej/ejndx.htm; Internet; accessed on 16 January 2002).
4. This is covered in Martin V. Melosi, *Effluent America: Cities, Industry, Energy, and the Environment* (Pittsburgh: University of Pittsburgh Press, 2001).
5. Daniel Farber, "The Political Economy of American Capitalism: New Challenges for the Environmental Justice Movement," in *The Struggle for Ecological Democracy: Environmental Justice Movements in the United States*, Daniel Farber (ed.) (New York: The Guilford Press, 1998), p. 38.
6. Elisabeth Rosenthal, "Smuggling Europe's Waste to Poorer Countries," *New York Times* (accessed online at www.nytimes.com on 27 September 2009).
7. Michael T. Klare, *Resource Wars: The New Landscape of Global Conflict* (New York: Metropolitan Books, 2000), p. 15.
8. *The CIA World Factbook* (accessed online at https://www.cia.gov/library/publications/the-world-factbook/ on 8 July 2013).
9. Jason Stearns, *Dancing in the Glory of Monsters: The Collapse of the Congo and the Great War of Africa*, Reprint Edition (New York: Public Affairs, 2012); Daniel Bergner, "The Most Unconventional Weapon," *The New York Times Magazine*, October 26, 2003, pp. 48-53; P.W. Singer, *Children at War* (Berkeley, Calif.: University of California Press, 2006).
10. *Ibid.*
11. Steven Solomon, *Water: The Epic Struggle for Wealth, Power, and Civilization* (New York: Harper, 2010).
12. Charles Fishman, *The Big Thirst: The Secret Life and Turbulent Future of Water* (New York: The Free Press, 2011).
13. Barlow, "Blue Gold."
14. Maude Barlow, *Blue Gold: The Global Water Crisis and the Commodification of the World's Water Supply*, Report to the International Forum on Globalization of Water (available at www.ifg.org/bgsummary.htm; Internet; 1999; accessed on 31 January 2002).
15. Jim Yardley, "For Texas Now, Water and Not Oil Is Liquid Gold," *New York Times* (electronic version) (available at http://nytimes.com 16 April 2001; accessed 31 January 2002).
16. Klare, *Resource Wars*, p. 145.
17. Tom Gorman, "Water May Be a Wet Blanket to New Growth," *L.A. Times* (electronic edition) (available at www.latimes.com; 8 July 2002; accessed on July 2002).

18. "Arizona Passes Limits on Growth," *L.A. Times* (electronic version) (available at www.latimes.com; 25 May 2007; accessed on 25 May 2007).
19. Larry Copeland, "Water Wars Brew in Southeast: Resource Is Nearing a Critical Point Because of Regional Growth," *U.S.A. Today*, 18 July 2001, p. 3A.
20. Dan McGraw, "A Boiling Tex-Mex Water War," *U.S. News & World Report*, 1 May 2000, p. 24.
21. *Ibid.*
22. Klare, *Resource Wars*, p. 19.
23. John M. Swomley, "When Blue Becomes Gold," *The Humanist* (September/October 2000), pp. 5-7; James F. Smith, "Testing the Waters of Cooperation," *L.A. Times* (electronic version) (available at www.latimes.com; 29 May 2001; accessed 29 May 2001).
24. Erling Hoh, "China's 'Mother River' Is Dying: Parched Yellow Portends Vast Ecological Doom," *Chicago Tribune,* 5 July 2001, p. 4.
25. Solomon, *Water: The Epic Struggle for Wealth, Power, and Civilization*, pp. 377-378.
26. Marla Dickerson, "Once-Grand Mexican Lake Is Being Drained of Its Life," *L.A. Times* (electronic version) (available at www.latimes.com; 18 April 2003; accessed 18 April 2003).
27. Marvin Cetron and Owen Davis, *Probable Tomorrows: How Science and Technology Will Transform Our Lives in the Next Twenty Years* (New York: St. Martin's Press, 1997).
28. Felicity Barringer, "In California, What Price Water?" *New York Times* (accessed online at www.nytimes.com on 28 February 2013).
29. Kate Galbraith, "Texas' Water Woes Spark Interest in Desalination," *The Texas Tribune* (accessed online at www.texastribune.org on 10 June 2012).
30. Gleick, "Making Every Drop Count."
31. Sandra Postel, "Growing More Food with Less Water," *Scientific American* (February 2001), pp. 46-47, 50-51.
32. "Hidden Water," *National Geographic* (April 2010, issue insert).
33. Laurie Goering, "Earth Sumit Clashes with World Realities," *Chicago Tribune,* 25 August, 2002, pp. 1, 12.
34. Got Mercury.org, *Operation Safe Seafood California 2010* (accessed online at www.GotMercury.org on 9 July 2013).
35. Maude Barlow, "Water Incorporated," *Earth Island Journal* 17, no. 1 (2002), pp. 30-31.
36. Deborah Schoch, "Dreams Dry Up in Klamath Basin: Public Policy Allowed Too Many Water-Reliant Interests to Come into Being," *L.A. Times* (electronic edition) (available at www.latimes.com/news/nationworld/nation/la-072301klamath.story; 23 July 2001; accessed on 23 July 2001).
37. Peter H. Gleick, "Making Every Drop Count," *Scientific American* (February 2001). pp. 40-45.
38. World Health Organization, *Global Water Supply and Sanitation Assessment 2000 Report* (available at www.who.int/water_sanitation_health/Globalassessment/GlobalTOC.htm accessed on 4 February 2002).
39. Solomon, *Water: The Epic Struggle for Wealth, Power, and Civilization,* p. 371.
40. Cited in Mike Pflanz, "Word Water Day: Dirty Water Kills More People Than Violence, Says UN," *The Christian Science Monitor* (accessed online at www.csmonitor.com on 22 March 2010).
41. Solomon, *Water: The Epic Struggle for Wealth, Power, and Civilization.*
42. Bill Flick, "Flick Fact," *The Pantagraph*, December 28, 2003.
43. Solomon, *Water: The Epic Struggle for Wealth, Power, and Civilization,* p. 469.
44. "Hidden Water."
45. *Ibid.*, p. 5.
46. The Blue Planet Project, *Fact Sheet 1: Facts on the World's Top Ten Water Companies* (available at www.canadians.org/blueplanet/pubs-fact1.html; Internet; accessed on 31 January 2002).
47. World Water Day 2001, *Water for Health—Taking Charge* (available at www.worldwaterday.org/report/index.html; Internet; accessed on 4 February 2002).
48. Barlow, *Blue Gold.*
49. *Ibid.*

50. World Water Day 2001.
51. Jim Schultz, "Water Fallout: Bolivians Battle Globalization," *In These Times* (available at www.inthesetimes.com/issue/24/12/shultz2412.html; Internet; 15 May 2000; accessed on 31 January 2002); William Finnegan, "Leasing the Rain: The World Is Running Out of Fresh Water, and the Fight to Control It Has Begun," *The New Yorker*, 8 April 2002, pp. 43-47, 50-53.
52. John Elvin, "Activists Attack Campbell for Privatizing Water Rights," *Insight on the News,* 15 (24 May 1999) (available at http://FirstSearch.oclc.org; Internet; accessed on 4 February 2002).
53. James Sterngold, "Private Sector May Sell Water to Southern California Agency," *New York Times* (electronic edition) (accessed at www.nytimes.com; 26 December 2000; accessed on 31 January 2002).
54. Yardley, "For Texas Now."
55. Barlow, "Water Incorporated."
56. Quoted in Swomley, p. 6.
57. Cited in Solomon, *Water: The Epic Struggle for Wealth, Power, and Civilization* , p. 372.
58. Klare, *Resource Wars*, p. 146.
59. *Ibid., p.* 147.
60. Peter H. Gleick, *The World's Water, 1998-1999: The Biennial Report on Freshwater Resources* (Washington, D.C.: Island Press, 1998).
61. *Ibid.*, p. 111.
62. Ibid.; Klare; Marq de Villers, *Water: The Fate of Our Most Precious Resource* (Boston: Houghton Mifflin Co., 2000); Thomas Homer-Dixon and Jessica Blitt (eds.), *Ecoviolence: Links Among Environment, Population and Security* (Lanham, Md.: Rowman & Littlefield, 1998).
63. Kimberly Kelly and Thomas Homer-Dixon, "The Case of Gaza," in *Ecoviolence: Links Among Environment, Population, and Security*, Thomas Homer-Dixon and Jessica Blitt (eds.) (New York: Rowman & Littlefield), pp. 67-107.
64. Klare, *Resource Wars.*
65. *Ibid.*
66. *Ibid.*, p. 171.
67. *Ibid.*
68. Kelly and Homer-Dixon, "The Case of Gaza."
69. De Villers, p. 189.
70. Gleick, *The World's Water, 1998-1999.*
71. Klare, *Resource Wars*, p. 196.
72. *Ibid.*
73. Barlow, "Water Incorporated."
74. United Nations, *Convention on International Trade in Endangered Species of Wild Fauna and Flora* (accessed online at http://cites.org/eng/disc./E-Text.pdf on 11 July 2013).
75. Mara E. Zimmerman, "The Black Market for Wildlife: Combatting Transnational Organized Crime in Illegal Wildlife Trade," *Vanderbilt Journal of Transnational Law* 36 (2003), pp. 1657-1689, cited in Jacqueline L. Schneider, *Sold into Extinction: The Global Trade in Endangered Species* (Santa Barbara, Calif.: Praeger, 2012).
76. World Wildlife Fund (WWF), "UN Recognizes Wildlife Crime as Threat to Rule of Law" (accessed online at www.wwf.panda/org on 11 July 2013).
77. Frank Langfitt, "Vietnam's Appetite for Rhino Horn Drives Poaching in Africa," *National Public Radio* (accessed online at www.npr.org/blogs/parallels/2013/05/14/181587969/Vietnams-Appetite-For-Rhino-Horn-Drives-Poaching-In-Africa on 14 May 2013).
78. *Ibid.*
79. United Nations Office on Drugs and Crime, *World Drug Report 2013* (accessed online at www.unodc.org/unodc/en/wildlife-and-forest-crime/index.html on 11 July 2013); Schneider, *Sold into Extinction.*
80. Schneider, *Sold into Extinction.*

81. Associated Press, "Thieves Destroying Walnut Trees for Valuable Wood" (available at http://sddt.com/files/librarywire/DN95_10_09/DN95_10_091.htm; Internet; accessed on 16 January 1997).
82. Michael R. Pendelton, "Looking the Other Way: The Institutional Accommodation of Tree Theft," *Qualitative Sociology* 20 (1997), pp. 325-340.
83. "The Ol' Naked Wife Diversion," *San Francisco Chronicle* (electronic edition) (available at www.sfgate.com; 12 December 2001; accessed on 15 February 2002).
84. "The Chocolate Industry: Slavery Lurking Behind the Sweetness," *Global Exchange Newsletter* (available at www.globalexchange.org/cocoa/gxWinter2002.htm; Internet; accessed on 11 February 2002).
85. Klare, *Resource Wars.*
86. *Ibid.*
87. *Ibid.*, p. 223.
88. Kevin Bales, *Disposable People: New Slavery in the Global Economy* (Berkeley: The University of California Press, 1999).
89. Brad Knickerbocker, "Eco-Terrorists, Too, May Soon Be on the Run," *The Christian Science Monitor* (electronic edition) (available at www.csmonitor.com; 15 February 2002; accessed on 15 February 2002).
90. Ed Hunt, "Ecoterror's Troubling Trend," *The Christian Science Monitor* (electronic edition) (available at www.csmonitor.com; 7 October 2002; accessed on 7 October 2002).
91. *Ibid.*
92. David Orr, "Floodgates of Terror," *Earth Island Journal* 17 no. 1 (2002), p. 38.
93. Harvey Wasserman, "Nuclear Power and Terrorism," *Earth Island Journal* 17 no. 1 (2002), p. 37; Simson Garfinkel, *Database Nation: The Death of Privacy in the 21st Century* (Cambridge, Mass.: O'Reilly, 2000).

PART

Strategies for Achieving Justice

Earlier sections of this book have considered the difficulty of defining justice, examined some of the key formal systems that pursue legal justice, and described a sampling of contemporary issues concerning justice. A discussion of justice is incomplete, however, without also considering how justice might be achieved—particularly when we move beyond traditional criminal justice to consider justice more generally. This section of the book examines how individuals and nongovernment organizations can pursue justice. It also considers the emerging issue of global justice, in which there is increasing recognition of laws and rights that transcend any single national boundary.

Injustice is pervasive and the scale of injustice can, at times, seem overwhelming. It may seem that individuals are powerless to stop injustice, but history has proven that belief wrong. There are many instances in which a single individual has changed the course of history for the better. The first chapter in this part of the book suggests some of the ways in which individuals have helped achieve justice, with a particular focus on the use of public education, civil disobedience, lawsuits, and guerilla tactics. The examples of the successful use of each approach may serve as blueprints for action that may be utilized by others.

Although individuals can make a difference, there are also advantages to using organizations to achieve justice. Organizations, like individuals, may use public education and civil disobedience to achieve justice. Organizations have also made effective use of civil action in court and of violence to achieve their objectives. This chapter provides examples of organizations that have used each of these approaches to systematically and successfully work for justice.

The final chapter, "Global Justice," concentrates on international efforts to recognize human rights that should be accorded to everyone and to correct injustices that cross national boundaries. The chapter discusses rules of war, such as the Lieber Code, and the creation of definitions of war crimes to use to judge those who violate those rules. This chapter also discusses the creation of the Universal Declaration of Human Rights and the subsequent creation of the European Court of Human Rights, temporary tribunals, and the Permanent International Criminal Court. This chapter highlights the ways in which justice has gradually come to be viewed as an issue of international concern meriting an international response.

The chapters in this section show that achieving justice is possible, but success often requires hard work, dedication, and patience. The battle for justice is never ending, but it is a battle that must be fought for the sake of our humanity. Giving up the quest reduces us to little more than animals.

CHAPTER 14

Individual Strategies for Achieving Justice

Never doubt that a small group of thoughtful committed citizens can change the world. Indeed, it is the only thing that ever has.[1]

Margaret Mead

History is full of people who have worked to achieve justice. Some have brought about advances in justice purely through the power of their personalities. Others have worked tirelessly in their local communities. Some have taken issues of injustice to court. Still others have used their positions of power to advance justice. All four types are to be applauded, but in the larger scheme of things, each type has its own limitations. The charismatic reformer may have difficulty duplicating her success elsewhere, and when she is gone, a similarly charismatic leader may be impossible to find. Those who work tirelessly to change their local communities are to be admired for their efforts, but their work is often unnoticed outside of the communities in which they work. Victories in court can be hard to win as well, and most people do not occupy positions of power from which justice might be advanced. In fact, it is often those in power who stand to gain from injustice.

This chapter focuses on individual actions to achieve justice, and it includes a discussion of people who have made a direct difference in their pursuit of justice, while leaving behind blueprints for action by others, whether explicitly in their writings or by the power of their example. Any such list is arbitrary by nature, and out of necessity, this particular list is incomplete. The intention is to select a few strategies for achieving justice that have had a lasting impact. The chosen strategies also represent a range of approaches to achieving justice.

There are many general approaches to achieving justice that individuals might take. This chapter has selected four approaches to advancing justice: (1) educating the public, (2) civil disobedience, (3) civil procedures, and (4) guerilla tactics. For purposes of our discussion, each is discussed separately, but it should be clear that effective strategies for bringing about justice might combine these approaches. The discussion does not attempt to include every strategy an individual might use. For example, it does not include the use of violence as a tactic. It is difficult to find examples of individuals who have successfully used violence as a tactic for positive social change *and* who have articulated the principles of this strategy so that others may apply it to their own situations. Examples of individuals using violence for negative purposes abound (e.g., Hitler), and it is possible to find examples of violence engaged in by groups or nations that led to a positive social change (e.g., the American Revolution). However, this chapter focuses on articulated strategies that have been advanced by individuals.

EDUCATING THE PUBLIC

There are times when injustices exist and continue because the public is uninformed about the nature and extent of the problem. Individuals can make a difference by bringing injustice to light, but several conditions must be met for this strategy to work effectively. First, the problem must be one with which the public can relate, an issue that touches their daily lives. It can be difficult to mobilize people to act against child labor, torture, and even genocide in other countries, particularly if those countries are far away and inhabited by people with whom there are limited interactions, and if those countries have very different cultures and customs.

Second, the educator must have an effective medium for reaching the public. This means that the educational materials must be presented in a way that the public can understand, as when complicated medical issues are presented using everyday language. For an individual to inform the public, there must also be a mechanism for physically distributing the materials to the public. A powerful documentary about child prostitution in the United States will have little impact if the public never sees the film.

Third, the public must believe the problem is one for which there is a solution. If, for example, people believe that nothing they do will stop a nation's use of torture, it will be very difficult to mobilize them, regardless of how they personally view the problem or how well informed they are about the issue.

There are numerous examples of using education to bring about change. Abraham Lincoln himself said that Harriet Beecher Stowe's 1852 book, *Uncle Tom's Cabin*, the story of the brutality of life under slavery, played a key role in starting the Civil War. Upton Sinclair's 1906 book, *The Jungle*, exposed the horrendous sanitary and working conditions in meat-packing plants and led directly to the passage of the Pure Food and Drug Act. Ralph Nader's 1972 book, *Unsafe at Any Speed*, disclosed the unwillingness of the automobile industry to incorporate even the simplest safety measures into the construction of automobiles. The book had a major impact on the automotive industry, causing it to emphasize building safety features into automobiles, thus saving tens of thousands of lives.

Rachel Carson's *Silent Spring*

To illustrate the power of the educational approach, this discussion focuses on the work of Rachel Carson, whose 1962 book, *Silent Spring*, has been credited with starting the modern environmental movement. Carson grew up with a love of nature, an inquiring scientific mind, and a yearning to be a writer. Her interests led her to study zoology and English at Johns Hopkins University. From there, she began writing materials for the U.S. Bureau of Fisheries. She eventually became editor-in-chief for the U.S. Fish and Wildlife Service. Throughout her time in government service, she continued to write articles and books. Her book, *The Sea Around Us*, was a critical and public success, staying on the *New York Times'* bestseller list for 81 weeks.[2] This led to the reprinting of an earlier book, *Under the Sea-Wind*, which also became a bestseller. These books led to numerous honors and awards from both the scientific and the literary community. Rachel Carson had a rare gift for understanding complex scientific issues, while writing about them in a language that everyday people could understand and in a style that has been described as poetic.

While her earlier materials were educational, even inspiring, it was *Silent Spring* that started a revolution in the way we think about the environment. The idea for the book was triggered by a letter from a friend who had observed a mosquito control plane flying over her bird sanctuary, spraying the insecticide DDT. Shortly after the spraying, the friend found some of her songbirds dead.[3] Rachel immediately began investigating the use of pesticides, which at the time were commonly sprayed from airplanes to kill insects on crops. On the ground, trucks drove through neighborhoods spraying a fog of DDT to kill mosquitoes, leaving large clouds of the poison floating in the air. It was known that "just a few millionths of parts too much DDT could cause fish and birds to produce eggs that wouldn't hatch, or to hatch offspring that couldn't live."[4] Much less was known about the impact of DDT on people. Most of the information about the safety of these chemicals for humans was provided by the chemical industry itself, which was making millions each year from the sale of their products. To reassure the public that these chemicals were safe, films were distributed, including one showing school children eating picnic lunches while being enveloped in a cloud of DDT.[5]

The title, *Silent Spring*, reflected Carson's image of a springtime in which there were no songbirds left to sing. She realized that the chemical industry would attack any criticism of their products, and that they had the resources to investigate any claims she might make. She examined all of the scientific research she could find concerning the effects of these chemicals. "Carson first demonstrates the pollution of our water system and soil, then damage to plants and wildlife, and finally the more obvious kills of birds and fish."[6] She also focused on the tendency of some chemicals to accumulate in the body and the effects of these chemicals on key organs, offering the most current thinking on the connection between cancer, radiation, and industrial chemicals. Critics were quick to accuse her of trying to ban all toxic chemicals, but that was never her position. What Carson opposed was society's willingness to freely and perhaps excessively use these chemicals without extensive research on their long-term impact.

Carson's attack on the use of industrial chemicals was so detailed, so systematic, and so carefully researched, while at the same time being so accessible to the average reader, that the book became a best-seller within a few days of its release. Within just three months, the book sold more than 250,000 copies.[7] Parts of her book were read into the *Congressional Record. Silent Spring* eventually led to Congressional hearings, as well as the formation of a Presidential Committee to investigate the use of pesticides, and the book has been credited with changing the way Americans think about the toxic chemicals they use. Just as importantly, Carson's book influenced important policy makers, including Interior Secretary Morris Udall and Al Gore, who would eventually become Vice President. Although the initial impact of her book was felt in America, *Silent Spring* was also published in Great Britain, France, Germany, Italy, Denmark, Sweden, Norway, Finland, Holland, Spain, Brazil, Japan, Iceland, Portugal, and Israel.[8]

Chemical manufacturers saw the book as a direct attack on their industry and launched an all-out assault on the book and on Rachel Carson herself. They tried unsuccessfully to stop publication of the book, and when that failed, they launched a media campaign to discredit it. To undermine the credibility of the book, the chemical industry enlisted the aid of agricultural journals and magazines, trade associations connected to the chemical industry, and universities conducting research funded by the chemical industry.[9] *Time* and *Reader's Digest* both drew on materials provided by the chemical industry to criticize *Silent Spring*, although each magazine would in later years change its view, pointing with pride to articles they had published warning of the dangers of pesticide.[10] One testament to the care with which Carson had done her work was the frequency with which critics would eventually come to accept most of the key points she presented.

Two years after the publication of *Silent Spring*, Rachel Carson died of breast cancer and heart disease at the age of 57. The problems she exposed in 1962 persist. Today more chemicals are being used than ever, and they are still used with too little knowledge about their long-term consequences. However, because of Rachel Carson, chemicals are used more carefully, and the public, lawmakers, and industry now have an awareness that long-term consequences cannot be ignored. Just as importantly, Carson's book has provided a roadmap to guide our search for those consequences.

Contemporary Examples: There are many contemporary examples of seeking social change through educating the public. Books are still a common medium for public education. A sample of more recent books addressing injustice and social problems follows. Kevin Bales' book, *Disposable People*, is a powerful description of contemporary slavery. Eric Schlosser's *Fast Food Nation* uncovers the practices of the fast food industry and, much like *The Jungle*, provides an expose of conditions in the meatpacking industry. In *The American Way of Death*, Jessica Mitford exposes the dark side of the funeral industry in the United States and has led a number of states to enact legislation protecting consumers. In *Nickel and Dimed,* Barbara Ehrenreich gives the reader a firsthand look at the world of the working poor, showing the difficulty of getting by on a minimum wage job. And, in *A Long Way Gone,* Ishmael Beah paints a chilling portrait of life as a child soldier.

While books remain a powerful tool for educating the public about injustice, the contemporary activist has the ability to utilize resources not available in the past. Films, particularly documentary films, can have an impact on public perceptions of an issue. Oscar nominees in the categories of documentary (both feature and short films) have created a number of films that address issues of justice. For example, *The Invisible War* focuses on the sexual abuse of female soldiers in the U.S. military. *Saving Face* exposes the practice of Pakistani men throwing acid on the faces of women in their communities, and *Food, Inc.* reveals the process by which food is manufactured in America. Television news magazines, such as *60 Minutes*, have also served a powerful education function, as has the PBS documentary series *Frontline*.

Activists have also discovered the internet as a tool for disseminating information and for organizing activities. To this point, the internet has not produced materials with the impact of *Uncle Tom's Cabin* or *Silent Spring*, but it has come close with the March 2012 release of the 20-minute film *Kony 2012* on YouTube.[11] The film, created and released by the group *Invisible Children*, documents the atrocities committed by Joseph Kony, leader of the Lord's Resistance Army (LRA) in Uganda, Africa. Under his direction, the LRA forced children into military service, compelling them to engage in murder, rape, and mutilation. The film *Kony 2012* was seen by nearly 100 million people and led the U.S. Congress to pass a resolution supporting efforts to stop Kony and the LRA.[12] While the film is not without its controversy, and it is unclear whether it can ultimately be credited with stopping the LRA, it represents an example of the potential for using the internet as a tool for pursuing justice.

CIVIL DISOBEDIENCE

Civil disobedience is the intentional and public refusal to obey a law with which one disagrees, and it has been a powerful tool for bringing about change throughout history. There are Biblical accounts of citizens refusing to follow the orders of their government, and civil disobedience played an important role in the founding of America. Although the idea has been around for some time, it was articulated as an explicit strategy in a speech given by the author Henry David Thoreau in 1848.[13] This speech, later published under the title "Resistance to Civil Government," recounts his experiences during a night in jail after he refused to pay a local tax that he believed supported a government that condoned slavery and that was involved in an unjust war with Mexico. Although Thoreau objected to the war with Mexico and to government support for slavery, the opening statement of his speech suggests that his contempt was for government more generally:

> *I heartily accept the motto, "That government is best which governs least"; and I should like to see it acted upon more rapidly and systematically. Carried out, it finally amounts to this, which also I believe,—"That government is best which governs not at all"; and when men are prepared for it, that will be the kind of government which they will have.*[14]

In practice, Thoreau did not sacrifice much for his beliefs. He spent only one night in jail protesting the tax. Someone else paid the tax for him that year and for several years after. His speech was important, however, because it outlined the justifications for refusing to cooperate with unjust laws, and it has inspired others to consider civil disobedience as a strategy for change. However, few of those who were inspired by Thoreau seem to share his belief that government should be done away with altogether.

Gandhi: Among those purportedly influenced by the writings of Thoreau was Gandhi, a man who almost single-handedly led India to independence from Great Britain, thereby providing the world with a model for using civil disobedience as a tactic for change. While other individuals had practiced civil disobedience before him, Gandhi provided a living example of its use, and he left behind extensive writings about civil disobedience and nonviolence.

Mohandas Karamchand Gandhi was born in 1869 in India. He was a mediocre student who was so shy that he ran home from school to avoid talking with other students.[15] He was greatly influenced by both parents. His mother was deeply religious, and as a follower of Hinduism, she was also a vegetarian. His father was a local official who was known for his honesty and fairness.

When Gandhi was only 16 years old, his father died, leaving the family in poverty. It was decided that Gandhi would borrow money to study law in England as a way to eventually support the family.[16] He finished his law degree and returned to India. However, he was still quite shy and failed as a lawyer. In one court case, he "was literally too shy to open his mouth in court and gave the brief to a colleague."[17] A failure as an independent attorney, he began writing legal briefs and doing odd legal work for other attorneys.

Gandhi was soon invited to South Africa to handle legal cases involving business transactions between Indians living in South Africa and English-speaking residents. While in South Africa, Gandhi first developed his method of nonviolent resistance or civil disobedience, a method he called *satyagraha*.[18] Some suggest that Ghandi's activism was initially inspired by an incident in which he was thrown out of the first class section of a train because a fellow passenger thought he was Black—Blacks were forbidden from riding in first class. The incident made Gandhi more fully realize the oppressive nature of British colonial rule and started him on a path to improve living conditions for Indians in South Africa.

In 1907, 14 years after he arrived in South Africa, a law was passed there "requiring the registration and fingerprinting of all Indians and giving the police the power to enter their houses to ensure that the inhabitants were registered."[19] Gandhi helped organize "peaceful picketing of registration centers, burning registration cards, courting arrest, and gracefully accepting punishment and police harassment."[20] These efforts produced only limited success, but a short time later, he organized women and miners against immigration regulations, indentured labor, a local tax, and the government's failure to recognize Indian marriages. This time his efforts were more successful, leading to the Indian Relief Act in 1914.[21] Gandhi also appreciated the power of the written word to change people, and he began a weekly newspaper devoted to airing the concerns of Indians in South Africa.

In 1915, having been in South Africa for more than 20 years, Gandhi returned to India. He had left for South Africa a shy and little-known failure, but was returning a hero for his work to advance Indian rights. Soon after his return to India, he came to be called "Mahatma," which means "great soul." Some in India even considered him a reincarnation of God.[22] Although he was given parties and testimonials by wealthy Indians, he was strongly drawn to the plight of the poor. When he traveled, Gandhi walked or traveled third class on the train. He abandoned western dress in favor of simple peasant clothing made from homespun cloth, took a vow of celibacy, rejected material goods, and restricted his diet.

For years, Gandhi worked to improve conditions in India and to undermine the authority of the British, while always remaining true to his philosophy of nonviolence and passive resistance. Gandhi's belief in nonviolence should not be confused with cowardice. Rather, it demanded extraordinary bravery. His commitment to nonviolence included demanding that protesters willingly submit to the blows of police batons, without even raising their arms in self-defense. Gandhi himself said that, if he had to choose between cowardice and violence, he would choose violence, because cowardice takes away from a man's self-respect.[23]

Gandhi's activities in support of Indian independence are too numerous to mention here, but there were several events that served as turning points on India's road to freedom and that highlight Gandhi's strategy for bringing about change. The first event occurred in 1919, one year after World War I ended. During the war, many liberties of Indians had been suspended by the British. Thousands of Indians who spoke against the British and for an independent India were tried in secret tribunals and sent to prison. Similarly, Indian newspapers were censored.[24] Many Indians hoped that, when the war ended, civil liberties would be restored. Instead, in 1919, the Rowlatt Act was passed, extending the wartime restrictions.

Gandhi's response to the Rowlatt Act was to call for a *hartal*—a work stoppage that would shutter shops, shut down factories, and close banks. He also called for distributing banned political literature.[25] The strategy was initially a success, but soon violence among his followers broke out in several cities, much to Gandhi's dismay. In one city, Amritsar, a British schoolteacher was attacked and pushed around by a group of Indian youth. The government responded to the violence by calling in troops and banning public meetings. Defying the law, a crowd met in a courtyard to protest the Rowlatt Act. Soldiers arrived and, without warning, fired into the crowd of men, women, and children. They were ordered to keep shooting until they ran out of ammunition. In all, 1650 rounds were fired, 379 people were killed, and 1137 wounded. The general in charge issued an order that none of the injured were to receive medical treatment for 72 hours, even if they faced death without treatment. He also ordered any Indians traveling on the lane in front of the schoolteacher's house to crawl on all fours or risk being beaten to death.[26]

Gandhi responded to the massacre at Amritsar by calling for a boycott of British goods, British schools, and British jobs.[27] He traveled the countryside, encouraging Indians to burn imported clothing and to only wear fabric made in India. Thousands of his countrymen were imprisoned for political dissent, and Gandhi himself was soon arrested and sentenced to prison for publishing articles calling for a free India. Throughout these ordeals, Gandhi held firm to his belief in nonviolence. There were times when his followers seemed to lose faith in nonviolence and lashed out against the British. When his words were not enough to stop violence against the British, Gandhi fasted—sometimes to the point of near death. Gandhi insisted that fasts were only used to instruct his followers and would have been useless as a tool for reforming the British.[28] In many instances, the possibility that their aggressive acts might lead to the death of their revered leader was enough to prevent Gandhi's followers from becoming violent.

The second turning point in Gandhi's quest for an independent India came in 1930 and is among the best known examples of his use of civil disobedience. At that time, the world economy was in decline, and farmers in India were in economic trouble. Gandhi decided to use the British government's tax on salt to both defy the British government and to unite his followers. Salt was a commodity that all citizens needed, and for the poor, a tax on salt was particularly oppressive. Although salt was easy to gather along the seashore, it was illegal to possess salt that was not obtained from the government.[29] Gandhi announced to the British that he would begin a 240-mile march on foot from his camp to the sea, where he would intentionally harvest salt without paying a tax. The march lasted 24 days, and along the way, Gandhi stopped each day at villages to give speeches urging civil disobedience and asking citizens to join his march. For the convenience of the police, the names of the 79 original marchers were printed in the newspaper.

Gandhi's salt march attracted international attention. Reporters from around the world followed the march and reported on the large crowds that gathered to greet Gandhi in each village. Along the way, at Gandhi's urging, local Indian officials working for the British government resigned their jobs. By the time Gandhi reached the sea, the marchers numbered in the thousands. Arriving at the ocean, Gandhi walked along the sand until he found a spot where the salt was thick. He picked it up and gave a speech urging other Indians to ignore the law and gather salt. Thousands followed his example, and within a week, police were arresting people selling salt on the street and beating those who refused to use government salt.[30] Despite his insistence on nonviolence, some anti-British acts of violence did occur, and Gandhi was arrested and jailed. While he was in jail, Gandhi's followers marched on the saltworks, where government salt was produced. The crowd of 2500 was met by 400 police. The unarmed marchers peacefully approached the saltworks in rows of 24 men. They were beaten by the police, but refused to defend themselves in any way, not even raising their arms to deflect the blows of the batons. Within a few hours, more than 300 protesters were wounded, and several had died. There were not enough stretchers to carry the injured away, but still the rows of protesters kept advancing. This continued for days, and Indians staged raids on other salt facilities throughout the country.[31] The salt protests showed the world and the British themselves the brutal nature of British rule in India, as well as the determination of the Indian people to be free.

A free India was on the horizon, but internal strife between Muslims and Hindus meant continued unrest. One issue was whether there should be one India or whether land with large concentrations of Muslims should be broken off into a separate country, Pakistan. Gandhi believed there should be only one country but some extremists erroneously believed he had secretly agreed to a separate Pakistan. In November of 1948, when Gandhi was 79 years old, an extremist shot and killed him as he was preparing to conduct prayer services. Thirty-three years had passed between his return from South Africa and his death, but in that time he had engineered independence for India and provided the rest of the world with a model for using nonviolent means to bring about change.

Several points about Gandhi's approach are worth noting. First, Gandhi always refused to follow the law openly and for a purpose. Before engaging in a specific act of civil disobedience, Gandhi respectfully notified authorities of his intention. Throughout his life, he remained optimistic about the nature of human beings and was always hopeful that, if told of his plans in advance, authorities might be willing to negotiate for change.

Second, Gandhi was always willing to pay for his civil disobedience by going to jail. In fact, there were many occasions when he expressed disappointment because he was not jailed, or because he was released from jail early. Jail showed his followers his dedication to their cause, gave him a chance to rest and to plan further actions, and allowed him time to write. Throughout his lifetime, Gandhi spent 2338 days, or 6.4 years, in jail.

Third, Gandhi and his followers were willing to suffer beatings and other physical punishments without returning violence or treating the attackers with contempt or disrespect. Violence or any demeaning of others was, in Gandhi's view, something that diminished the person practicing it. For Gandhi, violence was both morally reprehensible and, ultimately, an ineffective strategy for change.

Fourth, Gandhi's faith in his approach gave him great patience. His work to free India lasted 32 years, during which time he never gave up on peaceful civil disobedience as a strategy for change. While an independent India was always the long-term goal, he was a patient man who was willing to negotiate for smaller short-term steps toward that goal. Finally, Gandhi appreciated the value of using every available medium to spread his ideas. He not only led his followers by direct example, but he also gave speeches and was a prolific writer. He was constantly writing letters and essays for newspapers, and he even published his own newspapers. After his death, the government of India began collecting his writings. To date, there are 90 volumes of his work, each over 500 pages long. Because Ghandi committed so many of his thoughts to writing, we have a clear guide to the principles underlying his approach to social change.

Contemporary Examples: There are many examples of civil disobedience as a strategy for change. During the 1950s and 1960s, the American civil rights movement used several strategies developed by Gandhi, including peaceful marches, boycotts, and sit-in demonstrations. Dr. Martin Luther King, Jr. was among those in the civil rights movement who studied the work of Gandhi. In the 1950s, the Reverend Leon Sullivan successfully led boycotts of 29 companies that had refused to hire Blacks in Philadelphia. He also established training programs to prepare Blacks for the jobs newly opened to them. Sullivan recognized, just as Gandhi had in India, that full equality for American Blacks would depend ultimately on economic equality. By the 1970s, Sullivan's church had grown to over 6000 members and he was nationally known for his civil rights work. Sullivan treated government and corporate leaders with respect, while offering them workable strategies for improving the economic condition of Blacks. In 1971, he became the first Black on the board of directors at General Motors. He used his position to first improve the standing of women and Blacks at General Motors and then to attack racism in South Africa. He developed "The Global Sullivan Principles," a set of guidelines for South African companies that might break down the system of racial segregation known as apartheid. He was able to persuade major corporations to only do business with South African companies that agreed to follow the Sullivan Principles. In 1990, apartheid was revoked in South Africa, due in part to his efforts.[32]

There are dozens of issues to which the principles of civil disobedience have been applied. In 2001, two elderly nuns (one 88, the other 68) were sentenced to federal prison for trespassing at the School of the Americas (renamed the Western Hemisphere Institute for Security Cooperation in January 2001). Through the School of the Americas in Georgia, the United States has trained a number of brutal South American dictators. Also in 2001, protesters at the Navy training base on Viques Island in Puerto Rico were arrested while trying to stop bombing exercises. Among those arrested were prominent members of Congress and noted political activists. In 2011, the group Occupy Wall Street took over Zuccotti Park in New York to protest growing income inequality in the United States, as well as the power of major banking institutions.[33] Members of the group refused to leave the park and were willing to be arrested for their beliefs. Their efforts were copied by other groups around the country. Protesters have also disrupted meetings of the World Trade Organization, boycotted merchants selling products made with slave labor, blocked access to abortion clinics, and perched in trees to prevent logging. There is now an organization, The Rukus Society, that runs camps for the purpose of training activists to protest without injuring others or being injured themselves.[34] Civil disobedience is a powerful tool that is still evolving. Perhaps, as a glimpse into the future of this tactic, there has already been discussion of electronic civil disobedience.[35]

CIVIL PROCEDURES

Civil action represents an important way for individuals to pursue justice. Technically, civil procedures address a wide array of issues, including family relations (divorce, child custody, adoption, etc.), inheritance, contracts, and disputes about property. This discussion focuses on one particular aspect of civil law, the law of *torts*. The word tort is derived from the Latin word *torquere*, which means wrong or twisted.[36] Those found blameworthy in civil court are called "tortfeasors."[37] Under tort law, an individual who has been injured sues another to compensate for that injury and uses the court as a neutral arbitrator between the two sides. Sometimes the courts are asked to order the accused to take a particular action or to stop a particular behavior, as when a shopkeeper sues a local gang to stop loitering on the sidewalk outside his shop. More commonly, people who sue under tort law are generally seeking money to compensate for their injuries, or to punish the wrongdoer. For example, a customer who slips on the wet floor of a restaurant might sue the store owner for damages.

Americans have a love–hate relationship with civil suits. They justifiably mock cases they consider absurd, such as:

- The man who sued the devil for causing evil in his community.[38]
- The overweight children who sued McDonald's for their own obesity.[39]
- The man who sued the American Dental Association for not warning consumers about the risk of "toothbrush-related injury."[40]
- The Texas cattle industry which sued Oprah Winfrey for $12 million for disparaging beef.[41]

They also call for tort reform, pointing out that civil suits, whether real or threatened, add to the cost of medical care, forcing some doctors out of business.[42] Civil suits also add to the cost of products we buy every day.

Yet, despite the many justifiable criticisms of tort law, it can serve as an important tool for pursuing justice. For example, in the state of New York, women who are raped are encouraged to report the crime, cooperate with a criminal prosecution, and then bring a separate civil suit against their attackers.[43] Because civil and criminal procedures are considered separate legal systems, such actions are not considered double jeopardy under the law. In many jurisdictions, shoplifters are not arrested and charged for their crimes, but are instead sued by the store.[44] Residents of Los Angles brought lawsuits against street gang members, compelling them to limit their activities.[45] In Peoria, Illinois, residents of one neighborhood sued men who cruised their neighborhood looking for prostitutes.[46] To understand why someone might use civil justice instead of, or in addition to, criminal justice, it is necessary to understand the difference between the two systems of justice.

Under criminal law the crime is a public offense. Under civil law the offense is a private matter. Suppose Fred Smith is arrested for assaulting Jim Jones in California. The case appears in court as the State of California versus Fred Smith. Technically, the state is the victim seeking justice. Jim Jones is almost incidental to the criminal proceedings, although his testimony may be important in gaining a conviction. If Jim Jones sues Fred Smith in civil court, the case is titled Jones versus Smith. In civil court, the case is a matter of dispute between two individuals.

The criminal law punishes the guilty, whereas the civil law repairs the damage done to the victim. Thus, under criminal law, the primary question is what should be done *to* the offender. In civil law the primary question is what should be done *for* the victim. The judgment handed down in a criminal case is called a sentence, while in a civil case, it is called a remedy.

Under criminal law the state brings the wrong to the attention of the court. In civil law the individual brings the wrong to the attention of the court. This is an important distinction. If a prosecutor decides not to bring charges, there is little the victim can do. Similarly, if an abused woman decides she does not want charges brought, the prosecutor is free to ignore her wishes and go forward with criminal charges. In civil court it is the individual victim's responsibility to bring the matter to court, and it is the wishes of the injured person that take priority.

The sentence or fine is paid to the court in a criminal case. In a civil case the individual receives the fine or damage award. Thus, someone convicted of shoplifting in a criminal court may be required to pay a fine to the court, but the store is likely to gain nothing but the return of its stolen merchandise. If the store, instead, sues the shoplifter, it will receive any financial penalty imposed on the offender, potentially including all of its legal costs for taking the case to court. The store may even be awarded extra money as punishment of the offender, something known as punitive damages.

The standard of proof is higher in criminal cases than in civil cases. In criminal cases one must be found guilty "beyond a reasonable doubt." In most civil cases, one need only be found accountable by the "preponderance of evidence." To convict in a criminal case, there must be no reasonable doubt that the person is guilty, but in a civil case, it is only necessary to show that the defendant is more likely to be responsible than to be not responsible. In other words, the judge or jury need be only 51% certain of guilt.[47] The O.J. Simpson case illustrates why this distinction makes a difference. After Simpson was acquitted in a criminal proceeding, the Goldman family, whose daughter was allegedly killed by Simpson, sued in civil court and won a substantial judgment against him. It might appear that the criminal and civil findings were contradictory, but given the very different standards for conviction, there may not be a contradiction at all.

Someone accused of doing harm in civil court has fewer constitutional protections than someone accused in criminal court. Many people are familiar with the constitutional protections provided to the accused in criminal court. The defendants in criminal court have the right to an attorney, and if they cannot afford an attorney, one will be provided for them. All criminal defendants have the right to a speedy trial. The criminal court defendant has the right to remain silent and the right to face his or her accusers. These rights, as detailed in the Bill of Rights to the Constitution (see Chapter 4), were designed to protect the accused from the power of the government. However, in civil cases the accuser is not the government but another individual. For this reason, many constitutional protections available to criminal defendants do not apply to defendants in civil court. For example, the accused in a civil proceeding are not provided with an attorney if they cannot afford one, and there is no right to a speedy trial. Someone facing civil charges does not have the right to remain silent. Should they refuse to testify, their silence can be considered in the decision about their case. Furthermore, whatever a defendant says in the civil proceeding can be used against that party in any criminal action.[48] Witnesses who are some distance away do not have to appear in court, but may give a deposition, which is testimony under oath that is taken outside of the courtroom. And, while double jeopardy protections do apply in civil cases, double jeopardy does not apply across criminal and civil cases. In other words, someone found guilty of a crime in a criminal case can still be sued in civil court for the same behavior. This is not considered double jeopardy, because the civil and criminal justice systems are considered separate.[49] Similarly, entering a guilty plea in criminal court may be used as evidence in a civil proceeding. When money is involved, the defendant in a civil suit has the right to a trial by jury. Juries in civil cases vary in size from 4 to 12 members. In some jurisdictions the defense and prosecution can negotiate the size of the jury. Some jurisdictions require jury verdicts to be unanimous, but others require only a majority.[50]

Some people believe that civil suits are primarily about greed and money. Money can be an important part of justice, as when an innocent accident victim sues to have his medical bills paid by a reckless driver. It is also true that greed is sometimes a motivating factor. It would be a mistake, however, to focus on money and fail to see the other respects in which civil law can be used to achieve justice. Civil justice can give the injured a sense of having a voice in exacting justice. Civil procedures can help victims who feel that the criminal justice system has failed them. Finally, civil procedures provide a mechanism for imposing punishments beyond those provided by the criminal justice system. Consider the example of O.J. Simpson mentioned above. When the Goldman family sued O.J. Simpson for the death of their daughter, they were probably not motivated by money. Instead, they appear to have been motivated by a desire to exact justice. In Chapter 15, we will see how organizations have also recognized the value of civil justice as a tool for pursuing justice.

GUERILLA TACTICS

Education, civil disobedience, and civil suits can be powerful tools for bringing about social change. There are occasions, however, when none of these tools seem effective. When conventional tactics fail, it can be useful to turn to the unconventional, what we describe here as guerilla tactics. As described here, guerilla tactics are very different from acts of terrorism. The tactics described here do not use violence and are usually, though not always, within the law. Where violations of the law do occur, they are designed not to harm others. On the other hand, we define unusual or outrageous approaches that use violence or harm others as acts of terrorism.

The use of guerilla tactics has been largely defined by the work of one man, Saul Alinsky. Alinsky died in 1972, but he left behind a rich legacy of examples of his approach, a set of written materials describing his philosophy, and an institute to train others hoping to follow in his footsteps.

Alinsky spent much of his career as a community organizer, working to help poor neighborhoods obtain basic city services and to help local residents get jobs. In his terms, he worked to help the Have-Nots take power away from the Haves. Alinsky grew up in one of the poorest slums of Chicago and that's where he began his work. By the time of his death, he was known throughout the world for using tactics that were outrageous but highly effective.

There were several key elements to Alinsky's work. We first list these elements and then give an example of how he used them to better local communities.

First, Alinsky assumed that *people always act out of self-interest*, so, one way to gain their cooperation was to appeal to their self-interest rather than to higher moral principles. He argued that the principle even applied to ministers and priests. For example, when he approached them for help he found that appeals to justice and moral principles were far less effective than emphasizing how a better standard of living would put parishioners in a better position to contribute to the church.

Second, Alinsky firmly believed that communities and groups could only produce long-term change if residents were committed to that change; *a desire for change must come from the local community itself.* As an outsider he could mobilize them, but he would not impose on them his idea of what changes were needed.[51] It was important to him to be seen as legitimate by local residents, and there were several ways in which he accomplished this. He never spoke down to them or treated them with paternalism. He also found that being insulted or attacked by those in power made him more credible to the Have-Nots. Perhaps the most effective way to show his solidarity with them was to be arrested and jailed. Alinsky looked forward to being jailed because it gave him instant credibility with the Have-Nots, and it also gave him time to reflect on strategies and to write.

Third, Alinsky's tactics *centered around the idea of power*. Unlike Gandhi, Alinsky saw conflict as a positive force essential to a free society. For him the challenge was always to find ways to pressure those in power to make concessions. He says, for example, that his book, *Rules for Radicals* (1971), was written for people without power who wanted to take it away from people with power. While the Haves have access to the power that comes with money, the Have-Nots have power in their large numbers of people.

Fourth, Alinsky believed that *ethical standards of right and wrong must change to fit the times*. He noted that, in war, the ends justify almost any means, and he viewed his efforts to help the poor as a battle against those in power. In his view, any effective means is automatically judged by the opposition to be unethical, and people who spend a great deal of time worrying about the ethics of the tactics used by the Have-Nots are really allies of the Haves.

Fifth, Alinsky *used humor as a weapon*. Gandhi often used gentle humor to endear himself to those with whom he was negotiating. Alinsky also used humor, but he relied more on ridicule and humor at the expense of the Haves as a tool to gain their cooperation. As we will see in the example that follows, humor was one of the more powerful tools he used.

Sixth, Alinsky knew that *for unconventional tactics to work they had to be unanticipated* by the Haves. This meant doing things that were completely outside of the normal experiences of the Haves. It also meant not using the same tactic repeatedly, because the Haves would soon anticipate the tactic and act to neutralize it.

Finally, Alinsky always *organized communities with specific objectives in mind* and specific ways in which the Haves could meet those objectives. He would not, for example, focus on general unemployment in an impoverished community, but would target a specific company or group in the community and make clear to them how they would benefit from hiring local residents. If the Haves threw up their hands and said, "What do you expect us to do?" Alinsky had a very specific answer for them.

Thus, Alinsky took many of the essential elements of Gandhi and added a confrontational element to them. An example illustrates why his approach has been called radical.

Rochester, New York, was a city whose economy depended heavily on Kodak, but at that time, Kodak was doing little to hire or promote Blacks. After a race-riot in the community, a group of liberal clergymen invited Alinsky to organize the Black community in Rochester. Alinsky responded that the churches did not speak for Blacks in Rochester, and he would come only if local Blacks invited him. At first there was little interest among Black residents. Then the local press, the mayor, and others in the community power structure began publicly attacking Alinsky as a troublemaker who had no business coming to Rochester. After a series of these public attacks, the Black community came together and invited him to help them organize. As one Black later told Alinsky, "I just wanted to see somebody who could freak those mothers out like that."[52] Alinsky began attacking Kodak immediately upon his arrival. When asked at the airport why he was meddling in the Black community after all Kodak had done for it, he replied, "Maybe I'm uninformed, but as far as I know the only thing Kodak has done on the race issue in America is to introduce color film."[53]

Realizing that a traditional local boycott of an international corporation would be unlikely to bring about change, Alinsky formed a plan. At the time, the Rochester Philharmonic was a symbol of cultural pride for Rochester and for Kodak. Alinsky suggested they select a performance with quiet music. They would buy 100 seats for that performance and give them to Blacks from the local community. Before the performance, the group would be given a large baked bean dinner, leading to a "fart-in" at the performance. Alinsky intended that the details of the plan be leaked to Kodak in the hope that they would make concessions before the plan was implemented. The plan was brilliant in that it would publicly embarrass Kodak, while giving them few options to save face. Arresting the Blacks involved would only draw national ridicule to Kodak and raise questions about its hiring practices. As it happened, Alinsky decided not to employ this strategy, but it remains a classic example of his approach.

Today there are few community organizers as outrageous as Saul Alinsky, but his name and tactics are well known among those who try to bring about positive social change. Those who directly involve the community in the development and implementation of strategies seldom utilize techniques as outrageous as those conceived by Alinsky. Conversely, those who utilize outrageous techniques for drawing attention to problems—such as the Biotic Baking Brigade[54] that throws cream pies in the faces of important business and political leaders—seldom seem to be involved in representing a grassroots constituency and often lack a pragmatic strategy for change.

Despite the fact that no single person has emerged as a successor to Alinsky, his work is largely regarded as a success. Alinsky succeeded in many of the individual projects he undertook, but he also succeeded on a much larger level, in that he has challenged activists everywhere to think more creatively about the strategies they might adopt to bring about change.

One creative and highly controversial guerilla tactic is "hactivism," which is the nonviolent accessing and disrupting of computer systems for political or social reasons. The individuals involved are known as hactivists and tend to be a loosely coordinated group of individuals without any clear leadership structure. Many of their cyber attacks are launched by a single hacker, rather than an organized group. However, when multiple hackers join forces and act as a group, they can be a powerful force.

Perhaps the best known hactivist group is Anonymous. Anonymous began in 2003, and over time its members have engaged in a wide range of actions targeting major corporations, religious groups, and government agencies.[55] Anonymous members used their skills to launch cyber attacks against Tunisia's brutal dictator, disrupting government web sites and providing citizens with software to circumvent the Tunisian government's censorship of on-line information. Within a month the dictator fled the country. In the United States, computers for the CIA and the U.S. Senate were targeted, as were major banks after the economic slowdown in 2011.

The activities of Anonymous members have also included aid to victims of rape.[56] In one case a high school girl was photographed being raped by two football players while she was passed out drunk. Two players were arrested, but 11 others who watched the rape and did nothing were not publicly identified. One of the bystanders was videotaped laughing and joking about the rape. Anonymous members warned they would release the phone numbers and social security numbers of the football team if those present at the rape did not come forward. It found and posted the video of the laughing bystander, and the video quickly went viral. As a result, there were public demonstrations at which women stood up and recounted their experiences of sexual assault. The two football players were convicted, and the school board was investigated for a possible cover-up of the rape.

While the activities of hactivists can bring to light injustices, their techniques can also be abused, leading to vigilante justice in which the innocent are mistakenly targeted. In the case described above, one football player was mistakenly listed as present at the rape, and as a result, he was too terrified to go to school. Still, hactivism is likely here to stay, and only time will tell if its potential for good is realized, outweighing any harm from its abuse.

CONCLUSION

Individuals can bring about positive social change, and as this chapter has shown, there are a variety of ways of doing this. The four approaches highlighted here—education, civil disobedience, civil suits, and guerilla tactics—represent a continuum of approaches from the least to the most confrontational. Education is often the first tactic tried. When education fails, civil disobedience or civil suits may prove effective. Finally, guerilla tactics may be necessary when other strategies have failed. Whether using education, civil disobedience, civil suits, or guerilla tactics, the people profiled in this chapter not only worked for change, but also committed themselves fully to change.

DISCUSSION QUESTIONS

1. What are the disadvantages associated with each of the four approaches that individuals might use to achieve justice?
2. How might advances in technology shape the strategies that individuals might use to achieve justice?
3. What is the difference between Gandhi's form of civil disobedience and simple lawlessness? What is the difference between guerilla tactics and terrorism?

Endnotes

1. Cited on p. 281 of Thom Hartman, *Unequal Protection: The Rise of Corporate Dominance and the Theft of Human Rights* (Cincinnati, Ohio: Rodale, 2002).
2. For one of the best biographies, see Philip Sterling, *Sea and Earth: The Life of Rachel Carson* (New York: Thomas Y. Crowell Company, 1970).
3. *Ibid.*
4. *Ibid.*, p. 159.
5. Neil Goodwin (Producer), *Rachel Carson's Silent Spring* (Alexandria, Va.: PBS Video, 1993).
6. Carol B. Gartner, *Rachel Carson* (New York: Frederick Ungar Publishing Company, 1983), p. 89.
7. Sterling, *Sea and Earth.*
8. For the international impact, see Paul Brooks, *The House of Life: Rachel Carson at Work* (Boston: Houghton Mifflin Company, 1972).
9. *Ibid.*
10. *Ibid.*
11. The film can be accessed online at: https://www.youtube.com/watch?v=Y4MnpzG5Sqc.
12. "Kony 2012," *Wikipedia* (accessed online at http://en.wikipedia.org on July 18, 2013).
13. William Rossi (ed.), *Henry David Thoreau: Walden and Resistance to Civil Government* (New York: W.W. Norton & Company, 1992).
14. *Ibid.*, p. 226.
15. Louis Fischer, *Gandhi: His Life and Message for the World* (New York: Mentor Books, 1982).
16. Yogesh Chadha, *Gandhi: A Life* (New York: John Wiley & Sons, 1997).
17. Fischer, *Gandhi*, p. 20.
18. Bhikhu Parekh, *Gandhi* (New York: Oxford University Press, 1997).

19. *Ibid.*, p. 3.
20. *Ibid.*
21. *Ibid.*
22. Fischer, *Gandhi.*
23. *Ibid.*
24. *Ibid.*
25. *Ibid.*
26. Indian Freedom Fighters, *Gandhi, Mohandas Karamchand* (online at http://swaraj.net/iffw/profiles/gandhi_mk.htm; accessed April 13, 2001); Fischer; Chadha.
27. Fischer, *Gandhi.*
28. *Ibid.*
29. Chadha, *Gandhi.*
30. *Ibid.*
31. Fischer, *Gandhi.*
32. Mike Sager, "A Tribute to the Reverend Leon Sullivan, 1922-2001," *Rolling Stone*, July 5, 2001, pp. 87-90, 92, 155; also see Leon Sullivan, *Moving Mountains: The Principles and Purposes of Leon Sullivan* (New York: Judson Press).
33. "Occupy Wall Street," *Wikipedia* (accessed online at https://en.wikipedia.org on July 18, 2013).
34. Dan Baum, "You Say You Want a Revolution?" *Rolling Stone*, July 5, 2001, pp. 82-83, 85.
35. Stefan Wray, "On Electronic Civil Disobedience," paper presented to the 1998 Socialist Scholars Conference, New York, N.Y. (online at www.nyu.edu/projects/wray/oecd.html; accessed on November 14, 2001).
36. *West Legal Directory* (2001), Torts (online at www.wld.com/conbus/weal/wtorts.htm on September 27, 2001).
37. James Calvi and Susan Coleman, *American Law and Legal Systems* (4th ed.) (Upper Saddle River, N.J.: Prentice Hall, 2000).
38. Clarence Petersen, "Satan Gets a Lawyer in Arkansas," *Chicago Tribune*, November 30, 1986, Section 2, p. 1.
39. Amity Shales, "Lawyers Get Fat on McDonald's: New York Lawsuit Alleges Chain Is Responsible for Obesity," *Chicago Tribune*, November 27, 2002, p. 13.
40. Bruce Jaspen, "Toothbrush Injury Charges Have No Bite, Judge Decides," *Chicago Tribune*, July 25, 2000, Section 3, p. 3.
41. "Can You Libel an Emu?" *Chicago Tribune*, January 20, 1998, p. 12A.
42. Tom Gorman, "Physicians Fold Under Malpractice Fee Burden," *Los Angeles Times*, March 4, 2002 (online at www.latimes.com on March 4, 2002).
43. Maureen Balleza, "Many Rape Victims Finding Justice Through Civil Courts," *New York Times*, September 20, 1991, pp. A1, B8.
44. Melissa Davis, Richard J. Lundman, and Ramiro Martinez, Jr., "Private Corporate Justice: Store Police, Shoplifters, and Civil Recovery," *Social Problems*, 38(3) 1991, pp. 395-411.
45. David A. Price, "Got Gang Problems? Sue-Em," *USA Today*, January 2, 1997, p. 11A.
46. Douglas Fruehling, "Group Suing Man Convicted of Soliciting," *Peoria Journal Star*, January 30, 1995, pp. A1, A7.
47. For a good overview of civil law issues, see Howard Abadinsky, *Law and Justice: An Introduction to the American Legal System* (5th ed.) (Upper Saddle River, N.J.: Prentice Hall, 2003).
48. Robert G. McCampbell, "Parallel Civil and Criminal Proceedings: Six Legal Pitfalls," *Criminal Law Bulletin*, 31(6) 1995, pp. 483-501.
49. *Ibid.*
50. Carol J. DeFrances and Marika F.X. Litras, *Civil Trial Cases and Verdicts in Large Counties, 1996* (Bulletin Number NCJ 173426) (Washington, D.C.: Bureau of Justice Statistics, 1999).

51. For a readable and remarkable guide, see Saul Alinsky, *Reveille for Radicals* (Chicago: University of Chicago Press, 1946).
52. Eric Norden, "Saul Alinsky: A Candid Interview with the Feisty Radical Organizer." *Playboy*, March 1972, p. 173.
53. *Ibid.*
54. Biotic Baking Brigade (online at www.asis.com/~agit-prop/bbb; accessed on December 17, 2001).
55. Brian B. Kelly, "Investing in a Centralized Cybersecurity Infrastructure: Why 'Hactivism' Can and Should Influence Cybersecurity Reform," *Boston University Law Review* 92(5) 2012, pp. 1663-1710.
56. Josh Harkinson, "Cyberbullies with a Cause." *Mother Jones*, July/August 2013, pp. 12, 14-15.

CHAPTER 15

Organizations Seeking Justice

In Chapter 14, it is argued that individuals can make a difference, and much of the chapter illustrates ways in which justice can be pursued by individuals. This chapter continues the emphasis on pursuing justice but focuses on the use of organizations as instruments for achieving that goal. While individuals can do much to correct injustices, there are several advantages to organizations. Organizations can perpetuate themselves over time and continue a fight for justice long after their founders depart. Organizations often have a wider range of resources and staff and can simply do more than an individual. For example, an organization dealing with environmental issues may have a staff of scientists, political lobbyists, and legal experts who together can provide a range of expertise not usually available from a single individual. And, the individuals on the staff can collectively put many more hours into addressing an injustice than would ever be possible for one person.

Many organizations deal with the issue of justice, and there are many approaches to addressing injustices. The discussion in this chapter emphasizes several important strategies but cannot begin to cover every approach. This discussion leaves out the many charities that seek to have an impact on such things as poverty, disease, or education. Organizations such as the Bill and Melinda Gates Foundation[1] and the organization Free the Children[2] provide essential services that improve the lives of millions around the world. Similarly, there are many church groups that deal with these issues of injustice as part of their broader missions. However, it can be argued that they focus only indirectly on the issue of justice. For this reason, they are not given extensive coverage in this chapter.

The organization-level strategies included here are public education, civil disobedience, the use of civil action in the courts, and the use of violence or the threat of violence to achieve justice. While individuals may express frustration and a sense of injustice through the use of violence, this is not the same as using violence as a calculated strategy. While the use of aggression to address social issues is not common, it is easier to identify groups that have used violence as a strategic tool for bringing about justice. Discussing the use of violence by organizations does not condone it, nor does the attention given to this strategy suggest that it is particularly effective. Organizations can have difficulty correctly anticipating the response to violence. In some situations, violence may bring about change, whereas in others the response to violence is a backlash that only makes change less likely.

The categories used in this chapter are intended as a tool for organizing the discussion. In reality organizations do not always fit into simple categories. Many organizations use more than one strategy for dealing with a problem. An organization might, for example, publicize injustices as a method for educating the public while simultaneously providing legal services to take perpetrators to court and lobbying members of Congress for new legislation. Organizations may also change the strategies they use to meet changing environments.

EDUCATING THE PUBLIC

One of the most common organizational approaches to achieving justice is to draw public attention to injustices. The hope is that those committing the injustices will be shamed into changing their behavior or that the publicity will apply pressure for change. A large number of organizations use this approach. Two such organizations, Amnesty International (AI) and Human Rights Watch, are described here to give the reader a sense of how these groups work.

Amnesty International

In 1961, a British lawyer, Peter Benenson, read a newspaper account of two Portuguese students who were dining in a restaurant. During their meal, they made remarks critical of Portugal's dictator and then raised their glasses in a toast to freedom. Their comments were overheard and reported to Portuguese authorities. As a result, the two were sent to prison for 7 years for committing treason.[3] In the absence of any formal legal mechanism for freeing the prisoners, Benenson hoped that drawing the world's attention to the problem might help. He appealed for help from the public in a newspaper editorial describing the plight of eight people from different countries imprisoned for their religious or political beliefs.[4] Benenson described people imprisoned for expressing their religious or political views as "prisoners of conscience," and he urged readers to contact his office and write letters seeking the release of these prisoners. With the help of friends, Benenson soon expanded the focus of his work to include additional prisoners in other countries, and his office was quickly flooded with letters from people wanting to help.[5]

Benenson's initial success led him to launch a year-long campaign to free religious and political prisoners around the world. He called the campaign "Appeal for Amnesty, 1961." The year 1961 seemed particularly fitting because it was the 100th anniversary of the beginning of the civil war and thus the end of slavery in the United States, as well as the freeing of serfs in Russia.[6] As offers to help came in, Benenson adopted a practice of having small groups of volunteers "adopt" particular prisoners. The volunteers then contacted the prisoner and the prisoner's family and wrote letters to authorities on their behalf.

Benenson's organization grew quickly and came to be known as AI. Eventually, the types of cases taken on by AI expanded, as did the alternatives for dealing with each case. Missions were sent into countries where prisoners of conscience were being held to directly observe conditions and to gain facts firsthand. The key to the organization's success remains "the collection, organization, preparation, and presentation of information."[7] When AI was first founded, some considered the idea of using public attention to end injustices to be ridiculous. The organization was dubbed "one of the larger lunacies of our time."[8] However, the strategy has proven its effectiveness. Even oppressive regimes sometimes change their behavior in the face of public scrutiny and condemnation. In 1977, AI was awarded the Nobel Peace Prize for its efforts.

Today, AI has more than 2.8 million members in more than 150 countries. There are more than 7500 local chapters throughout the world, as well as national-level sections in 80 countries. The organization's home office remains in London, where its staff now numbers more than 170 people.[9]

The mandate for AI includes freeing prisoners of conscience, making certain that political prisoners have fair and prompt trials, abolishing the death penalty, and putting an end to extrajudicial executions and "disappearances."[10] AI also works to end torture, detention without charges, and human rights abuses by armed opposition groups. Although AI lobbies and campaigns for international treaties to stop human rights abuses, its primary work involves issuing reports detailing human rights violations. These reports are summarized in press releases, printed for distribution, and posted on their web site, a site that now contains more than 10,000 files.[11] In addition, AI continues the tradition of sponsoring "adoption groups," citizens who volunteer to take on or adopt a particular human rights case. They regularly write governments urging the release of individual political prisoners, and they maintain contact with the prisoners and their families.

The story of AI is the story of how an organizational structure can give life to one motivated individual's ideas about correcting injustices. As an organization, AI has been able to address human rights issues on a scale far beyond what Peter Benenson might have hoped to accomplish by acting alone.

Human Rights Watch

The model established by AI has been adopted by other groups, most notably Human Rights Watch. Human Rights Watch has the following explicit objective:

> *. . . the embarrassment of governments to halt human rights violations. Publicity—pitiless, potent and persistent—has been the continuing and ultimate aim of the organization's numerous projects. And, at this specialty, HRW has developed an expertise unrivaled in the human rights business.*[12]

Human Rights Watch began in 1978. It was originally formed as Helsinki Watch and was designed to "monitor the compliance of Soviet bloc countries with the human rights provisions of the landmark Helsinki Accords."[13] In the 1980s, Americas Watch was established to publicize human rights violations in South America, particularly those cases involving violations by governments that the United States supported, while seemingly ignoring their abuses.[14] In 1985, Asia Watch was created, followed by Africa Watch in 1986 and Middle-East Watch in 1989. Finally, these various committees joined to form Human Rights Watch.[15]

As with AI, Human Rights Watch focuses on human rights violations by governments and organized political groups, rather than on individuals acting on their own. Both organizations report on human rights abuses around the world, and both organizations refuse to take money from any government, believing that government money might compromise their objectivity. Although AI and Human Rights Watch use the United Nations' Universal Declaration of Human Rights (see Appendix) as the basis for their work, Human Rights Watch takes a somewhat broader approach, addressing such issues as freedom of the press, academic freedom, the use of child soldiers, and the production and deployment of land mines. As an organization formed in the United States, Human Rights Watch also devotes a considerable amount of energy to publicizing human rights violations in the United States, including conditions in U.S. prisons, the detention of immigrants, and racial disparities in the enforcement of drug laws. In addition, Human Rights Watch places more emphasis than does AI on pressuring the U.S. government to use its clout to influence other nations to modify behaviors that violate human rights.[16]

At present Human Rights Watch has a staff of 280 professionals, monitoring human rights issues in more than 90 countries.[17] Although Human Rights Watch is significantly younger than AI and has a smaller staff, it has become a potent force. Some argue that it now surpasses AI in its ability to publicize human rights violations and shame governments into taking corrective action.[18]

It is, perhaps, a sad statement about the human condition that two organizations can together identify thousands of human rights violations each year around the world. A review of the projects identified by these two groups shows that they are not concerned with trivial or minor issues of justice, but with serious violations of human rights by governments and organized groups—rape, torture, slavery, and murder. Both AI and Human Rights Watch have proven effective at publicizing human rights violations and using the attendant publicity to shame authorities into modifying their practices. As the technology for disseminating information improves, these organizations will be able to reach a wider audience and will be able to do so more quickly. Thus, the effectiveness of this strategy is likely to only improve over time.

When existing laws do not allow for the punishment of governments that violate human rights, public shame may be among the only tools available to human rights groups. There are times, however, when injustices involve behaviors that are subject to existing laws. In these situations, more direct action may be necessary. Our focus now shifts to illustrating how this direct action might be carried out.

CIVIL ACTION

While education can be a powerful tool, it is not always enough. Organizations may need to work within the framework of existing laws and regulations to bring about change. This strategy requires that the necessary laws and regulations be in place and that groups have the legal skills to fight the battle in court. While it is possible to identify several organizations that have successfully used the law to bring about justice, one organization, the American Civil Liberties Union (ACLU), has been particularly effective at utilizing this tactic.

From 1917 to 1920, America was engaged in the First World War. During that war, many basic civil rights, including freedom of speech, had little meaning. The 1918 Sedition Act made it a crime to criticize the government. For giving a speech critical of war, Socialist Party leader Eugene Debs was sentenced to ten years in prison, and a film maker was prosecuted for making a film about the American Revolution that was critical of the British, who were our allies in World War I.[19] The U.S. Post Office refused to deliver magazines or other materials that in any way questioned the war. Conscientious objectors were often kept in solitary confinement in military prisons, where they were fed bread and water diets and subjected to brutality.[20]

Basic liberties were also restricted in response to a series of bombings by anarchists. In 1919, bombs went off in eight cities, including one at the doorstep of Attorney General A. Mitchell Palmer. In response, Congress passed new laws further restricting freedom. It became a crime to send anything written in German through the U.S. mail, or to fly a red flag—the Communists had just staged a successful revolution in Russia.[21] Foreigners, in particular, were targets, and after the bombing, approximately 4000 people in 33 cities were rounded up, beaten, and arrested without warrants in what were known as the Palmer Raids. Many had no connection to radical movements, but appeared foreign. "Thousands were held without charges and were not permitted to see either counsel or family."[22]

Among those protesting the war was Roger Baldwin, who had himself served a year in prison for his antiwar views. Baldwin was outraged that the "land of the free" allowed people to express only those views supportive of the government and that the government would so freely ignore the basic principles outlined in the Constitution. In 1920, Roger Baldwin formed the ACLU as a private voluntary organization with the sole purpose of defending the Bill of Rights to the Constitution. The case of Roger Baldwin and the ACLU is an excellent example of not only the power of an individual to shape an organization, but also the power of an organization to accomplish more than could be done by any single individual. As Walker has observed:

> *Without Baldwin, the ACLU would not have survived its early years, and as a consequence, the law of civil liberties probably would have developed differently. In his thirty years as director of the ACLU he created something that transcended his own efforts—both an organization that carried on long after he retired and, more important, an idea that inspired countless other people over the years. The defense of the rights of everyone, the downtrodden and even the advocates of the most hateful ideas, became the guiding principle of Baldwin's life and that of the ACLU.*[23]

One of the continuing challenges facing the ACLU, and the nation, has been to determine just what is meant by the provisions granted in the Bill of Rights. Each of the freedoms listed in the Bill of Rights is really freedom from the long arm of the government, but the Bill of Rights is a relatively short document that gives few clues as to how its principles are to be applied to everyday situations. What words and behaviors are protected by "freedom of speech" and "freedom of religion"? What does it mean to be "free from unreasonable searches"? Even today, more than 90 years after the ACLU began its quest to defend these basic rights, society is still grappling with these issues. For example, is burning the flag in protest a form of free speech that is protected by the first amendment, or is it behavior that should be treated as criminal?

The ACLU was formed in 1920, after the excesses of the Palmer Raids. Its immediate task was to decide which civil liberties issues to take on and how to best make a difference. Now that the war was over, some of the most glaring violations of basic liberties were practiced against the newly emerging labor unions. In many communities it was illegal for workers to hold meetings to simply discuss labor conditions and the possibility of organizing. Wealthy businessmen spent a great deal of money spreading propaganda that equated union membership with radicalism and un-American activity.[24] Any behavior that even suggested a protest might subject the actor to arrest. In Los Angeles, for example:

> *When author Upton Sinclair and five friends marched up "Liberty Hill" to read the First Amendment, the police chief warned them to "cut out that Constitution stuff." Before they could finish they were arrested and charged with criminal syndicalism.*[25]

The link between the ACLU and labor would last until the 1930s, "when the Wagner Act established labor's right to organize."[26] By then the ACLU had begun taking on other issues.

Within the ACLU there were two differing opinions about how the organization could best improve civil liberties in America. Baldwin and several others thought that civil disobedience and other direct action was the best strategy. Others in the organization believed that the best long-term prospects for change would come from taking cases to court. Within the organization, each side followed its own approach. Those who worked through the courts did not achieve a victory until 1931, 11 years after the organization was founded.[27] While their strategy was less dramatic and may have drawn fewer headlines, it proved more successful in the long run. Eventually, civil action became the primary strategy used by the ACLU. Figure 15.1 shows some of the more visible cases in which the ACLU has been involved, either directly, or in a supporting role.

Today the ACLU is supported by donations from its more than 500,000 members and from private donors. It describes itself as the nation's largest public interest law firm. The ACLU has independent affiliate offices in all 50 states and handles thousands of cases each year. It has a staff that includes more than 200 ACLU staff attorneys and thousands of attorneys who volunteer their time to the

1925: Represented John Scopes who was accused of teaching evolution. Scopes was convicted but the ACLU had its first experience as a legal advocate
1933: Successfully fought a U.S. Customs Service ban on James Joyce's novel *Ulysses*
1939: Successfully fought a ban on union organizing in Jersey City
1942: Was one of the few groups to oppose the internment of American citizens of Japanese descent during World War II
1950: Fought against the "loyalty oaths" required of federal workers during the cold war of the 1950s
1954: Joined the legal battle against school desegregation in the case of *Brown v Board of Education*
1960: Supported the peaceful nonviolent tactics of the civil rights movement throughout the 1960s
1973: The case of *Roe v Wade* in which a woman's right to an abortion was upheld
1981: Successfully challenged an Arkansas law requiring that the biblical story of creation be taught as a scientific alternative to the theory of evolution
1989: Successfully overturned a Texas statute punishing flag desecration, which the ACLU argued was a form of political speech protected by the constitution
1996: Supreme Court recognized civil rights of lesbians and gay men by invalidating Colorado statute prohibiting gay rights laws

FIGURE 15.1

The ACLU goes to court.

Source: American Civil Liberties Union (2002).

organization.[28] It also appears before the Supreme Court more often than any other organization, except the Justice Department.[29] As Walker has observed:

> *The ACLU can legitimately claim much of the credit—or be assigned the blame, if you prefer—for the growth of modern constitutional law. Consult a standard constitutional law textbook and note the cases deemed important enough to be listed in the table of contents—the proverbial "landmark" cases. The ACLU was involved in over 80 percent of them; in several critical cases the Supreme Court's opinion was drawn directly from the ACLU brief. As even its critics have charged, the ACLU has exerted "an influence out of all proportion to its size."*[30]

There is a common perception that the ACLU is a "liberal" organization, but that is inaccurate. One might even argue that its commitment to limiting the power of government is quintessentially conservative. Politically, the organization strives to remain nonpartisan. It is more accurate to describe the ACLU as "absolutist" due to its absolute commitment to the Bill of Rights, or as libertarian because of its belief that the government must be kept in check. This is why an organization that supports the rights of women to have access to abortions also goes to court to defend the rights of anti-abortion protesters. The ACLU defends the right American Nazis and members of the Ku Klux Klan to stage public demonstrations, but it also stands against racial profiling by the police. For the ACLU the question is not whether the party they represent has morally correct views, or is even likeable. The question is whether the government is unjustly restricting that party's rights. Because it is so absolutist in its defense of civil liberties, the ACLU has taken positions that sometimes outrage conservatives and liberals alike. Their absolutist position means they are willing to defend people whose views they find offensive. As the organization puts it:

We do not defend them because we agree with them; rather, we defend their right to free expression and free assembly. Historically, the people whose opinions are the most controversial or extreme are the people whose rights are most often threatened. Once the government has the power to violate one person's rights, it can use that power against everyone.[31]

The fact that the ACLU is more libertarian than liberal was evident when two of the most conservative Republican members of Congress—Representative Dick Armey of Texas and Representative Bob Barr of Georgia—announced that they would become lobbyists for the ACLU when they left Congress in January 2003. Both representatives expressed concerns that, after the September 11, 2001, attacks on the World Trade Center, the U.S. Government had gone too far in restricting the rights of American citizens. Barr also reported that he had been working with the ACLU since the Oklahoma City bombing in 1995.[32]

The ACLU's primary efforts are in the courtroom, but it also engages in other activities to further civil liberties. The organization lobbies for and against legislation that may impact civil liberties, publishes books and other materials explaining basic rights, and takes public positions on issues related to civil liberties. However, it is in the courtroom that the organization has met its greatest success. The ACLU is an excellent example of how much more can be done when an individual's vision for justice is pursued by an organization. It would be hard to find an organization that has been more successful at using the courts to achieve justice, has had that success over such a long period of time, and has done so in a way that will have a lasting impact.

Baldwin's belief that civil disobedience was the best way to bring about justice eventually lost out to the strategy of taking justice issues to court. For some organizations, civil disobedience remains an important strategy for change, however. Our attention now turns to a sample of these organizations.

CIVIL DISOBEDIENCE

Civil disobedience is the intentional violation of the law, either because the law is seen as unjust, or to draw attention to a perceived injustice. For the action to qualify as civil disobedience, it must be public, and the individual must be willing to face any legal or social consequences that follow the act. In Chapter 14, it is suggested that Gandhi's work provides a model for the effective use of civil disobedience. Gandhi's approach involved more than simply breaking the law. His approach required that the lawbreaking take place as part of a strategy designed to achieve some higher purpose and that each act of civil disobedience had a very specific objective. In response to the question "What do you hope to gain by this?" Gandhi was always able to provide a list of very specific things that realistically could be done by those in power. Gandhi's vision of civil disobedience also required that participants be willing to accept the legal consequences of their actions, and it required a commitment to nonviolence.

Many organizations and movements have experimented with civil disobedience, usually as only one of several strategies. Thus far, no organization has had enough success with civil disobedience to be considered a model by others. In other words, no organizational counterpart to Gandhi has emerged thus far. There is no group that has done for civil disobedience what AI has done for public education or what the ACLU has done for civil action. Yet, there are groups that make periodic forays into civil disobedience. During the civil rights movement, for example, several groups effectively used civil disobedience to challenge racial inequalities in the law.[33] However, the use of civil disobedience by those groups was relatively short-lived, and those organizations eventually moved on to other, less confrontational strategies. The discussion now turns to some illustrative examples of the ways in which organizations have used civil disobedience to pursue their visions of justice.

Civil disobedience has become a tool used by organizations from both ends of the political spectrum. Anti-abortion demonstrators have been arrested for blocking clinic entrances, and environmental activists have engaged in sit-down demonstrations intended to disrupt international trade discussions. Two brief examples demonstrate the use of civil disobedience by groups from each end of the political spectrum.

Operation Rescue

In 1973, the United States Supreme Court, in the case of *Roe v. Wade*, ruled that women had a right to have an abortion. While there had been opposition to abortion before *Roe v. Wade*, the decision mobilized many who opposed abortion. However, efforts were scattered and largely uncoordinated until 1986. In that year antiabortion activist Randall Terry was serving a short jail sentence for blocking an abortion clinic when he hit upon the idea of organizing abortion foes around the country. He called his organization Operation Rescue (OR), and in 1987, he assembled more than 200 supporters to block the entrance to a New Jersey clinic.[34] Soon blockades were organized around the country, and thousands were being arrested. Between May of 1988 and August of 1990, Operation Rescue had organized 683 "rescue operations," leading to more than 60,000 arrests and the jailing of nearly 41,000.[35] Despite OR's success in garnering public attention and in hampering the operation of clinics, the organization's strategy of civil disobedience fell into decline after the early 1990s. Lawler (1992) attributes this decline to two factors: the failure of Operation Rescue to develop a long-term commitment to civil disobedience in its followers, and the increased legal penalties facing both individual protesters and the organization itself. The web site for Operation Rescue shows a very different organization that no longer has civil disobedience as the focus of its work and now distances itself from those who might resort to violence to end abortion. The organization's focus now is on peaceful and legal approaches to ending abortion in the United States.[36]

Greenpeace

Greenpeace is an environmental organization that began in 1971 in a Vancouver Unitarian church. A group of concerned citizens wanted to stop the United States from testing nuclear weapons on the island of Amchitka, which is part of the Aleutian Islands off the coast of Alaska.[37] A small group boarded a boat with the intention of parking it at the test site. They didn't arrive in time to stop the testing, but they did gain substantial media attention and, over time, honed their skills at conducting civil disobedience and at gaining publicity. As Wapner has observed:

> *Greenpeace chiefly wages its campaigns in world civic politics through "direct actions." These include positioning activists between harpooners and whales, plugging up industrial discharge pipes, parachuting from smokestacks and floating a hot-air balloon into a nuclear test site. None of these activities involves lobbying a government per se or calling for a particular policy change on the part of specific countries. Instead, the aim is to instill a sense of outrage among the largest audience possible.*[38]

The work of Greenpeace is based on the Quaker notion of "bearing witness."[39] "Having observed a morally objectionable act, one cannot turn away in avoidance. One must either take action to prevent further injustice, or stand by and attest to its occurrence."[40]

Today, Greenpeace has offices in 30 countries. It also has a fleet of ships, inflatable boats, and a hot air balloon.[41] It employs more than a thousand full-time staff members, hundreds of part-time staff members, and thousands of volunteers.[42] Although many people think of Greenpeace as an organization that focuses on saving the whales, their mandate is much broader, including saving ancient forests, ending global warming, stopping the dumping of toxic pollutants, controlling overfishing of the oceans, eliminating genetically engineered crops, and putting an end to "all phases of nuclear production and use."[43] The organization makes extensive use of modern technology to provide the press with video images of environmental harm.

Although the use of civil disobedience by organizations has not always met with long-term success, the strategy has great potential, and there are signs that it may be maturing as a tool for change. In 1995, an organization called the Ruckus Society emerged with an approach to civil disobedience that made it unique. Although members of the Ruckus Society periodically engage in civil disobedience themselves, the organization is unique because it provides training to others who wish to use civil disobedience to bring about social change. According to the Society, its mission is to provide "training in the skills of non-violent civil disobedience to help environmental and human rights organizations achieve their goals."[44] The Society provides week-long training programs across the country, in what are known as "Action Camps." Participants in these camps learn a variety of skills related to nonviolent civil disobedience, including using the media, advance planning, scouting out locations, climbing (trees, construction cranes, etc.), and filming with video cameras. Participants are also expected to stay for the duration of the camp, with the hope that networks will form to be useful in future actions. The Ruckus Society is adamant in its emphasis on nonviolence. As its literature states, "Wherever the location, regardless of the subject, we condemn and do not train activists in any technique that will harm any being."[45]

As organizations go, the Ruckus Society is quite young. It is possible that people being trained by the Ruckus Society today will help some organization become a model for the use of nonviolent civil disobedience, a model as powerful as the example provided by Gandhi.

VIOLENCE

Vandalism and violence have long been tools of individual extremists, the mentally unstable, or those who have been forced into violence out of desperation. Individual radical environmentalists have engaged in arson, and individual radical anti-abortionists have bombed abortion clinics and killed doctors. However, the extent to which these actions are coordinated and directed by organizations is not always clear. Individual members of organizations like Earth First! may have voiced their approval of the $12 million arson fire that destroyed a Colorado ski resort, and members of the Army of God may believe that justice has been served when an abortion doctor is killed. However, expressing sympathy or approval for such actions is very different from directing or coordinating them. Even when organizations have a direct hand in violence, they are generally reluctant to publicly admit to their role, probably because they are unwilling to suffer the legal consequences of their actions. It is also true that admitting to violence can drive away moderate supporters and undermine the credibility of the organization, as well as any claim it has to holding the moral high ground. Although disclaiming any involvement with violence is the general rule, there are highly visible exceptions. Two types of exceptions are worth noting here. First, there are groups for which violence is one component of a larger ideology of hate. The Ku Klux Klan, Aryan Nations, the American Nazi Party, and the Jewish Defense League (JDL) are examples of groups purported to view violence as an acceptable strategy for achieving their vision of justice. The Ku Klux Klan, Aryan Nations, and the American Nazi Party are discussed in Chapter 10. The discussion here focuses on the example of the JDL, given the group's willingness to openly express its belief in the necessity of violence.

The JDL

Members of the JDL have been particularly willing to publicly express their belief that violence is both justified and necessary. Founded in 1968, the JDL views the Jewish people as under attack, and it has lashed out against minorities and other Jewish groups that take a more moderate stance. Violence is considered necessary in self-defense, or to preserve the Jewish people.[46] One of the five principles upon which the JDL was founded makes it clear that violence is to be considered a viable option:

> *JDL upholds the principle of* Barzel*—iron—the need to both move to help Jews everywhere and to change the Jewish image through sacrifice and all necessary means—even strength, force and violence.*[47]

In his book *The Story of the Jewish Defense League*, JDL founder Meir Kahane devotes an entire chapter to justifying the use of violence. He concludes by arguing that "violence is never good but sometimes necessary and Jewish violence to protest Jewish interests is *never* bad."[48]

The issue of violence continues to swirl around the JDL. The web site for the Anti-Defamation League, one of the moderate Jewish organizations often criticized by the JDL, provides an extensive listing of violent acts attributed to the JDL. In 1990, Meir Kahane was assassinated in New York City by an Arab extremist.[49] In December of 2001, the chairman of the JDL and another member were arrested for plotting to bomb the offices of an Arab-American U.S. Representative, as well as a Los Angeles-area mosque.[50]

For hate-based groups, violence can serve some useful functions. It can solidify membership by having members engage in actions that reinforce their commitment to the organization. It can also point to attacks on its methods and ideas to show members that they are a noble, embattled group. It is less clear, however, that the violence conducted by these groups does much to advance their causes. To the contrary, their violence can do much to energize groups opposed to them. Furthermore, when the leaders of organizations that utilize violence are unwilling to step forward and take responsibility for their actions, questions emerge about their true level of commitment and their genuine interest in achieving justice.

Aside from the violence of hate-based groups, this discussion includes a second category of organizations that employ violence. These organizations are not driven by hate, but by nationalism and the desire to create a new nation. Numerous examples can be found. The United States was formed through the use of violence, as was the state of Israel. When these revolutionary groups begin their actions, they are often defined as terrorists, but if they succeed, they come to be viewed as visionaries. One example of a modern-day organization that uses violence with the aim of creating an independent nation is the Irish Republican Army (IRA).

The IRA

Tensions between Ireland and England go far back in time, perhaps as much as 1000 years before Columbus came to America.[51] During much of that period, the tensions have led to violence. Over time, a number of Irish organizations have arisen in opposition to the British. Today, one of the more visible organizations is the IRA. The IRA first emerged in 1916, when seven men seized a government post office in Dublin and posted a signed proclamation declaring them the "Provisional Government of the Irish Republic."[52] A number of organizations preceded the IRA, and over time, it split into a number of factions. Furthermore, the influence of the IRA has periodically waxed and waned.[53] Still, the impact of the IRA has been considerable, and it remains an important player in the effort to create an independent Ireland.

Throughout its history, the IRA has used violence to frustrate what it views as an occupying force. "Basically, the IRA man felt that he was fighting for freedom, for an end to injustice, while his opponents sought superiority, so the end justified the means."[54] The IRA has used car bombs, radio-controlled bombs, bank robbery, and murder to further their cause. With financial support from Irish people living outside the contested area, particularly the United States, the IRA also assembled an impressive assortment of weapons, including automatic weapons and rocket launchers. In addition, it has been claimed that extremists in the IRA and their supporters have stolen enough weapons and munitions from the U.S. military to arm 8000 men.[55]

In the latter part of the 1900s, the organization became more sophisticated in its operation. First, it abandoned its more traditional military structure in favor of small cells. These cells were usually made up of four people, with only the leader having contact with higher authority. Cell members were cautioned to keep their activities secret, even from family and friends. Thus, individual cell members had very limited knowledge of larger operations or of other people involved in the movement.[56] This protected the organization by making it difficult for informers to foil plans and by making captured operatives of little use to British authorities, because those operatives knew little about larger plans for the organization. The use of cells has also been adopted by anti-government extremist organizations in the United States (see Chapter 8) and may have been an element in the 1995 bombing of the Alfred P. Murrah building in Oklahoma City.

In order to educate members about the purpose and philosophy of the IRA without revealing their identity to other members, the IRA produced the *Green Book*, an explicit statement of the IRA's position on violence:

> *Volunteers are expected to wage a military war of liberation against a numerically superior force. This involves the use of arms and explosives. Firstly the use of arms. When volunteers are trained in the use of arms they must fully understand that guns are dangerous, and their main purpose is to take human life, in other words to kill people, and volunteers are trained to kill people. . . . [The volunteer must have] convictions which are strong enough to give him confidence to kill someone without hesitation and without regret.*[57]

After untold thousands of deaths over more than 1500 years, Ireland and Britain continue to fight over the issue of Irish independence. In the 1990s, there was talk of peace and agreements to end the violence (or at least that violence sponsored by organizations), but as of this writing, Ireland is still not an independent country, and violence is still a feature of daily life in Ireland. Should independence come to Ireland, it is will likely be facilitated by the use of violence, and after peace does occur, groups such as the IRA will probably be defined by the world as patriots rather than as terrorists.

CONCLUSION

There are many ways in which organizations can work to bring about justice. This chapter has only scratched the surface regarding the methods that might be used. Constraints on space have precluded a discussion of the many organizations that work to organize local communities and neighborhoods,[58] or the vast network of organizations that promote peace,[59] to mention just two examples. This chapter is not intended to provide a comprehensive listing of organizations that work for justice, or to provide step-by-step instructions on how to build such organizations. Rather, the purpose of this chapter is to provide illustrative examples of organization-level approaches that have been used with some success.

While Chapters 14 and 15 discuss the power of individuals and organizations to address injustices, Chapter 16 introduces yet another concern in the pursuit of justice. What is to be done with nations or national leaders who grossly and intentionally violate human rights? When does the interest of the world community take precedence over the interests of a nation to govern itself, even if that process of governing involves unspeakable horrors?

DISCUSSION QUESTIONS

1. How might the strategy an organization adopts be shaped by the particular problem they are addressing? That is, under what conditions would each of the four strategies described in this chapter be the most appropriate?
2. Think of organizations not described in this chapter that have had success at pursuing justice. What strategies do they use?
3. What are the circumstances under which violence might be a morally acceptable strategy for an organization seeking justice?

Endnotes

1. Information about the Bill and Melinda Gates Foundation can be found at www.gatesfoundation.org.
2. Information about Free the Children can be found at www.freethechildren.com.
3. William Korey, *NGOs and the Universal Declaration of Human Rights* (New York: St. Martin's Press, 1998).
4. Ann Marie Clark, *Diplomacy of Conscience: Amnesty International and Changing Human Rights Norms* (Princeton: Princeton University Press, 2001).
5. *Ibid.*
6. Korey, *NGOs.*
7. *Ibid.*, p. 166.
8. Jonathan Power, *Like Water on Stone: The Story of Amnesty International* (Boston: Northeastern University Press, 2001), p. xi; Amnesty International (accessed July 21, 2013 at www.amnesty.org).
9. Amnesty International United Kingdom (available from www.amnesty.org.uk/; Internet; accessed July 21, 2013). Also see Power, *Like Water on Stone.*
10. Amnesty International.
11. *Ibid.*
12. Korey, *NGOs*, p. 340.
13. Human Rights Watch, *Human Rights Watch: Our History* (available from www.hrw.org/node/75134; Internet; accessed July 21, 2013).

14. *Ibid.* and Korey, *NGOs.*
15. Korey, *NGOs.*
16. *Ibid.*
17. Human Rights Watch, *Human Rights Watch: FAQ* (available from www.hrw.org/node/75138; Internet; accessed July 21, 2013).
18. Korey, *NGOs.*
19. Samuel Walker, *In Defense of American Liberties: A History of the ACLU* (New York: Oxford University Press, 1990).
20. Diane Garey, *Defending Everybody: A History of the American Civil Liberties Union* (New York: TV Books, 1998).
21. *Ibid.*
22. *Ibid.*, p. 58.
23. Walker, *In Defense of American Liberties*, p. 30.
24. *Ibid.*
25. *Ibid.*, p. 54.
26. *Ibid.*, p. 55.
27. *Ibid.*
28. The American Civil Liberties Union, *About the ACLU* (available from www.aclu.org/about-aclu-0; Internet; accessed July 23, 2013).
29. American Civil Liberties Union, *A Brief History and Overview of the ACLU* (available from www.aclu.org/about/about.html; Internet; accessed August 13, 2002).
30. Walker, *In Defense of American Liberty*, p. 4.
31. American Civil Liberties Union.
32. Jill Lawrence, "Conservative Favorites to Join ACLU," *USA Today*, November 25, 2002, p. 2A.
33. Peter Ackerman and Jack Duvall, *A Force More Powerful: A Century of Nonviolent Conflict* (New York: Palgrave, 2000).
34. Philip E. Lawler, *Operation Rescue: A Challenge to the Nation's Conscience* (Huntington, Ind.: Our Sunday Visitor, Inc., 1992).
35. *Ibid.*
36. Operation Rescue's position can be found on their web site (available from www.operationrescue.org; Internet; accessed on July 23, 2013).
37. Paul Wapner, "Environmental Activism and Global Civil Society," *Dissent* (summer 1994), pp. 389-393.
38. *Ibid.*, p. 390.
39. Michael Brown and John May, *The Greenpeace Story* (New York: Dorling Kindersley, Inc., 1991).
40. Wapner, "Environmental Activism," p. 391.
41. Greenpeace (available from www.greenpeace.org; Internet; accessed on July 23, 2013).
42. *Ibid.*
43. Greenpeace, *Inside Greenpeace: History and Mission* (available from www.greenpeace.org/inside/historytext .htm; Internet; accessed on March 11, 2002).
44. The Ruckus Society, *About the Ruckus Society* (available from http://ruckus.org/about.html; Internet; accessed on March 7, 2002).
45. *Ibid.*
46. Anti-Defamation League, *Backgrounder: The Jewish Defense League* (available from www.adl.org; Internet; accessed on July 21, 2013).
47. Jewish Defense League, *The Five Principles of the Jewish Defense League* (available from www.jdl.org; Internet; accessed on 13 March 2002).
48. Rabbi Meir Kahane, *The Story of the Jewish Defense League* (Radnor, Pa.: Chilton Book Company, 1975), p. 144, emphasis in the original.

49. Anti-Defamation League
50. Vincent J. Schodolski, "2 Jewish Militants Jailed on Bomb Plot," *Chicago Tribune*, March 13, 2002 (available from www.chicagotribune.com; Internet; accessed on March 13, 2002).
51. Tim Pat Coogan, *The Troubles: Ireland's Ordeal 1966-1996 and the Search for Peace* (Boulder, Colorado: Roberts Rinehart Publishers, 1996).
52. J. Bowyer Bell, *The Secret Army: The IRA,* 3rd ed. (New Brunswick, N.J.: Transaction Publishers, 1997).
53. Tim Pat Coogan, *The IRA*, 5th ed. (New York: St. Martin's Press, 2000).
54. *Ibid.,* p. 381.
55. *Ibid.*
56. *Ibid., The Troubles: Ireland's Ordeal 1966-1996 and the Search for Peace.*
57. Cited in *ibid.*, p. 547.
58. For a more extensive discussion of these, see Robert Fisher, *Let the People Decide: Neighborhood Organizing in America* (New York: Twayne, 1994).
59. A nice overview of organizations that promote peace can be found in Elise Boulding, *Cultures of Peace: The Hidden Side of History* (Syracuse, N.Y.: Syracuse University Press, 2000).

CHAPTER

Global Justice

16

Chapters 14 and 15 have focused on a variety of ways in which individuals and organizations might pursue justice. Unlike individual- and organization-level approaches to justice, the concept of global justice is an emerging area in which a variety of fundamental issues have yet to be resolved. To date, there are no examples that illustrate this approach at its best. Despite this lack of models, global justice is of great importance. Improved transportation and communication have aided the movement of goods and ideas between nations, but these technologies have also aided the spread of war crimes, genocide, slavery, and other serious human rights violations. As nations become increasingly interdependent, events in one country impact events in others. As a result, nations have struggled to find alternative ways to define acts of injustice that threaten the stability of other nations and to penalize violators.

This chapter focuses on international efforts to pursue justice, in which nations collectively respond to injustices committed either by other nations or by individuals in formal leadership positions within nations. The challenge is to identify acts that violate universal standards of justice while also respecting the ability of nations to handle their own affairs and make their own judgments about what behaviors are acceptable.

The idea that universal standards of justice exist and that nations and national leaders can be held accountable for violating those standards is a relatively recent development. Even the notion of human rights is relatively new. Robertson[1] argues that the first modern notion of human rights enforceable through the courts was the1688 Bill of Rights in England. By claiming these rights, the British formally ended the notion that the king ruled by divine right, and Parliament gained the ability to veto royal decisions. Similar to the rights later enumerated in the Bill of Rights to the U.S. Constitution, the British rights included the right to have the lawfulness of imprisonment tested by the courts, also known as habeas corpus, and:

> *. . . the right of subjects to live under the law as approved by parliament without arbitrary royal interference; the right to due process in the selection of jurors; the right not to lose liberty through excessively high fixing of bail; and the right not to be inflicted with "cruel and unusual punishment."*[2]

These rights, enacted in 1688, were viewed as basic rights of British citizens and eventually provided the justification for the American Revolution. However, their focus was on rights *within* the British Empire. The notion of basic human rights that transcend national boundaries would come later.

The discussion of global justice begins with a discussion of war. Chapter 9 discussed issues of justice surrounding the initiation and conduct of war. This chapter shows how modern efforts to achieve global justice have emerged as a result of wartime atrocities. Furthermore, as discussed in Chapter 12 on genocide, war is sometimes used to justify behaviors that would otherwise be indefensible.

WAR

There is little basis in reality for the popular saying "All's fair in love and war." Both courtship and war have recognized rules. As discussed in Chapter 9, St. Augustine delineated the criteria for a "just war." St. Augustine's rules focused on the circumstances under which it was morally justifiable to engage in war and on the treatment of civilians.[3] Written rules placing restrictions on the treatment of enemy combatants and the practice of war itself did not emerge until the mid-1800s during the American Civil War. President Abraham Lincoln recognized that the manner in which the Civil War was fought would have a lasting impact on the ability of the warring factions to peacefully coexist when the war was over. In 1863, he directed Dr. Franz Lieber to develop rules of war to guide the actions of Union soldiers.

Issued as General Orders Number 100 from the Adjutant General's Office in 1863, the Lieber Code is a remarkable document both in the range of issues it includes and in the succinctness of its writing. The Lieber Code is the source for modern military law and has been used as the basis for military codes in other countries. It also has been used to develop international law on war crimes.[4] The Lieber Code is divided into 10 sections, with a total of 157 Articles (major points) across those 10 sections, but it is only about 25 pages long. To provide just a few examples, the Code includes a discussion of the following: what martial law is and when it applies to occupied territories; what occupying armies are forbidden from doing to property, civilians, and enemy soldiers; how deserters, traitors, spies, and prisoners of war are to be handled; and flags of truce, prisoner exchanges, and the procedures for reaching a peace settlement.[5]

In St. Petersburg in 1868, at the Hague in 1899, and again at the Hague in 1907, nations reached a general agreement on the rules of war, including a ban on weapons that inflicted unnecessary suffering; attacks on undefended towns; attacks on hospitals, churches, universities, and historic buildings; and the use of poison or poison gas. There also was agreement that prisoners of war were to be treated humanely.[6] A series of additional international meetings expanded and clarified the rules of war. Most well known, perhaps, are the rules for engagement, the treatment of prisoners, and the treatment of civilians outlined in the 1949 Geneva Conventions.[7]

In 1949, there was a series of conventions regarding the rules of war. These meetings, held in Switzerland, came to be known as the Geneva Conventions. The first convention provided guidelines for the treatment of sick and wounded combatants on land. The second convention focused on sick and wounded combatants at sea. The third convention provided guidelines for the handling of prisoners of war, and the fourth concerned the treatment of civilians in occupied territories.[8]

In 2001, when the United States held Afghan fighters in Guantanamo Bay, Cuba, concerns were raised about whether these captives were treated according to the Geneva Conventions, but most Americans probably had little idea of what the Geneva Conventions required. According to the Conventions, prisoners of war cannot be tortured to extract information or used for military labor. In addition:

> *The prisoner must give his name, rank, regimental number and date of birth: on thus achieving POW status he is entitled to be "quartered under conditions as favorable as those for the forces of the detaining power" and to have nutritious food, warm clothing and bedding, and permission to pray and to smoke. POWs are to receive monthly pay . . . and must be allowed to receive food parcels and send and receive mail. They must be permitted to organize discipline in their own camps, and to make formal complaints about their treatment.*[9]

Over time, each of these agreements, from the 1868 meeting in St. Petersburg to the 1949 Geneva Convention, was more detailed than the last, but they all shared a failure to establish any enforcement mechanism. Without an enforcement mechanism, the prohibitions outlined in the various commissions and conventions had little meaning. During both World War I and World War II, the agreed-upon rules of war were systematically violated by both sides.[10] Creating these rules of war was not sufficient to change the behavior of nations, but it was a necessary step in the creation of an enforcement mechanism. Such a mechanism has still not fully evolved, but it is possible to identify early attempts. Perhaps the most important of these attempts was the series of trials at Nuremberg.

THE NUREMBERG TRIALS

At the end of World War I, there was a feeble attempt to hold the German leadership accountable for Germany's actions during the war. Articles 228 and 229 of the Versailles Treaty:

> *. . . provided that Germany should try its own war criminals: evidence against 901 of its nationals was handed over . . . 888 were acquitted, and of the thirteen convicted several were allowed to escape by prison officers who were publicly congratulated for assisting them.*[11]

After World War II, there was a renewed call for the victorious nations to hold tribunals to try the vanquished, but this time the process and the outcome were quite different. The victorious Allied nations—the United States, England, France, and the Soviet Union—reached an agreement and produced the 1945 Charter of the Nuremberg Tribunal, while also establishing a Tokyo tribunal to deal with Japanese war crimes. This charter provided relatively detailed rules of procedure under which leaders of the Nazi regime would be tried and punished.[12] The Nuremberg Trials were heavily stacked in favor of the prosecution:

> *. . . all prosecutors and judges were nationals of the Allied powers, and all defendants and, more regrettably, their lawyers were German . . . . The German defense lawyers, floundering in the alien Anglo-American environment of the adversary trial, were given limited facilities to prepare their cases and little notice of prosecution evidence.*[13]

Some defense attorneys suffered reprisals from their local bar associations for having worked too aggressively in the defense of their clients. Even the location, the site of the German anti-Semitic laws, gave the prosecution a psychological advantage.[14] The German defendants, accused of wartime atrocities, were not allowed to present evidence of numerous Allied atrocities during the war, including the 30,000 executed following what were transparently show trials in the Soviet Union between 1936 and 1938.[15] Charges at Nuremberg included "subverting the League of Nations," although the United States had never joined the League of Nations, and the Soviet Union had been expelled from it.[16] Furthermore, the trial was an ex-post facto prosecution. That is, defendants were tried for behaviors they engaged in *before* those acts were defined as crimes.[17] This violated a fundamental principle of fairness recognized in most legal systems.

Perhaps the most unfortunate feature of the Nuremberg Trials was the manner in which justice was dispensed. As Robertson has observed:

> *In its end lay the negation of its beginning: it created crimes against humanity and then punished them inhumanely. Twelve defendants were sentenced to death by hanging, after which—by some grisly irony appealing to the Allied high command—the bodies were cremated in the ovens at Dachau. The ashes were consigned to an unidentified fast-flowing river so no grave would ever serve as a place of neo-Nazi pilgrimage.*[18]

The trials were also notable for the small number of defendants who were charged with war crimes. Thousands of offenders were never charged by the tribunal, and, if the Nuremberg Trials were to serve as a deterrent to prevent future atrocities, they failed. Numerous instances of state-sponsored atrocities have occurred since Nuremberg, some of which are noted in Chapter 12 on genocide. Most of these horrendous acts have elicited only a tepid response from the international community.

Despite these limitations, the Nuremberg proceedings were much more than show trials. The defendants faced clearly articulated charges of crimes against humanity, and the proceedings followed a detailed series of legal procedures. Most importantly, the Nuremberg Trials laid the groundwork for later efforts at defining war crimes, for conducting war crime tribunals, for the principle that individuals could be held accountable for the acts of nations, and that "I was just following orders" was not an acceptable defense for all wartime atrocities. It has also been argued that the Nuremberg Trials inspired the development of the United Nations and the rise of non-government organizations that pursue human rights.[19]

THE UNIVERSAL DECLARATION OF HUMAN RIGHTS

Although Allied war atrocities were substantial, those of the Nazis were particularly horrific, causing nations to more formally recognize fundamental human rights and to move to establish a framework for punishing nations that flagrantly violated those rights. The United Nations, which had been formed in 1945, was a logical organization to direct this international effort. The Charter for the United Nations placed considerable emphasis on human rights, and the UN quickly established a Commission on Human Rights. The Commission on Human Rights included 18 member nations and was chaired by Eleanor Roosevelt, wife of president Franklin D. Roosevelt, with a Canadian, John Humphrey, serving as secretariat. One of the first items on the Commission's agenda was the creation of the Universal Declaration of Human Rights (see Appendix). It was fitting that Eleanor Roosevelt should serve as chair, because the direction of the Commission may have been influenced by a speech given by President Franklin D. Roosevelt, in which he spoke of four fundamental freedoms—the freedoms of speech and worship and the freedoms from want and fear—ideas that had been outlined in the writings of science fiction author H.G. Wells.[20]

Although the practical work of constructing the Universal Declaration of Human Rights was in the hands of an American and a Canadian, there was a serious effort to include the perspectives of many cultures from countries representing a broad range of economic development.[21] Altogether, the Commission received input from 250 delegates representing fifty-six countries, in addition to seeking the advice of recognized authorities, including H.G. Wells himself. Giving a back-handed testimonial as to its multi-cultural appeal, Robertson notes:

> *That over the following half-century the Declaration would be flouted without regard to geography, by governments of every creed and color and often by or with the connivance of the U.S. and its European allies, amply demonstrates that its guarantees are not "Western" in any meaningful sense. "Liberal" the Declaration is not, in any consistent way . . . .*[22]

The broad appeal of the Declaration is all the more surprising given the wide range of issues it includes among basic human rights. Aside from the obvious prohibitions against such things as slavery and torture, the Universal Declaration of Human Rights also includes the rights to marry, work, join labor unions, have rest and leisure, free education, and the enjoyment of the arts. It is perhaps ironic that this wide-ranging list does not include the right to two of the most basic human needs, food and water.

The document was groundbreaking in another way. Influenced by what the Germans had done to their own people, the Universal Declaration of Human Rights also addressed the problems of human rights violations *within* nations. The United Nations justified interfering with a nation's sovereignty by arguing that serious human rights violations within a single nation threatened international peace and stability.[23] This created a precedent for subsequent international tribunals and interventions in what might previously have been considered purely internal matters.

The Universal Declaration of Human Rights was high on principles, but made no effort to outline a mechanism for holding nations or individuals accountable for living up to those principles. Thus, the document was an important step toward global justice, but left the hard part for those who would follow.

Although the Universal Declaration of Human Rights has never had the force of law, it has been tremendously influential as a model of what nations should aspire to achieve. As Robertson has observed:

> *What amazes today is the contemporaneity of the document, over half a century on. Roosevelt and her drafting committee produced an imperishable statement that has inspired more than 200 international treaties, conventions and declarations, and the bills of rights found in almost every national constitution adopted since the war.*[24]

THE EUROPEAN COURT OF HUMAN RIGHTS

In 1950, a group of 12 European nations, known as the Council of Europe and eventually the Council of the European Union, held the European Convention on Human Rights. Signatory nations agreed to abide by the principles outlined in the Universal Declaration of Human Rights and, where necessary, to modify their legal codes to be consistent with the Universal Declaration.[25] More importantly, the European Convention on Human Rights created the European Court of Human Rights, which began hearing cases in 1959. The Convention also established rules and procedures for bringing alleged offenders to trial and for providing the accused with basic procedural rights drawn from the English common law tradition (see Chapter 5 for a discussion of that tradition). The most contentious of the procedural rights granted in the European Court has been the right of individuals and organizations to directly bring charges against a country before the court. This right has meant that individuals could bring international charges against their own country. The reluctance of nations to accept this provision delayed the active use of the court for nearly two decades.

Concerns about procedural issues were eventually worked out, and the frequency with which the court was used has increased dramatically over time. In 1983, there were about 500 cases brought before the court. By the year 2000, there were over 10,000 cases brought before the court, and nearly 16,000 cases were pending.[26] By 2012, over 65,000 cases were brought before the court, and 128,000 cases were pending.[27] After the Berlin wall came down in 1989, many nations that had been under the control of the Soviet Union now sought to join the European Union and were willing to abide by the rules of the European Court of Human Rights.[28]

The European Court has been criticized for sometimes turning cases back to the country standing accused before it, as well as for its requirement that, whenever a nation is tried before it, the panel of judges deciding the case will have at least one of its judges drawn from the accused nation.[29] Despite these weaknesses the European Court has been quite successful at persuading member nations to incorporate basic human rights protections into their laws. As Robertson has observed:

> *The European Court of Human Rights has become the model human rights court, proof positive that international law can work to enforce fundamental freedoms across a swathe of countries, as every one of its original member governments has made changes in its laws for the benefit of groups such as immigrants, transvestites, prisoners, and mental patients—reforms which would not have been sufficiently vote-winning in the absence of a decision from Strasbourg [France, where the court is housed].*[30]

By the late 1990s, the court was used frequently, creating a 6-year backlog of cases. In 1998, the Council of Europe expanded the European Court, making its judges permanent and paying them respectable wages. At present, 47 member nations have willingly placed themselves under the jurisdiction of the European Court of Human Rights.[31] Ideally, the model presented by the European Court could be expanded to include nations from every continent to create a court with truly global jurisdiction. While there has been some movement in this direction, the discussion that follows makes it clear that the process will be a long one.

TEMPORARY TRIBUNALS

Between 1945 and 1950, there was a flurry of international activity focused on human rights. The United Nations was formed, the Nuremberg Trials were held, the Universal Declaration of Human Rights was adopted, the Geneva Conventions issued rules of war, the Genocide Convention formalized the UN position on genocide, and there was a European Convention on Human Rights. Given all of the developments during this period, it is surprising that international war crimes tribunals did not emerge for at least another 40 years, and it was not until 1998 that the United Nations set in motion the process for establishing a permanent International Criminal Court (ICC) to prosecute war crimes and the most egregious human rights violations.

The single biggest obstacle to setting up international courts with true enforcement power is that, for such a court to be effective, participating nations must agree in advance to abide by its findings and thus to give up some of their sovereignty. A nation that agrees to be under the jurisdiction of such a court may easily find itself accused and tried by nations it does not trust.

The international human rights activities described above fell far short of what was needed to hold people and nations fully accountable for war crimes and acts of genocide. These were, however, important steps toward the creation of a structure that would have the ability to examine specific cases and hand out punishments. The next significant steps toward a system of justice to deal with global atrocities did not occur until 43 years later when, in 1993, when the United Nations established a temporary war crimes tribunal in the Hague to hear cases of war crimes and genocide in Bosnia. Just one year later, it established another temporary tribunal to hear cases of war crimes in Rwanda. The Rwandan genocide was described in some detail in Chapter 12, as was the genocide in Bosnia.

The Hague Tribunal for War Crimes in Bosnia was the first international tribunal since the 1945 Nuremberg Trials. Unlike Nuremberg, the Hague Tribunal was truly international and not simply a situation in which the victors held the vanquished in judgment. The legal basis for creating the Hague Tribunal was not explicit, but was inferred from the UN Charter, which gave the United Nations authority to act where there were threats to international peace and security. The Tribunal was authorized to hear cases against individuals whose acts were committed after 1991 in what had formerly been Yugoslavia. It was given the authority to prosecute and punish serious violations of the laws of war outlined in the 1949 Geneva Conventions and in the 1907 Hague Convention. It was also authorized to punish genocide and crimes against humanity.[32] In 1994, the UN Security Council created an extension of the Hague Tribunal to hear charges against those involved in the genocide in Rwanda. This Tribunal was conducted in Arusha, Tanzania, and as with the Tribunal in the Hague, there were three trial chambers, each with an international panel of judges to hear the cases. To provide consistency across cases, the same body served as the Appeals Chamber for both the Hague and the Arusha Tribunals.

Someone accused of an international crime is arrested by one of the countries that has agreed to cooperate with the international tribunals. The Hague and the Arusha Tribunals each have three courtrooms. In each courtroom, there is a panel of three judges hearing each case, with a simple majority necessary for a conviction. Defendants are provided with the attorneys of their choice, and if they cannot afford an attorney, the fees are paid for them. The accused is provided with many of the rights granted in common law courts. The only penalty that can be imposed by the Tribunals is imprisonment and the return of improperly seized property to victims. Prison time is served in a country willing to take the offender and the length of sentence is determined by the gravity of the offense.[33]

The Hague Tribunal was initially underfunded and understaffed. The first Serb was not arrested until two years after the tribunal was formed, although the whereabouts of Serbs accused of war crimes were well known. Over time more resources came to the Tribunal, and it became more aggressive in its pursuit of cases. By 2001, what began, in 1993, as an operation with one deputy prosecutor had expanded to a prosecutor's staff of 300 and a total staff of more than 1000.[34] By April 2002, the Tribunal's detention facility held 40 inmates, with eight individuals on provisional release and another 30 remaining at large.[35] By 2013, 161 people had been indicted by the court, and 136 had their proceedings completed.[36]

The Arusha Tribunals have processed even fewer cases arising from the Rwandan genocide than have been processed in the Hague Tribunals. Formed in 1994, the Arusha Tribunals did not hear their first case until 1996, and by early 2002, the Tribunals had only tried nine of 50 suspects held in custody. By 2013, the Tribunals had heard just 75 cases, and of those, there were 63 convictions.[37] There is no fixed predetermined ending date for these Tribunals, and some years are likely to pass before they have finished their work. Considering that at least some of those on trial will be found not guilty, there are questions about the fairness of holding suspects in jails for years before their trials—a problem for which there is no obvious solution.

Critics have argued that, if the Nuremberg Trials were used by victors to punish the vanquished, then the temporary tribunals for Bosnian and Rwandan war crimes were created to be little more than symbolic gestures allowing other nations to do nothing.[38] Inadequate funding may reflect the ambivalence that nations of the world feel toward these acts of genocide. The number of prosecutions is small considering the number of people who might be charged. While it is true that resources have improved over time, these tribunals remain short on cash, short on personnel, and short on time. For example, in Rwanda, the government has taken to holding its own trials. An additional 120,000 people have been arrested and are on trial in Rwanda's courts. By 2002, only 6000 of these had been tried.[39] It is estimated that, at the current pace, the Rwandan government will take 200 years to try the remaining suspects.[40]

What is the verdict on these temporary tribunals? Their weaknesses are many. They have received inadequate financial support from UN member nations. They have handled only a tiny fraction of the cases that fall within their jurisdiction. There is no evidence that the functioning of these courts has done much to prevent genocide. Many of the acts of genocide committed by the Serbs took place after the Hague Tribunal was called into being, as were the acts of genocide in Rwanda. Finally, it is not clear that the Tribunals have helped heal the emotional wounds of survivors. As Power has noted:

> *Despite the presence of high-powered defendants in UN custody, none of the early trials had the effect on survivors that the 1961 trial of Adolf Eichmann, the Nazi official in charge of Jewish deportations, for instance, had on Israelis. Citizens in Rwanda and Bosnia paid almost no attention to the court proceedings. Israelis recall the days when they huddled around their radios to hear for the first time the details of Nazi horrors, whereas Bosnians and Rwandans just shrug when the courts are mentioned. They are deemed irrelevant to their daily lives.*[41]

Viewed in isolation, the Hague and Arusha Tribunals would appear to be of limited utility. Their value, however, can only be appreciated when they are viewed within a larger context. Both tribunals represent a small but important step in the evolution of a system of global justice. The tribunals have served an educational function, making it clear to the world that shared definitions of unacceptable behavior exist and holding up examples in which these shared rules have been violated. The tribunals have also clarified the boundaries of behavior falling within the jurisdiction of international courts through decisions in individual cases. For example, in February of 2001, the Hague Tribunal ruled that sexual enslavement was a war crime, convicting three Serbs of "crimes against humanity for repeatedly raping and torturing Muslim women in 'rape camps.'"[42] Finally, aside from those facing trial, there have been no serious challenges to the authority of the tribunals, nor have there been questions about their fairness. In 2013, a ceremony was held marking the launch of the Hague branch of the Mechanism for International Tribunals—putting into place a more formal mechanism to continue the work of the tribunals.[43] The tribunals have been a success if viewed as steps in a longer journey rather than as the final destination. The next step in this journey is the development of a permanent ICC that has the authority to deal with cases wherever they might occur.

A PERMANENT ICC

In July of 1998, 120 nations reached an agreement detailing the creation of a permanent ICC to hear cases of the most extreme human rights violations and to dispense punishments to those found guilty. The agreement, signed in Rome, Italy, was known as the Rome Statute,[44] and would go into effect 1 year after it had been ratified by at least 60 nations. On April 11, 2002, that threshold was passed, bringing the total number of ratifying countries to 65 and setting in motion the creation of the ICC. On March 11, 2003, opening ceremonies were held for the court, and the first judges were sworn in.[45] In protest, the United States sent no representative to the ceremony.

The Rome Statute drew heavily on the experiences of Nuremberg and the Hague, as well as from the examples of the many perpetrators of genocide and war crimes who had successfully evaded punishment.[46] The ICC is authorized to hear cases involving four types of crime: genocide, crimes against humanity, war crimes, and the crime of aggression. Each category of crime is defined in the Rome Statute, except for "crimes of aggression," which will be included when participating nations come to an agreement on the acts to be included within this category.[47]

The rules of the ICC generally follow those in common law adversarial systems.[48] Trials are open to the public, defendants are presumed innocent, and the burden of proof is on the prosecutor to show guilt beyond a reasonable doubt. Defendants have a right to remain silent, and if they cannot afford an attorney, one is provided for them. Those standing accused before the court have a right to review the evidence against them, to confront witnesses against them, and to call witnesses in their behalf. Convicted defendants have the right to appeal their conviction and their sentence, and contrary to most common law systems, the prosecution also has the right to appeal.

The ICC, consistent with an emerging world standard, cannot impose the death penalty on convicted offenders. Punishments are limited to life imprisonment for the most serious cases, up to 30 years in prison for the majority of serious offenses, and five years in prison for lesser offenses. The court can also order defendants to return gains from their crimes, and there are provisions for reparations to victims and fines. Criminal procedures are conducted by the ICC, but the enforcement of the court's rulings is left to the states that have signed onto the Statute.[49]

Although the ICC has great promise, some are skeptical of its ability to have any meaningful authority. Robertson, for example, suggests that the final version of the Rome Statute included so many compromises that it will render the court largely ineffective.[50] He is particularly critical of the United States, which had opposed an ICC from the very beginning, indicating it could support such an institution only if there were absolute guarantees that no United States citizen would ever be subject to the ICC. In 1998, 120 nations agreed to the Rome Statute, creating a permanent ICC, and seven nations voted to oppose the court. In its vote against the ICC, the United States aligned itself with nations that have questionable records for protecting human rights, including China, India, and Israel. Many modifications were made to weaken the authority of the court in the hopes of gaining the support of the United States, but that support did not materialize.

Here are a few of the many ways that Robertson believes the ICC was unnecessarily weakened.[51] First, cases can only be pursued if they are sent to the court through the UN Security Council, which is made up of the world's superpowers, or with the permission of the nation in which the state-sponsored atrocities occurred. Thus, major nations can block a prosecution, as can oppressors who remain in power. Second, the jurisdiction of the court and the rules that govern it cannot be modified until its review seven years after it has been put in place. Third, no individuals can be charged for actions that took place before their country ratified the Rome Statute. Fourth, states have the ability to ratify the ICC, but any time after ratification, the states may receive exemptions from the jurisdiction of the court for seven years. Thus, state officials planning to engage in war crimes or genocide may, prior to committing the acts, request a seven-year exemption from prosecution by the ICC. Fifth, under the ICC, individuals can be charged with international crimes, but nations, political groups, or corporations cannot. Finally, the court cannot proceed in cases prosecuted within a nation, unless it can be shown that the national prosecution was a show trial or was otherwise conducted in a way to avoid justice. In fact, a number of nations, including the Netherlands, Germany, and Australia, have enacted their own laws that mirror those of the ICC.[52]

On March 11, 2003, ceremonies were held at the Hague, officially opening the permanent ICC. Eighteen judges were sworn in before diplomats, politicians, and judges from more than 100 nations. The United States, a long-time opponent of the court, sent no representatives and has no judges sitting on the court.[53]

By 2013, the Rome Statute had been ratified by 122 countries. At that time, the court had 18 cases brought before it and was investigating another 8 cases.[54] From the beginning, the ICC has been controversial.[55] The ICC holds the promise of a judicial body that will hold criminally accountable those who engage in genocide and war crimes. In its present configuration, the ICC is unlikely to fully meet this promise. However, the ICC is of tremendous symbolic importance, and despite its limitations, it is a very small but important step toward the development of a more complete system of international justice. The same powerful nations that have shown little interest in stopping war crimes or genocide in developing countries have little interest in establishing a legal structure that would hold offenders accountable—at least for the moment.

TRUTH AND RECONCILIATION COMMISSIONS

Many times courts do not have the resources to handle all of the cases of human rights violations before them. In other cases convictions are not possible because the perpetrators successfully destroy evidence or because the authorities now in power block efforts to gather evidence of past atrocities. Justice for gross human rights violations does not only mean legal prosecution and punishment. An alternative is the truth and reconciliation commission.[56] Between 1974 and 2000, there were at least 21 truth commissions,[57] usually following a transition from a brutal authoritarian regime to a more democratic system. By 2013, there were truth commissions in more than 30 countries around the world, though most could be found in Africa and South America.[58]

The structure of these commissions has varied, as has the extent to which they were deemed a success. Sometimes they have been conducted in conjunction with prosecutions, while other times, they have been conducted in place of prosecutions. All truth and reconciliation commissions represent a shared belief that a full accounting of atrocities in the recent past is necessary to reach closure and move forward. As Rotberg has observed:

> *Truth commissions thus seek, whatever their mandate from a new government, to uncover the past in order to answer questions that remain unanswered: What happened to husbands, sons, wives, and lovers at the hands of the ousted regime? Who executed the orders? What was the grand design? Who benefitted? Getting the facts provides closure, at least in theory.*[59]

Minow argues that:

> *. . . the working hypothesis is that testimony of victims and perpetrators, offered publicly to a truth commission, affords opportunities for individuals and the nation as a whole to heal. . . . truth commissions presume that telling and hearing truth is healing.*[60]

A common strategy is to allow offenders to publicly describe their crimes in full in exchange for amnesty. Sometimes this means amnesty for anyone who fully cooperates, and sometimes amnesty is granted for admission of lesser offenses, while any serious offenses that are uncovered are forwarded for prosecution. Victims are also allowed to testify and may find it therapeutic to have their victimization publicly recognized. Thus, the focus is on healing and reconciliation rather than on vengeance and punishment. This is particularly appropriate where the victims and offenders are from the same country and, of necessity, must cooperate for the country to function smoothly. Not every instance of gross human right violations is amenable to a truth commission, but there are many circumstances where it is a viable alternative to focusing on punishment.

CONCLUSION

As the world moves toward a global economy and nations are increasingly interdependent, it is becoming more difficult to view genocide and war crimes as purely internal matters. In the past nations have not been moved to stop such atrocities on purely moral grounds, but now these same nations are increasingly finding that intervention is necessary for their own economic and social stability. Thus, despite the reluctance of the United States, China, and others to embrace an international system of justice, it will be in their interest to do so in the long run. The development of an international justice system has progressed at a glacial pace, but it has steadily progressed. The key will be to devise a system that can address the most serious atrocities, while allowing nations as much independence as possible.

DISCUSSION QUESTIONS

1. What are the arguments for and against having rules of war and defining war crimes for those who violate the rules?
2. Why was the Universal Declaration of Human Rights important, even though it did not have the force of law?
3. What are the arguments for and the arguments against the U.S. position opposing an ICC?

Endnotes

1. Geoffrey Robertson, *Crimes Against Humanity: The Struggle for Global Justice* (New York: The Free Press, 1999).
2. *Ibid.*, p. 3.
3. Richard Norman, *Ethics, Killing and War* (New York: Cambridge University Press, 1995).
4. Robertson, *Crimes Against Humanity.*
5. Richard Shelly Hartigan, *Lieber's Code and the Law of War* (Chicago: Precedent, 1983).
6. Robertson, *Crimes Against Humanity.*
7. Norman, *Ethics, Killing and War.*
8. Robertson, *Crimes Against Humanity.* For an excellent discussion of what constitutes a war crime, also see Roy Gutman and David Rieff (eds.), *Crimes of War: What the Public Should Know* (New York: W.W. Norton & Company, 1999).
9. *Ibid.*, p. 176.
10. *Ibid.*
11. *Ibid.*, pp. 210-211.
12. See the Avalon Project, *Nuremberg Trial Proceedings, Volume I: Rules of Procedure* (available from www.yale.edu/lawweb/avalon/imt/proc/imtrules.htm; Internet; accessed on March 26, 2002).
13. Robertson, *Crimes Against Humanity,* p. 214.
14. Martha Minnow, *Between Vengeance and Forgiveness: Facing History after Genocide and Mass Violence* (Boston: Beacon Press, 1998).
15. Robertson, *Crimes Against Humanity.*
16. *Ibid.*
17. Minnow, *Between Vengeance and Forgiveness.*
18. Robertson, *Crimes Against Humanity.*

19. Minnow, *Between Vengeance and Forgiveness.*
20. Robertson, p. 23; Susan Waltz, "Universalizing Human Rights: The Role of Small States in the Construction of the Universal Declaration of Human Rights," *Human Rights Quarterly* 23 (2001), pp. 44-72.
21. *Ibid.*
22. Robertson, *Crimes Against Humanity*, p. 32.
23. *Ibid.*
24. *Ibid.*, p. 29.
25. *Ibid.*
26. European Court of Human Rights, *Analysis of Statistics 2012* (available from www.echr.coe.int/Documents/Stats_analysis_2012_ENG.pdf; Internet; accessed on August 12, 2013).
27. *Ibid.*
28. Robertson, *Crimes Against Humanity.*
29. *Ibid.*
30. *Ibid.*, p. 58.
31. European Court of Human Rights, *Questions and Answers* (available from http://www.echr.coe.int/Documents/Questions_Answers_ENG.pdf; Internet; accessed on August 12, 2013).
32. Robertson, *Crimes Against Humanity.*
33. *Statute of the International Tribunal* (available from www.un.org/icty/basic/statut/stat2000.htm; Internet; accessed on April 18, 2002).
34. Power, *A Problem With Hell.*
35. International Tribunal, *Outstanding Public Indictments* (available from www.un.org/icty/glance/indictlist-e.htm; Internet; accessed on April 18, 2002).
36. United Nations, *ICTY Digest #134* (available from http://www.icty.org/x/file/About/Reports%20and%20Publications/ICTYDigest/2013/icty_digest_134_en.pdf; Internet; accessed on August 13, 2013).
37. International Criminal Tribunal for Rwanda, *Status of Cases* (available from www.unictr.org/Cases/tabid/204/Default.aspx; Internet; accessed on August 13, 2013).
38. Robertson, *Crimes Against Humanity.*
39. Arthur Asiimwe, *Arusha Tribunal to Move Some Genocide Cases* (available from http://allafrica.com/stories/200202180774.html; Internet; accessed on April 18, 2002).
40. Danna Harman, "Rwanda Turns to Its Past for Justice," *Christian Science Monitor* (30 January 2002 edition) (available from www.csmonitor.com/2002/0130/p09s01-woaf.html; Internet; accessed on January 30, 2002).
41. Power, *A Problem With Hell*, p. 496.
42. Lauren Comiteau, "'Sexual Enslavement' Established as a War Crime," *USA Today,* February 23, 2001, p. 10A.
43. United Nations, *ICTY Digest #134.*
44. *Rome Statute of the International Court* (available from www.un.org/law/icc/statute/99_corr/cstatute.htm; Internet; accessed on February 21, 2002).
45. Stevenson Swanson, "1st Global War Crimes Court Poised to Open," *Chicago Tribune*, 11 March 2003, p. 3.
46. William A. Schabas, *An Introduction to the International Criminal Court* (New York: Cambridge University Press, 2001).
47. *Rome Statute of the International Court*
48. *Ibid.*
49. Hirad Abtahi and Steven Arrig Koh, "The Emerging Enforcement Practice of the International Criminal Court," *Cornell International Law Journal*, 45 (2012), pp. 1-23.
50. Robertson, *Crimes Against Humanity.*
51. *Ibid.*
52. Hiromi Sato, "Modes of International Criminal Justice and General Principles of Criminal Responsibility," *Goettingen Journal of International Law*, 4 (2012), pp. 765-807.

53. Marlise Simons, "World Court for Crimes of War Opens in the Hague," *New York Times*, March 12, 2003 (available from www.nytimes.com; Internet; accessed on March 12, 2003).
54. The International Criminal Court, "Situations and Cases" (available from http://www.icc-cpi.int/en_menus/icc/situations%20and%20cases/Pages/situations%20and%20cases.aspx; Internet; accessed on August 13, 2013).
55. See Sarah B. Sewall and Carl Kaysen, *The United States and the International Criminal Court* (New York: Rowman & Littlefield, 2000); Alton Frye, *Toward an International Criminal Court: A Council Policy Initiative* (New York: Council on Foreign Relations Books, 1999).
56. See Minow, *Between Vengeance and Forgiveness*; Priscilla B. Hayner, *Unspeakable Truths: Confronting State Terror and Atrocity* (New York: Routledge, 2001); Robert I. Rotberg and Dennis Thompson (eds.), *Truth v. Justice: The Morality of Truth Commissions* (Princeton, N.J.: Princeton University Press, 2000).
57. Hayner, *Unspeakable Truths.*
58. Amnesty International, "Truth Commissions" (available from www.amnesty.org/en/international-justice/issues/truth-commissions; Internet; accessed on August 13, 2013); United States Institute of Peace, "Truth Commission Digital Collection" (available from www.usip/org/publications/truth-commission-digital-collection; Internet; accessed on August 13, 2013).
59. Robert I. Rotberg, "Truth Commissions and the Provision of Truth, Justice, and Reconciliation," in Robert I. Rotberg and Dennis Thompson (eds.), *Truth v. Justice: The Morality of Truth Commissions* (Princeton, N.J.: Princeton University Press, 2000), p. 3.
60. Minow, *Between Vengeance and Forgiveness,* p. 61.

Conclusion: Justice as an Evolving Concept

Justice has been hard to define and even harder to implement. It would be a mistake, however, to view justice as something with a fixed definition whose achievement is objectively measurable. Rather than a destination, justice should be viewed as a journey and as a mirror reflecting the development of a particular people over time. As societies advance, injustices may continue, but sensitivity to injustice grows and the list of issues considered under the umbrella of justice expands.

Evidence of concern over justice and institutions that support justice can be found in the earliest cultures. In William Golding's book, *Lord of the Flies*, a group of children are stranded on an island with no adults to supervise them.[1] They form their own society, but that society quickly breaks into violent groups. The book illustrates the primitive instincts in man and the brutality of mankind, but it also illustrates that mankind requires laws and structure to overcome those baser instincts. It might be argued that the pursuit of justice is a natural response to man's violent instincts. Golding wrote that book following the atrocities perpetrated by the Nazis during the Holocaust, and although not everyone shares the author's dark view of human nature, it is a reminder that justice is a human construct raised in response to human injustices.

For early societies, and some modern ones, that emphasized religion as central to life, definitions of justice came from holy documents and prophets. Angry or merciful gods dispensed justice and gave humans guidance in dispensing their own justice. All humans would have their own judgment days when they died. Even secular leaders looked to priestly classes to justify their actions. When Moses and Pharaoh battled over the fate of an enslaved class, both called upon gods and religious arguments to justify their actions. Pilate and Herod bowed to the chief priests and scribes in the pre-trial of Jesus. Subsequent monarchs in Europe laid claim to the Divine Right of Kings. Even in a highly secular society like the United States, Presidents routinely use religious rhetoric to justify their positions.

When some advanced civilizations subsumed religion into mythology, a long history of philosophical discussion on justice resulted. The importance of justice to Greek, Roman, and early Catholic thinkers attests to both its perennial attraction and to the difficulty of fully understanding the concept. Philosophers who have pondered the great human mysteries have found that one of the great mysteries concerns what constitutes a just life, a just government, and a just society. The fact that discussions begun thousands of years ago continue today attests to the staying power and complexity of the concept.

As civilizations evolved and the nation state became more prominent, the legacy of religion lingered in the Divine Right of Kings. Pronouncements about justice from these leaders were accepted by the citizenry as having come directly from God. Only after secular forces took over the state during the Renaissance did philosophers and politicians discuss justice in new ways. The state, needing the support of its citizens, focused on issues of the responsibility of government to its own citizens and to other countries. In doing so ideas developed on political legitimacy, the nature of leadership, just wars, and law.

[1]William Golding, *Lord of the Flies* (New York: Perigee, 1959).

About this time the most dramatic expression of political justice, criminal justice, was taken from religious and private hands and placed with the state. The development of criminal justice mirrored the development of society with harsh and unspeakably cruel punishments first couched in religious terms and institutions. When the state took over criminal justice, punishments became public spectacles, demonstrating for all the recently acquired power of the government. Criminal law reflected the nature of the state in which it emerged, leading to variations in criminal law in France and England in Europe, Muslim societies in the Middle East, and Asian culture in the Far East. Generally, courts emerged first with police and prisons only developing later, or being connected to the military.

Political and economic revolutions of the eighteenth, nineteenth, and twentieth centuries assured an ever increasing development and expansion of democracy and capitalism. With some exceptions feudalism and monarchies became less valid. These changes gave rise to questions of liberty and equality, and there were questions regarding the appropriate division of wealth. Political justice became increasingly important and there was a growing focus on economic justice, and still later this evolved into a concern with social justice.

As the state became more involved in justice, a variety of justice systems emerged. In Europe the classic delineation was between common law and civil law. In the Middle East the influence of Islam was pronounced. These justice systems reflected the particular values of the countries in which they emerged. For example, England was a highly stratified country with upper classes in firm control and judges were empowered to dispense law and justice. These elites were answerable to no one but the monarch. Even Parliament, which had a hard time getting started itself, was divided between Lords and Commons. Courts, with judges wearing aristocratic wigs and a stratified lawyer class of barristers, reflected the country's values. Even the police, which did not emerge in England until the early 1800s, was organized as a magisterial force. In contrast, France had experienced a spectacular revolution in which peasants took power from the aristocracy. Under such conditions there was a strong interest in having a public check on those who made law, placing such power in the hands of elected legislators. Further, because Catholicism had a stronger place in France, and the state was more bureaucratized, the transformation of canon law into civil law was relatively easy. The justice system and its practitioners were more centralized. These two systems, largely through colonialism, spread and predominated throughout much of the western world. However, particular ideologies, such as Islam and later Communism, put a different spin upon the law and on the meaning of justice.

The American justice system is interesting because it shows how a country's particular value system shapes the form a dominant justice system takes, and it reflects the tendency of many societies to draw selectively from different models of justice. On the one hand the American system is built upon the traditions of English common law. Founding members of the United States crafted a Constitution and Bill of Rights owing much to common law traditions and to earlier documents developed in England. The American Revolution was never as radical as the revolutions in France or Russia, and many of the English views of justice were adopted wholesale in America.

Although America was a democracy with common law roots, elements of civil law crept in and over time statutes became as important as judicial pronouncements in defining law and establishing punishments. Even today, through such things as mandatory minimum sentences, Congress continues to erode the power of judges, shifting that power to legislators. However, the influence of common law remains strong, particularly as seen through the importance placed on process. In most cases, for example, people convicted in court can only base an appeal of their conviction on mistakes made in the trial process, not on new evidence showing their innocence. In the U.S. criminal justice system, justice really means fairness in procedure, but this emphasis on procedure is not absolute. There is a continuous tension between thorough procedures (common law) and efficiency (civil law). In the last half century a "Due Process Revolution" has occurred to make certain that the system does not place so much emphasis on efficiency that the rights of offenders are sacrificed. In spite of these safeguards, numerous injustices have occurred. In this book we have highlighted just two: racial profiling and wrongful convictions.

The many injustices that exist throughout the world suggest that justice remains a work in progress. We have selected just a few to illustrate how persistent and pervasive some of these justice issues can be. The United States has a long history of radical dissent. Significant numbers of people have lost faith in the national government and have joined groups bent on revolution. A dramatic example of this issue was the bombing of the federal building in Oklahoma City in 1995, in which 167 people were killed. By the end of the nineteenth century most countries had ended slavery, and yet there are more slaves in the world today than at any other time. The particular form taken by slavery has changed and in many ways is far more brutal than the outlawed practices of the past. Similarly, genocide in the past 100 years has been more widespread than in any 100-year period in history. Despite the hollow promises of "Never Again," people continue to be slaughtered because of their religious beliefs, tribal affiliations, or the color of their skin. Finally, the world has seen an unprecedented assault on the environment and that assault has led to war, disease, and untold brutality—bringing out the very worst in mankind.

How is it possible for society to advance while injustices seem to multiply? That is a question that in one form or another has arisen throughout the book but for which there is no obvious answer. One might just as well turn the question around. Is a world in which injustices are multiplying truly a world in which civilization is advancing?

Well, then, how is justice to be attained? Considerable religious, intellectual, and political energy has been expended but injustice remains. Perhaps this has to do with the nature of humans, a notoriously self-serving species. Perhaps mankind is as primitive and violent as is assumed in *Lord of the Flies*. Perhaps ignorance or lethargy might explain the growth of injustice, or perhaps justice cannot be achieved.

The name of this book is suggestive. The pursuit of justice may be as important as attaining it. Several remarkable individuals and organizations seek to achieve a just world. Indeed, in another evolutionary step, there have been several international organizations working to achieve global justice. Just as the United Nations works toward international cooperation in politics and the World Trade Organization tries to deal with multinational corporations, there have been several organizations working to achieve global justice. Still, injustice persists, even in more advanced nations like the United States. Religious exhortations, academic discourses, political statements, individual activists, reformist groups, nonprofit organizations, and World Courts all testify that justice has not been achieved but that the pursuit of justice continues to be a human obsession.

Perhaps there will never be true justice in the world. Even if justice remains elusive, it is such an important objective and the benefits of reaching it are so great that the pursuit of justice must continue. To say we should give up on justice because we have been unable to achieve it is like saying that because we have spent billions of dollars and millions of man-hours without successfully finding a cure for cancer, we should stop looking. Like the failed search for a cancer cure, we cannot define past failures to achieve justice as wasted efforts—those past failures may someday become the building blocks for a lasting answer. Ultimately, the old saying rings true—"No Justice No Peace."

APPENDIX

The United Nations' Universal Declaration of Human Rights

THE UNIVERSAL DECLARATION OF HUMAN RIGHTS

Adopted by the General Assembly of the United Nations on December 10, 1948

Preamble

Whereas recognition of the inherent dignity and of the equal and inalienable rights of all members of the human family is the foundation of freedom, justice and peace in the world,

Whereas disregard and contempt for human rights have resulted in barbarous acts which have outraged the conscience of mankind, and the advent of a world in which human beings shall enjoy freedom of speech and belief and freedom from fear and want has been proclaimed as the highest aspiration of the common people,

Whereas it is essential, if man is not to be compelled to have recourse, as a last resort, to rebellion against tyranny and oppression, that human rights should be protected by the rule of law,

Whereas it is essential to promote the development of friendly relations between nations,

Whereas the peoples of the United Nations have in the Charter reaffirmed their faith in fundamental human rights, in the dignity and worth of the human person and in the equal rights of men and women and have determined to promote social progress and better standards of life in larger freedom,

Whereas Member States have pledged themselves to achieve, in co-operation with the United Nations, the promotion of universal respect for and observance of human rights and fundamental freedoms,

Whereas a common understanding of these rights and freedoms is of the greatest importance for the full realization of this pledge,

Now, Therefore THE GENERAL ASSEMBLY proclaims THIS UNIVERSAL DECLARATION OF HUMAN RIGHTS as a common standard of achievement for all peoples and all nations, to the end that every individual and every organ of society, keeping this Declaration constantly in mind, shall strive by teaching and education to promote respect for these rights and freedoms and by progressive measures, national and international, to secure their universal and effective recognition and observance, both among the peoples of Member States themselves and among the peoples of territories under their jurisdiction.

Article 1

All human beings are born free and equal in dignity and rights. They are endowed with reason and conscience and should act towards one another in a spirit of brotherhood.

Article 2

Everyone is entitled to all the rights and freedoms set forth in this Declaration, without distinction of any kind, such as race, colour, sex, language, religion, political or other opinion, national or social origin, property, birth or other status.

Furthermore, no distinction shall be made on the basis of the political, jurisdictional or international status of the country or territory to which a person belongs, whether it be independent, trust, non-self-governing or under any other limitation of sovereignty.

Article 3
Everyone has the right to life, liberty and security of person.

Article 4
No one shall be held in slavery or servitude; slavery and the slave trade shall be prohibited in all their forms.

Article 5
No one shall be subjected to torture or to cruel, inhuman or degrading treatment or punishment.

Article 6
Everyone has the right to recognition everywhere as a person before the law.

Article 7
All are equal before the law and are entitled without any discrimination to equal protection of the law. All are entitled to equal protection against any discrimination in violation of this Declaration and against any incitement to such discrimination.

Article 8
Everyone has the right to an effective remedy by the competent national tribunals for acts violating the fundamental rights granted him by the constitution or by law.

Article 9
No one shall be subjected to arbitrary arrest, detention or exile.

Article 10
Everyone is entitled in full equality to a fair and public hearing by an independent and impartial tribunal, in the determination of his rights and obligations and of any criminal charge against him.

Article 11
(1) Everyone charged with a penal offence has the right to be presumed innocent until proved guilty according to law in a public trial at which he has had all the guarantees necessary for his defence.

(2) No one shall be held guilty of any penal offence on account of any act or omission which did not constitute a penal offence, under national or international law, at the time when it was committed. Nor shall a heavier penalty be imposed than the one that was applicable at the time the penal offence was committed.

Article 12
No one shall be subjected to arbitrary interference with his privacy, family, home or correspondence, nor to attacks upon his honour and reputation. Everyone has the right to the protection of the law against such interference or attacks.

Article 13

(1) Everyone has the right to freedom of movement and residence within the borders of each state.
(2) Everyone has the right to leave any country, including his own, and to return to his country.

Article 14

(1) Everyone has the right to seek and to enjoy in other countries asylum from persecution.
(2) This right may not be invoked in the case of prosecutions genuinely arising from non-political crimes or from acts contrary to the purposes and principles of the United Nations.

Article 15

(1) Everyone has the right to a nationality.
(2) No one shall be arbitrarily deprived of his nationality nor denied the right to change his nationality.

Article 16

(1) Men and women of full age, without any limitation due to race, nationality or religion, have the right to marry and to found a family. They are entitled to equal rights as to marriage, during marriage and at its dissolution.
(2) Marriage shall be entered into only with the free and full consent of the intending spouses.
(3) The family is the natural and fundamental group unit of society and is entitled to protection by society and the State.

Article 17

(1) Everyone has the right to own property alone as well as in association with others.
(2) No one shall be arbitrarily deprived of his property.

Article 18

Everyone has the right to freedom of thought, conscience and religion; this right includes freedom to change his religion or belief, and freedom, either alone or in community with others and in public or private, to manifest his religion or belief in teaching, practice, worship and observance.

Article 19

Everyone has the right to freedom of opinion and expression; this right includes freedom to hold opinions without interference and to seek, receive and impart information and ideas through any media and regardless of frontiers.

Article 20

(1) Everyone has the right to freedom of peaceful assembly and association.
(2) No one may be compelled to belong to an association.

Article 21

(1) Everyone has the right to take part in the government of his country, directly or through freely chosen representatives.
(2) Everyone has the right of equal access to public service in his country.
(3) The will of the people shall be the basis of the authority of government; this will shall be expressed in periodic and genuine elections which shall be by universal and equal suffrage and shall be held by secret vote or by equivalent free voting procedures.

Article 22

Everyone, as a member of society, has the right to social security and is entitled to realization, through national effort and international co-operation and in accordance with the organization and resources of each State, of the economic, social and cultural rights indispensable for his dignity and the free development of his personality.

Article 23

(1) Everyone has the right to work, to free choice of employment, to just and favourable conditions of work and to protection against unemployment.
(2) Everyone, without any discrimination, has the right to equal pay for equal work.
(3) Everyone who works has the right to just and favourable remuneration ensuring for himself and his family an existence worthy of human dignity, and supplemented, if necessary, by other means of social protection.
(4) Everyone has the right to form and to join trade unions for the protection of his interests.

Article 24

Everyone has the right to rest and leisure, including reasonable limitation of working hours and periodic holidays with pay.

Article 25

(1) Everyone has the right to a standard of living adequate for the health and well-being of himself and of his family, including food, clothing, housing and medical care and necessary social services, and the right to security in the event of unemployment, sickness, disability, widowhood, old age or other lack of livelihood in circumstances beyond his control.
(2) Motherhood and childhood are entitled to special care and assistance. All children, whether born in or out of wedlock, shall enjoy the same social protection.

Article 26

(1) Everyone has the right to education. Education shall be free, at least in the elementary and fundamental stages. Elementary education shall be compulsory. Technical and professional education shall be made generally available and higher education shall be equally accessible to all on the basis of merit.
(2) Education shall be directed to the full development of the human personality and to the strengthening of respect for human rights and fundamental freedoms. It shall promote understanding, tolerance and friendship among all nations, racial or religious groups, and shall further the activities of the United Nations for the maintenance of peace.
(3) Parents have a prior right to choose the kind of education that shall be given to their children.

Article 27

(1) Everyone has the right freely to participate in the cultural life of the community, to enjoy the arts and to share in scientific advancement and its benefits.
(2) Everyone has the right to the protection of the moral and material interests resulting from any scientific, literary or artistic production of which he is the author.

Article 28

Everyone is entitled to a social and international order in which the rights and freedoms set forth in this Declaration can be fully realized.

Article 29

(1) Everyone has duties to the community in which alone the free and full development of his personality is possible.

(2) In the exercise of his rights and freedoms, everyone shall be subject only to such limitations as are determined by law solely for the purpose of securing due recognition and respect for the rights and freedoms of others and of meeting the just requirements of morality, public order and the general welfare in a democratic society.

(3) These rights and freedoms may in no case be exercised contrary to the purposes and principles of the United Nations.

Article 30

Nothing in this Declaration may be interpreted as implying for any State, group or person any right to engage in any activity or to perform any act aimed at the destruction of any of the rights and freedoms set forth herein.

Source: http://www.un.org/Overview/rights.html

Index

Note: Page numbers followed by *b* indicate boxes, *f* indicate figures, and *t* indicate tables.